A Source Book of Advaita Vedānta

A Source Book of

ADVAITA VEDĀNTA

ELIOT DEUTSCH

J. A. B. VAN BUITENEN

THE UNIVERSITY PRESS OF HAWAII
HONOLULU
1971

Library of Congress Catalog Card Number 75-148944

(formerly University of Hawaii Press; ISBN 0-87022-189-2)

Manufactured in the United States of America

Contents

Source Selections vii
Preface ix

Part I BACKGROUND IN TRADITION: THE THREE DEPARTURES

1. Revelation 5
   Selections from the *Ṛgveda* and Upaniṣads
2. Recollection 33
   Selections from the *Bhagavadgītā*
3. System 51
   Contents-summary of the *Brahmasūtras*

Part II PHILOSOPHICAL AND CULTURAL BACKGROUND

4. Early History and Cultural Values of Vedānta 65
5. Common Philosophical Problems 72
6. Criticisms of Rival Systems 77
   Selections from Śaṁkara's *Brahmasūtrabhāṣya*

Part III SOURCES OF ADVAITA VEDĀNTA

7. Gauḍapāda 119
8. Śaṁkara 122
9. Sureśvara 223
10. Maṇḍana Miśra 229
11. Padmapāda 242
12. Vācaspati Miśra 252
13. Sarvajñātman 267

14. Vimuktātman 278
15. Vidyāraṇya 281
16. Madhusūdana Sarasvatī 288
17. Sadānanda 294
18. Dharmarāja 302
19. Appaya Dīkṣita 304
20. Summary 308
Bibliography 313
Index 319

Source Selections

I. BACKGROUND IN TRADITION

Ṛgveda X, 129 (trans. A. A. Macdonell)

Chāndogya Upaniṣad VI; V, 3–10 (trans. J. A. B. van Buitenen); *Taittirīya Upaniṣad* II, 1–8 (trans. J. A. B. van Buitenen); *Bṛhadāraṇyaka Upaniṣad* III, 7, 8; IV, 2, 3, 4 (trans. Franklin Edgerton); *Bhagavadgītā* I, 26–35, 40–44; II, 11–25, 46–53; III, 3–9, 22–30, 36–41; IV, 6–8, 16–23, 36–42; V, 1–7, 15–26; VII, 1–7, 24–30; VIII, 16–22; IX, 1–10, 13–14, 25–31; XI; XII, 1–7; XIII, 1–6, 12–17, 19–27; XV, 16–20; XVIII, 45–63 (trans. Eliot Deutsch)

II. PHILOSOPHICAL AND CULTURAL BACKGROUND

Śaṁkara, *Brahmasūtrabhāṣya* II, 2: 1, 2, 4–10, 12, 15, 17–21, 25–33, 37–44 (trans. George Thibaut)

III. SOURCES OF ADVAITA VEDĀNTA

Gauḍapāda, *Kārikās on the Māṇḍūkya Upaniṣad* I, 16–18; II, 1, 4, 11–13, 17, 18, 31, 32; III, 15, 19, 28, 46, 48 (trans. Eliot Deutsch)

Śaṁkara, *Upadeśasāhasrī*, Part I (trans. Sengaku Mayeda)

Śaṁkara, *Brahmasūtrabhāṣya*. Introduction; I, 1: 1–2, 4, 5, 9, 11, 17, 19–20, 24, 31; I, 2: 6, 8, 18, 20, 21; I, 3: 19, 22, 28, 30, 34; I, 4: 14, 15, 22, 23; II, 1: 1, 6, 9, 11, 13–16, 18, 21–24, 27, 32–36; II, 3: 18, 32, 42, 46, 48, 50; III, 2: 3, 4, 11, 14, 15, 18, 20–22, 32; III, 3: 9, 53, 54; IV, 1: 2, 3, 13, 15 (trans. George Thibaut)

Śaṁkara, *Bṛhadāraṇyakopaniṣadbhāṣya* I, 4, 7; IV, 3, 7 (trans. Swāmī Mādhavānanda)

Śaṁkara, *Bhagavadgītābhāṣya* III, 3, 4, 8, 9; IV, 18, 19; V (Introduction); XIII, 2 (trans. A. Mahādeva Śāstri)

Sureśvara, *Naiṣkarmya Siddhi* I, 68–79, 107–110; III, (Comm.); IV, 49–51, 56–58 (trans. A. J. Alston)

Maṇḍana Miśra, *Brahma Siddhi*, Chapter I (parts) (trans. R. Balasubramanian)

Padmapāda, *Pañcapādikā* II, 2–4; III, 8, 9; IV, 12; V, 13; VI, 16; VII, 17, 18; IX, 24; XXI, 70; XXIX, 107–111; XXX, 112–114; XXXI, 115–117; XLII, 159–160; XLVII, 180, 181 (trans. D. Venkataramiah)

Vācaspati Miśra, *Bhāmatī*, I, (Superimposition) (trans. S. S. Suryanarayana Sastri and C. Kunhan Raja); *Bhāmatī* II, 1.22, 1.26, 27 (trans. P. K. Sundaram)

Sarvajñātman, *Saṁkṣepaśārīraka* I, 20–24, 31–37, 319–330, 452–454, 464–465, 513–526; II, 9–15, 25–40, 60–68, 132, 134–139, 183–187, 218–220; III, 105–109, 115, 125–131, 139–140 (trans. T. Mahadevan)

Vimuktātman, *Iṣṭa Siddhi*, III, 22–24; IV, 17–21 (trans. P. K. Sundaram)

Vidyāraṇya, *Pañcadaśī*, I, 15–23, 33–37, 44, 45; II, 47–49, 59; III, 13, 17, 18, 26–30, 37–42; IV, 12–13, 19–22, 29–31, 34–37; VI, 1–10, 74–76, 128–142 (trans. Hari Prasad Shastri)

Madhusūdana Sarasvatī, *Vedāntakalpalatikā*, 19–22; 46–47; 49–50 (trans. R. D. Karmarkar)

Sadānanda, *Vedāntasāra* I, 6, 15; II, 32–56, 122–123; IV, 137–157, 159–180 (trans. Swami Nikhilananda)

Dharmaraja, *Vedāntaparibhāṣā* VII (trans. S. S. Suryanarayana Sastri)

Appaya Dīkṣita, *Siddhāntaleśasaṁgraha* 2:32; 3:711 (trans. S. S. Suryanarayana Sastri)

Preface

The purpose of this book is to help make possible a study of Advaita Vedānta in its classical form as this great tradition of thought actually functioned in Indian culture and as this tradition represents distinctive philosophical achievements. We are concerned in short to understand Advaita Vedānta both in terms of cultural history and philosophy.

We are presenting translations of selections from the major Sanskrit writings of some of the most important advaitic thinkers, together with the appropriate background materials. We have not included in this work any material from the neo-Vedānta that has developed in India in recent decades (e.g., Vivekananda, Aurobindo, Radhakrishnan) as the literature of this movement, having been written in English, is readily accessible.

In a collaboration of this sort the authors, while standing behind the entire work, have naturally divided it into areas of special individual responsibility. Van Buitenen has worked primarily with chapters 1–4, and Deutsch with chapters 5–20.

The authors wish to express their gratitude to Professors Richard Brooks, N. K. Devaraja, T. M. P. Mahadevan, Sengaku Mayeda, and K. N. Upadhyaya for many helpful suggestions made and courtesies extended. They also wish to thank Gerald Schwartz for assistance in correcting galleys and preparing the Index and Floris Sakamoto for the graciousness with which she carried out many secretarial tasks.

The authors also wish to acknowledge their appreciation to the University Research Council, University of Hawaii, for the research and travel support that was generously provided.

The authors are extremely grateful to the publishers of the selected Sanskrit translations for their permission to use material previously published by them. Publishers are cited in the publication information preceding each quoted passage. Notes, footnotes, and some translator's interpolations have been deleted from the quoted material and diacritic marks have been altered where necessary to conform with contemporary usage.

A Source Book of Advaita Vedānta

PART I

Background in Tradition: The Three Departures

Vedānta means in the first place the "Conclusion of the Veda" in the double sense that the Veda has come to an end here and that it has come to a conclusion. This final portion of the Veda comprises principally the Upaniṣads, which form the last tier in the monument we call the Veda.

In the second place, Vedānta is an abbreviation of Vedāntamīmāṁsā, *or the "Enquiry into the Vedānta"—the name of the most interesting, most influential, and most diverse of the philosophical traditions of Hindu India. Its very name implies a program: it is a tradition which intends to base itself on the Vedānta in the primary sense, the Upaniṣads.*

The Upaniṣads, however, are not the only foundation of Vedānta. Classical Vedānta recognizes three "points of departure" (prasthānatraya) *for its philosophy; that is to say that all Vedānta true to its name accepts the authority of three texts, or sets of texts, which authenticate its conclusions. There is, then, first the set of Upaniṣadic texts; further, the text of the* Bhagavadgītā; *and finally, the text of the* Brahmasūtras. *Each adds a new dimension to the others.*

It is clear, therefore, that any investigation into Vedānta must be preceded by an enquiry into its traditional sources. These sources may appear to be difficult and at times indeed abstruse; but they set up the problems to which Vedānta addresses itself and which it intends to resolve through its commentaries on these sources.

The basic works of the founders of the different Vedānta schools present themselves as commentaries on the traditional sources; while most of their works are original to a high degree and often seem to owe little more to the admitted sources than an inspiration, nevertheless the philosophers themselves in all honesty present themselves as commentators only. It is not for them to "find" the truth; the truth is already there. It is enough for them to explicate the available truth. We shall briefly sketch the three Departures under the headings of "Revelation," "Recollection," and "System."

CHAPTER 1

Revelation

If we are to form a proper understanding of the meaning and scope of "Revelation," we do well to forget at once the implications of the term in the Mediterranean religions, Judaism, Christianity, and Islām. Strictly speaking, "revelation" is a misnomer, since ultimately there is no revealer. The Sanskrit term for it is *śruti*, literally "the hearing," which means an erudition acquired by listening to the instruction of a teacher. This instruction itself had been transmitted to the teacher through an uninterrupted series of teachers that stretches to the beginning of creation.

Revelation, therefore, is by no means God's word—because, paradoxically, if it were to derive from a divine person, its credibility would be impugned. It is held to be authorless, for if a person, human or divine, had authored it, it would be vulnerable to the defects inherent in such a person. It is axiomatic that revelation is infallible, and this infallibility can be defended only if it is authorless.

Then from where does it come? The answer is stark and simple: it is given with the world. For some of the Mīmāṁsā (or orthodox, exegetical) thinkers who have addressed themselves to this problem, the world is beginningless and the assumption of a creator is both problematic and unnecessary. And even if a beginning of the world is assumed, as in later Hindu thought when it is held that the universe goes through a pulsating rhythm of origination, existence, and dissolution, it is also held that at the dawn of a new world the revelation reappears to the vision of the seers, who once more begin the transmission.

Revelation, then, comes with the world, and it embodies the laws which regulate the well-being of both world and man. It lays down first and foremost what is our *dharma*, our duty. This duty is more precisely defined as a set of acts which either must be done continuously (*nitya*), or occasionally (*naimittika*), or to satisfy a specific wish (*kāmya*).

While we would be inclined to look upon the Revelation as a more or less continuous series of historic texts, spanning close to a millennium from ca. 1400 B.C. till 500 B.C., orthodoxy looks upon it as eternal and therefore simultaneous. Also, the Mīmāṁsā Exegetes laid down rather rigorous criteria for its authority. Orthodox consensus recognizes three fundamental means of knowledge, each of which has its own scope. Of these means (pramāṇas), sensory perception (*pratyakṣa*) holds the first place, for it is through perception that the world is evident to us. Built upon perception is inference (*anumāna*), in which a present perception combines with a series of past perceptions to offer us a conclusion about a fact which is not perceptibly evident. While these two means of knowledge, perceiving and reasoning, tell us everything about the world that we wish to know, they cannot give us any knowledge about matters that are suprasensory. It is here that the force of Revelation comes in. Revelation, then, is authoritative *only* about matters to which neither perception nor inference gives us access; but then it is fully authoritative. This authority, as pointed out, is primarily concerned with one's duties. To give a contrastive example, the orthodox Exegetes would reject most of the Bible as Revelation: most of it they would classify as *itihāsa* or *purāṇa*, "stories about things past," describing events which were accessible to perception and hence require only the authority of perception; but, for example, the chapters dealing with the Law in Deuteronomy would be considered Revelation in the true sense, since here rules are laid down and results are set forth which escape human perception and inference.

Led by this principle, the Exegetes classified Revelation under three basic rubrics, "injunction" (*vidhi* or *niyoga*, including prohibition or *niṣedha*), "discussion" (*arthavāda*), and "spell" (*mantra*). Spells comprise the mass of formulae, metric or in prose, which were employed at the execution of the rites. Discussion comprises all the texts which describe, glorify, or condemn matters pertaining to rites. Injunction comprises all the statements, direct or indirect, which lay down that certain rites or acts must be done or must not be done.

The stock example is *svargakāmo jyotiṣṭomena yajeta*, "he who wishes for heaven should sacrifice with the soma sacrifice." It is in such statements that the authority of Revelation finally resides. It enjoins an action (offering up a sacrifice), the nature of which escapes human invention, for a purpose (heaven) whose existence neither perception nor inference could have acknowledged, upon a person (the sacrificer) who stands qualified for this action on the basis of the injunction. Declarations which accompany the description of the sacrifice, e.g., "the sacrificial pole is the sun," while strictly speaking untrue and carrying no authority, have a derivative authority insofar as they are subsidiary to and supportive of the injunction, and may be condemnatory or laudatory of facts connected with the rite laid down in the injunction (e.g., the sacrificial pole is compared to the sun in a laudatory fashion for its central function at the rite). The spells accompanying the festive celebration of the rite have their secondary, even tertiary, significance only within the context of the rite laid down in the injunction.

From the exegetical point of view, then, much of what is generally described as Revelation holds little authority. For example, the Four Vedas as we call them, the Veda of the hymns (*ṛk*), the formulae (*yajus*), the chants (*sāma*), and the incantations (*atharva*), are almost entirely under the rubric of "spell." The large disquisitions of the Brāhmaṇas are almost entirely "discussion," except for the scattered injunctions in them; and the same largely holds for the third layer of texts, the Āraṇyakas. Generally speaking, Vedānta will go along with this view.

It is, however, with the last layer of text (the Vedānta or the Upaniṣads) that Exegetes and Vedāntins come to a parting of ways. For the Exegetes the Upaniṣads are in no way an exception to the rules that govern the Revelation as a whole. Nothing much is enjoined in them nor do they embody marked spells. In fact, they are fundamentally "discussion," specifically discussion of the self; and such discussion certainly has a place in the exegetical scheme of things, for this self is none other than the personal agent of the rites and this agent no doubt deserves as much discussion as, say, the sacrificial pole.

Basically therefore the Exegetes find the Revelation solely, and fully, authoritative when it lays down the Law on what actions have to be undertaken by what persons under what circumstances for which purposes. Vedānta accepts this, but only for that portion of Revelation which bears on ritual acts, the *karmakāṇḍa*. But to relegate the portion dealing with knowledge, the *jñānakāṇḍa*, to the same ritual context is unacceptable. It is taken for granted that *karmakāṇḍa* indeed defines the principle of authority in injunctions of acts to be done, but Vedānta declines on the one hand that the Upaniṣads embody an injunction (e.g., that Brahman or the self must be studied and known, or that the world must be dephenomenalized) and declines on the other hand that if the Upaniṣads bear on no injunction they have simply the limited authoritative standing of a discussion. The consensus of the Vedānta is that in the Upaniṣads significant and authoritative statements are made concerning the nature of Brahman.

From the foregoing it will have become clear that very little of the Revelation literature preceding the Upaniṣads was of systematic interest to the Vedāntins. For example, Śaṁkara quotes less than twenty verses from the entire *Ṛgveda* in his commentary on the *Brahmasūtras*, about fourteen lines from the largest Brāhmaṇa of them all, the *Śatapatha Brāhmaṇa*, but no less than thirty-four verses from the *Muṇḍaka Upaniṣad*, a fairly minor and short Upaniṣad. This is not to say that Vedānta rejects the previous literature, but that it considers all the relevant wisdom of the Veda concerning these issues to have been embedded in the Upaniṣads.

HYMN OF CREATION

Ṛgveda X, 129

Among the hymns of the *Ṛgveda* that are clearly philosophical both in character and influence none is more important than the "Hymn of Creation." This hymn exhibits a clear monistic or nondualistic concern, an account of creation that gives special attention to the role of desire, and a kind of skeptical or agnostic attitude concerning man's (and even god's) knowledge of creation. The following translation is from *Hymns From the Rig Veda*, translated by A. A. Macdonell, Heritage of India Series (Calcutta: Association Press, n.d.).

Non-being then existed not nor being:
There was no air, nor sky that is beyond it.
What was concealed? Wherein? In whose protection?
And was there deep unfathomable water?

Death then existed not nor life immortal;
Of neither night nor day was any token.
By its inherent force the One breathed windless:
No other thing than that beyond existed.

Darkness there was at first by darkness hidden;
Without distinctive marks, this all was water.
That which, becoming, by the void was covered,
That One by force of heat came into being.

Desire entered the One in the beginning:
It was the earliest seed, of thought the product.
The sages searching in their hearts with wisdom,
Found out the bond of being in non-being.

Their ray extended light across the darkness:
But was the One above or was it under?
Creative force was there, and fertile power:
Below was energy, above was impulse.

Who knows for certain? Who shall here declare it?
Whence was it born, and whence came this creation?
The gods were born after this world's creation:
Then who can know from whence it has arisen?

None knoweth whence creation has arisen;
And whether he has or has not produced it:
He who surveys it in the highest heaven,
He only knows, or haply he may know not.

The authority of the statements of the Upaniṣads is final for Vedānta. But inevitably there are portions in the Upaniṣads that are more influential than others. This influence is of two kinds. One kind of influence is that exerted through the *Brahmasūtras* which, when referring to an Upaniṣadic passage, makes it incumbent upon the commentator to interpret and accommodate the passage in his thinking. Perhaps the most quoted Upaniṣad in the Sūtras is the *Chāndogya.* Another kind of influence is the predilection of a commentator for certain passages which for him express the final thoughts of the Upaniṣads.

The selection of Upaniṣadic texts which follows hereunder does not pretend to be exhaustive, either as far as their occurrence in the Sūtras goes, or in their appeal to the individual commentators. But they are all basic to the Vedānta as a whole.

THE WISDOM OF THE EXISTENT

Chāndogya Upaniṣad VI

This text portion, which comprises the entire sixth chapter of the *Chāndogya Upaniṣad,* is no doubt the most influential of the entire corpus of the Upaniṣads. It is presented in the form of an instruction by Uddālaka Āruṇi Gautama (nickname, patronymic, family name) to his son Śvetaketu, both of whom, we shall see, reappear in other important selections of the Upaniṣads. The significance of the present "wisdom" is threefold:

a. It lays down for Vedānta that creation is not *ex nihilo,* that the phenomenal world is produced out of a preexistent cause. This cause is the substantial or material cause (*upādāna*), which, by the example of the clay and its clay products (section 1), provides the authority for the tenet that the phenomenal world is non-different from its cause. Although the text does not use the term *brahman,* the Vedānta tradition is that the Existent (*sat*) referred to is no other than Brahman. The tenet implies the important doctrine of *satkāryavāda,* viz., that the product does not emerge as a completely new entity, but preexists in its substantial cause.

This doctrine is common to both Sāṁkhya and Vedānta, but while the former treats the cause as the subtle unconscious *prakṛti*, the material germ of the material cause which is totally different from the conscious order of selves (*puruṣa*), the latter understands the substantial cause to be identical with the principle of consciousness in the phenomenal world. Thus this text presents us with the basic problem of Vedānta, the relation between the plural, complex, changing phenomenal world and the Brahman in which it substantially subsists.

b. It teaches that "You are That," and thus, for Vedānta, lays down that there is an identity (however to be understood) between the Brahman and the individual self. This makes the text one of the "great statements" (*mahāvākya*) for Śaṁkara, who reads in it the ultimate denial of any difference between the consciousness of the individual self and the consciousness that is Brahman.

c. It is quoted several times in the *Brahmasūtras*, which adduces its evidence in 1. 1. 5 ff. to prove that the universal cause is conscious and thus to disprove the assumption of an unconscious causal *prakṛti* of the Sāṁkhyans, and in 2. 1. 14 to prove that the produced world is non-different from Brahman. Therefore all Vedāntins have to confront themselves with this text while commenting on the Sūtras, and the commentaries on 2. 1. 14 will state their basic positions—whether this non-difference signifies a complete non-dualism (Śaṁkara), a difference-non-difference (Bhāskara), or a non-difference in a differentiated supreme (Rāmānuja).

The text is presented in a new translation by J. A. B. van Buitenen. It differs in many instances from previous translations which, he believes, have been unduly influenced by the interpretation of Śaṁkara. For example in section 4, the repeated "fireness has departed from fire," "sunness has departed from sun," "moonness has departed from moon," "lightningness has departed from lightning" do not signify that there is in reality no fire, sun, moon, and lightning, but rather that these four entities, which previously had been considered irreducible principles, can be further analyzed into compounds of the Three Colors or Elements that Uddālaka sets up.

The interpretation of *vācārambhaṇaṃ vikāro; nāmadheyaṃ . . . satyam* (here rendered "creating is seizing with Speech, the Name is *Satyam*, namely . . .") is an old crux. The traditional explanation, which can be traced to Śaṁkara's, is that "any product is no more than a verbal handle, a name given to it, but that only the cause is real." Once more this explanation implies that the produced phenomenal world is not quite as real as its cause—the basic assumption of Śaṁkara. The interpretation here presented is that the process of creation (*vikāra*) proceeds by naming entities by speech (entities which are "names-and-forms"), and that the statement "the Name is *Satyam*" is best understood in context with similar speculations on the name *satyam.*

The Indian commentators generally break up the sentence as follows: *vācārambhaṇaṃ vikāro nāmadheyam; . . . satyam,* but differ widely on what is to be understood by *vācārambhaṇaṃ,* and on the explanation of what is *satyam* "real" or "true."

Since a source book should avoid presenting sources in a controversial manner, the reader is urged to consult, e.g., Franklin Edgerton's translation in *Beginnings of Indian Philosophy,* Hume's in *Thirteen Principal Upaniṣads,* Radhakrishnan's in *The Principal Upaniṣads,* to quote the more accessible ones, for further reference.

1. There was Śvetaketu, the grandson of Aruṇa. His father said to him, "Śvetaketu, you must make your studies. Surely no one of our family, my son, lives like a mere Brahmin by birth alone, without having studied."

At the age of twelve he went to a teacher and after having studied all the Vedas, he returned at the age of twenty-four, haughty, proud of his learning and conceited.

His father said to him: "Śvetaketu, now that you are so haughty, proud of your learning and conceited, did you chance to ask for that Instruction by which the unrevealed becomes revealed, the unthought thought, the unknown known?"

"How does this Instruction go, sir?"

"Like this for example: by a single lump of clay everything is known that is made of clay. 'Creating is seizing with Speech, the Name is Satyam,' namely clay.

"Like this for instance: by one piece of copper ore everything is known that is made of copper. 'Creating is seizing with Speech, the Name is Satyam,' namely copper.

"Like this for instance: by one nail-cutter everything is known that is iron. 'Creating is seizing with Speech, the Name is Satyam,' namely iron."

"Certainly my honorable teachers did not know this. For if they had known, how could they have failed to tell me? Sir, you yourself must tell me!"

"So I will, my son," he said.

2. "The *Existent* was here in the beginning, my son, alone and without a second. On this there are some who say, 'The *Nonexistent* was here in the beginning, alone and without a second. From that Nonexistent sprang the Existent.'

"But how could it really be so, my son?" he said. "How could what exists spring from what does not exist? On the contrary, my son, the *Existent* was here in the beginning, alone and without a second.

"It willed, 'I may be much, let me multiply.' It brought forth Fire. The Fire willed, 'I may be much, let me multiply.' It brought forth Water. Hence wherever a person is hot or sweats, water springs in that spot from fire.

"The Water willed, 'I may be much, let me multiply.' It brought forth Food. Hence wherever it rains, food becomes plentiful: from water indeed spring food and eatables in that spot."

3. "Of these beings indeed there are three ways of being born: it is born from an egg, it is born from a live being, it is born from a plant.

"This same deity willed, 'Why, I will create separate names-and-forms by entering entirely into these three deities with the living soul.

" 'I will make each one of them triple.' This deity created separate names-and-forms by entering entirely into these three deities with the living soul.

"Each of them he made triple. Now learn from me how these three deities each became triple."

4. "The red color of fire is the Color of Fire, the white that of Water, the black that of Food. Thus fireness has departed from fire. 'Creating is seizing with Speech, the Name is Satyam,' namely the Three Colors.

"The red color of the sun is the Color of Fire, the white that of Water, the black that of Food. Thus sunness has departed from the sun. 'Creating is seizing with Speech, the Name is Satyam,' namely the Three Colors.

"The red color of the moon is the Color of Fire, the white that of Water, the black that of Food. Thus moonness has departed from the moon. 'Creating is seizing with Speech, the Name is Satyam,' namely the Three Colors.

"The red color of lightning is the Color of Fire, the white that of Water, the black that of Food. Thus lightningness has departed from lightning. 'Creating is seizing with Speech, the Name is Satyam,' namely the Three Colors.

"As they knew this, the ancients of the great halls and of great learning said, 'Now no one can quote us anything that is unrevealed, unthought, unknown,' for they knew it by these Three Colors.

"If something was more or less red, they knew it for the Color of Fire; if it was more or less white, they knew it for the Color of Water; if it was more or less black, they knew it for the Color of Food.

"If something was not quite known, they knew it for a combination of these three dieties. Now learn from me, my son, how these three deities each become triple on reaching the person."

5. "The food that is eaten is divided into three: the most solid element becomes excrement, the middle one flesh, the finest one mind.

"The water that is drunk is divided into three: the most solid element becomes urine, the middle one blood, the finest one breath.

"The fire that is consumed is divided into three: the most solid element becomes bone, the middle one marrow, the finest one speech.

"For the mind, my son, consists in Food, the breath consists in Water, the speech consists in Fire."

"Sir, instruct me further."

"So I will, my son," he said.

6. "The fineness of milk which is being churned rises upward, my son, and that becomes butter.

"In the same way, my son, the fineness of the food that is eaten rises upward, and that becomes the mind.

"The fineness of the water that is drunk rises upward, my son, and that becomes the breath.

"The fineness of the fire that is consumed rises upward, my son, and that becomes speech.

"For the mind, my son, consists in Food, the breath consists in Water, the speech consists in Fire."

"Sir, instruct me further."

"So I will, my son," he said.

7. "Man consists of sixteen parts, my son. Do not eat for fifteen days. Drink water as you please. The breath will not be destroyed if one drinks, as it consists in Water."

He did not eat for fifteen days. Then he came back to him. "What should I say, sir?"

"Lines from the *Ṛgveda*, the *Yajurveda* and the *Sāmaveda*, my son."

"They do not come back to me, sir."

He said to him, "Just as of a big piled-up fire only one ember may be left, the size of a firefly, and the fire does not burn much thereafter with this ember, thus of your sixteen parts one part is left and with that you do not remember the Vedas. Eat. Afterwards you will learn from me."

He ate. Then he returned to him, and whatever Veda he asked, he responded completely. He said to him, "Just as one ember, the size of a firefly, that remains of a big piled-up fire will blaze up when it is stacked with straw and the fire will burn high thereafter with this ember, so, my son, one of your sixteen parts remained. It was stacked with food and it blazed forth, and with it you now remember the Vedas. For the mind consists in Food, my son, the breath in Water, speech in Fire." This he learnt from him, from him.

8. Uddālaka son of Aruṇa said to his son Śvetaketu, "Learn from me the doctrine of the sleep. When a man literally 'sleeps' [*svapiti*], then he has merged with Existent. He has 'entered the self' [*svamapītaḥ*], that is why they say that he 'sleeps'. For he has entered the self.

"Just as a bird which is tied to a string may fly hither and thither without finding a resting place elsewhere and perches on the stick to which it is tied, likewise the mind may fly hither and thither without finding a resting place elsewhere and perches on the breath. For the breath is the perch of the mind, my son.

"Learn from me hunger and thirst. When a man literally 'hungers' [*aśiśiṣati*], water conducts the food he eats. And just as we speak of a cow leader, a horse leader, a man leader, so we speak of water as 'food leader' [*aśanāyā,* but first: hunger]. You must know a shoot has sprung up there, my son. This shoot will not lack a root.

"Where would this root be but in food? Thus indeed, my son, search by way of the food, which is a shoot, for the fire, its root. Search, my son, by way of the fire as a shoot, for the Existent, its root. All these creatures, my son, are rooted in the Existent, rest on the Existent, are based upon the Existent.

"And when a man literally 'thirsts' [*pipāsati*], fire conducts the liquid which is drunk. Just as we speak of a cow leader, a horse leader, a man leader, we speak of fire as 'water leader' [*udanyā,* but first: thirst]. You must know that a shoot has sprung up there, my son. This shoot will not lack a root.

"Where would this root be but in water? Search, my son, by way of the water as the shoot, for the fire, its root. Search, my son, by way of the fire as the shoot, for the Existent, its root. All these creatures, my son, are rooted in the Existent, rest on the Existent, are based upon the Existent. It has been said before how these three deities each become triple on reaching man. Of this man when he dies, my son, the speech merges in the breath, the breath in the Fire, the Fire in the supreme deity. That indeed is the very fineness by which all this is ensouled, it is the true one, it is the soul. *You are that,* Śvetaketu."

"Instruct me further, sir."

"So I will, my son," he said.

9. "Just as the bees prepare honey by collecting the juices of all manner of trees and bring the juice to one unity, and just as the juices no longer distinctly know that the one hails from this tree, the other from that one, likewise, my son, when all these creatures have merged with the Existent they do not know, realizing only that they have merged with the Existent.

"Whatever they are here on earth, tiger, lion, wolf, boar, worm, fly, gnat, or mosquito, they become that.

"It is this very fineness which ensouls all this world, it is the true one, it is the soul. *You are that,* Śvetaketu."

"Instruct me further, sir."

"So I will, my son," he said.

10. "The rivers of the east, my son, flow eastward, the rivers of the west flow westward. From ocean they merge into ocean, it becomes the same ocean. Just as they then no longer know that they are this river or that one, just so all these creatures, my son, know no more, realizing only when having come to the Existent that they have come to the Existent. Whatever they are here on earth, tiger, lion, wolf, boar, worm, fly, gnat or mosquito, they become that.

"It is this very fineness which ensouls all this world, it is the true one, it is the soul. *You are that,* Śvetaketu."

"Instruct me further, sir."

"So I will, my son," he said.

11. "If a man would strike this big tree at the root, my son, it would bleed but stay alive. If he struck it at the middle, it would bleed but stay alive. If he struck it at the top, it would bleed but stay alive. Being entirely permeated by the living soul, it stands there happily drinking its food.

"If this life leaves one branch, it withers. If it leaves another branch, it withers. If it leaves a third branch, it withers. If it leaves the whole tree, the whole tree withers. Know that it is in this same way, my son," he said, "that this very body dies when deserted by this life, but this life itself does not die.

"This is the very fineness which ensouls all this world, it is the true one, it is the soul. *You are that,* Śvetaketu."

"Instruct me further, sir."

"So I will, my son," he said.

12. "Bring me a banyan fruit."

"Here it is, sir."

"Split it."

"It is split, sir."

"What do you see inside it?"

"A number of rather fine seeds, sir."

"Well, split one of them."

"It is split, sir."

"What do you see inside it?"

"Nothing, sir."

He said to him, "This very fineness that you no longer can make out, it is by virtue of this fineness that this banyan tree stands so big.

"Believe me, my son. It is this very fineness which ensouls all this world, it is the true one, it is the soul. *You are that,* Śvetaketu."

"Instruct me further, sir."

"So I will, my son," he said.

13. "Throw this salt in the water, and sit with me on the morrow." So he did. He said to him, "Well, bring me the salt that you threw in the water last night." He looked for it, but could not find it as it was dissolved.

"Well, taste the water on this side.—How does it taste?"

"Salty."

"Taste it in the middle.—How does it taste?"

"Salty."

"Taste it at the other end.—How does it taste?"

"Salty."

"Take a mouthful and sit with me." So he did.

"It is always the same."

He said to him, "You cannot make out what exists in it, yet it is there.

"It is this very fineness which ensouls all this world, it is the true one, it is the soul. *You are that,* Śvetaketu."

"Instruct me further, sir."

"So I will, my son," he said.

14. "Suppose they brought a man from the Gandhāra country, blindfolded, and let him loose in an uninhabited place beyond. The man, brought out and let loose with his blindfold on, would be turned around, to the east, north, west, and south.

"Then someone would take off his blindfold and tell him, 'Gandhāra is that way, go that way.' Being a wise man and clever, he would ask his way from village to village and thus reach Gandhāra. Thus in this world a man who has a teacher knows from him, 'So long will it take until I am free, then I shall reach it.'

"It is this very fineness which ensouls all this world, it is the true one, it is the soul. *You are that,* Śvetaketu."

"Instruct me further, sir."

"So I will, my son," he said.

15. "When a man is dying, his relatives crowd around him: 'Do you recognize me? Do you recognize me?' As long as his speech has not merged in his mind, his mind in his breath, his breath in Fire, and Fire in the supreme deity, he does recognize.

"But when his speech has merged in the mind, the mind in the breath, the breath in Fire, and Fire in the supreme deity, he no longer recognizes.

"It is this very fineness which ensouls all this world, it is the true one, it is the soul. *You are that,* Śvetaketu."

"Instruct me further, sir."

"So I will, my son," he said.

16. "They bring in a man with his hands tied, my son: 'He has stolen, he has committed a robbery. Heat the ax for him!' If he is the criminal, he will make himself untrue. His protests being untrue, and covering himself with untruth, he seizes the heated ax. He is burnt, and then killed.

"If he is not the criminal, he makes himself true by this very fact. His protests being true, and covering himself with truth, he seizes the heated ax. He is not burnt, and then set free.

"Just as he is not burnt—that ensouls all this world, it is the true one, it is the soul. *You are that,* Śvetaketu."

This he knew from him, from him.

THE WISDOM OF THE FIVE FIRES

Chāndogya Upaniṣad V, 3–10

This is another selection from the *Chāndogya Upaniṣad,* presenting Śvetaketu and his father Uddālaka Gautama in a different role. Here Śvetaketu, almost always the incompletely instructed pupil, complains to his father that he is unable to answer the riddles posed by a baron (*kṣatriya*).

This text, along with one closely related in the *Bṛhadāraṇyaka*

Upaniṣad, presents the fullest account of the doctrine of transmigration, which on the whole is rather understated in the Upaniṣads. The views held by the Sūtras on the subject is based on the present account. The text is further remarkable in that it presents this doctrine as special knowledge of the *kṣatriya* class. This has given rise to the hypothesis that there was a lively ambience of philosophy among the barons from which the brahmins were excluded. While this hypothesis is no doubt extreme, the question remains alive.

This and the following sections are new translations by J. A. B. van Buitenen unless otherwise indicated.

3. Śvetaketu, the grandson of Aruṇa, went to the assembly of the Pañcālas. Pravāhana Jaivali said to him, "Boy, has your father instructed you?"

"He has, sir."

"Then do you know where the creatures go from here?"

"No, sir."

"Do you know the bifurcation of the two paths, the Way of the Gods and the Way of the Ancestors?"

"No, sir."

"Do you know why the world beyond does not fill up?"

"No, sir."

"Do you know how the water in the fifth oblation becomes known as man?"

"Not at all, sir."

"Then how do you call yourself instructed? How could one call oneself instructed if he does not know the answers?"

Upset, he went back to his father. He said to him, "To be sure, your reverence told me, without having instructed me, that you had instructed me! Five questions did that accursed baron ask me, and I could not resolve a single one of them!"

. . . He said, "The way you have stated them, my son, I do not know any one of them. If I had known the answers, why would I not have told you?"

So Gautama went to the king. The latter received him with honor on his arrival. The next morning he went up to sit in the audience hall. He said to him, "Reverend Gautama, ask a boon of human wealth."

He replied, "Keep your human wealth, king! Relate to me the discourse which you mentioned before the boy!"

The king was cornered. He ordered him, "Stay a while." He said, "This wisdom, as you state it to me, Gautama, has never before you gone to the brahmins. That is why the rule in all the worlds belongs to the baronage."

4. He said to him,

"The world beyond, Gautama, is a fire. Of it the sun is the kindling, the rays the smoke, the glow the day, the embers the moon, the sparks the constellations.

"In this fire the gods offer up faith; from the oblation springs King Soma."

5. "The monsoon, Gautama, is a fire. Of it the wind is the kindling, the cloud the smoke, the lightning the glow, the thunderbolt the embers, the hail stones the sparks.

"In this fire the gods offer up King Soma. From this oblation springs the rain."

6. "The earth, Gautama, is a fire. Of it the year is the kindling, space the smoke, night the glow, the compass points the embers, the intermediate points the sparks.

"In this fire the gods offer up the rain. From this oblation springs food."

7. "Man, Gautama, is a fire. Of him speech is the kindling, breath the smoke, the tongue the glow, the eye the embers, the ear the sparks.

"In this fire the gods offer up food. From this oblation springs the seed."

8. "Woman, Gautama, is a fire. Of her the womb is the kindling, the proposition the smoke, the vagina the glow, intercourse the embers, pleasure the sparks.

"In this fire the gods offer up the seed. From this oblation springs the child."

9. "Thus in the fifth oblation water becomes known as man. The embryo, enveloped by its membrane, lies inside for ten months, or however long, then it is born.

"Once born he lives for as long as he has life. When he has died his appointed death, people carry him from here to the fire, from which he had come forth and was born."

10. "They who know it thus and in the forest devote themselves to faith and austerity, they go into the fire's glow, from the glow to day, from day to the fortnight of waxing moon, and from that fortnight to the six months when the sun goes the northern course. From these months to the year, from the year to the sun, from the sun to the moon, from the moon to lightning. There is a person who is not human; he conducts them to Brahman. This is the Way of the Gods as described.

"Now those who in the village devote themselves to rites and charity, they go into the fire's smoke, from the smoke to night, from night to the other fortnight, from the other fortnight to the six months when the sun goes the southern course. They do not reach the year.

"From the months they go to the world of the ancestors, from that world to space, from space to the moon: he is the King Soma, it is the food of the gods, the gods eat it.

"There they stay out the remainder, then they return by the same way, namely to space, from space to wind. Having become wind, they become smoke. Having become smoke, they become mist.

"Having become mist, they become the cloud, and having become the cloud, they rain forth. They are born on earth as barley and rice, herbs and trees. From thence escape is indeed difficult. If a person eats that food and then ejaculates his semen, then one becomes once more.

"They who in this world have been of pleasant deeds, the expectation is that they attain to pleasant wombs, of a brahmin, or a baron, or a clansman. But if they have been of putrid deeds, the expectation is that they attain to putrid wombs, of a dog, or a swine, or an outcaste.

"But by neither of these paths go the lowly creatures that again and again come back. That is the third level, that of: Be Born! Die! Therefore the world beyond does not fill up. Hence one should watch out. There is this verse:

> The thief of gold, the drinker of wine,
> The corruptor of his teacher's bed, a brahmin-killer,
> Those four fall, and so the fifth who consorts with them.

"If one does know these five fires, then one is not smeared with evil, even though consorting with them. Clean, pure, and of auspicious domain becomes he who knows it thus, who knows it thus."

THE WISDOM OF THE FIVE SHEATHS

Taittirīya Upaniṣad II, 1–8

The present selection is important for all Vedāntins in several respects:

1. Its lapidary opening sentence "He who knows Brahman attains the most high" lays down that the primary pursuit of Vedānta must be the knowledge of Brahman.
2. It presents a definition of Brahman in the famous assertion *satyaṃ jñānam anantam brahma,* "Brahman is truth, knowledge, and endless."
3. It outlines, even though in primitive terms, a hierarchy of the person—five "sheaths" (*kośa*) of increasing interiority.
4. And it declares, perhaps more emphatically than any other text, that the realization of the innermost self, which is tantamount to Brahman, is bliss.

1. OṂ! He who knows Brahman attains to the Most-High. On this there is the verse:

Brahman is truth, knowledge, and endless. He who knows what is hidden in the cave in the highest heaven partakes of all desires with the wise Brahman.

From this very self sprang space, from space the wind, from the wind the fire, from the fire water, from water the earth, from the earth the herbs, from the herbs food, from food man. Thus man indeed is made up of the sap of food. This is his head, this his right side, this his other side, this his trunk, this his tail, his foundation. On this there is the verse:

2. From food arise the creatures, whichsoever live on earth, and through food alone do they live, and to it they return in the end. Of all elements, food indeed is the best, hence it is called the best medicine. They forsooth attain to all food who contemplate on Brahman as food. From food are the creatures born, and once born they grow through food. It is eaten and eats the creatures, hence it is called food.

Other than this self consisting in the sap of food and within it is the self which consists of breath. It is filled by it. This has the shape of a person; it has the shape of a person according to the personal shape of the other. The *prāṇa* is its head, the *vyāna* its right side, the *apāna* its left side, space the trunk, earth its tail, its foundation. On this there is the verse:

3. After breath do the gods, men, and cattle breathe. For breath is the life of the creatures, hence it is called the all-life. To all-life go those who contemplate on Brahman as breath. For breath is the life of the creatures, hence it is called the all-life.

This self is embodied in the previous one. Other than this self consisting in breath and within it is the self consisting of mind. It is filled by it. This has the shape of a person: it is shaped like a person according to the personal shape of the other. The *yajus* formula is its head, the *rc* verse the right side, the *sāman* chant the other side, the instruction the trunk, the *atharva* hymns the tail, the foundation. On this there is the verse:

4. He who knows the Brahman which is bliss—from which both words and mind turn back without reaching it—he has no fear any more.

This self is embodied in the previous one. Other than this self consisting in mind and within it is the self consisting of knowledge. It is filled by it. This has the shape of a person: it is shaped according to the personal shape of the other. Faith is its head, order the right side, truth the other side, discipline the trunk, *mahas* the tail, the foundation. On this there is the verse:

5. Knowledge performs the sacrifice, and it performs the rites. All the gods contemplate on knowledge as the oldest Brahman. When one knows Brahman as knowledge and when one doest not become distracted from it, then, giving up the evils in the body, he attains to all desires.

This self is embodied in the previous one. Other than this self consisting in knowledge and within it is the self consisting in bliss. It is filled by it. This has the shape of a person; it is shaped according to the personal shape of the other. Happiness is its head, joy its right side, rapture its other side, bliss its trunk, Brahman its tail, its foundation. On this there is the verse:

6. Nonexistent becomes he when he knows Brahman as nonexistent. When he knows that Brahman exists, they know him by that to exist.

This self is embodied in the previous one. Next then arise the further questions: Does anyone who does not possess the knowledge go to yonder world after his death? Or does the wise man attain to yonder world after his death?

He willed, "Let me be much, I will procreate." He performed austerities. Having performed austerities he created all this, whatever is here. Having created it he entered into it, and having entered into it, he became both the Existent and the Yon [*say-tyat*], the spoken and the unspoken, the abode and the non-abode, knowledge and ignorance, truth and falsehood, he became Satyam, whatever there is. That is why they call him Satyam. On this there is the verse:

7. In the beginning the Nonexistent was here, from it was born the existent. It made itself into a self, that is why it is called well-made. That which is well-made is the sap. For upon attaining to this sap one becomes blissful. For who would breathe in and breathe out if there were no bliss in his space? That indeed makes blissful. For when one finds security, foundation in this invisible, impersonal, unspoken non-abode, then he has become fearless. When he makes in it a differentiation, then he becomes fearful. But it is a terror to the wise man who does not think. On this there is the verse:

8. For fear of it blows the wind, from fear of it rises the sun, from fear of it run Agni and Indra, and Death as the fifth.

THE WISDOM OF THE INNER RULER

Bṛhadāraṇyaka Upaniṣad III, 7

This Upaniṣadic passage is a favorite of Rāmānuja. It once more introduces Uddālaka Gautama, now as challenger of Yājñavalkya who is the principal teacher in the *Bṛhadāraṇyaka Upaniṣad* as Uddālaka is in the *Chāndogya*. The following selections from the *Bṛhadāraṇyaka* are reprinted by permission of the publishers from Franklin Edgerton, *The Beginnings of Indian Philosophy* (Cambridge, Mass.: Harvard University Press) Copyright, 1965, by George Allen & Unwin Ltd. Some of the translator's parenthetical additions to the text have been omitted.

Then Uddālaka son of Aruṇa questioned him. Yājñavalkya, said he, we were dwelling among the Madras, studying the sacrifice in the house of Patañcala son of Kapi. His wife was possessed of a gandharva (spirit). We asked him: Who are you? He said: Kavandha of the Atharvan family.

He said unto Patañcala son of Kapi and the students of the sacrifice: Do you know, pray, son of Kapi, that thread on which this world and the world beyond and all creatures are strung together?—Patañcala son of Kapi said: I do not know it, reverend sir.

He said unto Patañcala son of Kapi and the students of the sacrifice:

Do you know, pray, son of Kapi, that inner controller which controls this world and the world beyond and all creatures within?—Patañcala son of Kapi said: I do not know it, reverend sir.

He said unto Patañcala son of Kapi and the students of the sacrifice: Verily, son of Kapi, whosoever knows that thread and that inner controller, he knows Brahman, he knows the worlds, he knows the gods, he knows the Vedas, he knows the sacrifice, he knows creatures, he knows the Self, he knows everything.—Thus he spoke unto them. This I know. If you, Yājñavalkya, without knowing that thread and that inner controller, are driving away the brahmans' cows, your head shall fall off!

I know, verily, that thread, Gautama, and that inner controller.—Anyone whatsoever might say 'I know, I know.' Say, how you know it!

Wind, verily, Gautama, is that thread. By wind, verily, Gautama, as by a thread, this world and the world beyond and all creatures are strung together. Therefore, verily, Gautama, they say of a man that is dead, that his limbs have fallen apart. For by the wind, Gautama, as a thread, they are strung together.—That is just so, Yājñavalkya. Say (what) the inner controller (is).

That which rests in the earth, and is distinct from the earth, which the earth knows not, of which the earth is the body, which controls the earth within, that is thy Self, the immortal inner controller.

That which rests in water, and is distinct from water, which water knows not, of which water is the body, which controls water within, that is thy Self, the immortal inner controller.

That which rests in fire, and is distinct from fire, which fire knows not, of which fire is the body, which controls fire within, that is thy Self, the immortal inner controller. . . . So far with respect to the (cosmic) potencies. Now with respect to the worlds.

That which rests in all the worlds, and is distinct from all the worlds, which all the worlds know not, of which all the worlds are the body, which controls all the worlds within, that is thy Self, the immortal inner controller. So far, again, with respect to the worlds. Now with respect to the Vedas.

That which rests in all the Vedas, and is distinct from all the Vedas, which all the Vedas know not, of which all the Vedas are the body, which controls all the Vedas within, that is thy Self, the immortal inner controller. So far, again, with respect to the Vedas. Now with respect to sacrifices.

That which rests in all sacrifices, and is distinct from all sacrifices, which all sacrifices know not, of which all sacrifices are the body, which controls all sacrifices within, that is thy Self, the immortal inner controller. So far, again, with regard to sacrifices. Now with regard to creatures.

That which rests in all creatures, and is distinct from all creatures, which all creatures know not, of which all creatures are the body, which controls all creatures within, that is thy Self, the immortal inner controller. So far, again, with regard to creatures. Now with regard to the (individual) self.

That which rests in the breath, and is distinct from the breath, which the breath knows not, of which the breath is the body, which controls the breath within, that is thy Self, the immortal inner controller.

The Unseen Seer; the Unheard Hearer; the Unthought Thinker; the Unknown Knower. There is no other Seer; there is no other Hearer; there is no other Thinker; there is no other Knower. This is thy Self, the immortal inner controller. Whatever is other than this is evil.—Then Uddālaka son of Aruṇa subsided.

THE WISDOM OF THE IMPERISHABLE

Bṛhadāraṇyaka Upaniṣad III, 8

This selection from the *Bṛhadāraṇyaka Upaniṣad* is of great importance to Śaṁkara in that it appears to give scriptural authority to the postulate of a completely undifferentiated supreme being, of which nothing phenomenal can be predicated. The text eases into the following one (IV, 2) in which King Janaka of Videha, a patron of Yājñavalkya and himself a royal seer, interrogates the brahmin. It culminates in the famous description of Brahman as "Not, Not" (*neti neti*), perhaps the most succinct statement of the unqualified supreme as held by Śaṁkara.

Then (Gārgī) the daughter of Vacaknu said: Reverend Brahmans, look now! I will ask this Yājñavalkya two questions. If he solves them for me, of a certainty not one of you could overcome him in a *brahmodya* (theological debate). If he does not solve them for me, his head will fall off.—Ask, Gārgī! he said.

Said she: Verily I, Yājñavalkya—as a chief's son of Kāśī or Videha would string his unstrung bow and take in his hand two arrows to smite his enemies and stand forth (to combat)—just so I stand forth against you with two questions. Answer me them!—Ask, Gārgī, he said.

Said she: That which, Yājñavalkya, is above the heaven, that which is beneath the earth, that which is between heaven and earth here, that which they call past and present and future; on what is this strung and threaded?

Said he: That which, Gārgī, is above the heaven, that which is beneath the earth, that which is between heaven and earth here, that which they call past and present and future; on the ether that is strung and threaded.

Said she: Homage be yours, Yājñavalkya! For you have solved me this (question). Prepare yourself for the other.—Ask, Gārgī! he said.

Said he: That which, Yājñavalkya, is above the heaven, that which is beneath the earth, that which is between heaven and earth here, that which they call past and present and future; on what, I repeat, is this strung and threaded?

Said he: That which, Gārgī, is above the heaven, that which is beneath the earth, that which is between heaven and earth here, that which they call past and present and future; on the ether, I repeat, that is strung and threaded.—But on what, say, is the ether strung and threaded?

Said he: This verily, Gārgī, is what brahmans refer to as the Imperishable. It is not coarse, not fine; not short, not long; without blood, without fat; without shadow, without darkness; without wind, without ether; without contact, without touch, without smell, without taste, without sight, without hearing, without speech, without thought-organ, without heat; without breath, without mouth; without name, without family; ageless, deathless, fearless, immortal; without dust, without sound; not opened, not closed; without first, without last; without inside, without outside; it consumes no one, no one consumes it.

In the control of this Imperishable, Gārgī, heaven and earth stand severally fixed. In the control of this Imperishable, Gārgī, sun and moon stand severally fixed. In the control of this Imperishable, Gārgī, days and nights, half-months, months, seasons, and years stand severally fixed. In the control of this Imperishable, Gārgī, some rivers flow eastward from the white mountains, others westward, and in whatsoever direction they each may flow. In the control of this Imperishable, Gārgī, men praise the generous giver, the gods are dependent on the sacrifice-patron, and the departed ancestors on the spoon-offering.

Whosoever without knowing this Imperishable, Gārgī, sacrifices, gives gifts, or practices austerities for even many thousands of years, for him that (heavenly) world (which he gains) is only finite. Whosoever without knowing this Imperishable, Gārgī, passes away from this world, he is wretched. But he who knowing this Imperishable, Gārgī, passes away from this world, he is a (true) Brāhmaṇa.

It is just this Imperishable, Gārgī, which is the unseen seeing one, the unheard hearing one, the unthought thinking one, the unknown knowing one. There is nothing else that sees; there is nothing else that hears; there is nothing else that thinks; there is nothing else that knows. It is even this Imperishable, Gārgī, whereon the ether is strung and threaded.

Said she: Reverend Brahmans! Think it a great enough thing, if you can get free of him with a rendering of homage! Of a certainty not one of you will ever overcome him in a *brahmodya* (theological debate).—Then Gārgī the daughter of Vacaknu subsided.

"NOT, NOT"

Bṛhadāraṇyaka Upaniṣad IV, 2, 3, 4

2. Then Janaka of Videha descended humbly from his seat and said: Homage to you, Yājñavalkya! Instruct me! Said he: As, O king, one about to go on a long journey would provide himself with a car or a boat, so your Self is fitted out with these mystic doctrines. Being so eminent and rich, after you have studied the Vedas and heard the mystic doctrines recited, where will you go when you are released from this world?—I do not know, reverend sir, where I shall go.—Then I will tell you this, where you will go.—Speak, reverend sir!

He said: This person in the right eye is called Indha (the kindler). He, who is Indha, is called Indra, cryptically as it were; for the gods may be said to love the cryptic and dislike the obvious.

Now this that has the form of a person in the left eye is his consort, Virāj ('queen' or 'majesty'). The concert of these two is this space within the heart. Their food is this mass of blood within the heart. Their covering is this net-like thing within the heart. Their path, which is traversible, is this channel which goes upward from the heart.

He (the Self, union of Indha and Virāj) has these channels called *Hitā*, (as fine) as a hair split in a thousand parts. By these flows in to him (the food) that flows in. Therefore he has, so to say, more delicate food than this corporeal Self.

Of this same person, the eastern (-going) vital powers are the eastern quarter, the southern (-going) vital powers are the southern quarter, the western (-going) vital powers are the western quarter, the northern (-going) vital powers are the northern quarter, the upward (-going) vital powers are the zenith, the downward (-going) vital powers are the nadir; all his vital powers are all the quarters.

This is the Self that is (described as) 'not, not.' It is ungraspable, for it is not grasped; it is indestructible, for it is not destroyed. It has not attachment and is unfastened; it is not attached, and (yet) is not unsteady. You have truly attained freedom from danger, Janaka! said Yājñavalkya.—Said Janaka of Videha: Homage to you, Yājñavalkya! May freedom from danger come to you, inasmuch as you, reverend sir, announce freedom from danger for me. Here are the Videhas, and here am I (as your servants).

3. Yājñavalkya approached Janaka of Videha, thinking: I will converse with him. Now when Janaka of Videha and Yājñavalkya had conversed together at an Agnihotra sacrifice, Yājñavalkya had given him a wish. The wish which he chose was just to ask any desired question. And he had granted this (wish) to him. Therefore the king himself spoke first to him.

Yājñavalkya, what serves as light to man here?—The sun, O king, said he. It is by the light of the sun that he sits down, walks about, does his work, and returns home.—Just so it is, Yājñavalkya.

When the sun has set, Yājñavalkya, what serves as light, I repeat, to man here?—The moon, O king, said he. It is by the light of the moon that he sits down, walks about, does his work, and returns home.—Just so it is, Yājñavalkya.

When the sun has set, Yājñavalkya, and the moon has set, what serves as light, I repeat, to man here?—The fire, O king, said he. It is by the light of the fire that he sits down, walks about, does his work, and returns home.—Just so it is, Yājñavalkya.

When the sun has set, Yājñavalkya, and the moon has set, and the fire is extinguished, what serves as light, I repeat, to man here?—Speech, O king, said he. It is by the light of speech that he sits down, walks about, does his work, and returns home. Therefore it is, O king, that when even his own hand cannot be made out, then wherever Speech is uttered, one goes towards that.—Just so it is, Yājñavalkya.

When the sun has set, Yājñavalkya, and the moon has set, and the fire is extinguished, and speech has ceased, what serves as light, I repeat, to man here?—The Self, O king, said he. For it is by the light of the Self that he sits down, walks about, does his work, and returns home.

What is the Self?—It is that Spirit (*puruṣa*), consisting of intelligence, the inner light within the vital powers, within the heart. Being common (to the two worlds), it traverses both worlds, and seems to think (in the other, intellectual world), and seems to move about (in this world). Becoming a dream, endowed with intelligence (characteristic of the other world), it transcends this world.

This same Spirit, upon being born and attaining a body, is conjoined to evils; passing forth, dying, it abandons evils, the forms of death.

Now of this same Spirit there are (primarily) just two states; this one, and the other-world state. There is a third, a twilight state, the state of dream. When he is in this twilight state, he sees both states, this one, and the other-world state.

Now as this (dream-state) is an approach to the other-world state, entering on this approach, he sees both the evils (of this world's state) and the joys (of the other world's state). When this (Spirit) dreams, he takes material from this world with all its contents, and cutting it down himself, building it up himself, by his own radiance, by his own light, he dreams. Under these circumstances his own self serves as light to man (Spirit, *puruṣa*) here.

There are no wagons there (i.e. in the sleeping state), no teams, no roads; on the contrary he creates for himself wagons, teams, and roads. There are no joys, delights, and happinesses there; on the contrary he creates for himself joys, delights and happinesses. There are no pools, rivers and lakes there; on the contrary he creates for himself pools, rivers and lakes. For he is the Creator.

On this subject also there are these verses:

Subduing the bodily (state; or self?) with sleep—not sleeping, he gazes intently on those that are asleep. Assuming brightness, he comes back again to his (waking) state—the golden, Single Swan of the Spirit.

Protecting by the life-breath his other nest, roaming immortal outside of the nest, he wanders, immortal, wherever he wills—the golden Single Swan of the Spirit.

Wandering manifoldly in the state of dream, he makes for himself many forms, the God; now apparently indulging in pleasures with women (and so) laughing; now again apparently seeing terrors.

They see his pleasure-garden; *himself* no one sees. Therefore they say, Let one not waken one that is stretched out (in sleep); hard to cure is he to whom this (Spirit) does not return.

On this subject, moreover, they say: This (dream condition) is just (the same as) the waking condition of him. For the same things that one sees when he is awake, even these (he sees) when dreaming. Under these circumstances this man (Spirit) serves for himself as light.—Just so it is, Yājñavalkya. I now give your reverence a thousand (cows). From henceforth speak (on that which leads) unto salvation.

When, in this condition of dream, this (Spirit) has indulged in pleasures, has roamed about, only after he has seen the good (beyond) and the evil (here), according to his way of procedure (his 'rule', particular course of action), according to his origin (i.e. to the particular body which he left), he runs back precisely to the waking condition. And whatever he sees there (in dream), it does not follow after him; for nothing clings to this Spirit.—Just so it is, Yājñavalkya. I now give your reverence a thousand (cows). From henceforth speak (on that which leads) unto salvation.

Just as a great fish follows along both banks, the nearer and the farther (alternately); even so this Spirit follows along both states, the dream state, and the waking state.

Just as in the ether here, an eagle, or a falcon, after flying about in various places, being weary, folds its wings and settles down precisely on its nest; just so this Spirit makes for that state in which, asleep, he desires no desire, sees no dream (i.e. the state of deep, dreamless sleep).

He has these channels called *Hitā*, as fine as a hair split in a thousand parts, and they are full of white, blue, yellow, green and red. Now whenever (in a dream, as previously described; this resumé of dream-state prepares for the contrast with deep sleep) he seems to be smitten, or overpowered, or an elephant seems to cut him to pieces, or he seems to fall into a pit; whatever he looks upon as a terror when awake, even that in this state (of dream) he looks upon as a terror, through ignorance. On the other hand, (the state) in which (one is) like a king, like a god, one thinks 'I myself am this whole universe' (this describes the closest possible approach, in empiric waking life, to the author's notion of the state of deep sleep)—this (state of deep sleep) is his highest heaven.

Now when, asleep, he desires no desire and sees no dream, even this is his form (aspect, practically 'state') that desires (only) the Self, that has attained desires, that has no desires. Just as a man who is embraced by a beloved woman knows nothing outer or inner, even so this bodily Self (*ātman*), when it is embraced by the Self consisting-of-intelligence, knows neither outer nor inner.

Even this is his form that is beyond desire, that has sloughed off evil, that knows no fear, that is free from sorrow. In this state father is no father, mother no mother, worlds no worlds, gods no gods, Vedas no Vedas, sacrifices no sacrifices (to him): in this state a thief is no thief, a procurer of abortion no procurer of abortion, a Paulkasa no Paulkasa, a Cāṇḍāla no Cāṇḍāla, a mendicant no mendicant, an ascetic no ascetic. He is unaffected by good, unaffected by evil; for then he has transcended all sorrows of the heart.

If, then, he does not see—though seeing (having the power of sight), he sees no object of sight. For there cannot be any separation of the seer from sight, since it (or he?) is indestructible. But there is not, then, any second thing, other and separate from him, which he might see.

He is (like) water (?), the One Seer, with no second. This is realized, the Heaven of the Brahman, O king!—Thus he said to him.—This is his highest attainment, this is his highest heaven, this is his highest joy; it is just this joy, on a small portion of which other creatures live.

Now this (joy) of men which is perfect and prosperous, which is overlord of other (joys), and most richly endowed with all human desires;—this is the highest joy of men.

But a hundred joys of men are one joy of the ancestors ('Fathers', Manes) who have won heaven.

But a hundred joys of the ancestors who have won heaven are one joy in the Gandharva heaven.

But a hundred joys in the Gandharva heaven are one joy of the karma-gods, who have attained unto godhood by karma (i.e. by ritual works).

But a hundred joys of the karma-gods are one joy of the gods from birth [and of one who is a scholar in the Veda, free from guile, and not affected by desire].

But a hundred joys of the gods from birth are one joy in the Heaven of Prajāpati [and of one who is a scholar in the Veda, free from guile, and not affected by desire].

But a hundred joys in the Heaven of Prajāpati are one joy in the Heaven of Brahman [and of one who is a scholar in the Veda, free from guile, and not affected by desire]. This is the Heaven of Brahman, O king!—Thus he instructed him.—This is immortality (or: nectar)! I now give your reverence a thousand (cows). From henceforth speak (on that which leads) unto salvation.—

When, in this condition of peace, this (Spirit) has indulged in pleasure, has roamed about, has seen good and evil, according to his way of procedure (as above) according to his origin (as above) he returns again to the waking condition. And whatever he sees there (in deep sleep), it does not follow after him; for nothing clings to this Spirit.—Just so it is, Yājñavalkya. I now give your reverence a thousand (cows). From henceforth speak (on that which leads) unto salvation.—

Then Yājñavalkya became afraid (thinking): The king is clever; he has driven me out of all my conclusions.—(He continued): When one wastes away (literally 'goes to thinness'), it is on account of either old age or afflicting (disease) that he wastes away. Just as a mango or fig or peepal fruit is released from its stem, even so this corporeal Self is released from these members and returns according to its way of procedure, according to its origin (as above)—namely, to nothing but the (life-) breath.

Now just as a wagon when it is completely loaded starts out creaking, just so this corporeal Self, when the Intelligent Self (*see* 4. 4. 2, 3) has mounted upon it, starts out creaking.

Now just as when a king arrives his nobles, responsible heirs, marshals, and chief men of the towns prepare for him with food, drink, and lodging, saying: Here he comes, here he arrives!—just so all the elements (of the body, viz. the vital powers or sense-faculties and their material objects) prepare for him who has this knowledge, saying: Here (at the time of approaching death) comes the Brahman, here he arrives!

Now just as when a king intends to set out on a journey his nobles, responsible heirs, marshals and chief men of the towns gather together unto him, just so all the vital powers (*prāṇāḥ*) gather together unto this Self at the time of death, when he is on the point of breathing forth (his life) upward.

4. Now when this corporeal Self becomes weak and enters a state of seeming insensibility, then these vital powers (*prāṇāḥ*; here the various organic functions) gather together unto it. It takes unto itself those particles of radiance and departs into the Heart.

Now when this Spirit (*puruṣa*) of the Eye, leaving (the eye), turns away from it (to the Bodily Self in the heart), then he (the dying man) becomes incapable of distinguishing forms. He is unified: and they say, he cannot see. He is unified, and they say, he cannot smell. He is unified, and they say, he cannot taste. He is unified, and they say, he cannot speak. He is unified, and they say, he cannot hear. He is unified, and they say, he cannot think. He is unified, and they say, he cannot touch. He is unified, and they say, he cannot understand.

Now the tip of this heart becomes illuminated (by the 'particles of radiance'). By this light this Self (*ātman*) departs, either from the eye, or from the head, or from other parts of the body. When it departs the life (-breath; *prāṇa*) departs along with it; and when the life (-breath) departs all the vital powers (of the several organs, which have previously been united with it, in the state of coma; the word used is *prāṇāḥ*) depart along with it. It is simply consciousness (*saṁjñāna*, which must mean or include the *prāṇa* and the several prāṇas) that follows along with it; this same (Self) becomes knowing, endowed with intelligence (*vijñāna*). His knowledge and (past) deeds and memory ('knowledge of the past') take hold of him.

Then just as a grass leech, when it comes to the end of a blade of grass, gathers itself up together (to go over to something else), even so this Spirit, when it has rid itself of this body and cast off ignorance, gathers itself up together (to go over to another body).

Just as an embroiderer takes off a part from an embroidered garment and weaves for himself another, newer and more beautiful, pattern, even so this Spirit, when it has rid itself of this body and cast off ignorance, weaves for itself another newer form—either of a departed spirit (*pitar*) or of a gandharva or of (an inhabitant of) Brahma ('s world) or of (an inhabitant of) Prajāpati ('s world) or of a god or of a man or from other creatures.

Now this Self (*ātman*), verily, is Brahman. It is composed of intelligence, thought, speech, life (vital power or breath), sight, hearing, ether, wind, heat (fire), water, earth, anger and non-anger, joy and non-joy, right and non-right; it is composed of everything (i.e. contains everything within itself, because it is identical with the Brahman or Soul of the universe). Now whenever it is composed of this thing or of that thing,—however it acts, however it operates, so it becomes (in the next life). Acting well it becomes good; acting ill it becomes evil. As a result of right action it becomes what is good; as a result of evil action it becomes what is evil.

Now in this connection they say: This Spirit (man, *puruṣa*) consists simply of desire. As is his desire, so is his resolve; as is his resolve, so is the deed he does; as is the deed he does, so is that which he attains unto.

So there is this verse:

That upon which his characteristic mark (tag, namely) his thought, is intent—being just that, man goes unto that along with deeds. Having come to the end of (the effects of) that action, of all whatsoever he does in *this* world, he returns again from that world (beyond) unto this world, unto action.

So far one who is desirous. Now one who no longer desires. He who is desireless, who is without desire, who desires (only) the Self, who has attained his desires—from him the vital powers (of the body) do not mount upward; they are collected together right in him. Being just the Brahman, unto the Brahman he (the Soul) arrives.

Now on this there is this verse:

When all desires are expelled, which lurk within his heart, then a mortal becomes immortal; he attains the Brahman here (in this world).

Just as the slough of a snake lies dead, thrown down upon an ant-hill, even so this body lies (dead). Then this boneless, bodiless, intelligent Self (*ātman*) *is* just the Brahman—*is* just Heaven, O king! Thus said Yājñavalkya.—I now give your reverence a thousand (cows)! Thus said Janaka of Videha.

Now in this connection there are these verses:

Narrow is the way—penetrating (Kāṇva text 'extended'), ancient; it has reached unto me, by me likewise has it been discovered; by this way the wise knowers of the Brahman, rising upward, arrive at the heavenly world, released from this world.

Therein, they say, is white and blue, yellow, green, and red (fluid); this way was discovered, verily, by the Brahman; on it travels the Brahman-knower, the radiant, and the doer of right.

Into blind darkness enter they who are devoted to not-coming-into-being (who believe in no rebirth); into what seems even greater darkness than that, those who take delight in coming-into-being (who crave rebirth, further existence).

Those worlds are called the demons' worlds; they are enveloped in blind darkness. Ignorant, foolish folk enter into them after death.

Being just that, even that we become; dire disaster comes to him who knows it not! Those who know it become immortal; on the other hand the others attain naught but suffering.

If a man should well understand the Self, saying 'I am it'—seeking after what, for desire of what, should he pursue (Kāṇva, crave after, be troubled about) the body?

He who has found and awakened his Self, that is entered into this thicket of a bodily mold (impenetrable bodily complex), he is the All-creator; for he is the Maker of everything. Heaven is his; nay rather, he *is* Heaven outright!

When one looks upon this, the Self, directly as God, the Lord of past and future, then he shall not falter.

That Self, in which the five-fold creatures and the ether have their foundation, even that I, intelligent and immortal, hold for the immortal Brahman.

On this side of whom the year revolves with the days, that the gods worship as the light of lights—yes, as life, as immortality.

The life (-power) of life (-power), the eye of the eye likewise, and the ear of the ear, the food of food, the mind of mind—those who know this, they have understood the Brahman, the ancient, the primal.

By the mind alone must it be understood, that there is nothing manifold in this world. Death after death attains he who thinks he sees manifoldness in this world.

That imperishable, constant one must be perceived only with the mind; (it is) the unborn, great, constant Self, free from impurity, higher than the ether.

A man of insight, a brāhmaṇa, by understanding this (Self) should make knowledge for himself. Let him not muse on many words; for that is only wearing out the voice.

Now it is this Self that is the controller of all, the lord of all, the sovereign of all; it governs all this universe, whatever is at all. It becomes not greater by good deed, nor less by evil deed. It is overlord of creatures; it is the lord of the world(s); it is the guardian of the world(s); it is the dyke that holds apart these worlds, lest they should crash together (i.e. it keeps the world order from falling into chaos).

This it is which they seek to know through repetition of the Vedas, through celibate life, through asceticism, through faith, through sacrifice, and through fasting. When one knows this he becomes a Muni (silent sage). This it is which wandering ascetics seek as their heavenly world when they wander forth as ascetics.

Therefore those Brāhmaṇas of old, learned and wise, desired no offspring, thinking: What shall we do with offspring, we who possess this Self, this (equivalent of the) Heavenly World (which is the traditional object of begetting sons)?—Abandoning both the desire for sons and the desire for possessions and the desire for heaven, they wandered forth a-begging. For the desire for sons is the same as the desire for possessions, and the desire for possessions is the same as the desire for heaven; for both are nothing but desires.

This Self is (simply described as) 'Not, not'. It is ungraspable, for it is not grasped. It is indestructible, for it is not destroyed. It has no attachment, and is unfastened; it is not attached, and (yet) is not unsteady. For it, immortal, passes beyond both these two states (in which one thinks) 'For this reason I have done evil', 'For this reason I have done good'. It is not disturbed by good or evil things that are done or left undone; its heaven is not lost by any deed.

This is meant by this verse:

This is the constant greatness of the brāhmaṇa (knower of Brahman); he increases not nor becomes less by deed. This (greatness) it is, the basis of which one should seek to find; having found it, one is not stained by evil deed.

Therefore one who knows this, becoming pacified, controlled, at peace, patient, full of faith, should see the Self in the Self alone. He looks upon everyone as it. Everyone comes to be his Self; he becomes the Self of everyone. He passes over all evil; evil does not pass over him. He subdues all evil; evil does not subdue him. He is free from evil, free from age (Kāṇva, from impurity), free from hunger (Kāṇva, from doubt), free from thirst (Kāṇva omits), a Brāhmaṇa, who so has this knowledge.

This verily is that great unborn Self, the eater of (sacrificial) food, the giver of wealth (i.e. who has the functions of the Vedic gods). Whosoever knows thus this great unborn Self, the eater of food, the giver of wealth, he finds wealth.

This is that great unborn Self, ageless, deathless, fearless, immortal —the Brahman. You have attained fearlessness, O Janaka! Thus spoke Yājñavalkya.—I now give unto your reverence the Videhas, and myself too along with them, in servitude.—

This is that great unborn Self, ageless, deathless, fearless, immortal, the Brahman. The Brahman, in sooth, is fearlessness; fearlessness surely he becomes, he becomes Brahman, who has such knowledge.

CHAPTER 2

Recollection

After *śruti* or Revelation, Vedānta accepts a second point of departure, *smṛti* or Recollection. No Revelation is enough, and all Revelation is too plentiful. Every tradition that bases itself on revealed truth makes its selection, and in the end it is often no more than a few handfuls of assertions that finally constitute the scriptural foundation of a faith. At the same time, however great be the guidance of scripture in matters of high truth and ultimate destiny, it frequently is insufficient to guide the conduct of the believer. The Christian Church recognizes Tradition next to Revelation. Islām has formed a large collection of ḥadīth, traditions concerning Muhammad's reactions and responses to problems and questions that were not completely provided for by the *Qur'ān.* Likewise Indian religion has added to the monument of *śruti* the hostel of *smṛti.*

Literally the word means "memory" or "recollection." Generally it has become a technical term to describe an enormous corpus of texts and treatises. The transition between the two usages is not too difficult. We have seen that Revelation, which is beginningless and authorless, came to the vision of the seers at the dawn of creation. The seers thereupon started an uninterrupted transmission to a series of pupils that stretches until today. At the same time these seers conducted themselves in certain ways: in the first place their conduct was in accordance with the dictates of the Vedas, but they observed also customs and practices not explicitly mentioned in the Vedas. Such behavior they also transmitted to their pupils and it is such behavior, not explicitly Vedic but inferrable from the Vedas, which is deemed *smṛti,* "recollection." This behavior was subsequently written up as *dharma* in the smṛtis, for instance the *smṛti* of Manu—here the word practically approaches the notion of a book of law. The usage was extended to any work that dealt with the *dharma,* and indeed hardly any work from early Sanskrit literature does not qualify as such.

Nevertheless, these smṛtis do not have an independent authority as the Upaniṣads have. They are authored and therefore fallible.

The only bases of their authority are that they are put into practice by those who also adhere to the precepts of the Veda and that they are not in conflict with the Veda. Thus the smṛtis of Manu and Yājñavalkya are authoritative, but the *smṛti* of the Buddha, for instance, is not.

While Vedānta accepts as a matter of course the authority of a number of smṛtis, it gives first place to one text, the *Bhagavadgītā*, thus bowing to the popularity the text had acquired. The *Bhagavadgītā* is referred to in the *Brahmasūtras*, and the fact that all the early Vedāntins of the classical period, Śaṁkara, Bhāskara, and Rāmānuja, felt called upon to write a commentary on it—even Śaṁkara to whom the text is not at all congenial—shows that it had acquired an authority so wide that it could not be overlooked by Vedānta.

The *Gītā* is in many respects very dissimilar to the Upaniṣads. There is first the fact that it forms part of the huge epic of the *Mahābhārata*, which gives it a very different tone. It is not a "mystery," accessible only to those whose birth and education had singled them out for the study of it, but, as part of the popular epic, in principle within the scope of all and sundry (although Bhāskara will object to that). It is a discourse from one warrior to another, even if one of them will be discovered to be God himself. Although there are some discontinuities in it, it presents itself as, and largely is, a continuous discourse which is more extensive than any such in the Upaniṣads. As part of a different tradition, it could without difficulty draw on a far larger reality of beliefs and practices than the Upaniṣads, which remain tied to the Vedic tradition of sacerdotalism.

The *Gītā* is a dialogue. It is a dialogue, formally, between the warrior Arjuna who, when finally faced with a family war in which he finds close relatives, friends, and gurus drawn up against him and his party, has second thoughts and refuses to engage in the battle. But beyond that it is a dialogue, sometimes approaching a debate, between diverging attitudes concerning and methods toward the attainment of release (*mokṣa*).

Transmigration, still muted in the Upaniṣads, is now completely axiomatic. But having become axiomatic it has raised new questions. The entire thrust of the Vedic tradition, only partly parried by the Upaniṣads, was the supreme significance of ritual action, which was seen to be for the benefit of the world. There is an underlying assumption that this world is a good world and that the meticulous performance of the appointed ritual tasks are essential to the proper operation of this world. This world view can do comfortably without any assumptions of transmigration and the necessity to seek release from the world. Yet these very assumptions have now intersected with the established tradition.

The *Gītā* can be placed roughly about the beginning of the Christian era, within a margin of two centuries, and the authors must have seen the appeal of the soteriologies both of the "heterodox" traditions of Buddhism and Jainism and of the more "orthodox" ones of Sāṁkhya and Yoga. Given the variations even within each of these traditions, they had in common an ultimate rejection of the world, a final renunciation, in favor of an individual search for release without it.

Still, the Brahminist tradition, down from Vedic times, had exalted the significance of *dharma* as the instrument of goodness. The tenet of transmigration now has come to hold that a man who acts perpetuates, by his very action, the cycle of rebirth, even if the acts he accomplishes are *good* acts. This ethics of duty has been transcended by a different, seemingly incompatible ethics of release, which demands that man quit acting at all and rise "beyond the good and evil" of being of this world.

Formally, Arjuna's dilemma is to choose between conflicting dharmas: as a warrior his *dharma* is to fight a just war; as a man of honor, facing on the battlefield his kinsmen and betters, this war, however just, is unjust and against *dharma* since it attacks the family, the basic unit of *dharma* ethics. This dilemma is a real one, but Kṛṣṇa transforms it to restate the newer dilemma of whether to act at all, and by so doing condemn oneself to transmigration, or renounce all actions in favor of a solitary, unbeholden pursuit of release. While apparently forbearing to judge between the Way of the Task (*karma-yoga*) and the Way of the Insight (*jñāna-yoga*), Kṛṣṇa's emphasis is very strongly on the Task, and he offers the solution that the Task, if accomplished without detachment to its reward, leads equally to an escape from bondage as does the Way of the Insight, which harbors its own hypocrisies. Kṛṣṇa reveals himself as a practician of the Task, descending to this world not for any unfulfilled wish of his own, but to restore *dharma* and hold the world together.

He also reveals himself as the paramount God in the theophany of chapter eleven. And an even more novel attitude interjects itself in the dialogue between that of the *dharma* and that of the solitary insight—the attitude of *bhakti* or devotion. There is a godhead, both transcendent like a supreme God and immanent, or within the individual self itself, to which one should offer up one's actions in a rapture of glorification and thus attain unity with it in release.

In outlining these attitudes and methods and attempting to

forge a harmony between them, the *Gītā* at the same time presents us with a typology of Vedānta, if not of all Indian thought. There is the strand that holds the world so lightly that it can conceive of release only as the utter negation of it, and the only way to be pursued is that which leads to the liberating insight into the absolute otherness of the Brahman; this is exemplified by Śaṁkara. There remains the strand that *dharma* must not be ignored, that the world must be kept together, and if indeed the insight in Brahman's nature is necessary, this nature cannot be absolutely other than this world. There must be a continuity between this and that as there must be between living in this world and fulfilling one's task, and the insight that liberates from bondage; this is exemplified by Bhāskara. And finally there is the strand which holds that the very purpose of Vedānta is to explicate and glorify God and that both task and insight come together and are sublimated in devotion; this is exemplified by Rāmānuja.

It may well be *this* universalism of the *Gītā* which gave rise to its popularity, which in turn demanded that Vedānta, whose intentions became more and more universal, deal with it. It is in no way a systematic treatise, although it has a greater inner cohesion than the Upaniṣads. It reveals the influences of schools other or later than those represented by the earlier texts. It adds a new dimension to Vedānta which henceforth is not content to limit itself to the Upaniṣads, but needs respect the more open, popular, theistic assertions that have since been made.

The following selections are from *The Bhagavad Gītā*, translated by Eliot Deutsch. Copyright © 1968 by Eliot Deutsch. Reprinted by permission of Holt, Rinehart and Winston, Inc.

THE *BHAGAVADGĪTĀ*

Arjuna saw standing there fathers and grandfathers, teachers, uncles, brothers, sons and grandsons, and also companions;

And fathers-in-law and friends in both the armies. Seeing all these kinsmen thus arrayed, Arjuna,

Filled with the utmost compassion, sorrowfully spoke: Seeing my own kinsmen, O Kṛṣṇa, arrayed and wishing to fight,

My limbs collapse, my mouth dries up, there is trembling in my body and my hair stands on end;

The bow Gandiva slips from my hand and my skin also is burning; I am not able to stand still, my mind is whirling.

And I see evil portents, O Kṛṣṇa, and I foresee no good in slaying my own kinsmen in the fight.

I do not desire victory, O Kṛṣṇa, nor kingdom, nor pleasure. Of what use is kingdom to us, O Kṛṣṇa, of what use pleasure or life?

Those for whose sake we desire kingdom, pleasures and happiness, they are arrayed here in battle, having renounced their lives and riches.

Teachers, fathers, sons, and also grandfathers; uncles, fathers-in-law, grandsons, brothers-in-law and other kinsmen;

These I do not wish to kill, though they kill me, O Kṛṣṇa; even for the kingdom of the three worlds; how much less then for the sake of the earth! (I, 26–35)

In the ruin of a family, its immemorial laws perish; and when the laws perish, the whole family is overcome by lawlessness.

And when lawlessness prevails, O Kṛṣṇa, the women of the family are corrupted, and when women are corrupted, O Kṛṣṇa, mixture of caste arises.

And this confusion brings the family itself to hell and those who have destroyed it; for their ancestors fall, deprived of their offerings of rice and water.

By the sins of those who destroy a family and create a mixture of caste, the eternal laws of the caste and the family are destroyed.

The men of the families whose laws are destroyed, O Kṛṣṇa, assuredly will dwell in hell; so we have heard. (I, 40–44)

The Blessed Lord said:

Thou grievest for those thou shouldst not grieve for, and yet thou speakest words that sound like wisdom. Wise men do not mourn for the dead or for the living.

Never was there a time when I did not exist, nor thou, nor these rulers of men; nor will there ever be a time hereafter when we shall all cease to be.

As the soul in the body passes through childhood, youth and old age, so (after departure from this body) it passes on to another body. The sage is not bewildered by this.

Contacts with the objects of the senses, O Arjuna, give rise to cold and heat, pleasure and pain. They come and go, they are impermanent; endure them, O Arjuna.

The man who is not troubled by these contacts, O Arjuna, who treats alike pleasure and pain, who is wise; he is fit for immortality.

Of non-being there is no coming to be; of being there is no ceasing to be. The truth about both is seen by the seers of truth.

Know that by which all this is pervaded is indestructible, and that no one can cause the destruction of this immutable being.

It is said that (only) these bodies of the eternal embodied soul, which is indestructible and incomprehensible, are perishable. Therefore fight, O Arjuna!

He who thinks that this soul is a slayer, and he who thinks that this soul is slain; both of them are ignorant. This soul neither slays nor is slain.

It is never born, nor does it die, nor having once been, will it again cease to be. It is unborn, eternal, and everlasting. This primeval one is not slain when the body is slain.

He who knows that it is indestructible and eternal, unborn and unchanging, how can that man slay, O Arjuna, or cause another to slay?

Just as a man casts off worn-out clothes and takes on others that are new, so the embodied soul casts off worn-out bodies and takes on others that are new.

Weapons do not cut it, nor does fire burn it; waters do not make it wet, nor does wind make it dry.

It is uncleavable; it cannot be burnt, it can neither be wetted nor dried. It is eternal, omnipresent, unchanging and immovable. It is everlasting.

It is called unmanifest, unthinkable and immutable; therefore, knowing it as such, thou shouldst not grieve. (II, 11–25)

As much use as there is for a pond when there is everywhere a flood, so much is there in all the Vedas for a Brahmin who understands.

In action only hast thou a right and never in its fruits. Let not thy motive be the fruits of action; nor let thy attachment be to inaction.

Fixed in *yoga,* O Arjuna, perform actions, abandoning attachment and remaining evenminded in success and failure; for serenity of mind is called *yoga.*

Mere action is far inferior to the discipline of intelligence, O Arjuna. Seek refuge in intelligence; pitiful are those whose motive is the fruit of action.

One who has disciplined his intelligence leaves behind in this world both good and evil deeds. Therefore strive for *yoga,* for *yoga* is skill in action.

Having disciplined their intelligence and having abandoned the fruit born of their action, the wise are freed from the bondage of birth and attain the state that is free from sorrow.

When thy intelligence shall cross the tangle of delusion, then thou shalt become indifferent to what shall be heard and to what has been heard (in the Veda).

When their intelligence, which is now perplexed by the Vedic texts, shall stand immovable and be fixed in concentration, then shalt thou attain *yoga.* (II, 46–53)

In this world, O Arjuna, a twofold path has been taught before by Me; the path of knowledge (*jñāna-yoga*) for men of discrimination (sāṁkhyas) and the path of works (*karma-yoga*) for men of action (yogins).

Not by abstention from actions does a man gain freedom, and not by mere renunciation does he attain perfection.

No one can remain, even for a moment, without performing some action. Everyone is made to act helplessly by the guṇas born of *prakṛti.*

He who controls his organs of action, but dwells in his mind on the objects of the senses; that man is deluded and is called a hypocrite.

But he who controls the senses by the mind, O Arjuna, and, without attachment, engages the organs of action in *karma-yoga*, he excels.

Perform thy allotted work, for action is superior to inaction; even the maintenance of thy body cannot be accomplished without action.

This world is in bondage to *karma*, unless *karma* is performed for the sake of sacrifice. For the sake of that, O Arjuna, perform thy action free from attachment. (III, 3–9)

There is nothing in the three worlds, O Arjuna, to be done by Me, nor anything unobtained that needs to be obtained; yet I continue in action.

For if I, unwearied, were not always in action, O Arjuna, men everywhere would follow my path (example).

If I did not perform action, these worlds would be destroyed, and I should be the author of confusion and would destroy these people.

As the ignorant act with attachment to their work, O Arjuna, so the wise man should act but without attachment, desiring to maintain the order of the world.

Let no wise man unsettle the minds of the ignorant who are attached to action. Acting with discipline, he should make all action attractive.

All actions are performed by the guṇas of *prakṛti* alone. But he who is deluded by egoism thinks, "I am the doer."

He who knows the true essence of the separation of the soul from both the guṇas and action, O Arjuna, and that it is the guṇas which act upon the guṇas, he is not attached to action.

Those who are deluded by the guṇas of *prakṛti* are attached to the action of the guṇas. But the man who knows the whole should not unsettle the ignorant who know only a part.

Surrendering all actions to Me, with thy consciousness fixed on the supreme Self, being free from desire and selfishness, fight freed from thy sorrow. (III, 22–30)

Then by what is a man impelled to (commit) sin against his will, as if compelled by force, O Kṛṣṇa?

The Blessed Lord said:

This is desire, this is wrath, born of the *guṇa* of passion, all-devouring and very sinful. Know that this is the enemy here.

As fire is covered by smoke, as a mirror by dust, and as an embryo is enveloped by the womb, so this knowledge is covered by that passion.

Knowledge is enveloped, O Arjuna, by this constant enemy of the knower, by this insatiable flame of desire.

The senses, the mind, the understanding are said to be its basis. With these it bewilders the embodied soul, covering its knowledge.

Therefore, O Arjuna, having in the beginning controlled thy senses, slay this evil destroyer of spiritual and practical knowledge. (III, 36–41)

Although unborn, although My self is imperishable, although I am

Lord of all beings, yet establishing Myself in My own (material) nature, I come into being by My own mysterious power (*māyā*).

Whenever there is a decay of righteousness and a rising up of unrighteousness, O Arjuna, I send forth Myself.

For the preservation of good, for the destruction of evil, for the establishment of righteousness, I come into being in age after age. (IV, 6–8)

What is action? What is inaction? About this even the wise are confused. Therefore I will declare to thee what action is, knowing which thou shalt be freed from evil.

One must understand the nature of action, and one must understand the nature of wrong action, and one must understand the nature of inaction: hard to understand is the way of action.

He who sees inaction in action and action in inaction, he is wise among men; he does all actions harmoniously.

He whose undertakings are all free from desire and will, whose actions are burned up in the fire of knowledge, him the wise call learned.

Having abandoned attachment to the fruits of action, always content and independent, he does nothing even though he is engaged in action.

Having no desires, with his mind and self controlled, abandoning all possessions, performing action with the body alone, he commits no sin.

He who is content with what comes by chance, who has passed beyond the pairs of opposites, who is free from jealousy and is indifferent to success and failure, even when he is acting he is not bound.

The action of a man who is rid of attachment, who is liberated, whose mind is firmly established in knowledge, who performs action as a sacrifice, is completely dissolved. (IV, 16–23)

Even if thou art among sinners the worst sinner of all, thou shalt cross over all evil by the boat of knowledge alone.

As the fire which is kindled makes its fuel into ashes, O Arjuna, so the fire of knowledge makes all actions into ashes.

There is no purifier in this world equal to wisdom. He who is perfected in *yoga* finds it in the self in the course of time.

He who has faith, who is intent on it (knowledge) and who has controlled his senses, obtains knowledge and having obtained it, goes quickly to the highest peace.

But the ignorant man who is without faith and of a doubting nature perishes. For the doubting self, there is not this world, nor the next, nor happiness.

Actions do not bind him who has renounced actions in *yoga*, who has cast away doubt by knowledge, who possesses himself, O Arjuna.

Therefore having cut away, with the sword of knowledge, this doubt in thy heart that is born of ignorance, resort to *yoga* and arise, O Arjuna. (IV, 36–42)

Arjuna said:

Thou praisest renunciation of actions, O Kṛṣṇa, and again (*karma*) *yoga*. Tell me definitely which one of these is the better.

The Blessed Lord said:

Renunciation (of works) and the unselfish performance of works (*karma-yoga*) both lead to the highest happiness. But of these two the unselfish performance of works is better than the renunciation of works.

He who neither hates nor desires should be known as the eternal renouncer; free from the pairs of opposites, O Arjuna, he is easily released from bondage.

Children, not the wise, speak of renunciation and *yoga* as separate; for he who is well established in one obtains the fruit of both.

That place which is obtained by the sāṁkhyas is also gained by the yogins. He who sees that *sāṁkhya* and *yoga* are one, he truly sees.

Renunciation, O Arjuna, is difficult to attain without *yoga*. The sage who is disciplined in *yoga* soon goes to Brahman.

He who is disciplined in *yoga* and is pure in soul, who is ruler of his self, who has conquered his senses, whose self becomes the Self of all beings, he is not affected by acting. (V, 1–7)

The all-pervading Spirit does not take on the sin or good work of anyone. Knowledge is enveloped by ignorance; by this creatures are bewildered.

But of those in whom ignorance is destroyed by knowledge, for them knowledge illumines the highest Self like the sun.

Thinking on that (highest Self), their self fixed on that, established in that, devoted to that, they go to where there is no returning, their sins destroyed by knowledge.

Sages look equally on a Brahmin endowed with knowledge and breeding, or on a cow, an elephant, and even a dog and an outcaste.

Even here on earth, creation is conquered by those whose minds are established in equality. Brahman is spotless and is the same to all. Therefore they are established in Brahman.

One should not rejoice when obtaining the pleasant, nor be agitated when obtaining the unpleasant. Unbewildered, with firm intelligence, the knower of Brahman is established in Brahman.

The self who is unattached to external contacts finds happiness in the Self. Being joined by *yoga* to Brahman, he attains imperishable happiness.

The enjoyments which are born of contacts with objects are only sources of sorrow. These have a beginning and end, O Arjuna; the wise man does not rejoice in them.

He who is able to endure here on earth, even before he is liberated from the body, the force that springs from desire and anger, he is disciplined, he is the happy man.

He who is happy within, whose joy is within and whose light is within; that *yogin* becomes Brahman and attains to the bliss of Brahman.

The seers whose sins are destroyed, whose dualities (doubts) are dispelled, whose selves are disciplined and who rejoice in the welfare of all beings, attain to the bliss of Brahman.

To these holy men who have destroyed desire and anger, who have controlled their minds, who know the Self, the bliss of Brahman is near. (V, 15–26)

Hear, O Arjuna, how, by attaching thy mind to Me, and by practicing *yoga*, with reliance upon Me, thou shalt know Me entirely, without doubt.

I will declare to thee in full this wisdom together with knowledge which, when known, nothing more in this world remains to be known.

Among thousands of men perchance one strives for perfection, and of those who strive and are successful, perhaps one knows Me in essence.

This is My divided eightfold nature: earth, water, fire, wind, ether, mind, intellect and self-consciousness.

This is My lower nature. Know My other higher nature, O Arjuna, which is the life-soul by which this world is supported.

Learn that all beings arise from this higher and lower nature of Mine. I am the origin of the whole world and also its dissolution.

Nothing exists higher than Me, O Arjuna. All this (universe) is strung on Me like jewels on a string. (VII, 1–7)

The foolish think of Me, the unmanifest, as having (only) come into manifestation; not knowing My higher nature which is immutable and supreme.

I am not revealed to all, being covered by My power of illusion. This world is deluded and does not recognize Me, the unborn and imperishable.

I know beings that are past, that are present and that are yet to be, O Arjuna, but no one knows Me.

All beings are born to confusion, O Arjuna, and are deluded by the dualities that originate from desire and hatred.

But those men of virtuous deeds whose sins are ended and who are freed from the delusion of opposites, worship Me with steadfast resolve.

Those who strive for liberation from old age and death and have taken refuge in Me know Brahman entirely and the Supreme Self and all action.

Those who know Me together with My material and divine domains and the highest sacrifice; they, of balanced mind, know Me even at the time of death. (VII, 24–30)

From the world of Brahmā downwards, all worlds are reborn, O Arjuna; but having come to Me, O Arjuna, there is no rebirth.

They who know that the day of Brahmā is of a thousand ages and that the night of Brahmā is of a thousand ages, they are the persons who know what day and night are.

From the unmanifest, all manifestations come forth at the coming of day, and at the coming of night, they dissolve in that same thing, called the unmanifest.

This same multitude of beings, coming forth repeatedly, dissolves helplessly in the coming of night, O Arjuna, and comes forth in the coming of day.

But higher than that unmanifest state, there is another unmanifested eternal being who does not perish when all beings perish.

This unmanifested state is called the Indestructible. They call that the highest goal which, having obtained, they return not. That is My highest abode.

This is the supreme spirit, O Arjuna, obtainable by unswerving devotion, in whom all beings abide and by whom all this is pervaded. (VIII, 16–22)

I will declare to thee, who are uncomplaining, this deepest secret of wisdom combined with knowledge, knowing which thou shalt be delivered from evil.

This is sovereign knowledge, a sovereign secret, the highest purifier, understood immediately, righteous, very easy to practice and imperishable.

Men who have no faith in this law, O Arjuna, do not attain Me but return to the path of ceaseless birth and rebirth.

By Me, in My unmanifested form, all this world is pervaded. All beings rest in Me but I do not rest in them.

And yet beings do not rest in Me: behold My divine mystery. My Self, which is the source of beings, sustains all beings but does not rest in them.

Just as the great wind, blowing everywhere abides in the ether, so all beings abide in Me; know thou that.

All beings, O Arjuna, enter into My material nature at the end of a world cycle, and I send them forth again at the beginning of a new cycle.

Taking hold of My own material nature, I send forth again and again all this multitude of beings which are helpless, by the force of My material nature.

And these actions do not bind Me, O Arjuna; I am seated as one who is indifferent, unattached to these actions.

With Me as supervisor, *prakṛti* sends forth all moving and unmoving things; by this cause, O Arjuna, the world revolves. (IX, 1–10)

But the great-souled, O Arjuna, who abide in the divine nature, worship Me with undeviating mind, knowing Me as the imperishable source of all beings.

Always glorifying Me and striving with steadfast resolve, and honoring Me with devotion, they worship Me ever-disciplined. (IX, 13–14)

The worshipers of the gods go to the gods; the worshipers of the ancestors go to the ancestors; sacrificers of the spirits go to the spirits; and those who sacrifice to Me come to Me.

Whoever offers Me a leaf, a flower, a fruit or water with devotion, I accept that offering of devotion from the pure in heart.

Whatever thou doest, whatever thou eatest, whatever thou offerest, whatever thou givest, whatever austerities thou performest, do that, O Arjuna, as an offering to Me.

Thus thou shalt be freed from the bonds of action which produce good and evil fruits; disciplined by the *yoga* of renunciation, thou shalt be liberated and come to Me.

I am equal to all beings, there is none hateful nor dear to Me. But those who worship Me with devotion, they are in Me and I am in them.

Even if a man of very evil conduct worships Me with undivided devotion, he too must be considered righteous, for he has resolved rightly.

Quickly he becomes a righteous self and obtains eternal peace; O Arjuna, know thou that My devotee never perishes. (IX, 25–31)

Arjuna said:

As a favor to me Thou hast spoken about the supreme mystery called the Self; and by Thy words my delusion is dispelled.

The origin and dissolution of beings have been heard by me in detail from Thee, O Lotus-eyed one, and also Thy imperishable greatness.

As Thou declarest Thyself, so it is, O Supreme Lord. I desire to see Thy goldly form, O Purushottama!

If Thou thinkest that it can be seen by me, O Lord, then reveal Thy immortal Self to me, O Lord of Yoga!

The Blessed Lord said:

Behold, O Arjuna, My forms, by hundreds and by thousands, manifold and divine, of various colors and shapes.

Behold the Ādityas, the Vasus, the Rudras, the two Aśvins, and also the Maruts. Behold, O Arjuna, many marvels not seen before.

Behold today the whole world, of moving and unmoving things, united in My body, O Arjuna, and whatever else thou desirest to see.

But thou canst not see Me with thine own eye. I give thee a divine eye. Behold My divine *yoga*.

Saṁjaya said:

Having spoken thus, O King, the great Lord of Yoga, Hari, then showed to Arjuna His supreme, divine form;

Of many mouths and eyes, of many marvelous visions, of many divine ornaments, of many uplifted weapons;

Wearing divine garlands and garments with divine perfumes and ointments, full of all wonders, radiant, infinite, His face is turned everywhere.

If the light of a thousand suns were to spring forth simultaneously in the sky, it would be like the light of that great Being.

There Arjuna beheld the whole world, divided into many parts, all united in the body of the God of gods.

Then filled with amazement, his hair standing erect, Arjuna bowed down his head to the God and with hands folded in salutation said:

Arjuna said:

I see all the gods in Thy body, O God, and also the various kinds of beings: Brahmā, the Lord, seated on the lotus seat, and all the sages and divine serpents.

I see Thee, with many arms, stomachs, mouths, and eyes, everywhere infinite in form; I see no end nor middle nor beginning of Thee, O Lord of all, O universal form!

I behold Thee with diadem, club and discus as a mass of light shining everywhere with the radiance of flaming fire and the sun, difficult to regard, beyond all measure.

Thou art the imperishable, the highest to be known; Thou art the final resting place of this universe; Thou art the immortal guardian of eternal law; Thou art, I think, the primal spirit.

I behold Thee without beginning, middle or end, of infinite power, of innumerable arms, the moon and sun as Thine eyes, Thy face as a shining fire, burning this universe with Thy radiance.

This space between heaven and earth and all the quarters of the sky is pervaded by Thee alone; seeing this Thy wondrous, terrible form, the triple world trembles, O great one!

These hosts of gods enter Thee and some, affrighted, invoke Thee with folded hands, and hosts of great seers and perfected ones crying "Hail!" praise Thee with magnificent hymns.

The Rudras, the Ādityas, the Vasus, the Sādhyas, the Viśvedevas, the two Aśvins, the Maruts and the Ushmapās, and the hosts of Gandharvas, Yakṣas, Asuras, and perfected ones all gaze at Thee in amazement.

Seeing Thy great form, of many mouths and eyes, O mighty-armed one, of many arms, thighs and feet, of many bellies, of many terrible tusks, the worlds tremble, and so do I.

Seeing Thee touching the sky and blazing with many colors, with opened mouths and shining enormous eyes, my inmost self is shaken and I find no strength nor peace, O Vishnu!

Seeing Thy mouths, terrible with tusks, like time's devouring fire, I know not the directions of the sky and I find no security. Have mercy, O Lord of gods, Abode of the world!

And these sons of Dhṛtarāṣṭra, all of them, together with the hosts of kings, Bhīṣma, Droṇa, and also Karṇa, together with our chief warriors

Are rushing into Thy mouths, dreadful with terrible tusks. Some are seen with pulverized heads, stuck between Thy teeth.

As the many water currents of rivers race headlong to the ocean, so these heroes of the world of men enter into Thy flaming mouths.

As moths swiftly enter a blazing fire and perish there, so these creatures swiftly enter Thy mouths and perish.

Swallowing all the worlds from every side, Thou lickest them up with Thy flaming mouths; Thy fierce rays fill the whole world with radiance and scorch it, O Vishnu!

Tell me who Thou art with so terrible a form! Salutation to Thee, O best of gods, be merciful! I wish to know Thee, the primal one; for I do not understand Thy ways.

The Blessed Lord said:

Time am I, the world destroyer, matured, come forth to subdue the worlds here. Even without thee, all the warriors arrayed in the opposing armies shall cease to be.

Therefore stand up and win fame. Conquering thy enemies, enjoy a prosperous kingdom. By Me they have already been slain. Be thou the mere instrument, O Arjuna.

Slay thou Droṇa, Bhīṣma, Jayadratha, Karṇa, and the other warrior-heroes too, who have already been slain by Me. Be not distressed, fight! Thou shalt conquer thy enemies in battle.

Saṁjaya said:

Having heard this utterance of Kṛṣṇa, Arjuna, trembling and with folded hands, saluated Him again, and bowing down fearfully said to Kṛṣṇa in a faltering voice,

Arjuna said:

It is right, O Kṛṣṇa, that the world rejoices and is pleased by Thy fame. Ogres flee in terror in all directions, and all the hosts of perfected ones bow down before Thee.

And why should they not prostrate themselves, O Great One, who art greater than Brahmā, the primal creator? O infinite one! Lord of the gods! O refuge of the worlds! Thou art the imperishable; Thou art being and non-being, and that which is beyond both.

Thou art the first of the gods, the primal spirit; Thou art the highest treasure-house of this world; Thou art the knower and that which is to be known, and the highest goal. By Thee this universe is pervaded, O Thou of infinite form!

Thou art Vāyu and Yama, Agni, Varuṇa, Śaśānka, and Prajāpati, the grandsire. Hail, hail to Thee a thousand times; hail, hail to Thee again and also again!

Hail to Thee in front and in the rear, hail to Thee on every side, O all; infinite in power and immeasurable in strength. Thou penetratest all and therefore Thou art all.

For whatever I said in rashness from negligence or even from affection thinking Thou art my friend, and not knowing Thy greatness, calling Thee "O Kṛṣṇa, O Yādava, O Comrade,"

And whatever disrespect I showed Thee for the sake of jesting, whether at play, on the bed, seated or at meals, whether alone or in the company of others, O sinless one, I pray forgiveness from Thee, the boundless one.

Thou art the father of this moving and unmoving world. Thou art the object of its reverence and its greatest teacher. There is nothing equal to Thee, how then could anyone in the triple-world surpass Thee, O Thou of incomparable power!

Therefore, bending down and prostrating my body, I ask Thy grace; Thou, O Lord, shouldst bear with me as a father to his son, as friend with friend, as a lover to his beloved.

Having seen what was never seen before, I am glad, but my mind is distraught with fear. Show me, O Lord, that other form of Thine; O Lord of gods, be gracious, O refuge of the world.

I wish to see Thee as before with Thy crown, mace and disk in hand. Be that four-armed form, O thousand-armed one of universal form!

The Blessed Lord said:

By My grace, O Arjuna, and through My great power, was shown to thee this highest form, full of splendor, universal, infinite, primal, which no one but thee has seen before.

Not by the Vedas, by sacrifices or study, not by gifts, nor ritual, nor severe austerities can I, in such a form, be seen in the world of men by any other but thee, O Arjuna.

Be not afraid nor bewildered in seeing this terrible form of Mine. Without fear and of satisfied mind, behold again my other form.

Saṁjaya said:

Having thus spoken to Arjuna, Kṛṣṇa revealed again His own form. The Great One, having become again the gracious form, comforted him in his fear.

Arjuna said:

Seeing again this Thy gracious human form, O Kṛṣṇa, I have become composed of mind and restored to my normal nature.

The Blessed Lord said:

This form of Mine which is very difficult to see, thou hast seen. Even the gods are constantly desiring the sight of this form.

In the form that thou hast seen Me, I cannot be seen by the Vedas, by austerity, by gift or sacrifice.

But by devotion to Me alone can I in this form, O Arjuna, be known and seen in essence, and entered into, O oppressor of the foe.

He who does My work, who regards Me as his goal, who is devoted to Me, who is free from attachment and is free from enmity to all beings, he comes to Me, O Arjuna. (XI, complete)

Arjuna said:

Those devotees who are always disciplined and honor Thee, and those who worship the Imperishable and the Unmanifest—which of these are more learned in *yoga*?

The Blessed Lord said:

Those who, fixing their mind on Me, worship Me with complete discipline and with supreme faith, them I consider to be the most learned in *yoga*.

But those who worship the Imperishable, the Undefinable, the Unmanifested, the Omnipresent, the Unthinkable, the Immovable, the Unchanging, the Constant,

And have restrained all their senses, and are equal-minded and rejoice in the welfare of all beings—they also obtain Me.

The difficulty of those whose minds are fixed on the Unmanifested is much greater; the goal of the Unmanifested is hard for the embodied to attain.

But those who renounce all actions in Me and are intent on Me, who worship with complete discipline and meditate on Me,

These, whose thoughts are fixed on Me, I quickly lift up from the ocean of death and rebirth, O Arjuna. (XII, 1–7)

The Blessed Lord said:

This body, O Arjuna, is called the field, and he who knows this is called the knower of the field by those who know him.

Know Me as the Knower of the field in all fields, O Arjuna; the knowledge of the field and the knower of the field, this I hold to be real knowledge.

Hear from Me briefly what the field is, what its nature is, what its modifications are, whence it comes, who he (the knower of the field) is and what his powers are.

This has been sung by the seers in many ways; in various hymns distinctly and also in the well-reasoned and definite words of the aphorisms about Brahman.

The gross elements, the I-sense, the intellect and also the unmanifested, the ten senses and one (the mind) and the five objects of the senses;

Desire, hatred, pleasure, pain, the organism, intelligence and firmness; this, briefly described, is the field together with its modifications. (XIII, 1–6)

I will declare that which is to be known, by knowing which one gains immortality. It is the beginningless supreme Brahman who is called neither being nor non-being.

With his hands and feet everywhere, with eyes, heads and mouths on all sides, with his ears everywhere; he dwells in the world, enveloping all.

Appearing to have the qualities of all the senses, and yet free from all the senses; unattached and yet supporting all; free from the guṇas and yet enjoying the guṇas,

It is outside and within all beings. It is unmoving and moving. It is too subtle to be known. It is far away and it is also near.

It is undivided and yet seems to be divided in all beings. It is to be known as supporting all beings and as absorbing and creating them.

It is also, it is said, the light of lights beyond darkness; it is knowledge, the object of knowledge, and the goal of knowledge; it is seated in the hearts of all. (XIII, 12–17)

Know that both *prakṛti* and *puruṣa* are beginningless; and know also that modifications and the guṇas are born of *prakṛti.*

Prakṛti is said to be the cause of the generation of causes and agents, and *puruṣa* is said to be the cause of the experience of pleasure and pain.

The *puruṣa* abiding in *prakṛti* experiences the guṇas born of *prakṛti.* Attachment to the guṇas is the cause of his births in good and evil wombs.

The highest spirit in this body is said to be the witness, the consenter, the supporter, the experiencer, the great Lord, the supreme Self.

He who knows the *puruṣa* and *prakṛti* together with its guṇas, though in whatever state he may exist, he is not born again.

Some by meditation see the Self in the self by the self; others by the *yoga* of discrimination, and still others by the *yoga* of action.

Yet others, not knowing this but hearing it from others, honor it, and they too cross beyond death through their devotion to the scripture which they have heard.

Whatever being is born, immovable or moving, know, O Arjuna, that it (arises) from the union of the field and the knower of the field.

He who sees the supreme Lord abiding equally in all beings, not perishing when they perish, he truly sees. (XIII, 19–27)

There are two spirits in this world: the perishable and the imperishable. The perishable is all beings and the imperishable is called Kūṭastha (the unchanging).

But there is another, the highest Spirit (*puruṣottama*) called the supreme Self, who, as the imperishable Lord, enters into the three worlds and sustains them.

Since I transcend the perishable and am higher even than the imperishable, I am renowned in the world and in the Vedas as the highest Spirit.

He who undeluded thus knows Me as the highest Spirit is the knower of all; he worships Me with his whole being, O Arjuna.

Thus the most secret doctrine has been spoken by Me, O sinless one. Being enlightened about this, one will have true enlightenment and will have done his work, O Arjuna. (XV, 16–20)

A man obtains perfection by being devoted to his own proper action. Hear then how one who is intent on his own action finds perfection.

By worshiping him, from whom all beings arise and by whom all this is pervaded, through his own proper action, a man attains perfection.

Better is one's own *dharma*, though imperfect, than the *dharma* of another, well performed. One does not incur sin when doing the action prescribed by one's own nature.

One should not abandon his natural-born action, O Arjuna, even if it be faulty, for all undertakings are clouded with faults as fire by smoke.

He whose intelligence is unattached everywhere, whose self is conquered, who is free from desire, he obtains, through renunciation, the supreme perfection of actionlessness.

Learn from me, briefly, O Arjuna, how he who has attained perfection, also attains to Brahman, the highest state of wisdom.

Disciplined with a pure intelligence, firmly controlling oneself, abandoning sound and other sense-objects and throwing aside passion and hatred;

Dwelling in solitude, eating little, controlling speech, body and mind, constantly engaged in the *yoga* of meditation and taking refuge in dispassion;

Freed from egotism, force, arrogance, desire, anger and possession; unselfish, peaceful—he is fit to become Brahman.

Having become Brahman, tranquil in the Self, he neither grieves nor desires. Regarding all beings as equal, he attains supreme devotion to Me.

By devotion he knows Me, what my measure is and what I am essentially; then, having known Me essentially, he enters forthwith into Me.

Ever performing all actions, taking refuge in Me, he obtains by My grace the eternal, imperishable abode.

Renouncing with thy thought all actions to Me, intent on Me, taking refuge in the *yoga* of intellect, fix thy mind constantly on Me.

If thy mind is on Me, thou shalt, by My grace, cross over all obstacles; but if, from egotism, thou wilt not listen, thou shalt perish.

If, centered in egotism, thou thinkest "I will not fight," vain is this thy resolution; *prakṛti* will compel thee.

That which thou wishest not to do, through delusion, O Arjuna, that thou shalt do helplessly, bound by thine own action born of thy nature.

The Lord abides in the hearts of all beings, O Arjuna, causing all beings to revolve by His power as if they were mounted on a machine.

Go to Him alone for shelter with all thy being, O Arjuna. By His grace, thou shalt obtain supreme peace and the eternal abode.

Thus the wisdom, more secret than all secrets, has been declared to thee by Me. Having considered it fully, do as thou choosest. (XVIII, 45–63)

CHAPTER 3

System (the *Brahmasūtras*)

The basic guide for all Vedānta thought is known under different names, *Vedāntasūtras* and *Brahmasūtras*, but its most official name is *Śārīraka-mīmāṁsā-sūtras.* It is from the last name that we shall depart and take the members of the compound backwards: "the Threads of the Enquiry into That which is embodied."

In Brahministic usage, the word *sūtra* has a rather different meaning than it acquired among the Buddhists. With the latter it became a general word for a doctrinaire disquisition, sometimes of considerable length, in which a body of doctrine was explicated in full detail. But in its orthodox use the word denotes something quite *sui generis.* It means primarily "thread"—the word is distantly related to our verb *to sew.* A thread, however, only has a provisional existence of its own; its purpose is to be sewn or woven into a cloth. It is this cloth-out-of-threads that covers the System.

Sūtras, whether of Vedānta or of any other body of knowledge, aim at the briefest possible exposition of the propositions of a topic. Exposition is already saying too much; indication would be closer. Parsimony of statement is pushed to the extreme; a common witticism has it that an author of sūtras takes greater delight in the saving of a vowel than in the birth of a son. In order to understand the phenomenon of sūtras, we must know the method of education. And here we must once more return to the Vedic tradition.

A person's education begins with his initiation, the *upanayana.* In return for his pupil's obedience the teacher vows that he will transmit to him his complete erudition. There is a total loyalty of pupil to teacher and of teacher to pupil. Education proceeds in the greatest possible personal intimacy. Originally, it proceeded without the aid of books; education declined their use. When, later, Śaṁkara looks for an illustration of the relation between the semireal world and the supreme, he quotes the relation between the written word and the spoken word. The written book is but a crutch for the scholar, a sign of defective learning or failing memory: there need be no intermediary for the learned man between the possession of erudition and the vocal expression of it. Knowledge is verbal, not typographical, and the teacher makes certain that the pupil is word-perfect.

There are two phases in this instruction. In the first phase is transmitted that which is unalterable and must be remembered perfectly—that is, primarily, if the instruction centers on the Vedas themselves, those texts of any one Veda in the "branch" of which the pupil is born. The pupil's first task is *śravaṇa* "listening" and *anuśravaṇa* "repeating." The second phase is the explication of what now is literally known. In those forms of education where a system is instructed, be it Grammar, or Logic, or Vedānta, generations of teachers have combined to draw from the wealth of material basic statements which, after the formation period of the scholarly discipline is over, will be consolidated by a master into a complete repertory of statements which exhaust the system. These basic statements, collected in a number of lessons, are as concise as possible to facilitate their being remembered. Ideally they should be able to stand by themselves. Step by step the sūtras take the pupil from the most general statements to the most specific as by a system of ordered rules, each one presupposing the previous one, so that the pupil has no difficulty supplying the needed terms to the economically elliptic sentences. Verbs are almost entirely supplanted by nouns, for it is not processes of change that are studied but matters of unalterable fact.

Practically, however, the sūtras do need explanation: examples, references to sources, explications of the arguments which may not have to be recalled perfect to the letter but which would inevitably be triggered by the keywords of the sūtras.

The *Śārīraka-mīmāṁsā-sūtras* provide such a System for Vedānta, that is, for the concluding part of the Veda, the Upaniṣads. They are therefore the System statements for an Enquiry into the Upaniṣads. But, as such, the system cannot stand on its own. The Upaniṣads are but the second part of the Veda, the crowning part no doubt, but essentially sequential. Vedānta is therefore also known as the *uttara-mīmāṁsā*, the "Second Enquiry," presupposing a First Enquiry into the First Part of the Veda.

Although the relation between the First and Second Enquiries became a matter of profound dispute, still, as a text, the *Brahma-sūtras* presuppose the existence of the sūtras of the first *mīmāṁsā*; we shall follow the custom and speak of Mīmāṁsā and Vedānta.

Mīmāṁsā pretends to deal with nothing but the canons of exegesis which explain what our tasks are. It therefore deals with acts, that is, with ritual acts; but insofar as a rite is taken to mean a recurrent act on the part of a human agent who is enjoined upon to perform this act by the transcendent authority of Revelation, it is redundant to speak of "ritual acts," for every act is a rite or immediately subservient to it. Vedānta, however, deals not with rites, but with insight, and the canons of Mīmāṁsā might therefore seem irrelevant to it. Nonetheless, Vedānta must equally deal with and from *śruti,* since for it, too, does the argument hold that no insight in matters suprasensible and therefore metaphysical can be had through our ordinary means of knowledge; and hence it, too, must rely on the Vedic texts that are self-validating.

The *Brahmasūtras* open with four lines stating this inevitable reliance on *śruti: athāto brahma-jijñāsā / janmādy asya yataḥ / śāstrayonitvāt / tat tu samanvayāt,* "next, therefore, the desire of knowing Brahman; from which [derives] the origin, etc. [i.e., existence and dissolution] of this [universe]; because its [i.e., the knowledge's] source is scripture; [that Brahman is the cause of the universe,] that in fact [follows] from the total agreement [of the statements of scripture]." These four sūtras not only illustrate how scripture is accepted as the source of Vedānta, they also show the highly elliptic form of the presentation.

If indeed all the scriptural statements agree that Brahman is the cause, what is a statement? It is here that the canons of exegesis, evolved by Mīmāṁsā, at once come into play. Vedānta takes them for granted. The rule is laid down in Mīmāṁsā: "As long as one single purpose is served by a number of words which, if broken up, are found wanting and incapable of effecting this purpose, these words constitute one statement," which, for this school of thought, is an injunction to do specific acts. This injunction is incumbent upon an individual actively engaged in acts. It is this primary conception of the soul as embodied and involved in acts which from the first has given the "soul" in Vedānta a character which it does not necessarily hold in all Indian thinking, however this entity is conceived of. For Vedānta the soul is *agent,* the one himself responsible for his acts, who is therefore also the one who undergoes the results of these acts. The soul as agent and experient is an assumption demanded by the Mīmāṁsā theory of task but productive of profound problems that faced the later philosophers.

In a way a commentary on the *Brahmasūtras,* in principle, does away with the need for a direct study of the Upaniṣads themselves; nevertheless, the major philosophers address themselves directly to the Upaniṣads, either in the form of commentaries or by a treatise about them. In the *Brahmasūtras* the *Chāndogya Upaniṣad* holds the central place, followed by the *Bṛhadāraṇyaka Upaniṣad* and the *Taittirīya Upaniṣad.* These belong to the oldest stratum of the

Upaniṣadic corpus. The next stratum is that of the early metrical Upaniṣads of which the most important ones are the *Kaṭha* and *Śvetāśvatara*; the latter betrays influences from proto-Sāṁkhya and from growing theistic thought.

Below follows a synopsis of the topics of the *Brahmasūtras* without consideration of the relative fidelity of the individual commentaries.

The text is divided into four lessons, each with four quarters. Each quarter is subdivided into a number of topic sections, which may cover a group of sūtras, but also a single one.

1. 1. 1–31

TOPIC: I (1). Brahman is the object of the study of Vedānta.

II (2). Brahman is the origin of the world.

III (3). The relevance of scripture for the study of Brahman.

IV (4). All scripture bears upon Brahman.

V (5–11). Brahman as cause is a spiritual entity different from the non-spiritual causal *prakṛti* postulated by Sāṁkhya.

VI (12–19). The Soul of Bliss of *Taittirīya Upaniṣad* (Taitt. Up.) 2. 5 is Brahman.

VII (20–21). So is the Golden Person of *Chāndogya Upaniṣad* (Ch. Up.) 1. 6.

VIII (22). So is the Ether mentioned in Ch. Up. 1. 9 as world cause.

IX (23). So is the Breath discussed in Ch. Up. 1. 11. 5.

X (24–27). So is the Light mentioned in Ch. Up. 3. 13. 7.

XI (28–31). So is the Breath mentioned in *Kauṣītaki Upaniṣad* (Kau. Up.) 3. 2.

1. 2. 1–32

I (1–8). The subject of Ch. Up. 3. 14 is not the individual soul but Brahman itself.

II (9–10). So is that of *Kaṭha Upaniṣad* (Ka. Up.) 1. 2. 25.

III (11–12). The two beings of Ka. Up. 1. 3. 1 are Brahman and the individual soul.

IV (13–17). The Person-in-the-Eye of Ch. Up. 4. 15. 1 is Brahman.

V (18–20). The Inner Ruler of *Bṛhadāraṇyaka Upaniṣad* (Bṛh. Up.) 3. 7. 3 is Brahman.

VI (21–23). The Invisible of *Muṇḍaka Upanisad* (Mu. Up.) 1. 1. 3 is Brahman.

VII (24–32). So is the *vaiśvānara* soul of Ch. Up. 5. 11. 6.

1. 3. 1–43

I (1–7). That on which heaven and earth are woven according to Mu. Up. 2. 2. 5 is Brahman.

II (8–9). So is the Muchness of Ch. Up. 7. 23.

III (10–12). And the Imperishable of Bṛh. Up. 3. 8. 8.

IV (13). So is the supreme Person of *Praśna Upaniṣad* (Pra. Up.) 5. 5.

V–VI (14–21). The Tiny Ether of Ch. Up. 8. 1 is in fact Brahman.

VII (22–23). The Luminous One of Ka. Up. 2. 5. 15 is Brahman.

VIII (24–25). The Thumb-sized Person of Ka. Up. 2. 4. 12 is not the individual soul but Brahman itself.

IX (26–33). Miscellaneous discussions starting from the question whether gods can know Brahman; the relation of words to their contents.

X (34–38). Śūdras are disqualified for the study of Brahman.

XI (39). The Breath of Ka. Up. 2. 6. 2 is Brahman.

XII (40). So is the Light of Ch. Up. 8. 12. 3.

XIII (41). The creative Ether of Ch. Up. 8. 14 is really Brahman.

XIV (42–43). So is the Soul of Knowledge of Bṛh. Up. 4. 3. 7.

1. 4. 1–28

I (1–7). The unmanifest of Ka. Up. 1. 3. 10–11 is not the unmanifest *prakṛti* of Sāṁkhya but the subtle and gross body.

II (8–10). The three-colored Unborn One of *Śvetāśvatara Upaniṣad* (Śve. Up.) 4. 5 is not the Sāmkhyan *prakṛti* but the creativeness of the Lord.

III (11–13). The Five Tribes of Five in Bṛh. Up. 4. 4. 17 are not the 25 principles of Sāṁkhya.

IV (14–15). Scripture is not self-contradictory concerning the spiritual Brahman as cause of the world.

V (16–18). The Maker of Kau. Up. 4. 19 is Brahman.

VI (19–22). The "soul that must be seen" of Bṛh. Up. 2. 4. 5 is likewise Brahman.

VII (23–27). Brahman is not only the efficient but also the substantial cause of the world which develops through internal modification.

VIII (28). This refutation of Sāṁkhya covers other views on the origination of the world.

2. 1. 1–37

I (1–2). Sāṁkhya may not quote *smṛti* against Vedānta.

II (3). Neither may Yoga quote its *smṛti* against Vedānta.

III (4–11). Brahman, though spiritual, may well be the cause of the non-spiritual world and still not be affected by its qualities when the world merges back into Brahman.

IV (12). The above arguments also hold against Vaiśeṣika.

V (13). It is not true that this makes Brahman subject to experience and thus to *karman*.

VI (14–20). The product is nondifferent from its cause.

VII (21–23). Identity of the soul with Brahman does not make Brahman a cause of evil.

VIII (24–25). Brahman needs no instrumentation for world production.

IX (26–29). Brahman does not entirely become world and remains one and undivided.

X (30–31). Brahman creates without instruments and by its own power.

XI (32–33). Brahman has no motivation in creating the world.

XII (34–36). As Brahman creates with a view to the souls' *karman* it cannot be imputed with partiality and cruelty.

XIII (37). Brahman's qualities enable it to create the world.

2. 2. 1–45

I (1–10). Arguments against the Sāṁkhyans.

II (11–17). Arguments against the Vaiśeṣikas.

III (18–27). Arguments against the Buddhist Realists.

IV (28–32). Arguments against the Buddhist Idealists.

V (33–36). Arguments against the Jainas.

VI (37–41). Arguments against theists maintaining that God is only the efficient cause.

VII (42–45). Arguments against the Pāñcarātra.

2. 3. 1–53

I (1–7). Ether springs from Brahman.

II (8). Wind from Ether.

III (9). Brahman cannot have originated.

IV–VI (10–12). Fire springs from Wind, Water from Fire, Earth from Water.

VII (13). This successive generation is due to Brahman.

VIII (14). Dissolution takes place in reverse order.

IX (15). Senses and mind originate and dissolve with the elements.

X (16). Birth and death apply only to the body.

XI (17). The individual soul is not created.

XII (18). The soul is intelligent.

XIII (19–32). On whether the soul is atomic in size or omnipresent.

XIV–XV (33–39; 40). The soul is an agent.

XVI (41–42). This agency is dependent on the supreme soul who impels it.

XVII (43–53). The soul is a portion of the supreme soul, which does not mean that Brahman is affected by the qualities of the soul or that one soul shares the experiences of others.

2. 4. 1–22

I–III (1–4, 5–6; 7). The sensory faculties, the motoric faculties, and the mind spring from Brahman; there are eleven faculties, and they are atomic.

IV–VI (8; 9–12; 13). Breath is derived from Brahman; it is different from wind and the faculties, and it is atomic.

VII–VIII (14–16; 17–19). The faculties are supervised by specific deities, and are independent of Breath.

IX (20–22). Brahman, not the soul, evolves names-and-forms.

3. 1. 1–27

I (1–7). The soul when departing from the body at death is enveloped by subtle elements in which the soul's faculties subsist.

II (8–11). The souls, having enjoyed the rewards of their good acts on the moon, have a remainder of *karman* left as they return to earth, which determines the quality of their rebirth.

III (12–21). Those who did not sacrifice may also go to the moon, others go to hell, of which there are seven varieties. There is a third class of heat-born animals that have no interval between death and rebirth.

IV–VI (22; 23; 24–27). The subtle body of the soul when descending from the moon goes through a number of phases, similar but not identical with natural phenomena. This descent is brief. The soul at last lies waiting in plants until the plants are eaten by a man who then impregnates a woman with it. Thus it is reborn.

3. 2. 1–41

I (1–6). The visions of the dreaming soul are illusions; the soul cannot create, though it is a portion of the supreme soul, because it is limited by its body.

II (7–8). In dreamless sleep the soul merges with the Brahman in the heart.

III (9). The awakening soul is the one that fell asleep.

IV (10). On the swoon.

V (11–21). The fact that the supreme soul sojourns in the individual soul does not affect its perfect nature.

VI (22–30). How the soul can have a double nature, that of the supreme and that of the individual soul.

VII (31–37). On the correct interpretation of passages apparently implying the existence of something different from Brahman.

VIII (38–41). The operations of *karman* are not self-fructifying; the supreme soul allots the rewards.

3. 3. 1–66

I–II (1–4; 5). On the construction of vidyās (a particular body of knowledge).

III (6–8). On the distinctness of apparently identical vidyās.

IV (9). On the *udgītha-vidyā* of Ch. Up. 1. 1. 1.

V (10). On the unity of the *prāṇa*-vidyās.

VI (11–13). In a meditation on a *vidyā* the specific qualities of Brahman there set forth should be meditated upon, along with the qualities of knowledge and bliss.

VII (14–15). Ka. Up. 3. 10. 11 constitutes one *vidyā.*

VIII (16–17). On the *vidyā* of *Aitareya Āraṇyaka* 2. 4. 1. 1.

IX (18). On the Discourse of the Faculties.

X (19). On the *Śāṇḍilya-vidyā.*

XI (20–22). On the two distinct vidyās of Bṛh. Up. 5. 5.

XII (23). On the *Rāṇāyanīya-vidyā.*

XIII (24). On the distinction of two *puruṣa*-vidyās.

XIV (25). On the exclusion of *mantra* and *brāhmaṇa* passages from the contiguous *vidyā.*

XV (26). On the extension of certain passages to others.

XVI (27–28). Good and evil acts vanish at once on the soul's departure from the body to the world of Brahman.

XVII (29–30). On the propriety of this view.

XVIII (31). Those who meditate on the vidyās follow the Course of the Gods.

XIX (32). On the possession of a body by those who have knowledge.

XX (33). Negative qualities of Brahman are part of all meditations.

XXI (34). Ka. Up. 3. 1 and Mu. Up. 3. 1 constitute one *vidyā.*

XXII (35–36). Bṛh. Up. 3. 4 and 3. 5 constitute one *vidyā.*

XXIII (37). But *Aitareya Āraṇyaka* 2. 2. 4. 6 comprise two vidyās.

XXIV (38). Bṛh. Up. 5. 4. 5 is a single *vidyā.*

XXV (39). Ch. Up. 8. 1 and Bṛh. Up. 4. 4. 22 comprise two different vidyās.

XXVI (40–41). On Ch. Up. 5. 11 ff.

XXVII (42). Vidyās mentioned in connection with rites are not part of these rites.

XXVIII (43). The Vāyu and Prāṇa of Bṛh. Up. 1. 5 and Ch. Up. 4. 3 are to be separated.

XXIX (44–52). The altars of the Agnirahasya chapters of the *Śatapatha Brāhmaṇa* are not ritual ones, but objects of meditation.

XXX (53–54). On the body of the one engaged in meditation.

XXXI (55–56). The *udgītha* and other meditations apply to all śākhās.

XXXII (57). The *vaiśvānara-vidyā* of Ch. Up. 5. 11 ff. is a *vidyā* as a whole.

XXXIII (58). Vidyās about one object but differently qualified are different vidyās.

XXXIV (59). Vidyās having the same reward are optional.

XXXV (60). Vidyās providing for special desires may be accumulated or treated as optional.

XXXVI (61–66). This applies also to meditations such as the *udgītha* one and others.

3. 4. 1–52

I (1–17). Knowledge of Brahman does not subserve rite; it is independent.

II (18–20). This is shown by the *pravrājikas* ("hermits") for whom knowledge is prescribed, not ritual.

III (21–22). Certain vidyās are not mere glorifications but actual injunctions.

IV (23–24). On the other hand certain legends are not subservient to ritual, but glorify the injunctions involved.

V (25). Thus ascetics need no ritual, only knowledge.

VI (26–27). Yet ritual action encourages the rise of a *vidyā* in one's mind.

VII (28–31). Indulgences in matters of purity only apply to emergency cases.

VIII (32–35). The rites of a particular stage of life are incumbent on one who is not an aspirant to release.

IX (36–39). Those without a life stage through no fault of their own are yet entitled to knowledge.

X (40). The ascetic may not renounce his vow.

XI (41–42). If he does, he may be expiated.

XII (43). Or in certain cases excluded.

XIII (44–46). The *udgītha*, etc., meditations are incumbent on the priests, not the *yajamāna* ("patron").

XIV (47–49). Bṛh. Up. 3. 5. 1 dictates Silence in addition to Childlikeness and Learning.

XV (50). Childlikeness betokens innocence of mind.

XVI (51). A *vidyā* that produces good fortune fructifies in the present life, unless there are karmic obstacles.

XVII (52). Hence there is no binding rule as to the time of fructification.

4. 1. 1–19

I (1–2). The meditation on the Spirit is not once and for all, but is to be repeated.

II (3). The Brahman meditated upon is to be regarded as one's own soul.

III (4). Except for the *pratīka* meditations.

IV (5). There the pratīkas are to be viewed as Brahman, not contrariwise.

V (6). In the *udgītha*, etc., meditations, the *udgītha*, etc., are to be viewed as the relevant deity, not contrariwise.

VI (7–10). One should sit while meditating.

VII (11). Anywhere and anytime, whenever circumstances are conducive.

VIII (12). Until death.

IX (13). One who has thus obtained knowledge is exempt from past evil *karman*.

X (14). As well as from past good *karman*, when he dies.

XI (15). This exemption applies to the results of such acts as have not yet fructified.

XII (16–17). This exemption does not apply to perpetual rites, which encourage knowledge.

XIII (18). Also those rites encourage knowledge which do not include vidyās.

XIV (19). Acts that have already fructified must be lived out, then the knower merges with Brahman.

4. 2. 1–21

I–III (1–6). On the knower's death his faculties merge in mind, mind in breath, breath in soul, soul with the subtle elements.

IV (7). Up to this point the course of one who knows and one who does not are the same.

V (8–11). The dissolution of the subtle body takes place at release, not on death.

VI (12–14). An apparently conflicting passage in fact states that the faculties, etc., do not depart from the soul.

VII–VIII (15–16). The faculties eventually dissolve in Brahman.

IX (17). The soul of the knower passes into the heart and from there into the *suṣumṇā* channel, while that of the non-knower passes through a different channel.

X (18–19). From this *suṣumṇā* channel it passes by way of a ray to the sun, day or night.

XI (20–21). During the southern course of the sun as well as the northern.

4. 3. 1–16

I–III (1–3). The way stations on the road to Brahman.

IV (4–6). These stations include also the psychopomps.

V (7–16). Discussion of whether the Brahman reached is the effected Brahman, thus Bādari; or the supreme Brahman, thus Jaimini. The latter is in the case, while Bādarāyaṇa further holds that those who meditated on the effected Brahman as well as on the supreme Brahman are both led to Brahman.

4. 4. 1–21

I (1–3). The soul does on release merge in its own form.

II (4). On merging it is inseparate.

III (5–7). Discussion on whether the soul merges while possessing all divine perfections, thus Jaimini; or solely possessing spirituality, thus Audulomi; Bādarāyaṇa decides with both.

IV (8–9). The released soul is active in a state of release on the strength of its will alone, and enjoys divine sovereignty.

V (10–14). It may assume bodies at will.

VI (15–16). The soul may animate simultaneously multiple bodies; the soul retains a general knowledge.

VII (17–21). While the Lord is active in world operations, the released soul shares in his perfection, and no more returns to transmigration.

This necessary summary synopsis does not pretend to bring out the original intention of the Sūtras, nor even the original number of the topics. The later commentators hold such diverging views about both that certainty is impossible to come by. On the whole it is assumed that when Śaṁkara and Bhāskara agree on a topic, that view is traditionally held. If Bhāskara and Rāmānuja agree, and if Śaṁkara's difference is prompted by his particular division of reality, the former view is probably more original. But this list of topics does not aim at more than to give the reader at least some table of contents of the *Brahmasūtras*.

PART II

Philosophical and Cultural Background

CHAPTER 4

Early History and Cultural Values of Vedānta

It is one of the distinctive peculiarities of Indian learned traditions that it is taken for granted, in a formal way, that the fundamentals of each of them are given at the very outset of the history of the discipline and hence that it is the task of successive generations simply to restate them and to explicate them. The textual history of the discipline thus takes on the form of a basic text with generations of commentaries written on this basic text and on the preceding commentary.

This textual tradition is a reflection of *disciplinary* traditions. A particular system of thought or of sect or of cult must be based on clearly definable predecessors if it is to carry the authority expected. In philosophy as well as religion we find a *guruparamparā*, a succession of gurus: the *sūtra* is the *guru* of the commentary. The *guru* is not merely a predecessor in the same field whose views might become antiquated and open to revision; he is an *ancestor*, worthy of a veneration inspired by faith. If he had not occurred, the discipline would not have existed at all, or the line of transmission would have been interrupted and the lineage of learning expired.

We emphasize the fact that in the Indian context the acquisition of knowledge is not looked upon as a gradual *discovery* of it, but as a gradual *recovery* of it. At the beginning of history stands knowledge, complete and available. This knowledge is passed on from generation to generation through a patient transmission from teacher to pupil, and this transmission is founded on faith. Learning, in the widest sense of the word, is a network of lifelines that reaches back to the beginning when learning was given. To a very large extent these traditions of learning are "oral" traditions; and this oral character is not superseded by the texts that emerge along the way. The texts themselves, it is felt, are only part of a tradition which is preserved in its purest form in the oral transmission as it has been going on. No doubt the actual physical perishability of Indian manuscripts has helped to encourage this ancient reliance on direct instruction and retention by memory. The continued existence of the manuscripts depended on continuous copying, each manuscript having little more than an average lifespan of a couple of centuries. Only that was assured perpetuity which was safely ensconced in the memory of a master. Although there is, as a matter of fact, a nearly indestructible textual tradition, it does not supplant the primacy of the oral tradition.

The Indian teacher has little truck with originality. Ideally, he is the encyclopedia of all the erudition of former generations, and it is his task to pass on this knowledge to his pupil as it was passed on to him by his own master. Only when the transmission is complete does the scholar have a right to strike out on his own, with the proud certainty that, if his views after careful probing have been considered useful and worthwhile by his fellow-scholars, they will become part of the disciplinary erudition of what is forever preserved. Learning therefore is highly verbal; the orally acquired disciplinary erudition, which in part may also have been laid down in a written manuscript, is followed by probing discussions and debates, which add to the erudition and perhaps to the textual history of the system.

Such a tradition was, of course, highly vulnerable. The very directness, from master to pupil, of the education made it vulnerable in two respects: the uncertainty of the complete fidelity of the pupil, however good his faith, and the limitation of the number of pupils. One pupil might bend an oral tradition in his new and original way, and so impress his own students that those pupils who more dully repeated the original teaching might well find their lines expired in one or two generations. If no records were kept, the more original teaching would be lost, apart from incidental survivals in quotations; if records were retained, the lesser prestige of them might well discourage later scholars from spending the time or the money on the transcription of these records, let alone on the commenting of them, and they would equally be lost. The limitation of the number of students of any one teacher made the continuity of a tradition as uncertain and arbitrary as the continuity of a family.

These considerations have to be kept in mind when we look at the early history of systematic Vedānta, that is, after the compilation of the *Brahmasūtras*. Here we have at once to introduce a distinction between the *Brahmasūtras* and the *continuing* Upaniṣadic tradition. The Sūtras place an interpretation on the main teachings of the older Upaniṣads, an authoritative interpretation no doubt, but not necessarily the only one. The Sūtras themselves have preserved a record of diverging opinions held by a variety of masters on some crucial problems which are then resolved—as far as we can judge from the cryptic and elliptic sentences—by a final opinion. Did all aupaniṣadas accept this opinion? There might well have been school traditions that considered themselves *aupaniṣada* and yet made little or passing use of the Sūtras as a standard work, preferring to deal directly with the texts themselves on which the Sūtras were based. We must keep in mind that in Vedānta the Sūtras are not *the* basic work, as the *Aṣṭādhyāyī* of Pāṇini is for Grammar and the Nyāya and Vaiśeṣika Sūtras for Logic and the Vaiśeṣika system. The basic text is the Upaniṣad *itself.*

It would seem then that prima facie the assumption is justified that from the very beginning Vedānta never was a unitary system at all. The authority of the Sūtras was considerable, but they occasionally reneged on their essential task of determination by being too vague and obscure about controversial topics. The Upaniṣads formed a small corpus of texts and it was perfectly possible to build a Vedānta directly on, for example, the *Chāndogya Upaniṣad.* Apparently it was such a divergence of opinion and the resulting comparatively lesser degree of authority of the *Brahmasūtras* which prevented the emergence of an early authoritative *sūtra.* That basic commentaries must have existed, orally or written, is certain. That they did not survive must be due to the limitations of their respective audiences. Apart from a handful of quotations in later works, our earliest surviving commentary on the Sūtras is by Śaṁkara, who lived at least five centuries after the likely date of the Sūtras.

Thus Vedānta as a philosophy was from the beginning far more open than many other systems of orthodoxy. Therefore it will be less than fruitful to enquire which of the later commentaries most faithfully reflects the teaching of the Sūtras, because these commentaries might well have come out of *aupaniṣada* traditions that were not too faithfully reflected in the Sūtras themselves. Vedānta as a whole implicitly endorses this conclusion by not starting from its Sūtras alone, as for instance Mīmāṁsā does, but from the Upaniṣads and the *Bhagavadgītā* as well—there are *three* departures.

We have evidence that there were early commentators on the Sūtras. The only ones whose quotations survive are the glossator quoted by Śaṁkara and the Bodhāyana quoted by Rāmānuja. Other authors from whose works quotations are given appear to have been commentators on the Upaniṣads, particularly the *Chāndogya* and *Bṛhadāraṇyaka,* another indication that Vedāntic thought never limited itself to the Sūtras. The views of the early *sūtra* commentators are too sparse to permit any conclusions; Rāmānuja asserts that Bodhāyana supports his interpretation, but he does not give evidence. Since this is all we have before Gauḍapāda, Bhartṛhari, and Śaṁkara, we must conclude that we do *not* know the systematic tradition of the Sūtras.

What this tradition *did* provide was general knowledge on what the Sūtras were about: what topics were being discussed where, and particularly what scriptural evidence was behind the individual Sūtras. In the expository parts of the Sūtras, statements are proved by a text to which there is a minimal reference: for example, the crucial *sūtra* on the nondifference of the world reads "there is non-differentness from it, on the strength of the text on Seizing, etc." This mention of "seizing" would have sufficed in this case to identify the text as that of *Chāndogya Upaniṣad*, chapter 6, but what of the others? And in many cases the Sūtras are satisfied with such references as "on the strength of the Word," without indicating which one. Since in general the commentaries of classical Vedānta accept the topics and the scriptural passages as we first find them in Śaṁkara's work, we may conclude that *this* tradition at least was firm enough not to excite any difference of opinion. This is about all that can be said with certainty.

We concluded that it was less than fruitful to investigate what the various commentators have in common in their interpretations of parts of the *Brahmasūtras* in order to arrive at a knowledge of "original" Vedānta. Several distinguished scholars have made attempts to distinguish between the relative fidelity of Śaṁkara and Rāmānuja, and between Śaṁkara, Rāmānuja, Madhva, Nimbarka, and Vallabha. At best, if at all, we arrive thus at a conjectural picture of the teaching of the Sūtras associated with Bādarāyaṇa without knowing how representative these Sūtras were of Vedāntic thought around the beginning of the Christian era. Even if we know what Bādarāyaṇa thought, what about Jaimini, Badari, Kāśakṛtsna, Auḍulomi, Ātreya, etc., fellow-Vedāntins cited by Bādarāyaṇa, or what about Upavarṣa, Bodhāyana, Ṭaṅka and Drāmiḍa? All these are ancient names with the true ring of Vedic masters, whose teachings are now irrecoverable but must in the abstract be kept in mind to keep our view of what Vedānta was or ought to be sufficiently complex. Barring new discoveries of ancient manuscripts, which is always possible, we do better to confess our inability to trace the history of Vedānta precisely and our need to rely on unsystematic sources as they are available in the *Mahābhārata*, the *Bhagavadgītā*, and the Purāṇas, and in the incidental references found in non-Vedāntic literature. It is from the whole range of Revelation and Recollection that Vedānta can draw and has drawn. From this point of view we may say that the lack of one precise tradition has enabled the classical Vedānta as a whole to become far more representative of all orthodox thought than it otherwise could have achieved.

It is also clear that the meaning of the word "Vedānta" cannot have the same precision in the history of Indian philosophy as such names as "Mīmāṁsā" and "Logic." It is a name like "Buddhism," which combines under one general concern and faith a variety of philosophies. The common ground that we are trying to discover is likely to be a similar one of faith and concern.

Whatever else the *Mahābhārata* and the Purāṇas were intended to do, what they did was notice the variety of beliefs and cults of popular culture and eventually to organize them in the catholic totality which we usually call Hinduism. This word is hard to define. Hinduism is not a church, nor a theology, nor entirely an agglomeration of popular lore and mores, but something in between. It has two foci, social behavior and the worship of Gods. It is Brahministic insofar as Brahmins have come to be regarded as the guides to this social conduct and as the priests of this worship.

The cardinal texts are written in Sanskrit, which is one of their more important features. The history of the use of Sanskrit in the last millennium B.C. and the first millennium A.D. is a complicated one. The language is closely related to the more ancient and arcane language of the Vedas and even more so to that of the expository portions of Brāhmaṇa and Upaniṣad.

There developed a popular Sanskrit, the language of the younger epic and of the Purāṇas. This was not a language more easily understood by the common man *then* than it is now. It was a superior language (even if to the purist it was rather inferior) in which the local beliefs, practices, and gods could achieve a universality that was otherwise denied them. In a civilization where North and South were separated by a language barrier, Sanskrit served as the bridge. In a land where the loyalties were on a less than subcontinental scale and limited by region, language, and village dialect, Sanskrit permitted the part to participate in a thus grown whole. Among a people differentiated into a large number of *castes*, the Brahmin belonged to the only universal *class*, and the prime instrument of this class in maintaining its universality and that of its culture was Sanskrit.

But the Brahmin equally participated in the local culture. He was bilingual and therefore bicultural, and could translate the mainstream of the large culture in terms of the village and the culture of the village in terms of the mainstream. His own class heritage of *śākhā* (Vedic branch) and *sūtra* had continued to relate him to this larger culture of which he deemed the "Veda" to be the foundation. It was his task to relate his smaller culture to the larger ones. The smaller gods themselves became bicultural, and so did the larger ones. The local god was no other than Viṣṇu, the Viṣṇu grew thereby; and Viṣṇu was no other than the local god, whose respectability was now assured.

The Brahmin families lived in their communities as it were like settlers from the larger culture, consciously if not actually separate in their conduct. Through this example of it as well as through the endless sermonizing of the Purāṇas they propagated the good life according to the *dharma*, of which they themselves were the sole custodians. And while Buddhism flourished in the great centers on which the monks depended for patronage, Brahminism kept moving across the countryside as Hinduism.

In the process these ancient ritual specialists began to become the ministers of the gods. Though their own dharma-śāstras prohibited them from professional priesthood for "godlings," it was hard for religious zeal to distinguish between a locally supreme god and the Supreme of the ancient texts. The litanies they composed in Sanskrit for these gods had the same convincing language as the ancient mantras, and their taking over, gradually and assuredly, the ministrations of local religion had an inevitability about it and a fine propriety.

And still there were Brahmins and there were Brahmins. In a system where purity of behavior is a living practice, it is always possible to be purer. And the purest were the vaidikas, who were the living conscience and the comfort of the others. There were those who lived more strictly according to the dictates of the smṛtis and distinguished themselves as smārtas from the new Brahmins who accepted the authority of other texts as well—if not in theory, certainly in practice.

It was in Southern India where this consciously Brahminic culture, interacting with Hindu culture and powerful enough to counteract heterodoxy, had its broadest base. And it was from there that all the major philosophies of Vedānta were to come forth. The Gupta culture had been assassinated by the inroads of the White Huns. The city culture declined with the insecurity of the countrysides and the unsafety of the roads, and with it declined Buddhism. There was a void of philosophical as well as religious leadership, and this, over the next four centuries, the South would fill. Some of the forms of leadership were traditionally Brahministic, as that of Bhāskara and the background of Śaṁkara; others such as Rāmānuja attempted, with a goodly degree of success, to re-ally the resurgent devotionalism with Brahminism and in so doing reformed Vedānta; others again, such as Madhva, departed from the Vedāntic acceptance of the three departures and gave a completely new reinterpretation of all Vedānta, from the *Ṛgveda* onward.

Each of these responses of Vedānta had its own long roots, conceivably as far down as the Upaniṣads themselves. In all their variety and mutual hostility they all shared the same Brahministic concern to build their system of metaphysics on the rockbed of perennial tradition and to accommodate the multiple demands of Hinduism. Taken together they represented *the* Brahmin thought that asserted itself between the waning of Buddhism and the imminent invasion of Islām. It was at once a summing up and a new beginning; it looked with as great a confidence to the past as it did to the future.

CHAPTER 5

Common Philosophical Problems

Before one can appreciate or even understand the solution to a philosophical problem, it is necessary to have a clear understanding of the problem to which the philosopher's thought is directed. And, as we have recently come to learn in Western philosophy, philosophical problems seldom, if ever, arise from "pure" intellectual concerns—rather they reflect and echo a particular existential situation and they seek, however implicitly it may sometimes seem, to ameliorate that situation. The existential situation of a philosopher, like that of everyone else, has both historical and personal boundaries. The nature of the period and culture in which he lives in terms of their values, their state of positive knowledge, their aspirations, and their most pressing problems, as well as the nature and kinds of experience that the philosopher has undergone and assimilated within himself, go to form the milieu, as it were, in which he thinks.

This "existentialism," if you will, is especially true of the Vedānta tradition. The philosophers associated with this tradition in its classical form worked within specific cultural and varied personal boundaries. They were committed in the first place, as we have seen, to *śruti* and *smṛti*. Each Vedāntic philosopher thus had the task of showing that the Upaniṣads, the *Bhagavadgītā*, and the *Brahmasūtras* represent a single consistent system. Vedāntic philosophers had, in short, the exegetical task of making coherent a wide diversity of philosophical-religious materials which they regarded as "authoritative." But together with, or in the process of, showing that these texts were consistent and coherent, the Vedāntic thinkers had to answer a number of strictly philosophical questions. These questions gave rise in turn to other issues and being philosophers as well as "theologians" they had to provide answers to or analyses of them.[1]

1. It is interesting to observe that it is the derivative rather than the primary Vedāntic problems which can properly be phrased in universal philosophical terms. One could, to be sure, subsume the primary problems under a more universal form of expression, but to do this would

The first and the most basic problem of Vedānta is: *What is the nature of Brahman?* or *What kind of reality corresponds to, or is meant by, the term "Brahman"?* This problem is given to Vedānta by *śruti* and *smṛti* and is the most basic in the sense that the kind of answer given to the question will shape and form all other major problems and will color or condition the answers given to them.[2] Now although several answers to this question are proffered by Vedānta (by Advaitins, Viśiṣṭādvaitins, Dvaitins, etc.), the solutions can, for our purposes, be reduced to two main forms. The first solution is that Brahman is One, without quality or distinction; that "Brahman" stands for undifferentiated being (*nirguṇa* Brahman), for a non-personal "oneness" or "ground" of being. The second answer is that Brahman contains within Itself a multiplicity of real attributes, that Brahman is "personal"; that "Brahman" stands for a divine being (*saguṇa* Brahman). The first answer is essentially monistic or non-dualistic (*a-dvaita*); the second is essentially "theistic" or dualistic (*dvaita*). Vedāntic thinkers to be sure combine these answers in various ways, but still these two stand as the basic alternatives given.

METAPHYSICAL

If Brahman is undifferentiated, without quality or distinction, then the Vedāntin is immediately confronted with the fact that ordinarily we do not realize Brahman as so conceived. We experience in our normal, rational, sense-based consciousness a world of multiplicity which we take to be real. The Vedāntin of a non-dualistic persuasion is thus presented with these problems: (1) Why do we fail to realize the true nature of Brahman?, or By what process does Brahman appear to man as a being with attributes?, or Why has Brahman escaped some men's attention entirely?; (2) What is the relation that obtains between Brahman and the world of multiplicity?; and (3) What, if anything, is the nature of Brahman's activity?

If, on the other hand, Brahman is said to contain within Himself

---

be to do violence to the spirit and method of Vedānta philosophy and would tend to blur all cultural differences between Indian philosophy and other philosophical traditions.

2. This first problem of Vedānta nicely illustrates the point about philosophical "universality." The problem to which the Vedāntin first addresses himself is not *What is reality?* (as this is phrased in universal philosophical terms) but *What is the nature of Brahman?* This question is distinctively Indian and in this case Vedāntic (one would look in vain for any extensive analysis of this question in the other Indian systems, e.g., Nyāya, Vaiśeṣika, Sāṁkhya).

an infinite number of attributes, to be a personal being, then a Vedāntin of this persuasion must answer these questions:[3] (1) In what sense is Brahman *the* fundamental reality?; (2) What realities other than Brahman have to be acknowledged?; (3) What is His relation to these?; and (4) How, or from what cause, motive, purpose, does Brahman manifest Itself to man?

The metaphysical or ontological questions which follow from these basic problems may be stated, and in universal philosophical terms, as:

1. What kinds and/or levels of being present themselves in human experience?
2. Do various orders of being arrange themselves in a hierarchy? If so, by what criterion?
3. What is the nature of time, space, and causation?

These questions arise in the context of the Vedāntin's bringing Brahman and the world together in his thought. The real question that he is asking is: What is the nature of the world which makes Brahman or Brahman-experience possible? And it is interesting to note the presuppositions that are operative in the question; namely, that experience of Brahman is possible (by which is meant direct intuitive identity or unity) and that there is such a thing as the "world" which stands in need of explanation in relation to Brahman.

META-PSYCHOLOGICAL

For some Vedāntic systems (viz., Advaita), another way of raising the question about the nature of Brahman is to ask about the Self; and in any event an inquiry into the nature of selfhood is of central importance to Vedānta, as it is to all systems of philosophy. In the context of *śruti*, the question is raised by the Vedāntin in this way: *What is the status of the self in relation to Brahman?*

If Brahman is One, it follows that the self, if it is to be admitted at all, is not-different from Brahman. These questions must then be answered: (1) By what process does our individual self and other selves appear to us in our experience?; (2) How do the empirical dimensions or aspects of selfhood relate to the Self which

3. These are among the classical "theistic" problems in all cultures. They have, though, a special form in Vedānta in terms of the manner in which they are given to Vedānta by *śruti*. For example, *śruti* insists that Brahman is the material as well as the efficient cause of the world, and this quite clearly introduces a dimension which is absent, for the most part, in the Judaeo-Christian theistic tradition.

is identical with Brahman?; and (3) Is the individual self, the *jīva*, one or many?

If Brahman contains many real attributes, and hence is not undifferentiated, then it follows that individual selfhood is not in essence identical with Brahman. These questions then stand in need of answers: (1) Is the relation that obtains between the self and Brahman one of complete separation, of one-sided dependence, or of mutual dependence?; (2) What are the relationships between the physical and non-material or spiritual dimensions of the individual human being?; and (3) Is the spiritual dimension or quality of selfhood infinite and eternal?, and, If so, what is the principle of individuation?

Some of the specific meta-psychological problems which arise from these basic problems are:

1. What is the nature of consciousness?
2. How are the different empirical dimensions of selfhood functionally related to each other?

EPISTEMOLOGICAL

Once the concept of Brahman is put forward (in whatever form) the Vedāntic philosopher is confronted with this formidable problem, *How may Brahman be known?*

If Brahman is One, then by definition it is "unknowable" by the usual means of conceptual or perceptual knowing. The Vedāntin who affirms this "unknowableness" of Brahman is then presented with these questions: (1) What is the non-rational or supra-rational means of knowledge by which Brahman or the Self is known?; (2) What are the limits and the proper domain of reason?; and (3) How does the non-rational understanding of Brahman relate to other forms of human knowing or kinds of human knowledge?

If Brahman is differentiated, then these questions arise: (1) By what mode of thought or feeling can Brahman be known?; (2) How does this mode or means of knowledge relate to ordinary demonstrative and perceptual knowing?; and (3) To what extent can reason be relied upon in understanding the relations that obtain between Brahman and the world?

The epistemological questions which further arise from these sets of problems are:

1. What is the means by which knowledge is validated?, or What is truth?

2. How are perception, inference, etc., justified as valid means of knowledge?
3. What is the nature of error?

AXIOLOGICAL

Even if a Vedāntin successfully answered all these various metaphysical, meta-psychological, and epistemological questions, there still would remain for him the practical question of how man may realize Brahman as the highest value in his own experience. *Śruti* puts forward the goal of *mokṣa*, of freedom or release from all bondage, as the highest aim of life. The Vedāntin must answer, then, this last major question (which is experientially prior to all other concerns): *How may man obtain mokṣa?*

If Brahman is One, then: (1) How can any act or effort of man lead to its realization?; and (2) Does the self who realizes Brahman attain complete release while living with his body in the world?

If Brahman contains attributes, then: (1) How is individuality retained in *mokṣa*?; and (2) Why does "evil" or "ignorance" exist in the world at all?

The axiological or ethical questions which arise from these problems are:

1. Is moral behavior a necessary and/or sufficient condition for man's obtaining a supreme value?
2. What obligations, if any, are imposed upon one in one's interpersonal or social relationships by the realization of a highest value?
3. What is the source, the nature, and validity of man's moral judgments?

In sum, Vedānta may be defined on its philosophical side as just that tradition in Indian thought which had these metaphysical, meta-psychological, epistemological, and axiological problems as its distinctive concern. The various Vedāntic solutions to these problems will reflect the different experiences and values of the individual Vedāntic philosopher; the problems themselves, however, were common property and were generated in a specific historical/cultural context.

CHAPTER 6

Criticisms of Rival Systems

Vedānta developed its philosophical doctrines, its answers to the problems outlined above, in close relationship with other Indian philosophical systems and religious traditions, both "orthodox" and "heterodox." The various Vedāntic schools attack these rival systems in a powerful way but they also freely borrow from these systems when it suits their purpose. Much of the cosmological and epistemological doctrine of Vedānta, as it pertains to an explanation of the world, is taken from the Sāṁkhya and Nyāya systems, and much of the exegetical methodology used by Vedānta, as noted previously, is taken over from Mīmāṁsā. Rather than rejecting the rival systems in toto Vedānta adopts many of their ideas and subordinates them to Vedāntic principles. In the larger historical context, then, it might be said that Vedānta did not so much demolish its rivals as it swallowed them up.[1]

It is impossible to know just when or by whom the Vedāntic arguments against the basic metaphysical principles of the rival systems were first formulated. By the time of Śaṁkara many of these arguments, it is believed, were set in the form in which we now have them. Śaṁkara, in this account, introduces certain original elements into the arguments while accepting a line of attack which had already been worked out.[2] In any event, the dialectical interplay between Vedānta and the other Indian systems, as it has

1. This does not mean that after Śaṁkara Indian philosophy is to be identified with Vedānta. Several schools maintained their tradition and at times offered counter arguments to the Vedāntic criticisms of their doctrines. (*See* for example *Sāṁkhyapravacanasūtra*, I, 150–152, for the arguments employed by the Sāṁkhya system against Vedānta.

2. *See* Daniel H. H. Ingalls, "Śaṁkara's Arguments Against the Buddhists," *Philosophy East and West*, vol. 3, no. 4, (Honolulu: University of Hawaii Press, 1954), pp. 291–306.

come down to us, does take place in a kind of non-historical setting. Śaṁkara treats each system as though it were a living intellectual force whereas in fact many of the systems were no longer active in the intellectual milieu of his time.

To give the reader a sense of the interplay between the Indian schools of philosophy and to get a clearer idea of what Vedāntic thinkers hold in common, we have selected a rather large portion of Śaṁkara's *Brahmasūtrabhāṣya*[3] wherein he attacks rival non-Vedāntic schools. For the most part he sums up the doctrines of his rivals in a fair and objective way, and the arguments which he brings to bear against them are accepted by and large by later Vedāntic thinkers whether they be followers of his or another's system of Vedānta.

The source material is from *The Vedānta-Sūtras: with the Commentary by Śankarācārya*, translated by George Thibaut, The Sacred Books of the East, vols. 34 and 38, edited by F. Max Müller (Oxford: The Clarendon Press, 1890, 1896).

SĀṀKHYA

The first system following the Sūtras which Śaṁkara attacks is the Sāṁkhya. This is one of the oldest and most important systems of Indian thought. According to tradition it was formulated by one Kapila in the seventh century B.C. The oldest text which is available on the Sāṁkhya, however, is the *Sāṁkhya-Kārikā* of Īśvarakṛṣṇa, written about the third century A.D.[4] The importance of the Sāṁkhya for Indian thought lies primarily in its theory of cosmic evolution. Its *description* of evolution is generally accepted by (i.e., is incorporated into) Vedānta, but not its metaphysical basis or its spiritual interpretation.

According to the Sāṁkhya, the evolution of the world is the result of an interraction between two primal and irreducible prin-

---

3. *See* pp. 150–151 for a description of the status of Śaṁkara's commentary on the *Brahmasūtras* in the Advaitic school of Vedānta.

4. Another important Sāṁkhyan work is the *Sāṁkhyapravacanasūtra*, once ascribed to Kapila but now believed to have been written in the fourteenth century. Vācaspati's *Tattvakaumudī*, Gauḍapāda's *Sāṁkhya-Kārikā-bhāṣya*, Aniruddha's *Sāṁkhyasūtravṛtti*, and Vijñānabhikṣu's *Sāṁkhyapravacanabhāṣya* are also part of the basic primary literature. A. B. Keith's *The Sāṁkhya System* (London: Oxford University Press, 1918) is a good exposition of the Sāṁkhya in its relations to other Indian systems of thought.

ciples called *puruṣa* and *prakṛti*. *Puruṣa* is the principle of "consciousness," "spirit," "personality," and is defined as wholly passive in essence. *Prakṛti* is the principle of "physical nature," "matter," "unconscious force," and is regarded as the seat of all activity.[5] In its primitive or original state *prakṛti* is said to be in a state of perfect equilibrium. Its constituent elements or "strands," the guṇas of *sattva* ("dynamic balance," "goodness"), *rajas* ("turbulent action," "passion"), and *tamas* ("inertness," "lethargy," "darkness"), are held in a static balance or equipoise. This balance gets upset by the "proximity" of *puruṣa* to *prakṛti* and an evolution of the universe is set in motion, with *prakṛti* being its material cause. The evolution thus is basically an emanation of the universe from *prakṛti*; it is a transformation of a primordial material principle into a universe of gross and subtle objects—the causal theory explaining it being known as *pariṇāmavāda*, the theory of the transformation of a cause into its effect.[6] Evolution takes place, according to the Sāṁkhya, for the "sake of the spirit"; for the enjoyment of the *puruṣa*, and for its eventual return to a state of pure isolation.

The first evolvement of *prakṛti* is called *mahat* or *buddhi*, the principle of intellect. From this the *ahaṁkāra* or principle of individuation evolves, and from this, under the influence of the *guṇa* of *sattva*, the sense mind (*manas*), the five organs of perception (buddhīndriyas: taste, smell, touch, seeing, hearing), and the five organs of action (karmendriyas: tongue, feet, hands, the ejective, and generative organs) evolve. This is followed by the five subtle elements (tanmātras: the essences of sound, touch, color, taste, and smell conceived of as fine or subtle material principles) and the five gross elements (bhūtas: earth, water, fire, air, ether) which

---

5. The existence of *prakṛti* is inferred, according to the Sāṁkhya, on grounds such as (1) the finite objects of the universe must be dependent upon something else because of their very finitude, and (2) all individual objects possess certain similar characteristics (e.g., their being subject to pleasure and pain) and this is intelligible only when they are referred to a common source. (*See Sāṁkhya-Kārikā*, XV) The existence of the *puruṣa* is also argued on grounds such as (1) experience is unintelligible without a coordinating consciousness; (2) all composite objects exist for the use of a spiritual principle; and (3) there is a tendency toward spiritual experience in beings and this presupposes the existence of a spiritual principle in those beings. (Ibid., XVII)

6. *Pariṇāmavāda* is one form of the more general theory of causation known as *satkāryavāda*—the theory that the effect is pre-existent in its (material) cause and is not, therefore, something which, ontologically speaking, is radically different from its cause.

arise from the predominance of the *guṇa* of *tamas*. We have, then, as the general categories of the Sāṁkhya evolutionary schema:

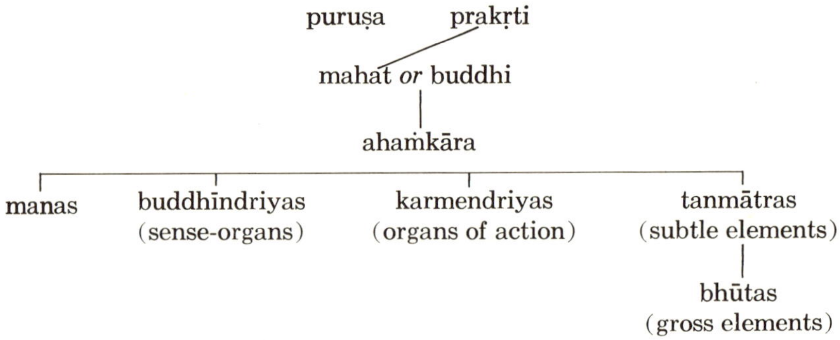

Once evolution takes place the principle of spirit, *puruṣa*, becomes pluralistic and many selves are then caught up in *prakṛti* in its evolved form. The goal of life, for the Sāṁkhya, is for the *puruṣa* to regain its pristine state, for the self to attain omniscience and bliss. *Puruṣa* is pure spirit, but it gets involved in *prakṛti* and forgets its true nature. The individual self, the *jīva*, is the *puruṣa* limited by its body and sense-experience. When a proper knowledge of *prakṛti* and the self's involvement with it is acquired, *puruṣa* regains its freedom.

Śaṁkara's attack against the Sāṁkhya system takes several forms. He argues first that the *arrangement* of the world in all its subtle intricacies is unintelligible on the assumption that a non-intelligent primal nature (*prakṛti* or the *pradhāna* as it is also called) is its sole cause. A purely naturalistic or materialistic account of the physical world is unable to provide a rational explanation of the world. It might give us "causes" but it cannot give us "reasons" for the order of the world. And the same applies, according to Śaṁkara, to the *activity* by which the world is produced. The efficient cause of an action never arises from the non-intelligent object which is affected (e.g., the pot), although it might belong to it, but from the intelligent agent (e.g., the potter) which acts upon the object. *Prakṛti*, in short, cannot undergo modification and give rise to an ordered universe through its own spontaneous activity. Further it is impossible to maintain on the basis of Sāṁkhyan principles that the evolution of *prakṛti* is guided by some purpose, for whether evolution takes place for the enjoyment or for the release of the *puruṣa* the goal turns out to be self-contradictory and impossible of attainment. Śaṁkara also criticizes the Sāṁkhyan assertion that evolution begins with the upsetting of the equipoise between the guṇas that constitute *prakṛti.* If one denies the existence of an external principle acting upon *prakṛti,* as the Sāṁkhya does, and at the same time maintains the absolute independence of the guṇas from each other, then it is impossible to show how evolution can commence.

Thus, the main line of Śaṁkara's attack against the Sāṁkhya system is that the cause of evolution is incomprehensible without a conscious, controlling agent, that primal nature could never by itself give rise to, or provide a purpose for, the intricate complexity of the world. The Vedānta argument against the Sāṁkhya is essentially a "theistic" criticism of a naturalistic world view. Although, as we will see later, Śaṁkara rejects the ultimacy of any theistic position, he is appealing to such a position in his critique of the Sāṁkhya.

Although it is the object of this [Vedāntic] system to define the true meaning of the Vedānta-texts and not, like the science of Logic, to establish or refute some tenet by mere ratiocination, still it is incumbent on thorough students of the Vedānta to refute the Sāṁkhya and other systems which are obstacles in the way of perfect knowledge. . . .
. . . For there is some danger of men of inferior intelligence looking upon the Sāṁkhya and similar systems as requisite for perfect knowledge, because those systems have a weighty appearance, have been adopted by authoritative persons, and profess to lead to perfect knowledge. Such people might therefore think that those systems with their abstruse arguments were propounded by omniscient sages, and might on that account have faith in them. For this reason we must endeavour to demonstrate their intrinsic worthlessness. . . .

The Sāṁkhyas, to make a beginning with them, argue as follows.—Just as jars, dishes, and other products which possess the common quality of consisting of clay are seen to have for their cause clay in general; so we must suppose that all the outward and inward (i.e. inanimate and animate) effects which are endowed with the characteristics of pleasure, pain, and dulness [the three guṇas—*sattva, rajas, tamas*] have for their causes pleasure, pain and dulness in general. Pleasure, pain, and dulness in their generality together constitute the threefold *pradhāna.* This *pradhāna* which is non-intelligent evolves itself spontaneously into multiform modifications, in order thus to effect the purposes (i.e. enjoyment, release, and so on) of the intelligent soul.—The existence of the *pradhāna* is to be inferred from other circumstances also, such as the limitation of all effects and the like.

Against this doctrine we argue as follows.—If you Sāṁkhyas base your theory on parallel instances [analogies] merely, we point out that a non-intelligent thing which, without being guided by an intelligent being, spontaneously produces effects capable of subserving the purposes of some particular person is nowhere observed in the world. We rather observe that houses, palaces, couches, pleasure-grounds, and the like—things which according to circumstances are conducive to the obtainment of pleasure or the avoidance of pain—are made by workmen endowed with intelligence. Now look at this entire world which appears, on the one hand, as external (i.e. inanimate) in the form of earth and the other elements enabling (the souls) to enjoy the fruits of their various actions, and, on the other hand, as animate, in the form of bodies which belong to the different classes of beings, possess a definite arrangement of organs, and are therefore capable of constituting the abodes of fruition; look, we say, at this world, of which the most ingenious workmen cannot even form a conception in their minds, and then say if a non-intelligent principle like the *pradhāna* is able to fashion it! . . . (II, 2, 1)

Leaving the arrangement of the world, we now pass on to the activity by which it is produced.—The three guṇas, passing out of the state of equipoise and entering into the condition of mutual subordination and superordination, originate activities tending towards the production of particular effects.—Now these activities also cannot be ascribed to a non-intelligent *pradhāna* left to itself, as no such activity is seen in clay and similar substances, or in chariots and the like. For we observe that clay and the like, and chariots—which are in their own nature non-intelligent—enter on activities tending towards particular effects only when they are acted upon by intelligent beings such as potters, &c. in the one case, and horses and the like in the other case. From what is seen we determine what is not seen. Hence a non-intelligent cause of the world is not to be inferred because, on that hypothesis, the activity without which the world cannot be produced would be impossible [unintelligible].

But, the Sāṁkhya rejoins, we do likewise not observe activity on the part of mere intelligent beings.—True; we however see activity on the part of non-intelligent things such as chariots and the like when they are in conjunction with intelligent beings.—But, the Sāṁkhya again objects, we never actually observe activity on the part of an intelligent being even when in conjunction with a non-intelligent thing.—Very well; the question then arises: Does the activity belong to that in which it is actually observed (as the Sāṁkhya says) or to that on account of the conjunction with which it is observed (as the Vedāntin avers)?—We must, the Sāṁkhya replies, attribute activity to that in which it is actually seen, since both (i.e. the activity and its abode) are matter of observation. A mere intelligent being, on the other hand, is never observed as the abode of activity while a chariot is. The existence of an intelligent Self joined to a body and so on which are the abode of activity can be established (by inference) only; the inference being based on the difference observed between living bodies and mere non-intelligent things, such as chariots and the like. For this very reason, viz. that intelligence is observed only where a body is observed while it is never seen without a body, the Materialists consider intelligence to be a mere attribute of the body.—Hence activity belongs only to what is non-intelligent.

To all this we—the Vedāntins—make the following reply.—We do not mean to say that activity does not belong to those non-intelligent things in which it is observed; it does indeed belong to them; but it results from an intelligent principle, because it exists when the latter is present and does not exist when the latter is absent. Just as the effects of burning and shining, which have their abode in wood and similar material, are indeed not observed when there is mere fire (i.e. are not due to mere fire; as mere fire, i.e. fire without wood, &c., does not exist), but at the same time result from fire only as they are seen when fire is present and are not seen when fire is absent; so, as the Materialists also admit, only intelligent bodies are observed to be the movers of chariots and other non-intelligent things. The motive power of intelligence is therefore incontrovertible. . . . (II, 2, 2)

The three guṇas of the Sāṁkhyas when in a state of equipoise form the *pradhāna*. Beyond the *pradhāna* there exists no external principle which could either impel the *pradhāna* to activity or restrain it from activity. The soul (*puruṣa*), as we know, is indifferent, neither moves to—nor restrains from—action. As therefore the *pradhāna* stands in no relation, it is impossible to see why it should sometimes modify itself into the great principle (*mahat*) and sometimes not. . . . (II, 2, 4)

Let this be (the Sāṁkhya resumes). Just as grass, herbs, water, &c. independently of any other instrumental cause transform themselves, by their own nature, into milk; so, we assume, the *pradhāna* also transforms itself into the great principle, and so on. And, if you ask how we know that grass transforms itself independently of any instrumental cause; we reply, 'Because no such cause is observed.' For if we did perceive some such cause, we certainly should apply it to grass, &c. according to our liking, and thereby produce milk. But as a matter of fact we do no such thing. Hence the transformation of grass and the like must be considered to be due to its own nature merely; and we may infer therefrom that the transformation of the *pradhāna* is of the same kind.

To this we make the following reply.—The transformation of the *pradhāna* might be ascribed to its own nature merely if we really could admit that grass modifies itself in the manner stated by you; but we are unable to admit that, since another instrumental cause is observed. How? 'Because it does not exist elsewhere.' For grass becomes milk only when it is eaten by a cow or some other female animal, not if it is left either uneaten or is eaten by a bull. If the transformation had no special cause, grass would become milk even on other conditions than that of entering a cow's body. Nor would the circumstance of men not being able to produce milk according to their liking prove that there is no instrumental cause; for while some effects can be produced by men, others result from divine action only. The fact, however, is that men also are able, by applying a means in their power, to produce milk from grass and herbs; for when they wish to produce a more abundant supply of milk they feed the cow more plentifully and thus obtain more milk from her.—For these reasons the spontaneous modification of the *pradhāna* cannot be proved from the instance of grass and the like. (II, 2, 5)

Even if we, accommodating ourselves to your (the Sāṁkhya's) belief, should admit what has been disproved in the preceding Sūtra, viz. that the *pradhāna* is spontaneously active, still your opinion would lie open to an objection 'on account of the absence of a purpose.' For if the spontaneous activity of the *pradhāna* has, as you say, no reference to anything else, it will have no reference not only to any aiding principle, but also to any purpose or motive, and consequently your doctrine that the *pradhāna* is active in order to effect the purpose of man will become untenable. If you reply that the *pradhāna* does not indeed regard any aiding principle, but does regard a purpose, we remark that in that case we must distinguish between the different possible purposes, viz. either enjoyment (on the part of the soul), or final release, or both. If enjoyment, what enjoyment, we ask, can belong to the soul which is naturally incapable of any accretion (of pleasure or pain)? Moreover, there would in that case be no opportunity for release.—If release, then the activity of the *pradhāna* would be purposeless, as even antecedently to it the soul is in the state of release; moreover, there would then be no occasion for the perception of sounds, &c.—If both, then, on account of the infinite number of the objects of *pradhāna* to be enjoyed (by the soul), there would be no opportunity for final release. Nor can the satisfaction of a desire be considered as the purpose of the activity of the *pradhāna*; for neither the non-intelligent *pradhāna* nor the essentially pure soul can feel any desire.—If, finally, you should assume the *pradhāna* to be active, because otherwise the power of sight (belonging to the soul on account of its intelligent nature) and the creative power (belonging to the *pradhāna*) would be purposeless; it would follow that, as the creative power of the *pradhāna* does not cease at any time any more than the soul's power of sight does, the apparent world would never come to an end, so that no final release of the soul could take place.—It is, therefore, impossible to maintain that the *pradhāna* enters on its activity for the purposes of the soul. (II, 2, 6)

Well then—the Sāṁkhya resumes, endeavouring to defend his position by parallel instances—let us say that, as some lame man devoid of the power of motion, but possessing the power of sight, having mounted the back of a blind man who is able to move but not to see, makes the latter move; or as the magnet not moving itself, moves the iron, so the soul moves the *pradhāna*.—Thus also, we reply, you do not free your doctrine from all shortcomings; for this your new position involves an abandonment of your old position, according to which the *pradhāna* is moving of itself, and the (indifferent, inactive) soul possesses no moving power. And how should the indifferent soul move the *pradhāna*? A man, although lame, may make a blind man move by means of words and the like; but the soul which is devoid of action and qualities cannot possibly put forth any moving energy. Nor can it be said that it moves the *pradhāna* by its mere proximity as the magnet moves the iron; for from the permanency of proximity (of soul and *pradhāna*) a permanency of motion would follow. The proximity of the magnet, on the other hand (to the iron), is not permanent, but depends on a certain activity and the adjustment of the magnet in a certain position; hence the (lame) man and the magnet do not supply really parallel instances. —The *pradhāna* then being non-intelligent and the soul indifferent, and there being no third principle to connect them, there can be no connexion of the two. If we attempted to establish a connexion on the ground of capability (of being seen on the part of the *pradhāna*, of seeing on the part of the soul), the permanency of such capability would imply the impossibility of final release. . . . (II, 2, 7)

For the following reason also activity on the part of the *pradhāna* is not possible.—The condition of the *pradhāna* consists in the three guṇas, viz. goodness, passion, and darkness, abiding in themselves in a state of equipoise without standing to one another in the relation of mutual superiority or inferiority. In that state the guṇas cannot possibly enter into the relation of mutual subserviency because thereby they would forfeit their essential characteristic, viz. absolute independence. And as there exists no extraneous principle to stir up the guṇas, the production of the great principle and the other effects—which would require for its operative cause a non-balanced state of the guṇas—is impossible. (II, 2, 8)

But—the Sāṁkhya resumes—we draw another inference, so as to leave no room for the objection just stated. We do not acknowledge the guṇas to be characterised by absolute irrelativity and unchangeableness, since there is no proof for such an assumption. We rather infer the characteristics of the guṇas from those of their effects, presuming that their nature must be such as to render the production of the effects possible. Now the guṇas are admitted to be of an unsteady nature; hence the guṇas themselves are able to enter into the relation of mutual inequality, even while they are in a state of equipoise.

Even in that case, we reply, the objections stated above which were founded on the impossibility of an orderly arrangement of the world, &c., remain in force on account of the *pradhāna* being devoid of the power of intelligence. And if (to escape those objections) the Sāṁkhya should infer (from the orderly arrangement of the world, &c.), that the primal cause is intelligent, he would cease to be an antagonist, since the doctrine that there is one intelligent cause of this multiform world would be nothing else but the Vedāntic doctrine of Brahman.—Moreover, if the guṇas were capable of entering into the relation of mutual inequality even while in the state of equipoise, one of two things would happen; they would either not be in the condition of inequality on account of the absence of an operative cause; or else, if they were in that condition, they would always remain in it; the absence of an operative cause being a non-changing circumstance. And thus the doctrine would be open to the objection stated before. (II, 2, 9)

VAIŚEṢIKA

The next system which the Sūtras and Śaṁkara criticize is the Vaiśeṣika. The main text of this school is the *Vaiśeṣika Sūtra* which was compiled in the first century A.D. and is ascribed to one Kaṇāda.[7] The Vaiśeṣika is a realistic and pluralistic system of cosmology and physics. It emphasizes an "atomic" theory of matter and a classification of all objects in the universe into six categories (padārthas). The categories are substance (*dravya*), quality (*guṇa*), activity (*karma*), generality (*sāmānya*), particularity (*viśeṣa*), and inherence (*samavāya*).[8] All objects of experience appear to us in these categories and these objects are "real"—the categories are features of the world as well as of thought.

A substance (*dravya*) is defined as a basic substratum which supports qualities. Nine substances are distinguished: earth (*pṛthivī*), water (*jala*), fire (*tejas*), air (*vāyu*), ether (*ākāśa*), time (*kāla*), space (*diś*), self (*ātman*), and mind (*manas*). Some of the substances are thus material, others are immaterial. The material substances are distinguished according to the qualities which are associated with them (e.g., air has the quality of touch, fire has the qualities of touch and color), and they are made up of partless atoms (paramāṇus). These atoms constitute then the composite things of the world.

The category of quality (*guṇa*) is defined as that which abides in substance and has no further qualities of its own. Qualities abide in substances but are logically and ontologically independent of them. Numerous qualities are identified; among them color, taste, smell, magnitude, and conjunction.[9]

The category of activity (*karma*) refers to the kinds of "movements" which subsist in corporeal substances—e.g., contraction and expansion—and is taken to be the cause of the conjunction

7. The *Padārthadharmasaṁgraha* of Praśastapāda is another important work of Vaiśeṣika thought. Commentaries were written on it by Vyomaśekhara, Śrīdhara, Udayana, and Śrīvatsa in the tenth and eleventh centuries.

8. Later Vaiśeṣikas add *abhāva* ("negation") to the list and so affirm seven basic categories.

9. *See Vaiśeṣika Sūtra,* I, 1, 6.

and disjunction of things. Generality (*sāmānya*), particularity (*viśeṣa*), and inherence (*samavāya*) are basically structural or relational categories. *Sāmānya* is the "universal" conceived as subsisting in itself and as apprehended in relation to particular things; *viśeṣa* is that which makes for the differences between things; *samavāya* is that which makes one entity present whenever another entity is present, it is that necessary relation which obtains, for instance, between a whole and its parts or between a substance and its qualities.[10]

In its account of the creation of the world the Vaiśeṣika maintains that the primal atoms combine first in dyads and then in molecules; the creative act (which follows regularly upon the state of universal destruction, *pralaya*) always has reference to the totality of merit and demerit (*adṛṣṭa*, the "unseen" principle) acquired by individual souls in previous lives. Although entities arise only from material substances of a like nature (i.e., the elements of one substance, say earth, can bring forth only those entities which are constituted by that substance), there is no limit to what may appear in existence. The Vaiśeṣika rejects *pariṇāmavāda*, the theory of the transformation of the cause into its effect accepted by Sāṁkhya, and holds to *asatkāryavāda*, the theory that the effect is not pre-existent in its cause and that the effect is ontologically different from its cause. All effects, according to the Vaiśeṣika, are impermanent; at some time they will cease to be.

In criticizing the Vaiśeṣika, Śaṁkara tries to disclose its inherent contradictions. He also employs the same argument which he used against the Sāṁkhya, viz., that the world is unintelligible without a conscious intelligent principle as its creative ground.[11] Śaṁkara further attacks the doctrine of relations put forth by the Vaiśeṣika and argues here that relations, such as conjunction, have no existence apart from the terms which they relate.

> Herewith we have refuted the doctrine which holds the *pradhāna* to be the cause of the world. We have now to dispose of the atomic theory. . . . (II, 2, 10)

---

10. *See Padārthadharmasaṁgraha*, II, 7–9, for a fuller description and explanation of these categories.

11. In the later development of Vaiśeṣika (when it became closely allied with the Nyāya system) the existence of God (Īśvara) is affirmed and it is held that it is by his will that the universe undergoes its periodic creations and destructions. God's will, though, always has reference to the total of merit and demerit—the "unseen" principle, *adṛṣṭa*—which is acquired by individuals in their previous lives. *Adṛṣṭa* also performs a creative function in the Vaiśeṣika by setting into motion the atoms of air from which the gross element of air arises—and so on throughout the creative process.

. . . This doctrine arises in the following manner. We see that all ordinary substances which consist of parts, as for instance, pieces of cloth originate from the substances connected with them by the relation of inherence, as for instance threads, conjunction co-operating (with the parts to form the whole). We thence draw the general conclusion that whatever consists of parts has originated from those substances with which it is connected by the relation of inherence, conjunction co-operating. That thing now at which the distinction of whole and parts stops and which marks the limit of division into minuter parts is the atom.—This whole world, with its mountains, oceans, and so on, is composed of parts; because it is composed of parts it has a beginning and an end; an effect may not be assumed without a cause; therefore the atoms are the cause of the world. Such is Kaṇāda's doctrine.—As we observe four elementary substances consisting of parts, viz. earth, water, fire, and air (wind), we have to assume four different kinds of atoms. These atoms marking the limit of subdivision into minuter parts cannot be divided themselves; hence when the elements are destroyed they can be divided down to atoms only; this state of atomic division of the elements constitutes the *pralaya* (the periodical destruction of the world). After that when the time for creation comes, motion (*karman*) springs up in the aerial atoms. This motion which is due to the unseen principle [*adṛṣṭa*] joins the atom in which it resides to another atom; thus binary compounds, &c. are produced, and finally the element of air. In a like manner are produced fire, water, earth, the body with its organs. Thus the whole world originates from atoms. For the qualities inhering in the atoms the qualities belonging to the binary compounds are produced, just as the qualities of the cloth result from the qualities of the threads.—Such, in short, is the teaching of the followers of Kaṇāda.

This doctrine we controvert in the following manner.—It must be admitted that the atoms when they are in a state of isolation require action (motion) to bring about their conjunction; for we observe that the conjunction of threads and the like is effected by action. Action again, which is itself an effect, requires some operative cause by which it is brought about; for unless some such cause exists, no original motion can take place in the atoms. If, then, some operative cause is assumed, we may, in the first place, assume some cause analogous to seen causes, such as endeavour or impact. But in that case original motion could not occur at all in the atoms, since causes of that kind are, at the time, impossible. For in the *pralaya* state endeavour, which is a quality of the soul, cannot take place because no body exists then. For the quality of the soul called endeavour originates when the soul is connected with the internal organ which abides in the body. The same reason precludes the assumption of other seen causes such as impact and the like. For they all are possible only after the creation of the world has taken place, and cannot therefore be the causes of the original action (by which the world is produced). If, in the second place, the unseen principle is assumed as the cause of the original motion of the atoms, we ask: Is this unseen principle to be considered as inhering in the soul or in the atom? In both cases it cannot be the cause of motion in the atoms, because it is non-intelligent. For, as we have shown above in our examination of the Sāṁkhya system, a non-intelligent thing which is not directed by an intelligent principle cannot of itself either act or be the cause of action, and the soul cannot be the guiding principle of the *adṛṣṭa* because at the time of *pralaya* its intelligence has not yet arisen. If, on the other hand, the unseen principle is supposed to inhere in the soul, it cannot be the cause of motion in the atoms, because there exists no connexion of it with the latter. If you say that the soul in which the unseen principle inheres is connected with the atoms, then there would result, from the continuity of connexion, continuity of action, as there is no other restricting principle.—Hence, there being no definite cause of action, original action cannot take place in the atoms; there being no action, conjunction of the atoms which depends on action cannot take place; there being no conjunction, all the effects depending on it, viz. the formation of binary atomic compounds, &c., cannot originate.

How, moreover, is the conjunction of one atom with another to be imagined? Is it to be total interpenetration of the two or partial conjunction? If the former, then no increase of bulk could take place, and consequently atomic size only would exist; moreover, it would be contrary to what is observed, as we see that conjunction takes place between substances having parts (*pradeśa*). If the latter, it would follow that the atoms are composed of parts.—Let then the atoms be imagined to consist of parts.—If so, imagined things being unreal, the conjunction also of the atoms would be unreal and thus could not be the non-inherent cause of real things. And without non-inherent causes effected substances such as binary compounds, &c. could not originate. And just as at the time of the first creation motion of the atoms leading to their conjunction could not take place, there being no cause of such motion; thus at the time of a general *pralaya* also no action could take place leading to their separation, since for that occurrence also no definite seen cause could be alleged. Nor could the unseen principle be adduced as the cause, since its purport is to effect enjoyment (of reward and punishment on the part of the soul), not to bring about the *pralaya*. There being then no possibility of action to effect either the conjunction or the separation of the atoms, neither conjunction nor separation would actually take place, and hence neither creation nor *pralaya* of the world.—For these reasons the doctrine of the atoms being the cause of the world must be rejected. (II, 2, 12)

Let us suppose, the Vaiśeṣikas say, all substances composed of parts to be disintegrated into their parts; a limit will finally be reached beyond which the process of disintegration cannot be continued. What constitutes that limit are the atoms, which are eternal (permanent), belong to four different classes, possess the qualities of colour, &c., and are the originating principles of this whole material world with its colour, form, and other qualities.

This fundamental assumption of the Vaiśeṣikas we declare to be groundless because from the circumstance of the atoms having colour and other qualities there would follow the contrary of atomic minuteness and permanency, i.e. it would follow that, compared to the ultimate cause, they are gross and non-permanent. For ordinary experience teaches that whatever things possess colour and other qualities are, compared to their cause, gross and non-permanent. A piece of cloth, for instance, is gross compared to the threads of which it consists, and non-permanent; and the threads again are non-permanent and gross compared to the filaments of which they are made up. Therefore the atoms also which the Vaiśeṣikas admit to have colour, &c. must have causes compared to which they are gross and non-permanent. Hence that reason also which Kaṇāda gives for the permanence of the atoms (IV, 1, 1, 'that which exists without having a cause is permanent') does not apply at all to the atoms because, as we have shown just now, the atoms are to be considered as having a cause. . . . (II, 2, 15)

. . . The Vaiśeṣikas assume six categories, which constitute the subject-matter of their system, viz. substance, quality, action, generality, particularity, and inherence. These six categories they maintain to be absolutely different from each other, and to have different characteristics; just as a man, a horse, a hare differ from one another. Side by side with this assumption they make another which contradicts the former one, viz. that quality, action, &c. have the attribute of depending on substance. But that is altogether inappropriate; for just as ordinary things, such as animals, grass, trees, and the like, being absolutely different from each other do not depend on each other, so the qualities, &c. also being absolutely different from substances, cannot depend on the latter. Or else let the qualities, &c. depend on substance; then it follows that, as they are present where substance is present, and absent where it is absent, substance only exists, and, according to its various forms, becomes the object of different terms and conceptions (such as quality, action, &c.); just as Devadatta, for instance, according to the conditions in which he finds himself is the object of various conceptions and names. But this latter alternative would involve the acceptation of the Sāṁkhya doctrine and the abandonment of the Vaiśeṣika standpoint.—But (the Vaiśeṣika may say) smoke also is different from fire and yet it is dependent on it.—True, we reply; but we ascertain the difference of smoke and fire from the fact of their being apperceived in separation. Substance and quality, on the other hand, are not so apperceived; for when we are conscious of a white blanket, or a red cow, or a blue lotus, the substance is in each case cognised by means of the quality; the latter therefore has its self in the substance. The same reasoning applies to action, generality, particularity, and inherence. . . .

Moreover, the distinction which the Vaiśeṣikas make between conjunction (*saṁyoga*) as being the connexion of things which can exist separately, and inherence (*samavāya*) as being the connexion of things which are incapable of separate existence is futile, since the cause which exists before the effect cannot be said to be incapable of separate existence. Perhaps the Vaiśeṣika will say that his definition refers to one of the two terms only, so that *samavāya* is the connexion, with the cause, of the effect which is incapable of separate existence. But this also is of no avail; for as a connexion requires two terms, the effect as long as it has not yet entered into being cannot be connected with the cause. And it would be equally unavailing to say that the effect enters into the connexion after it has begun to exist; for if the Vaiśeṣika admits that the effect may exist previous to its connexion with the cause, it is no longer *ayutasiddha* (incapable of separate existence), and thereby the principle that between effect and cause conjunction and disjunction do not take place is violated. And just as conjunction, and not *samavāya*, is the connexion in which every effected substance as soon as it has been produced stands with the all-pervading substances as ether, &c.—although no motion has taken place on the part of the effected substance—so also the connexion of the effect with the cause will be conjunction merely, not *samavāya*.

Nor is there any proof for the existence of any connexion, *samavāya* or *saṁyoga*, apart from the things which it connects. If it should be maintained that *saṁyoga* and *samavāya* have such an existence because we observe that there are names and ideas of them in addition to the names and ideas of the things connected, we point out that one and the same thing may be the subject of several names and ideas if it is considered in its relations to what lies without it. Devadatta although being one only forms the object of many different names and notions according as he is considered in himself or in his relations to others; thus he is thought and spoken of as a man, Brāhmaṇa, learned in the Veda, generous, body, young man, old man, father, son, grandson, brother, son-in-law, &c. So, again, one and the same stroke is, according to the place it is connected with, spoken of and conceived as meaning either ten, or hundred, or thousand, &c. Analogously, two connected things are not only conceived and denoted as connected things, but in addition constitute the object of the ideas and terms 'conjunction' or 'inherence,' which however do not prove themselves to be separate entities.—Things standing thus, the non-existence of separate entities (conjunction, &c.), which entities would have to be established on the ground of perception, follows from the fact of their non-perception. —Nor, again, does the circumstance of the word and idea of connexion having for its object the things connected involve the connexion's permanent existence, since we have already shown above that one thing may, on account of its relations to other things, be conceived and denoted in different ways. . . .

It thus appears that the atomic doctrine is supported by very weak arguments only, is opposed to those scriptual passages which declare the Lord to be the general cause, and is not accepted by any of the authorities taking their stand on Scripture, such as Manu and others. Hence it is to be altogether disregarded by highminded men who have a regard for their own spiritual welfare. (II, 2, 17)

BUDDHISM

Following his criticisms of the Sāṁkhya and the Vaiśeṣika, Śaṁkara attacks the "non-orthodox" tradition of Buddhism—and here one is confronted with several special problems. Adhering apparently to traditional Hindu classifications, Śaṁkara divides Buddhism into three types: the "realists" (sarvāstitvavādins), the "idealists" (vijñānavādins), and the "nihilists" (śūnyavādins); and he treats these Buddhist schools with a notable lack of sympathetic insight into their spiritual dimensions. Now few, if any, Buddhist scholars would classify the entire Buddhist tradition on its philosophical side, from Buddha through the rise and development of the Theravāda and Mahāyāna schools, in this simple threefold manner, and many would take great exception to the characterization of *śūnyavāda*, the "theory of the void" associated primarily with the Mādhyamika school of Nāgārjuna, as mere "nihilism."[12]

The problem of understanding the Vedāntic treatment of Buddhism is further compounded by the fact that Śaṁkara himself was called a crypto-Buddhist by other Vedāntins (viz., Bhāskara), who meant by this that much of Śaṁkara's metaphysics, especially his analysis of the world as *māyā*, was taken from Buddhist sources. In any event a close relationship between the Mahāyāna schools and Vedānta did exist with the latter borrowing some of the dialectical techniques, if not the specific doctrines, of the former.[13]

Śaṁkara's criticisms of Buddhism are nevertheless powerful and they exhibit clearly at least how Śaṁkara saw the difference between Buddhism and his own Vedāntic philosophy. He attacks the "realists"—who maintain that there exists an external world constituted by various "momentary" material aggregates and an internal world constituted by the five *skandhas* ("body," "feelings,"

12. *See* T. R. V. Murti, *The Central Philosophy of Buddhism* (London: George Allen & Unwin, 1955) and Th. Stcherbatsky, *The Conception of Buddhist Nirvāṇa* (Leningrad: Academy of Sciences of the USSR, 1927).

13. Śaṁkara might also have been influenced by Buddhism in his concern with, and success in, organizing monastic orders (maṭhs); monasticism having been otherwise quite foreign to the Hindu tradition.

"consciousness," "sensation," and "volitional dispositions")—mainly on the grounds that it is impossible to account on these principles for the formation of the aggregates, as there is nothing that can be admitted as their efficient cause, and that it is unintelligible how the self can be momentary in the face of the phenomenon of remembrance. Against the "idealists"—who reduce the external world to the internal—Śaṁkara argues that the very nature of consciousness implies a consciousness of objects that are external to it, and that without external objects no knowledge at all would be possible. The distinction between dreaming and waking consciousness further shows that the objects of waking experience must be given independently of the consciousness of them, for otherwise no distinction could be made between the two states. Śaṁkara's only attack on the Mādhyamikas is to argue that the entire world cannot be contradicted except by a principle or content of consciousness which is qualitatively different from it.

In a later selection from Śaṁkara's works, other criticisms put forward by him against Buddhism will be given.[14]

The reasons on account of which the doctrine of the Vaiśeṣikas cannot be accepted have been stated above. That doctrine may be called semi-destructive (or semi-nihilistic). That the more thorough doctrine which teaches universal non-permanency is even less worthy of being taken into consideration, we now proceed to show.

That doctrine is presented in a variety of forms, due either to the difference of the views (maintained by Buddha at different times), or else to the difference of capacity on the part of the disciples (of Buddha). Three principle opinions may, however, be distinguished; the opinion of those who maintain the reality of everything (Realists, *sarvāstitvavādin*); the opinion of those who maintain that thought only is real (Idealists, *vijñānavādin*); and the opinion of those who maintain that everything is void (unreal; Nihilists, *śūnyavādin*).—We first controvert those who maintain that everything, external as well as internal, is real. What is external is either element (*bhūta*) or elementary (*bhautika*); what is internal is either mind (*citta*) or mental

14. The ideas which Śaṁkara criticizes are without doubt part of the Buddhist tradition, but these ideas, as we have indicated, do not tell the whole story of Buddhism. And to tell this story with any completeness would require a separate text. The reader is advised, therefore, to consult any of the following surveys or histories for a more complete understanding of Buddhism:

Edward J. Thomas. *The History of Buddhist Thought.* New York: Barnes & Noble, 1959.

Edward Conze. *Buddhism: Its Essence and Development.* New York: Harper & Brothers, Torchbook Edition, 1959.

P. V. Bapat, ed. *2500 Years of Buddhism.* Delhi: Ministry of Information and Broadcasting, 1959.

(*caitta*). The elements are earth, water, and so on; elemental are colour, &c. on the one hand, and the eye and the other sense-organs on the other hand. Earth and the other three elements arise from the aggregate of the four different kinds of atoms; the atoms of earth being hard, those of water viscid, those of fire hot, those of air mobile.—The inward world consists of the five so-called 'groups' (*skandha*), the group of sensation (*rūpaskandha*), the group of knowledge (*vijñānaskandha*), the group of feeling (*vedanāskandha*), the group of verbal knowledge (*saṁjñāskandha*), and the group of impressions (*saṁskāraskandha*); which taken together constitute the basis of all personal existence.

With reference to this doctrine we make the following remarks.—Those two aggregates, constituting two different classes, and having two different causes which the Bauddhas assume, viz. the aggregate of the elements and elementary things whose cause the atoms are, and the aggregate of the five skandhas whose cause the skandhas are, cannot, on Bauddha principles, be established, i.e. it cannot be explained how the aggregates are brought about. For the parts constituting the (material) aggregates are devoid of intelligence, and the kindling (*abhijvalana*) of intelligence depends on an aggregate of atoms having been brought about previously. And the Bauddhas do not admit any other permanent intelligent being, such as either an enjoying soul or a ruling Lord, which could effect the aggregation of the atoms. Nor can the atoms and skandhas be assumed to enter on activity on their own account; for that would imply their never ceasing to be active. Nor can the cause of aggregation be looked for in the so-called abode (i.e. the *ālayavijñānapravāha*, the train of self-cognitions); for the later must be described either as different from the single cognitions or as not different from them. (In the former case it is either permanent, and then it is nothing else but the permanent soul of the Vedāntins; or non-permanent;) then being admitted to be momentary merely, it cannot exercise any influence and cannot therefore be the cause of the motion of the atoms. (And in the latter case we are not further advanced than before.)—For all these reasons the formation of aggregates cannot be accounted for. But without aggregates there would be an end of the stream of mundane existence which presupposes those aggregates. (II, 2, 18)

Although there exists no permanent intelligent principle of the nature either of a ruling Lord or an enjoying soul, under whose influence the formation of aggregates could take place, yet the course of mundane existence is rendered possible through the mutual causality of Nescience and so on, so that we need not look for any other combining principle.

The series beginning with Nescience comprises the following members: Nescience, impression, knowledge, name and form, the abode of the six, touch, feeling, desire, activity, birth, species, decay, death, grief, lamentation, pain, mental affliction, and the like. All these terms constitute a chain of causes and are as such spoken of in the Bauddha system, sometimes cursorily, sometimes at length. They are, moreover, all acknowledged as existing, not by the Bauddhas only, but by the followers of all systems. And as the cycles of Nescience, &c. forming uninterrupted chains of causes and effects revolve unceasingly like waterwheels, the existence of the aggregates (which constitute bodies and minds) must needs be assumed. as without such Nescience and so on could not take place.

This argumentation of the Bauddha we are unable to accept, because it merely assigns efficient causes for the origination of the members of the series, but does not intimate an efficient cause for the formation of the aggregates. If the Bauddha reminds us of the statement made above that the existence of aggregates must needs be inferred from the existence of Nescience and so on, we point out that, if he means thereby that Nescience and so on cannot exist without aggregates and hence require the existence of such, it remains to assign an efficient cause for the formation of the aggregates. But, as we have already shown—when examining the Vaiśeṣika doctrine—that the formation of aggregates cannot be accounted for even on the assumption of permanent atoms and individual souls in which the *adṛṣṭa* abides; how much less then are aggregates possible if there exist only momentary atoms not connected with enjoying souls and devoid of abodes (i.e. souls), and that which abides in them (the *adṛṣṭa*).—Let us then assume (the Bauddha says) that Nescience, &c. themselves are the efficient cause of the aggregate.—But how—we ask—can they be the cause of that without which—as their abode—they themselves are not capable of existence? Perhaps you will say that in the eternal *saṁsāra* the aggregates succeed one another in an unbroken chain, and hence also Nescience, and so on, which abide in those aggregates. But in that case you will have to assume either that each aggregate necessarily produces another aggregate of the same kind, or that, without any settled rule, it may produce either a like or an unlike one. In the former case a human body could never pass over into that of a god or an animal or a being of the infernal regions; in the latter case a man might in an instant be turned into an elephant or a god and again become a man; either of which consequences would be contrary to your system.—Moreover, that for the purpose of whose enjoyment the aggregate is formed is, according to your doctrine, not a permanent enjoying soul, so that enjoyment subserves itself merely and cannot be desired by anything else; hence final release also must, according to you, be considered as subserving itself only, and no being desirous of release can be assumed. If a being desirous of both were assumed, it would have to be conceived as permanently existing up to the time of enjoyment and release, and that would be contrary to your doctrine of general impermanency.—There may therefore exist a causal relation between the members of the series consisting of Nescience, &c., but, in the absence of a permanent enjoying soul, it is impossible to establish on that ground the existence of aggregates. (II, 2, 19)

We have hitherto argued that Nescience, and so on, stand in a causal relation to each other merely, so that they cannot be made to account for the existence of aggregate; we are now going to prove that they cannot even be considered as efficient causes of the subsequent members of the series to which they belong.

Those who maintain that everything has a momentary existence only admit that when the thing existing in the second moment enters into being the thing existing in the first moment ceases to be. On this admission it is impossible to establish between the two things the relation of cause and effect, since the former momentary existence which ceases or has ceased to be, and so has entered into the state of non-existence, cannot be the cause of the later momentary existence.—Let it then be said that the former momentary existence when it has reached its full development becomes the cause of the later momentary existence.—That also is impossible; for the assumption that a fully developed existence exerts a further energy, involves the conclusion that it is connected with a second moment (which contradicts the doctrine of universal momentariness).—Then let the mere existence of the antecedent entity constitute its causal energy.—That assumption also is fruitless, because we cannot conceive the origination of an effect which is not imbued with the nature of the cause (i.e. in which the nature of the cause does not continue to exist). And to assume that the nature of the cause does continue to exist in the effect is impossible (on the Bauddha doctrine), as that would involve the permanency of the cause, and thus necessitate the abandonment of the doctrine of general non-permanency. —Nor can it be admitted that the relation of cause and effect holds good without the cause somehow giving its colouring to the effect; for that doctrine might unduly be extended to all cases.—Moreover, the origination and cessation of things of which the Bauddha speaks must either constitute a thing's own form or another state of it, or an altogether different thing. But none of these alternatives agrees with the general Bauddha principles. If, in the first place, origination and cessation constituted the form of a thing, it would follow that the word 'thing' and the words 'origination' and 'cessation' are interchangeable (which is not the case).—Let then, secondly, the Bauddha says, a certain difference be assumed, in consequence of which the terms 'origination' and 'cessation' may denote the initial and final states of that which in the intermediate state is called thing.—In that case, we reply, the thing will be connected with three moments, viz. the initial, the intermediate, and the final one, so that the doctrine of general momentariness will have to be abandoned.—Let then, as the third alternative, origination and cessation be altogether different from the thing, as much as a buffalo is from a horse.—That too cannot be, we reply; for it would lead to the conclusion that the thing, because altogether disconnected with origination and cessation, is everlasting. And the same conclusion would be led up to, if we understood by the origination and cessation of a thing merely its perception and non-perception; for the latter are attributes of the percipient mind only, not of the thing itself. —Hence we have again to declare the Bauddha doctrine to be untenable. (II, 2, 20)

It has been shown that on the doctrine of general non-permanency, the former momentary existence, as having already been merged in non-existence, cannot be the cause of the later one.—Perhaps now the Bauddha will say that an effect may arise even when there is no cause. —That, we reply, implies the abandonment of a principle admitted by yourself, viz. that the mind and the mental modifications originate when in conjunction with four kinds of causes. Moreover, if anything could originate without a cause, there would be nothing to prevent that anything might originate at any time.—If, on the other hand, you should say that we may assume the antecedent momentary existence to last until the succeeding one has been produced, we point out that that would imply the simultaneousness of cause and effect, and so run counter to an accepted Bauddha tenet, viz. that all things are momentary merely. (II, 2, 21)

The philosopher who maintains that all things are momentary only would have to extend that doctrine to the perceiving person (*upalabdhṛ*) also; that is, however, not possible, on account of the remembrance which is consequent on the original perception. That remembrance can take place only if it belongs to the same person who previously made the perception; for we observe that what one man has experienced is not remembered by another man. How, indeed, could there arise the conscious state expressed in the sentence, 'I saw that thing, and now I see this thing,' if the seeing person were not in both cases the same? That the consciousness of recognition takes place only in the case of the observing and remembering subject being one, is a matter known to every one; for if there were, in the two cases, different subjects, the state of consciousness arising in the mind of the remembering person would be, 'I remember; another person made the observation.' But no such state of consciousness does arise.—When, on the other hand, such a state of consciousness does arise, then everybody knows that the person who made the original observation, and the person who remembers, are different persons, and then the state of consciousness is expressed as follows, 'I remember that that other person saw that and that.'—In the case under discussion, however, the Vaināśika himself—whose state of consciousness is, 'I saw that and that'—knows that there is one thinking subject only to which the original perception as well as the remembrance belongs, and does not think of denying that the past perception belonged to himself, not any more than he denies that fire is hot and gives light.

As thus one agent is connected with the two moments of perception and subsequent remembrance, the Vaināśika has necessarily to abandon the doctrine of universal momentariness. And if he further recognises all his subsequent successive cognitions, up to his last breath, to belong to one and the same subject, and in addition cannot but attribute all his past cognitions, from the moment of his birth, to the same Self, how can he maintain, without being ashamed of himself, that everything has a momentary existence only? . . . Nor can the hypothesis of mere similarity being cognised account for ordinary empirical life and thought; for (in recognising a thing) we are conscious of it being that which we were formerly conscious of, not of it being merely similar to that. We admit that sometimes with regard to an external thing a doubt may arise whether it is that or merely is similar to that; for mistakes may be made concerning what lies outside our minds. But the conscious subject never has any doubt whether it is itself or only similar to itself; it rather is distinctly conscious that it is one and the same subject which yesterday had a certain sensation and to-day remembers that sensation.—For this reason also the doctrine of the Nihilists is to be rejected. (II, 2, 25)

The system of the Vaināśikas is objectionable for this reason also that those who deny the existence of permanent stable causes are driven to maintain that entity springs from non-entity. This latter tenet is expressly enunciated by the Bauddhas where they say, 'On account of the manifestation (of effects) not without previous destruction (of the cause).' For, they say, from the decomposed seed only the young plant springs, spoilt milk only turns into curds, and the lump of clay has ceased to be a lump when it becomes a jar. If effects did spring from the unchanged causes, all effects would originate from all causes at once, as then no specifications would be required. Hence, as we see that young plants, &c. spring from seeds, &c. only after the latter has been merged in non-existence, we hold that entity springs from non-entity.

To this Bauddha tenet we reply, ('Entity does) not (spring) from non-entity, on account of that not being observed.' If entity did spring from non-entity, the assumption of special causes would be purportless, since non-entity is in all cases one and the same. For the non-existence of seeds and the like after they have been destroyed is of the same kind as the non-existence of horns of hares and the like, i.e. non-existence is in all cases nothing else but the absence of all character of reality, and hence there would be no sense (on the doctrine of origination from non-existence) in assuming that sprouts are produced from seeds only, curds from milk only, and so on. And if non-distinguished non-existence were admitted to have causal efficiency, we should also have to assume that sprouts, &c. originate from the horns of hares, &c. —a thing certainly not actually observed. . . . (II, 2, 26)

If it were admitted that entity issues from non-entity, lazy inactive people also would obtain their purposes, since 'non-existence' is a thing to be had without much trouble. Rice would grow for the husbandman even if he did not cultivate his field; vessels would shape themselves even if the potter did not fashion the clay; and the weaver too lazy to weave the threads into a whole, would nevertheless have in the end finished pieces of cloth just as if he had been weaving. And nobody would have to exert himself in the least either for going to the heavenly world or for obtaining final release. And which of course is absurd and not maintained by anybody.—Thus the doctrine of the origination of entity from non-entity again shows itself to be futile. (II, 2, 27)

There having been brought forward, in what precedes, the various objections which lie against the doctrine of the reality of the external world (in the Bauddha sense), such as the impossibility of accounting for the existence of aggregates, &c., we are now confronted by those Bauddhas who maintain that only cognitions (or ideas, *vijñāna*) exist. —The doctrine of the reality of the external world was indeed propounded by Buddha conforming himself to the mental state of some of his disciples whom he perceived to be attached to external things; but it does not represent his own true view according to which cognitions alone are real.

According to this latter doctrine the process, whose constituting members are the act of knowledge, the object of knowledge, and the result of knowledge, is an altogether internal one, existing in so far only as it is connected with the mind (*buddhi*). Even if external things existed, that process could not take place but in connexion with the mind. If, the Bauddhas say, you ask how it is known that that entire process is internal and that no outward things exist apart from consciousness, we reply that we base our doctrine on the impossibility of external things. For if external things are admitted, they must be either atoms or aggregates of atoms such as posts and the like. But atoms cannot be comprehended under the ideas of posts and the like, it being impossible for cognition to represent (things as minute as) atoms. Nor, again, can the outward things be aggregates of atoms such as pillars and the like, because those aggregates can neither be defined as different nor as non-different from the atoms.—In the same way we can show that the external things are not universals and so on.

Moreover, the cognitions—which are of a uniform nature only in so far as they are states of consciousness—undergo, according to their objects, successive modifications, so that there is presented to the mind now the idea of a post, now the idea of a wall, now the idea of a jar, and so on. Now this is not possible without some distinction on the part of the ideas themselves, and hence we must necessarily admit that the ideas have the same forms as their objects. But if we make this admission, from which it follows that the form of the object is determined by the ideas, the hypothesis of the existence of external things becomes altogether gratuitous. From the fact, moreover, of our always being conscious of the act of knowledge and the object of knowledge simultaneously it follows that the two are in reality identical. When we are conscious of the one we are conscious of the other also; and that would not happen if the two were essentially distinct, as in that case there would be nothing to prevent our being conscious of one apart from the other. For this reason also we maintain that there are no outward things.—Perception is to be considered as similar to a dream and the like. The ideas present to our minds during a dream, a magical illusion, a mirage and so on, appear in the twofold form of subject and object, although there is all the while no external object; hence we conclude that the ideas of posts and the like which occur in our waking state are likewise independent of external objects; for they also are simply ideas.—If we be asked how, in the absence of external things, we account for the actual variety of ideas, we reply that that variety is to be explained from the impressions left by previous ideas. In the beginningless *saṁsāra* ideas and mental impressions succeed each other as causes and effects, just as the plant springs from the seed and seeds are again produced from the plant, and there exists therefore a sufficient reason for the variety of ideas actually experienced. That the variety of ideas is solely due to the impressions left on the mind by past ideas follows, moreover, from the following affirmative and negative judgments: we both (the Vedāntins as well as the Bauddhas) admit that in dreams, &c. there presents itself a variety of ideas which arise from mental impressions, without any external object; we (the Bauddhas) do not admit that any variety of ideas can arise from external objects, without mental impressions.—Thus we are again led to conclude that no outward things exist.

To all this we (the Vedāntins) make the following reply.—The nonexistence of external things cannot be maintained because we are conscious of external things. In every act of perception we are conscious of some external thing corresponding to the idea, whether it be a post or a wall or a piece of cloth or a jar, and that of which we are conscious cannot but exist. Why should we pay attention to the words of a man who, while conscious of an outward thing through its approximation to his senses, affirms that he is conscious of no outward thing, and that no such thing exists, any more than we listen to a man who while he is eating and experiencing the feeling of satisfaction avers that he does not eat and does not feel satisfied?—If the Bauddha should reply that he does not affirm that he is conscious of no object but only that he is conscious of no object apart from the act of consciousness, we answer that he may indeed make any arbitrary statement he likes, but that he has no arguments to prove what he says. That the outward thing exists apart from consciousness, has necessarily to be accepted on the ground of the nature of consciousness itself. Nobody when perceiving a post or a wall is conscious of his perception only, but all men are conscious of posts and walls and the like as objects of their perceptions. That such is the consciousness of all men, appears also from the fact that even those who contest the existence of external things bear witness to their existence when they say that what is an internal object of cognition appears like something external. For they practically accept the general consciousness, which testifies to the existence of an external world, and being at the same time anxious to refute it they speak of the external things as 'like something external.' If they did not themselves at the bottom acknowledge the existence of the external world, how could they use the expression 'like something external?' No one says, 'Viṣṇumitra appears like the son of a barren mother.' If we accept the truth as it is given to us in our consciousness, we must admit that the object of perception appears to us as something external, not like something external.—But—the Bauddha may reply—we conclude that the object of perception is only like something external because external things are impossible.—This conclusion we rejoin is improper, since the possibility or impossibility of things is to be determined only on the ground of the operation or non-operation of the means of right knowledge; while on the other hand, the operation and non-operation of the means of right knowledge are not to be made dependent on preconceived possibilities or impossibilities. Possible is whatever is apprehended by perception or some other means of proof; impossible is what is not so apprehended. Now the external things are, according to their nature, apprehended by all the instruments of knowledge; how then can you maintain that they are not possible, on the ground of such idle dilemmas as that about their difference or non-difference from atoms?—Nor, again, does the non-existence of objects follow from the fact of the ideas having the same form as the objects; for if there were no objects the ideas could not have the forms of the objects, and the objects are actually apprehended as external.—For the reason (i.e. because the distinction of thing and idea is given in consciousness) the invariable concomitance of idea and thing has to be considered as proving only that the thing constitutes the means of the idea, not that the two are identical. Moreover, when we are conscious first of a pot and then of a piece of cloth, consciousness remains the same in the two acts while what varies are merely the distinctive attributes of consciousness; just as when we see at first a black and then a white cow, the distinction of the two perceptions is due to the varying blackness and whiteness while the generic character of the cow remains the same. The difference of the one permanent factor (from the two—or more—varying factors) is proved throughout by the two varying factors, and vice versa the difference of the latter (from the permanent factor) by the presence of the one (permanent factor). Therefore thing and idea are distinct. The same view is to be held with regard to the perception and the rememberance of a jar; there also the perception and the remembrance only are distinct while the jar is one and the same; in the same way as when conscious of the smell of milk and the taste of milk we are conscious of the smell and taste as different things but of the milk itself as one only. (II, 2, 28)

We now apply ourselves to the refutation of the averment made by the Bauddha, that the ideas of posts, and so on, of which we are conscious in the waking state, may arise in the absence of external objects, just as the ideas of a dream, both being ideas alike.—The two sets of ideas, we maintain, cannot be treated on the same footing, on account of the difference of their character. They differ as follows.—The things of which we are conscious in a dream are negated by our waking consciousness. 'I wrongly thought that I had a meeting with a great man; no such meeting took place, but my mind was dulled by slumber, and so the false idea arose.' In an analogous manner the things of which we are conscious when under the influence of a magic illusion, and the like, are negated by our ordinary consciousness. Those things, on the other hand, of which we are conscious in our waking state, such as posts and the like, are never negated in any state.—Moreover, the visions of a dream are acts of remembrance, while the visions of the waking state are acts of immediate consciousness; and the distinction between remembrance and immediate consciousness is directly cognised by every one as being founded on the absence or presence of the object. When, for instance, a man remembers his absent son, he does not directly perceive him, but merely wishes so to perceive him. As thus the distinction between the two states is evident to every one, it is impossible to formulate the inference that waking consciousness is false because it is mere consciousness, such as dreaming consciousness; for we certainly cannot allow would-be philosophers to deny the truth of what is directly evident to themselves. Just because they feel the absurdity of denying what is evident to themselves, and are consequently unable to demonstrate the baselessness of the ideas of the waking state from those ideas themselves, they attempt to demonstrate it from their having certain attributes in common with the ideas of the dreaming state. But if some attribute cannot belong to a thing on account of the latter's own nature, it cannot belong to it on account of the thing having certain attributes in common with some other thing. Fire, which is felt to be hot, cannot be demonstrated to be cold, on the ground of its having attributes in common with water. And the differences of nature between the waking and the sleeping state we have already shown. (II, 2, 29)

We now proceed to that theory of yours, according to which the variety of ideas can be explained from the variety of mental impressions, without any reference to external things, and remark that on your doctrine the existence of mental impressions is impossible, as you do not admit the perception of external things. For the variety of mental impressions is caused altogether by the variety of the things perceived. How, indeed, could various impressions originate if no external things were perceived? The hypothesis of a beginningless series of mental impressions would lead only to a baseless regressus ad infinitum, sublative of the entire phenomenal world, and would in no way establish your position. . . . (II, 2, 30)

If you maintain that the so-called internal cognition (*ālayavijñāna*) assumed by you may constitute the abode of the mental impressions, we deny that, because the cognition also being admittedly momentary, and hence non-permanent, cannot be the abode of impressions any more than the quasi-external cognitions (*pravṛtti-vijñāna*). For unless there exists one continuous principle equally connected with the past, the present, and the future, or an absolutely unchangeable (Self) which cognises everything, we are unable to account for remembrance, recognition, and so on, which are subject to mental impressions dependent on place, time, and cause. If, on the other hand, you declare your *ālayavijñāna* to be something permanent, you thereby abandon your tenet of the *ālayavijñāna* as well as everything else being momentary. —Or (to explain the Sūtra in a different way) as the tenet of general momentariness is characteristic of the systems of the idealistic as well as the realistic Bauddhas, we may bring forward against the doctrines of the former all those arguments dependent on the principle of general momentariness which we have above urged against the latter.

We have thus refuted both nihilistic doctrines, viz. the doctrine which maintains the (momentary) reality of the external world, and the doctrine which asserts that ideas only exist. The third variety of Bauddha doctrine, viz. that everything is empty (i.e. that absolutely nothing exists), is contradicted by all means of right knowledge, and therefore requires no special refutation. For this apparent world, whose existence is guaranteed by all the means of knowledge, cannot be denied, unless some one should find out some new truth (based on which he could impugn its existence) for a general principle is proved by the absence of contrary instances. (II, 2, 31)

No further special discussion is in fact required. From whatever new points of view the Bauddha system is tested with reference to its probability, it gives way on all sides, like the walls of a well dug in sandy soil. It has, in fact, no foundation whatever to rest upon, and hence the attempts to use it as a guide in the practical concerns of life are mere folly.—Moreover, Buddha by propounding the three mutually contradictory systems, teaching respectively the reality of the external world, the reality of ideas only, and general nothingness, has himself made it clear either that he was a man given to make incoherent assertions, or else that hatred of all beings induced him to propound absurd doctrines by accepting which they would become thoroughly confused.—So that —and this the Sūtra means to indicate—Buddha's doctrine has to be entirely disregarded by all those who have a regard for their own happiness. (II, 2, 32)

JAINISM

Following his sharp criticism of Buddhism Śaṁkara turns his attention to the philosophical-religious tradition of Jainism. Jainism has a long history in India. It maintains that its basic teachings are eternal, however, and that they are revealed in various periods of the world's evolution—with Mahāvīra, a contemporary of Buddha, being regarded as the last prophet (*tīrthaṅkara*) to espouse the creed.

The word "Jainism" comes from *jina* or "conqueror"—one who achieves enlightenment through the conquest of everything within oneself that stands in the way of it. On its religious side Jainism lays great stress on the doctrine of *ahiṁsā* or "non-injury" to any living creature. Being essentially a-theistic Jainism emphasizes that perfection is obtained only through self-effort: to be a *jina* is entirely up to oneself. At one time Jainism was immensely influential, being a strong competitor of Buddhism in many parts of India.[15]

Philosophically Jainism is characterized by a fundamental dualism between "soul" and "body" or between the categories of *jīva* ("spirit," "life") and *ajīva* ("inanimate nature," etc.). Each of these categories is taken as substantive (*drayva*) and is further sub-divided in various ways (e.g., under *ajīva*, space [*ākāśa*] and matter [*pudgala*] are classified). The philosophical doctrines of Jainism which are of greatest interest, however, are logical or epistemological—and it is mainly these doctrines which Śaṁkara criticizes.

According to the Jains, all affirmations or negations about something are true only within certain restricted frameworks: nothing can be affirmed with absolute certainty. Every object of experience appears to us with various qualities (those that it possesses and those that it lacks—e.g., a rose may be said to be red, not-blue, not-yellow, etc.) and in various relations to other objects and can be grasped, apprehended, or understood by us only from a certain number of "standpoints" or *nayas*. We may, for example, concentrate upon an object in terms of its universal characteristics, that which makes it a member of a class (*saṁgrahanaya*), or in our experience of it we may isolate its individual or particular features (*vyarahāranaya*), and so on. No one judgment exhausts the object and no single perspective of the world exhausts the complex richness of reality (*anekāntavāda*). This leads the Jains to formulate a kind of perspectival epistemology and a relativistic ordering of judgments. Since various, and from different standpoints contradictory, characteristics may be assigned to an object, any judg-

15. Today there are only approximately a million and a half Jains in India. For a description of the canonical literature of Jainism, see Surendranath DasGupta, *A History of Indian Philosophy*, vol. 1 (Cambridge: Cambridge University Press, 1957), pp. 171–172.

ment about an object may be true in one sense or from one standpoint and false in another sense or from a different standpoint. The doctrine which expresses this logical or epistemological teaching is called *syādvāda*—the doctrine of "maybe."

Seven forms of judgment (*saptabhaṅga*), each of which formally needs to be qualified by "maybe," are identified. They are:

1. S is P (*syāt asti*, "maybe it is")—"maybe the jug is red" (i.e., the jug is not always red but it is red under a set of presently given conditions).
2. S is not P (*syān nāsti*, "maybe it is not")—"maybe the jug is not red" (under a different set of conditions).
3. S is and is also not P (*syād asti ca nāsti ca*, "maybe it is and is not")—"the jug is red and it is not red" (i.e., the statement embodies the complex judgment that sometimes an object has a given quality and at other times it does not).
4. S is indescribable (*syād avaktavyaṃ*, "maybe it is indescribable")—"the real color of the jar is indescribable" (as it always appears to us in some restricted set of conditions).
5. S is P and is also indescribable (*syād asti ca avaktavyaṃ ca*, "maybe it is and is also indescribable")—"the jug is red here and now but its real color is indescribable."
6. S is not P and is indescribable (*syān nāsti ca avaktavyaṃ ca*, "maybe it is not and is indescribable")—"the jug is not red at this time and its real color is indescribable."
7. S is and is also not P and it is indescribable (*syād asti ca nāsti ca avaktavyaṃ ca*, "maybe it is and is not and is indescribable")—"sometimes the jug is red and sometimes it is not and its real color is indescribable."

In his criticism of this doctrine of relativity of judgments Śaṁkara assumes that the Jains are simply asserting contradictory judgments about an object under the same conditions, and that by insisting upon the relativity of all judgments the Jains condemn their own theory (i.e., the statements which put it forth must themselves have only relative validity).

Having disposed of the Bauddha doctrine we now turn to the system of the Gymnosophists (Jainas).

The Jainas acknowledge seven categories (*tattvas*), viz. soul (*jīva*), non-soul (*ajīva*), the issuing outward (*āsrava*), restraint (*saṁvara*), destruction (*nirjara*), bondage (*bandha*), and release (*mokṣa*). Shortly it may be said that they acknowledge two categories, viz. soul and the non-soul, since the five other categories may be subsumed under these two.—They also set forth a set of categories different from the two mentioned. They teach that there are five so-called *astikāyas* ('existing bodies,' i.e. categories), viz. the categories of soul (*jīva*), body (*pudgala*), merit (*dharma*), demerit (*adharma*), and space (*ākāśa*). All these categories they again subdivide in various fanciful ways.—To all things they apply the following method of reasoning, which they call the *saptabhaṅgīnaya*: somehow it is; somehow it is not; somehow it is and is not; somehow it is indescribable; somehow it is and is indescribable; somehow it is not and is indescribable; somehow it is and is not and is indescribable.

To this unsettling style of reasoning they submit even such conceptions as that of unity and eternity.

This doctrine we meet as follows.—Your reasoning, we say, is inadmissible 'on account of the impossibility in one thing.' That is to say, it is impossible that contradictory attributes such as being and non-being should at the same time belong to one and the same thing; just as observation teaches us that a thing cannot be hot and cold at the same moment. The seven categories asserted by you must either be so many and such or not be so many and such; the third alternative expressed in the words 'they either are such or not such' results in a cognition of indefinite nature which is no more a source of true knowledge than doubt is. If you should plead that the cognition that a thing is of more than one nature is definite and therefore a source of true knowledge, we deny this. For the unlimited assertion that all things are of a non-exclusive nature is itself something, falls as such under the alternative predications 'somehow it is,' 'somehow it is not,' and so ceases to be a definite assertion. The same happens to the person making the assertion and to the result of the assertion; partly they are, partly they are not. As thus the means of knowledge, the object of knowledge, the knowing subject, and the act of knowledge are all alike indefinite, how can the Tīrthakara (*Jina*) teach with any claim to authority, and how can his followers act on a doctrine the matter of which is altogether indeterminate? Observation shows that only when a course of action is known to have a definite result people set about it without hesitation. Hence a man who proclaims a doctrine of altogether indefinite contents does not deserve to be listened to any more than a drunken man or a madman. —Again, if we apply the Jaina reasoning to their doctrine of the five categories, we have to say that on one view of the matter they are five and on another view they are not five; from which latter point of view it follows that they are either fewer or more than five. Nor is it logical to declare the categories to be indescribable. For if they are so, they cannot be described; but, as a matter of fact, they are described so that to call them indescribable involves a contradiction. And if you go on to say that the categories on being described are ascertained to be such and such, and at the same time are not ascertained to be such and such, and that the result of their being ascertained is perfect knowledge or is not perfect knowledge, and that imperfect knowledge is the opposite of perfect knowledge or is not the opposite; you certainly talk more like a drunken or insane man than like a sober, trustworthy person.—If you further maintain that the heavenly world and final release exist or do not exist and are eternal or non-eternal, the absence of all determinate knowledge which is implied in such statements will result in nobody's acting for the purpose of gaining the heavenly world and final release. And, moreover, it follows from your doctrine that soul, non-soul, and so on, whose nature you claim to have ascertained, and which you describe as having existed from all eternity, relapse all at once into the condition of absolute indetermination.—As therefore the two contradictory attributes of being and non-being cannot belong to any of the categories—being excluding non-being and vice versa non-being excluding being—the doctrine of the Arhat must be rejected.—The above remarks dispose likewise of the assertions made by the Jainas as to the impossibility of deciding whether of one thing there is to be predicated oneness or plurality, permanency or non-permanency, separateness or non-separateness, and so on.—The Jaina doctrine that aggregates are formed from the atoms—by them called pudgalas—we do not undertake to refute separately as its refutation is already comprised in that of the atomistic doctrine given in a previous part of this work. (II, 2, 33)

NYĀYA

The Sūtras and Śaṁkara now turn to those theories which affirm that God is only the operative or efficient cause of the world and not the material cause as well—with special mention of the Nyāya system. This system was allegedly founded by the sage Gautama (also known as Akṣapāda), author of the *Nyāya-Sūtra.* The Nyāya became closely allied with the Vaiśeṣika school on its ontological or metaphysical side. It accepted the Vaiśeṣika analysis of matter, its account of causation in terms of *asatkāryavāda* (the theory that the effect is not pre-existent in its cause), etc., but in contrast to early Vaiśeṣika, the Nyāya system affirms and argues for the existence of a God who is the creator of the world. According to the Nyāya, God creates the world through the ordering of pre-existing categories—the atoms, space, time, etc. He is a demiurge, the efficient but not the material cause of the universe. Several "proofs" are offered by the Nyāya to support this affirmation. It is argued first of all that all objects of experience, being of the nature of effects, must have a cause for their existence. The atoms, etc., could never by themselves produce an ordered universe. Hence an ordering Deity is necessary.[16] The Nyāya also argues for the existence of God on the basis of *karman.* Without the existence of an intelligent cause who distributes the fruits of

16. *See Nyāya Kusumāñjali,* V, 1.

action to the actors over vast intervals of time, the whole notion of *karman* would be unintelligible. A moral universe, in short, demands and presupposes a creative moral force as its ground. Although Vedāntic thinkers occasionally make use of these arguments in criticizing a-theistic positions they do not ascribe finality to them. Reason, as Śaṁkara will show (somewhat in a Kantian fashion), is impotent when it comes to demonstrating the nature of reality.

But as with Jainism, the most important contributions of the Nyāya to Indian philosophy are not metaphysical or theological, rather they are epistemological and logical. The Nyāya system articulated the various means of knowledge (the pramāṇas) which, although sometimes added to, are accepted by the other orthodox systems; it codified a model of "inference" and set forth criteria for testing the validity of a rational argument. This model of correct reasoning was accepted, with minor qualifications, by all Vedāntic schools.[17]

It might be helpful at this point to digress somewhat from the Vedāntic criticisms of rival systems and examine briefly this model for inference. Subsequent arguments put forth in Vedāntic literature might profitably be tested by this model of correct reasoning, and in any event several of the arguments used by Vedāntins are cast according to the formal requirements of the model.

The Sanskrit term for "inference" is *anumāna* (*anu*=after; *māna*=measuring). It is defined as mediate and indirect knowledge which is acquired through observing that a "mark" is invariably present in an object. Three terms in an inference are identified: (1) *pakṣa* or the "minor term," the *subject* of the proposition to be proven; (2) *sādhya* or the "major term," that which is to be established in relation to the *pakṣa*, and (3) *liṅga* or *hetu* or the "middle term," that which indicates the presence of the *sādhya*. In the stock Indian textbook example of an inference

> There is a fire on the mountain
> Because the mountain smokes
> Wherever there is smoke there is fire, e.g. in the kitchen
> The mountain smokes
> Therefore it has fire

17. In a later phase of its development known as Navya-Nyāya, the Nyāya carried this "logic" further into a formal study of the relations between concepts and things. *See* Daniel H. H. Ingalls, *Materials for the Study of Navya-Nyāya Logic* (Cambridge: Harvard University Press, 1951), for the outstanding work in English on this school.

the *pakṣa* or minor term is "the mountain," the *sādhya* or major term is "fire" and the *liṅga* or *hetu* or middle term is "smoke." An inference is a kind of knowing which arises from the ascertainment of the presence of the major term, through the middle term, in the minor term. Between the middle and the major term there must exist an invariable concomitance (*vyāpti*). The term *vyāpti* literally means "pervasion": one thing, fact, or event is "pervaded" by another when it is always accompanied by the other, when no experience contradicts their "togetherness."

Two kinds of inference are distinguished in the Nyāya; *svārtha*, when it is carried out *for oneself* for the purpose of acquiring new knowledge, and *parārtha*, when *for others* one seeks to demonstrate some truth or fact. In the later case inference must follow a prescribed form. Five members or propositions are set forth:

1. the *pratijñā* or the proposition to be proven, the proposition being an assertion about a certain state of affairs—"the mountain has fire."
2. the *hetu* or the specific reason or cause for the assertion—"(because) the mountain smokes."
3. the *udāharaṇa* or the universal proposition which shows the connection between the first two propositions and an illustration of this connection with reference to a particular, familiar example—"wherever there is smoke there is fire, for example in the kitchen."
4. the *upanaya* or the application of the universal proposition to the case under consideration—"this mountain smokes."
5. the *nigamana* or the conclusion—"therefore this mountain has fire."

The Nyāya syllogism or model of inference, as we see, is at once "deductive" and "inductive." It is never purely "formal" in character as it recognizes no null classes. The ground of inference must be precisely that of *vyāpti* or invariable concomitance between the middle and major terms. The conclusion in the stock example given, that "this mountain has fire," is justified only if between smoke and fire a relation of invariable concomitance holds.[18] Apart

18. The Naiyāyikas make a distinction between two kinds of *vyāpti*; one which holds between terms of unequal extension (*asamavyāpti*), e.g., smoke and fire, the other between terms of equal extension (*samavyāpti*), e.g., knowable and nameable. In the first case one may infer one term from the other but not vice versa (fire may be inferred from smoke, but not smoke from fire); in the second case one may infer either from the other.

from the observation that the middle term is present in the minor term (*pakṣadharmatā*) in the specific case ("the smoke is present in this mountain"), one has also to show, then, the following:

1. that the middle term is present in all cases in which the major term is present;
2. that it is absent in all cases in which the major term is absent;
3. that it doesn't contradict the minor term;
4. that the relation is not qualified or determined by other conditions or reasons.[19]

In further testing the validity of an inference one can, in a negative way, see if any "fallacy" has been committed. A fallacy is called *hetvābhāsa*; it means that a *hetu* or reason appears to be real or appropriate but in fact is not. Five kinds of *material* fallacies are identified. These are:

1. *savyabhicāra* or *anaikāntika*. This fallacy occurs when the most general rule of inference, that the major term must be present in all cases in which the middle term is present, is violated. The middle term may be (*a*) too broad, making it possible for it to be present in negative cases (e.g., in "this mountain has fire because it is green," "green" is present in both objects which have fire and objects which do not); (*b*) too narrow (e.g., in "sound is eternal because it is audible," "audible" is associated only with sound and cannot be found anywhere else), and (*c*) non-exclusive, (e.g., in "all things are non-eternal because they are knowable," the minor term "all things" is simply all-inclusive).
2. *viruddha*. This fallacy occurs when the middle term disproves rather than proves the proposition to be established; e.g., in "air is heavy because it is empty," the middle term "empty" actually disproves the heaviness of air. (The stock Naiyāyika example is: in "sound is eternal because it is produced," the fact of being produced shows that sound is non-eternal, for only non-eternal things are produced.)
3. *satpratipakṣa*. In this fallacy one is put in the position of having the contradictory of one's conclusion proved by some other inference which is based on another middle term. With "sound is eternal because it is audible" we may also have "sound is non-eternal because it is produced."

19. This means that one must make repeated observations of the agreement in presence and in absence between the major and middle terms under varying circumstances. One must, in short, exclude the possibility that there is some other ("intermediary" or "intervening") sufficient condition which gives rise to the relation.

4. *asiddha* or *sādhyasama*. This occurs when the middle term, like the major term, requires proving. In the stock example "the sky-lotus is fragrant because it is a lotus like that found in water," the minor term is "unreal" and so the middle term has no place to stand.

5. *bādhita*. This fallacy occurs when the middle term is contradicted, not by another inference, but by another source of knowledge (*pramāṇa*). In "fire is cold because it is a substance," the middle term "substance" is contradicted because "cold," the major term, is contradicted by perceptual experience (*pratyakṣa*). We don't perceive that fire is cold; on the contrary we perceive that it is hot.

In sum, the model of inference codified by Nyāya, as we have briefly described it, is never just "formal" in character. An inference must be bound to actual experience. It is thus more of a quasi "scientific method" than it is a system of pure logic.[20]

In criticizing Nyāya and other theistic or deistic systems which affirm that God is only the efficient cause of the world, Śaṁkara puts himself in the rather curious position of having to argue against certain ideas which he himself will have to affirm in other contexts. In several instances here he is attacking not so much the ideas *per se* but the grounds upon which they are held.

The theories about the Lord which are independent of the Vedānta are of various nature. Some taking their stand on the Sāṁkhya and Yoga systems assume that the Lord acts as a mere operative cause, as the ruler of the *pradhāna* and the souls, and that *pradhāna*, soul, and Lord are of mutually different nature.—The Māheśvaras (Śaivas) maintain that the five categories, viz. effect, cause, union, ritual, the end of pain, were taught by the Lord Paśupati (Śiva) to the end of breaking the bonds of the animal (i.e. the soul); Paśupati is, according to them, the Lord, the operative cause.—Similarly, the Vaiśeṣikas and others also teach, according to their various systems, that the Lord is somehow the operative cause of the world.

Against all these opinions the Sūtra remarks 'the Lord, on account of the inappropriateness.' I.e. it is not possible that the Lord as the ruler of the *pradhāna* and the soul should be the cause of the world, on account of the inappropriateness of that doctrine. For if the Lord is supposed to assign to the various classes of animate creatures low, intermediate, and high positions, according to his liking, it follows that he is animated by hatred, passion, and so on, is hence like one of us, and

20. *See* Karl Potter, *Presuppositions of India's Philosophies*, chap. 5 (New York: Prentice-Hall, 1963) for a presentation of the Nyāya model of inference in greater detail.

is no real Lord. Nor can we get over this difficulty by assuming that he makes his dispositions with a view of the merit and demerit of the living beings; for that assumption would lead us to a logical see-saw, the Lord as well as the works of living beings have to be considered in turns both as acting and as acted upon. This difficulty is not removed by the consideration that the works of living beings and the resulting dispositions made by the Lord form a chain which has no beginning; for in past time as well as in the present mutual interdependence of the two took place, so that the beginningless series is like an endless chain of blind men leading other blind men. It is, moreover, a tenet set forth by the Naiyāyikas themselves that 'imperfections have the characteristic of being the causes of action' (*Nyāya Sūtra* I, 1, 18). Experience shows that all agents, whether they be active for their own purposes or for the purposes of something else, are impelled to action by some imperfection. And even if it is admitted that an agent even when acting for some extrinsic purpose is impelled by an intrinsic motive, your doctrine remains faulty all the same; for the Lord is no longer a Lord, even if he is actuated by intrinsic motives only (such as the desire of removing the painful feeling connected with pity).—Your doctrine is finally inappropriate for that reason also that you maintain the Lord to be a special kind of soul; for from that it follows that he must be devoid of all activity. (II, 2, 37)

Against the doctrine which we are at present discussing there lies the further objection that a Lord distinct from the *pradhāna* and the souls cannot be the ruler of the latter without being connected with them in a certain way. But of what nature is that connexion to be? It cannot be conjunction (*saṁyoga*), because the Lord, as well as the *pradhāna* and the souls, is of infinite extent and devoid of parts. Nor can it be inherence, since it would be impossible to define who should be the abode and who the abiding thing. Nor is it possible to assume some other connexion, the special nature of which would have to be inferred from the effect, because the relation of cause and effect is just what is not settled as yet.—How, then, it may be asked, do you—the Vedāntins—establish the relation of cause and effect (between the Lord and the world)?—There is, we reply, no difficulty in our case, as the connexion we assume is that of identity (*tādātmya*). The adherent of Brahman, moreover, defines the nature of the cause, and so on, on the basis of Scripture, and is therefore not obliged to render his tenets throughout conformable to observation. Our adversary, on the other hand, who defines the nature of the cause and the like according to instances furnished by experience, may be expected to maintain only such doctrines as agree with experience. Nor can he put forward the claim that Scripture, because it is the production of the omniscient Lord, may be used to confirm his doctrine as well as that of the Vedāntin; for that would involve him in a logical see-saw, the omniscience of the Lord being established on the doctrine of Scripture, and the authority of

Scripture again being established on the omniscience of the Lord.—For all these reasons the Sāṁkhya-yoga hypothesis about the Lord is devoid of foundation. Other similar hypotheses which likewise are not based on the Veda are to be refuted by corresponding arguments. (II, 2, 38)

The Lord of the argumentative philosophers is an untenable hypothesis, for the following reason also.—Those philosophers are obliged to assume that by his influence the Lord produces action in the *pradhāna,* &c. just as the potter produces motion in the clay, &c. But this cannot be admitted; for the *pradhāna,* which is devoid of colour and other qualities, and therefore not an object of perception, is on that account of an altogether different nature from clay and the like, and hence cannot be looked upon as the object of the Lord's action. (II, 2, 39)

Well, the opponent might reply, let us suppose that the Lord rules the *pradhāna* in the same way as the soul rules the organ of sight and the other organs which are devoid of colour, and so on, and hence not objects of perception.

This analogy also, we reply, proves nothing. For we infer that the organs are ruled by the soul, from the observed fact that the soul feels pleasure, pain, and the like (which affect the soul through the organs). But we do not observe that the Lord experiences pleasure, pain, &c. caused by the *pradhāna.* If the analogy between the *pradhāna* and the bodily organs were a complete one, it would follow that the Lord is affected by pleasure and pain no less than the transmigrating souls are.

Or else the two preceding Sūtras may be explained in a different way. Ordinary experience teaches us that kings, who are the rulers of countries, are never without some material abode, i.e. a body; hence, if we wish to infer the existence of a general Lord from the analogy of earthly rulers, we must ascribe to him also some kind of body to serve as the substratum of his organs. But such a body cannot be ascribed to the Lord, since all bodies exist only subsequently to the creation, not previously to it. The Lord, therefore, is not able to act because devoid of a material substratum; for experience teaches us that action requires a material substrate.—Let us then arbitrarily assume that the Lord possesses some kind of body serving as a substratum for his organs (even previously to creation).—This assumption also will not do; for if the Lord has a body he is subject to the sensations of ordinary transmigratory souls, and thus no longer is the Lord. (II, 2, 40)

The hypothesis of the argumentative philosophers is invalid, for the following reason also.—They teach that the Lord is omniscient and of infinite duration, and likewise that the *pradhāna,* as well as the individual souls, is of infinite duration. Now, the omniscient Lord either defines the measure of the *pradhāna,* the souls, and himself, or does not define it. Both alternatives subvert the doctrine under discussion. For, on the former alternative, the *pradhāna,* the souls, and the Lord, being all of them of definite measure, must necessarily be of finite duration;

since ordinary experience teaches that all things of definite extent, such as jars and the like, at some time cease to exist. The numerical measure of *pradhāna*, souls, and Lord is defined by their constituting a triad, and the individual measure of each of them must likewise be considered as defined by the Lord (because he is omniscient). The number of the souls is a high one. From among this limited number of souls some obtain release from the *saṁsāra*, that means their *saṁsāra* comes to an end, and their subjection to the *saṁsāra* comes to an end. Gradually all souls obtain release, and so there will finally be an end of the entire *saṁsāra* and the *saṁsāra* state of all souls. But the *pradhāna* which is ruled by the Lord and which modifies itself for the purposes of the soul is what is meant by *saṁsāra*. Hence, when the latter no longer exists, nothing is left for the Lord to rule, and his omniscience and ruling power have no longer any objects. But if the *pradhāna*, the souls, and the Lord, all have an end, it follows that they also have a beginning, and if they have a beginning as well as an end, we are driven to the doctrine of a general void. Let us then, in order to avoid these untoward conclusions, maintain the second alternative, i.e. that the measure of the Lord himself, the *pradhāna*, and the souls, is not defined by the Lord.—But that also is impossible, because it would compel us to abandon a tenet granted at the outset, viz. that the Lord is omniscient.

For all these reasons the doctrine of the argumentative philosophers, according to which the Lord is the operative cause of the world, appears unacceptable. (II, 2, 41)

THE BHĀGAVATAS

The last system which the *Brahmasūtras* and Śaṁkara take up for criticism is not so much a philosophical system (a *darśana*) in the Indian sense of the term as it is a popular religious movement which is supported by a "cosmology." Śaṁkara refers to it as "the doctrine of the Bhāgavatas."

The Bhāgavata movement was a religious cult which developed during the late Vedic period and was non-Brahmanic, and possibly non-aryan, in origin. It worshipped a transcendent deity, Vāsudeva, and believed that salvation could be obtained through fervent devotion (*bhakti*) to Him. The folk hero Kṛṣṇa became identified with Vāsudeva and became the center of a very rich and colorful mythology. Kṛṣṇa also came to be identified with the Vaiṣṇaivite *Viṣṇu-Nārāyaṇa* and thus also became an important feature in Vaiṣṇaivism. On its theological side the so-called Bhāgavatas incorporated the ancient philosophy known as the Pāñcarātra (whose origin is obscure), which had worked out an elaborate theory of the levels (vyūhas) of the divine nature. These are identified with Vāsudeva and members of his family and also with some of the categories of the Sāṁkhya system.[21]

Śaṁkara's criticisms here are quite mild and are focused mainly on the theory of vyūhas.

We have, in what precedes, refuted the opinion of those who think that the Lord is not the material cause but only the ruler, the operative cause of the world. We are now going to refute the doctrine of those according to whom he is the material as well as the operative cause.—But, it may be objected, in the previous portions of the present work a Lord of exactly the same nature, i.e. a Lord who is the material, as well as the operative, cause of the world, has been ascertained on the basis of Scripture, and it is a recognised principle that *smṛti*, in so far as it agrees with Scripture, is authoritative; why then should we aim at controverting the doctrine stated?—It is true, we reply, that a part of the system which we are going to discuss agrees with the Vedānta system, and hence affords no matter for controversy; another part of the system, however, is open to objection, and that part we intend to attack. The so-called Bhāgavatas are of opinion that the one holy (*bhagavat*) Vāsudeva, whose nature is pure knowledge, is what really exists, and that he, dividing himself fourfold, appears in four forms (*vyūha*), as Vāsudeva, Saṅkarśaṇa, Pradyumna, and Aniruddha. Vāsudeva denotes the highest Self, Saṅkarśaṇa the individual soul, Pradyumna the mind (*manas*), Aniruddha the principle of egoity (*ahaṁkāra*). Of these four Vāsudeva constitutes the ultimate causal essence, of which the three others are the effects.—The believer after having worshipped Vāsudeva for a hundred years by means of approach to the temple (*abhigamana*), procuring of things to be offered (*upādāna*), oblation (*īgyā*), recitation of prayers, &c. (*svādhyāya*), and devout meditation (*yoga*), passes beyond all affliction and reaches the highest Being.

Concerning this system we remark that we do not intend to controvert the doctrine that Nārāyaṇa, who is higher than the Undeveloped, who is the highest Self, and the Self of all, reveals himself by dividing himself in multiple ways; for various scriptural passages, such as 'He is onefold, he is threefold' (Ch. Up. VII, 26, 2), teach us that the highest Self appears in manifold forms. Nor do we mean to object to the inculcation of unceasing concentration of mind on the highest Being which appears in the Bhāgavata doctrine under the forms of reverential approach, &c.; for that we are to meditate on the Lord we know full well from *smṛti* and Scripture. We, however, must take exception to the doctrine that Saṅkarśaṇa springs from Vāsudeva, Pradyumna from Saṅkarśaṇa, Aniruddha from Pradyumna. It is not possible that from Vāsudeva, i.e. the highest Self, there should originate Saṅkarśaṇa, i.e. the individual soul; for if such were the case, there would attach to the

---

21. *See* J. A. B. van Buitenen, *Rāmānuja's Vedārthasaṃgraha* (Poona: Deccan College Monograph Series 16, 1956), pp. 36–37.

soul non-permanency, and all the other imperfections which belong to things originated. And thence release, which consists in reaching the highest Being, could not take place; for the effect is absorbed only by entering into its cause.—That the soul is not an originated thing, the teacher will prove later on (II, 3, 17). For this reason the Bhāgavata hypothesis is unacceptable. (II, 2, 42)

The Bhāgavata hypothesis is to be rejected for that reason also, that observation never shows us an instrument, such as a hatchet and the like, to spring from an agent such as Devadatta, or any other workman. But the Bhāgavatas teach that from an agent, viz. the individual soul termed Saṅkarṣaṇa, there springs its instrument, viz. the internal organ termed Pradyumna, and again from this offspring of the agent another instrument, viz. the *ahaṁkāra* termed Aniruddha. Such doctrines cannot be settled without observed instances. And we do not meet with any scriptural passages in their favour. (II, 2, 43)

Let us then—the Bhāgavatas may say—understand by Saṅkarṣaṇa, and so on, not the individual soul, the mind, &c., but rather Lords, i.e. powerful beings distinguished by all the qualities characteristic of rulers, such as pre-eminence of knowledge and ruling capacity, strength, valour, glory. All these are Vāsudevas free from faults, without a substratum (not sprung from *pradhāna*), without any imperfections. Hence the objection urged in Sūtra 42 does not apply.

Even on this interpretation of your doctrine, we reply, the 'non-exclusion of that,' i.e. the non-exclusion of the impossibility of origination, can be established.—Do you, in the first place, mean to say that the four individual Lords, Vāsudeva, and so on, have the same attributes, but do not constitute one and the same Self?—If so, you commit the fault of uselessly assuming more than one Lord, while all the work of the Lord can be done by one. Moreover, you offend thereby against your own principle, according to which there is only one real essence, viz. the holy Vāsudeva.—Or do you perhaps mean to say that from the one highest Being there spring those four forms possessing equal attributes?—In that case the objection urged in Sūtra 42 remains valid. For Saṅkarṣaṇa cannot be produced from Vāsudeva, nor Pradyumna from Saṅkarṣaṇa, nor Aniruddha from Pradyumna, since (the attributes of all of them being the same) there is no supereminence of any one of them. Observation shows that the relation of cause and effect requires some superiority on the part of the cause—as, for instance, in the case of the clay and the jar (where the cause is more extensive than the effect)—and that without such superiority the relation is simply impossible. But the followers of the Pāñcarātra do not acknowledge any difference founded on superiority of knowledge, power, &c. between Vāsudeva and the other Lords, but simply say that they all are forms of Vāsudeva, without any special distinctions. The forms of Vāsudeva cannot properly be limited to four, as the whole world, from Brahman down to a blade of grass, is understood to be a manifestation of the supreme Being. (II, 2, 44)

PART III

Sources of Advaita Vedānta

Advaita Vedānta is that school of Vedānta which affirms that Reality, or Brahman, is non-dual (a-dvaita), *that the world is false* (mithyā), *the product of a creative illusion* (māyā), *and that the human being* (jīva) *is essentially not-different from Brahman. Advaita has occupied the dominant position in Indian philosophy from the time of Śaṁkara (ninth century) to the present day. Its prestige, in fact, has been such that the very term "Vedānta" is often made synonymous with it. Many of the finest minds in India contributed to its rich and complex development and brought to the articulation of its basic principles their own special concerns. Further, more than any other school in Indian philosophy Advaita strives to incorporate within itself what it takes to be valid and significant in other systems and to integrate these materials according to its own distinctive metaphysical values.*

CHAPTER 7

Gauḍapāda

According to Vedāntic tradition the first available treatise on Advaita Vedānta is the *Kārikās on the Māṇḍūkya Upaniṣad,* written by Gauḍapāda, who was the *guru* of Śaṁkara's *guru* Govinda. The dates of Gauḍapāda's life are not known and the question has even been raised as to whether such a person lived at all. But if tradition is correct in maintaining that he was literally Śaṁkara's *paramaguru* then he must have lived no earlier than the seventh century. In the *Kārikās on the Māṇḍūkya Upaniṣad* (also called the *Āgamaśāstra*), Gauḍapāda sets forth, at times in a rather extreme form, what later becomes some of the main principles of classical Advaita.

There is a good deal of controversy over the degree to which the author of the *Kārikās* was influenced by Buddhist thought (viz., by the Vijñānavāda and Śūnyavāda schools of Mahāyāna Buddhism). Gauḍapāda rather clearly draws from Buddhist philosophical sources for many of his arguments and distinctions (e.g., his use of Nāgārjuna's distinction between two orders of truth—*paramārtha satya* and *saṁvṛtti satya*) and even for the forms and imagery in which these arguments are cast. Vedānta tradition maintains, though, that rather than presenting Buddhism as such in a Brahmanic guise, Gauḍapāda merely found it convenient to draw from Buddhism while maintaining allegiance to Upaniṣadic sources and to *śruti* in general.

The main doctrine that Gauḍapāda puts forth is called *ajātivāda* —the theory of no-origination. According to *ajātivāda* the entire world of duality is merely an appearance: nothing ever really comes into being, for nothing other than Brahman really exists—the whole world is an illusion like a dream. At times Gauḍapāda blurs the distinction between waking and dream consciousness, a distinction which Śaṁkara later insists upon, and suggests that the whole of our waking experience is exactly the same as an illusory and insubstantial dream (cf. Vasubandhu's arguments in *Viṁśatika* X, ff.). Gauḍapāda establishes this by a dialectical critique of causation and by an appeal to the doctrine of *māyā.*

The following brief selections from the *Kārikās* have been chosen simply to illustrate Gauḍapāda's contribution to Advaita and are newly translated by Eliot Deutsch. The most complete study of Gauḍapāda as an advaitic thinker has been made by T. M. P. Mahadevan in *Gauḍapāda: A Study in Early Advaita* (Madras: University of Madras, 1960).

KĀRIKĀS ON THE MĀṆḌŪKYA UPANIṢAD

I, 16. When the empirical self (*jīva*) is awakened from the sleep of beginningless illusion (*māyā*), it realizes the unborn, sleepless, dreamless non-dual (Reality).

I, 17. If the phenomenal world were (really) existing then it ought no doubt to disappear. But this (whole universe of) duality is mere illusion: the absolute truth is that of non-duality.

I, 18. If anyone merely imagined the world of diversity (to exist), it would disappear (upon the termination of his fancy). This talk (of duality) is only for instruction. There is no duality (when Reality) is known.

II, 1. The wise declare the insubstantiality of all things (seen) in a dream because they are within (the body) and are therein confined.

II, 4. As in the dream state so in the waking state, the objects seen are insubstantial because of their being perceived. The difference between them is only that the objects of dream are confined within the body.

II, 11. (Objector's question). If in both states the objects are unreal, who is it that perceives these objects? Who is it that imagines them?

II, 12. The self-luminous Self (Ātman) imagines Itself through Itself by the power of its own illusion. It is itself the cognizer of objects. This is the definite conclusion of the Vedānta.

II, 13. The Lord (Self) imagines in various forms the well-defined objects which are in His mind when His mind is turned outward, and (various ideas) when His mind is turned within.

II, 17. As a rope which is not clearly perceived is, in the dark, imagined to be a snake or a line of water, so the Self is imagined in different ways.

II, 18. As definite knowledge of the rope destroys all illusions about it and the conviction arises that it is nothing but a rope, so is the nature of the Self determined.

II, 31. As dream and illusion or a castle in the air are seen (to be unreal), so this whole universe is seen by those who are wise in Vedānta.

II, 32. There is no dissolution and no creation, no one in bondage and no one who is striving for or who is desirous of liberation, and there is no one who is liberated. This is the absolute truth.

III, 15. The creation which has been set forth in different ways by illustrations of earth, metal, sparks is only a means for introducing the truth. In no manner are there any real distinctions.

III, 19. The birthless One is differentiated only through illusion, and in no other way. For if differentiation were real then the immortal would become mortal (which is absurd).

III, 28. There is no birth for a non-existent thing either through illusion or in reality. The son of a barren woman is not born either through illusion or in reality.

III, 46. When the mind does not disappear nor again is dispersed, when it is motionless and without sense-images, then it becomes Brahman.

III, 48. No individual is born, for there is nothing to cause (its birth). This (Brahman) is that highest truth—where nothing is born.

CHAPTER 8

Samkara

Gauḍapāda may have been the "first" advaitin and his doctrine of *ajāti* may be a sound one. Nevertheless, according to Vedāntic tradition, the real founder of the school was Śaṁkara—whom many Westerners as well as Indians consider to be one of the greatest philosophers, East or West.

He was born in the village Kāladi in Kerala in 788, into a Brahmin family distinguished for its learning. His mother, who played a large part in his life, belonged to the Nambūdri Brahmin caste; about his father, whose name was Śivaguru, the stories are confused. (Some enemies of Śaṁkara contended that his birth was illegitimate.) He underwent the *upanayana* at seven in the traditional fashion. Pious tradition sings that he finished all his Vedic studies within two years. Śaṁkara, however, had resolved on *saṁnyāsa*, total renunciation. Legend has it that his mother did not wish to give her permission, for reasons of sentiment as well as of custom, for as a *saṁnyāsin* Śaṁkara would be unable to perform her funeral rites. But once when Śaṁkara was bathing, a crocodile pulled him by the foot and, on the point of drowning, he wrested from his mother permission for "emergency renunciation," often practiced when death is near. Śaṁkara survived the danger, but held his mother to her consent. He entrusted her care to his relatives, left them his property, and went forth from his village to find a *guru* to initiate him properly into *saṁnyāsa*. He joined a hermitage on the bank of the Narmadā River and was accepted as a pupil by Govinda (who was himself, as indicated previously, the pupil of Gauḍapāda). There are no records about the length of his stay there. His *guru* charged him with the peripatetic life of the teacher, and Śaṁkara soon departed for Benares. It was there that he did most of the debating that was to be instrumental in the formulation of his philosophy and probably much of his writing. Soon he had attracted a following and had found a patron in the king of Benares.

Śaṁkara then traveled south, converting thinkers and reforming aberrant practices; he built a temple to the Goddess of Wisdom,

Śāradā Sarasvatī, on the bank of the Tungabhadra. Along with it he founded, with the support of a chieftain, Vīrasena, the famous advaita monastery of Sringeri, which still flourishes today. It was from there he was called back to his native village, where his mother was dying.

Eventually Śaṁkara resumed his circumambulation of India, combating the Tantrism of the South, founding another *maṭh* or monastery in Puri in the East, still a third in Dwaraka in the West. In the extreme North he founded a temple of Nārāyaṇa at Bādarikāśrama where ever since a Nambūdri from Malabar has officiated. He died of an intestinal disorder at an early age, thirty-two or thirty-eight.

Śaṁkara was the great revolutionary in Vedānta. His emphasis upon *saṁnyāsa* and his teachings about the nature of Brahman and the world stand in sharp contrast to the more conservative Brahminism which prevailed up to his time. And the success of his teachings was nothing less than phenomenal. Here is a philosophy which insists upon *nirguṇa* Brahman—Brahman without qualities—as the sole reality, upon the absolute identity of man with this distinctionless Reality, and upon the relativity, if not falsity, of all empirical experience. And this philosophy, which is obviously meaningful to only an intellectual-spiritual elite, soon became the dominant philosophical system in the whole of India.

Śaṁkara not only convinced many thinkers of the rational correctness of his teachings, he also gave them a means of interpreting the scriptures in a consistent, if not sometimes forced, manner. He drew a sharp distinction between two kinds of materials to be found in Vedic literature, the *karmakāṇḍa* and the *jñānakāṇḍa.* The former applies to that portion of the Veda which is concerned with action in the world, with ethical injunctions, etc., and it is there for those who are incapable of reaching the highest truth at their present state of intellectual-spiritual development. The latter, the *jñānakāṇḍa,* applies to that portion of the Veda which does have enlightenment or *mokṣa* as its aim, and this is the portion of the Veda which alone has compelling force upon the real aspirant for knowledge. It teaches one about the ultimate nature of being and how one must be in order to realize it.

UPADEŚASĀHASRĪ

An enormous amount of written work has been attributed to Śaṁkara, but many of the attributions are of dubious worth (see Bibliography). It is reasonably certain, though, that Śaṁkara was the author of commentaries on the *Brahmasūtras*, the *Bhagavadgītā*, and several Upaniṣads. It is also reasonably certain that he wrote several small treatises wherein he set forth, in a concise and vivid manner, the central tenets of his advaitism.

Among these small treatises is a highly popular work called the *Upadeśasāhasrī.* It is divided into two parts: the first is in prose and explains "a method of teaching the means to liberation . . ."; the second is in verse. The following selection, which we use to introduce the thought of Śaṁkara, consists of the entire first part of this text. It is taken from an unpublished translation by Sengaku Mayeda, which is based on his critical edition.

How to Enlighten the Pupil

1. Now we shall explain how to teach the means to final release for the benefit of seekers thereafter with faith and desire.

2. The means to final release is knowledge [of Brahman]. It should be repeatedly related to the pupil until it is firmly grasped, if he is dispassionate toward all things non-eternal which are attained by any means [other than knowledge]; if he has abandoned the desire for sons, wealth and worlds and reached the state of a *paramahaṃsa* wandering ascetic; if he is endowed with tranquility, self-control, compassion and so forth; if he is possessed of the qualities of a pupil which are well known from the scriptures; if he is a Brahmin who is [internally and externally] pure; if he approaches his teacher in the prescribed manner; if his caste, profession, behavior, knowledge [of the Veda] and family have been examined.

3. The *śruti* also says,

> "Having scrutinized [the worlds that are built up by action, a Brahmin should arrive at indifference. . . . For the sake of this knowledge let him go, with fuel in hand, to a spiritual teacher who is learned in the scriptures and established in Brahman. To him who has approached properly, whose thought is calm, who has reached tranquility, the man of knowledge teaches] in its very truth that knowledge of Brahman [by which he knows the Imperishable]" (Mu. Up. I, 2, 12–13);

for when knowledge [of Brahman] is firmly grasped, it conduces to one's own beatitude and to the continuity [of knowledge of Brahman]. And the continuity of knowledge [of Brahman] is helpful to people, as a boat [is helpful] to one wishing to get across a river. The scripture also says,

> "[Verily, a father may teach this Brahman to his eldest son or to a worthy pupil, but to no one else at all.] Even if one should offer him this [earth] that is encompassed by water and filled with treasure, [he should say], 'This, truly, is more than that.'" (Ch. Up. III, 11 [5–] 6.),

since knowledge [of Brahman] is not obtained in any other way [than from a teacher] according to passages from the *śruti* and the *smṛti* such as

> "One who has a teacher knows . . ." (Ch. Up. VI, 14, 2), "The knowledge which has been learned from a teacher [best helps to attain his end]" (Ch. Up. IV, 9, 3), "A teacher is a boatman; his [right] knowledge is called a boat here."

4. When [the teacher] finds from some indications that the pupil has not grasped [this] knowledge, he should remove the causes which hinder his grasping it,—demerit, worldly laxity, absence of firm preliminary learning concerning the discrimination between things eternal and non-eternal, care about people's consideration, pride of caste and the like—by the means contrary to those causes and enjoined by the *śruti* and the *smṛti*, that is to say, non-anger, etc., non-injury and other abstentions, and the observances which are not contradictory to knowledge.

5. He should also let [him] properly achieve the virtues such as modesty which are the means to attain knowledge.

6. And the teacher is able to consider the pros and cons [of an argument], is endowed with understanding, memory, tranquility, self-control, compassion, favor and the like; he is versed in the traditional doctrine; not attached to any enjoyments, visible or invisible, he has abandoned all the rituals and their requisites; a knower of Brahman, he is established in Brahman; he leads a blameless life, free from faults such as deceit, pride, trickery, wickedness, fraud, jealousy, falsehood, egotism, self-interest and so forth; with the only purpose of helping others he wishes to make use of knowledge.

First of all, he should teach the śrutis which are concerned primarily with the oneness of Ātman [with Brahman], for example:

> "In the beginning, my dear, this universe was the existent only, one alone, without a second" (Ch. Up. VI, 2, 1); "Where one sees nothing else, [hears nothing else, understands nothing else—that is the Fullness]" (Ch. Up. VII, 24, 1);
> "Ātman, indeed, is this all" (Ch. Up. VII, 25, 2);
> "Brahman, indeed, is this all";
> "Ātman, verily, was this universe, one alone, in the beginning" (Ait. Up. I, 1, 1);
> "Verily, this all is Brahman" (Ch. Up. III, 14, 1).

7. And after teaching [these śrutis], he should help [him] by means of the śrutis to grasp the marks indicative of Brahman, for example:

> "Ātman, which is free from evil, . . ." (Ch. Up. VIII, 7, 1);
> "[Explain to me] what the manifest, unconcealed Brahman is" (Bṛh. Up. III, 4, 1; 5, 1);
> "That which transcends hunger and thirst (Bṛh. Up. III, 5, 1);
> "Not Thus! Not so!" (Bṛh. Up. II, 3, 6);
> "[It is] not coarse, not fine" (Bṛh. Up. III, 8, 8);

"This Ātman is [described as] 'not, not' " (Bṛh. Up. III, 9, 26; IV, 2, 4; 4, 22; 5, 15);
"[Verily, O Gārgī, that Imperishable is] the unseen Seer" (Bṛh. Up. III, 8, 1);
"[Brahman is] knowledge, bliss" (Bṛh. Up. III, 9, 28);
"[He who knows Brahman as the real,] as knowledge, as the infinite" (Taitt. Up. II, 1);
"[For truly, when one finds fearlessness as a foundation] in that (= Brahman) which is invisible, bodiless, [. . . then he has reached fearlessness]" (Taitt. Up. II, 7);

"This, verily, is [the great, unborn Ātman]" (Bṛh. Up. IV, 4, 22);
"[This Brahman is . . .] breathless, mindless" (Mu. Up. II, 1, 2);
"[This Brahman is] without and within, unborn" (Mu. Up. II, 1, 2);
"[This great Being . . .] is just a mass of knowledge" (Bṛh. Up. II, 4, 12);
"[This Brahman is . . .] without an inside and without an outside" (Bṛh. Up. II, 5, 19);
"It is, indeed, other than the known and than the unknown" (Ken. Up. I, 3);
"Verily, what is called 'Space' [is the accomplisher of name-and-form]" (Ch. Up. VIII, 14, 1).

8. [He should] also [help him grasp the marks indicative of Brahman] by means of the smṛtis, if they are not incompatible with the marks indicative [of Brahman] described by the śrutis and concerned primarily with teaching that the highest Ātman is not subject to transmigration and that It is identical with all—for example:

"He is not born, nor does he ever die" (BhG. II, 20; Ka. Up. II, 18);
"He does not receive [the effect of] anyone's evil" (BhG. V, 15);
"As [the great Wind] constantly abides in space [. . . so all beings abide in Me]" (BhG. IX, 6);
"Know also that I am the Field-Knower (= Ātman)" (BhG. XIII, 2);
"It is called neither existent nor non-existent" (BhG. XIII, 12);
"Because [He] is beginningless and attributeless" (BhG. XIII, 31);
"[The supreme Lord, abiding] alike in all beings" (BhG. XIII, 27);
"There is the highest *puruṣa* (= Ātman)" (BhG. XV, 17).

9. If the pupil who has thus grasped the marks indicative of the highest Ātman according to the śrutis and the smṛtis wishes to get out of the ocean of transmigratory existence, [the teacher] should ask him: "Who are you, my dear?"

10. If he answers: "I am a Brahmin's son belonging to such and

such a family. I was a student—or, I was a householder—, [but] now I am a *paramahaṃsa* wandering ascetic. I wish to get out of the ocean of transmigratory existence infested with great sharks of birth and death"—

11. [then] the teacher should say: "My dear, when you are dead your body will be eaten by birds or will turn into earth right here. How then do you wish to get out of the ocean of transmigratory existence? Because if you turn into ashes on this bank of the river you cannot get across to the other side of the river."

12. If he answers: "I am different from the body. The body is born, dies, is eaten by birds, turns into earth, is destroyed by weapons, fire and so forth, and suffers from disease and so on. I have entered this body as a bird enters a nest, by force of the merit and demerit accumulated by myself. Again and again by force of the merit and demerit, when this body perishes, I shall enter another body as a bird enters another nest when its previous one has been destroyed. Thus I am in beginningless transmigratory existence. I have been abandoning [old] bodies which have been obtained one after another in the spheres of gods, animals, men and hells by force of my own *karman* and I have been getting other new bodies over and over again. I am forced by my own *karman* to rotate in the incessant cycle of birth and death as in a water-wheel. I have obtained this body in the course of time. I am tired of this rotation in the wheel of transmigratory existence, so I have come to you, Your Holiness, in order to end the rotation in the wheel of transmigratory existence. Therefore I am eternal and different from the body. The bodies come and go like a person's garments"—

13. [then] the teacher should say: "You are right. Your view is correct. [Then] why did you say incorrectly, 'I am a Brahmin's son belonging to such and such a family. I was a student—or, I was a householder—, [but] now I am a *paramahaṃsa* wandering ascetic'?"

14. If he says: "Your Holiness, how have I spoken wrongly?"—

15. [then] the teacher should reply to him: "Because, through such statements as 'I am a Brahmin's son belonging to such and such a family', you have identified the Ātman, which is free from caste, family and purifying ceremonies, with the body, which has different caste, family and purifying ceremonies."

16. If he asks: "How does the body have different caste, family, and purifying ceremonies?" or, "How am I (= Ātman) free from caste, family and purifying ceremonies?"—

17. [then] the teacher should reply: "Listen, my dear, [this is] how this body, different from you (= Ātman), has different caste, family and purifying ceremonies and how you (= Ātman) are free from caste, family and purifying ceremonies."

Thereupon [the teacher] should remind him: "You should remember, my dear, that you have been taught the highest Ātman, the Ātman of all, is endowed with the marks described above according to such *śruti* and *smṛti* passages as

> '[In the beginning,] my dear, this universe was the existent only, [one alone, without a second]' (Ch. Up. VI, 2, 1)

and [that you have also been taught] the marks indicative of the highest Ātman according to *śruti* and *smṛti* passages."

18. When [the pupil] has recalled to mind the marks indicative of the highest Ātman, [the teacher] should tell him [in answer to his first question]: "This [highest Ātman] which is called 'Space' is something different from name-and-form, bodiless, characterized as 'not coarse', etc. and as 'free from evil', etc. It is not afflicted with any attributes of transmigratory existence;

> '[Explain to me] what the manifest, unconcealed Brahman is . . . It is your Ātman, which is within everything' (Bṛh. Up. III, 4, 1).

It is

> 'the unseen Seer, the unheard Hearer, the unthought Thinker, the unknown Knower' (Bṛh. Up. III, 7, 23).

It is of the nature of eternal knowledge,

> 'without an inside and without an outside' (Bṛh. Up. II, 5, 19), 'just a mass of knowledge' (Bṛh. Up. II, 4, 12).

It is all-pervading like ether, possessed of infinite power, the Ātman of all, free from hunger, etc., and free from appearance and disappearance. This [highest Ātman] is the Evolver of the unevolved name-and-form merely by being existent since It is possessed of inconceivable power. The unevolved name-and-form is different in their essence from this [Ātman] and it is the seed of the world, abiding in It, indescribable as this or something else, and known to It.

19. "[Originally] unevolved, this name-and-form took the name-and-form of 'ether' in the course of its evolution from this very Ātman. And in this manner this element named 'ether' arose from the highest Ātman as dirty foam from clear water. Foam is neither [identical with] water nor absolutely different from water since it is not seen without water. But water is clear and different from foam which is of the nature of dirt. Likewise, the highest Ātman is different from name-and-form which corresponds to foam; Ātman is pure, clear and different in essence from it. This name-and-form, which corresponds to foam, [originally] unevolved, took the name-and-form of 'ether' in the course of its evolution.

20. "Becoming grosser in the course of evolution, the name-and-form becomes air from ether, fire from air, water from fire, earth from water. In this order each preceding [element] entered each succeeding one and the five gross elements, [ether, air, fire, water and] earth, came into existence. Consequently earth is characterized by the qualities of the five gross elements. And from earth, rice, barley and other plants consisting of the five elements are produced; from them, when they are

eaten, blood and sperm are produced, related respectively to the bodies of women and men. Both blood and sperm, produced by churning with the churning stick of sexual passion, driven by nescience and sanctified with sacred formulas, are poured into the womb at the proper time. Through the penetration of fluid from the womb, they become an embryo and it is delivered in the ninth or tenth month.

21. "When it is born it obtains its name-and-form, sanctified with sacred formulas by means of a birth ceremony and other [purifying ceremonies]. Again it obtains the name of a student through the performance of the purifying ceremony for initiation. This same body obtains the name of a householder through the performance of the purifying ceremony for union with a wife. This same body obtains the name of an ascetic through the purifying ceremony of becoming a forest-dweller. This same body obtains the name of a wandering ascetic through the purifying ceremony which ends the ritual actions. Thus the body is different from you (= Ātman) and is possessed of different caste, family and purifying ceremonies.

22. "The mind and the sense-organs consist only of the name-and-form according to the śrutis such as

> 'For, my dear, the mind consists of food' (Ch. Up. VI, 5, 4; 6, 5; 7, 6).

23. "[The second question you asked me earlier was,] 'How am I (= Ātman) free from caste, family and purifying ceremonies?' Listen to what [I am going to say]. The Evolver (= the highest Ātman) of name-and-form, by nature different in essence from name-and-form, created this body in the course of evolving name-and-form. And [the Evolver] entered the name-and-form [of the body], Itself being free from the duties of purifying ceremonies. Itself unseen by others, [the Evolver] is seeing; unheard, It is hearing; unthought, It is thinking; unknown, It is knowing.

> 'The wise one who having distinguished all forms and having created [their] names, sits calling' (Taitt. Ā. III, 12, 7).

There are thousands of *śruti* passages which have this same meaning, for example:

> 'Having created it, It, indeed, entered into it' (Taitt. Up. II, 6, 1);
> 'The Ruler of creatures entered into [them]' (Taitt. Ā. III, 11, 1);
> 'It entered here, [even to the fingertips]' (Bṛh. Up. I, 4, 7);
> 'It is your Ātman, [which is in everything]' (Bṛh. Up. III, 4, 1; 5, 1);
> 'So, cleaving asunder this very top of the skull, It entered by that door' (Ait. Up. I, 3, 12);
> 'Though It is hidden in all things, that Ātman [does not shine forth]' (Ka. Up. III, 12);
> 'That divinity thought, "Come! Let me [enter] these three divini-

ties [i.e., heat, water, and food] with this living Ātman and evolve name-and-form]" ' (Ch. Up. VI, 3, 2);

'[Ātman which is] the bodiless among bodies' (Ka. Up. II, 22).

24. "There are also *smṛti* passages [which have this same meaning], for example:

'Ātman is truly all gods' (Manu XII, 119);

'The embodied Ātman in the city of nine gates' (BhG. V, 13);

'Know also that I am the Field-Knower (= Ātman)' (BhG. XIII, 2);

'[The supreme Lord abiding] alike in all beings' (BhG. XIII, 27);

'The onlooker and consenter, [the highest Ātman . . . is also declared to be the highest *puruṣa*, in this body]' (BhG. XIII, 22);

'But there is the highest *puruṣa*, different [from this]' (BhG. XV, 17).

It is, therefore, established that you (= Ātman) are free from caste, family and purifying ceremonies."

25. If he says: "I am one [and] He is another; I am ignorant, I experience pleasure and pain, am bound and a transmigrator [whereas] He is essentially different from me, the god not subject to transmigration. By worshipping Him with oblations, offerings, homage and the like and through the [performance of] the actions prescribed for [my] class and stage of life, I wish to get out of the ocean of transmigratory existence. How am I He?"—

26. [then] the teacher should reply: "My dear, you should not hold such a view since it is prohibited to understand that [Ātman] is different [from Brahman]."

[The pupil may say:] "How is it prohibited to understand that [Ātman] is different [from Brahman]?"

Then the teacher replys:

" 'So whoever worships another divinity [than his Ātman], thinking that He is one and I another, he does not know' (Bṛh. Up. I, 4, 10);

'Brahmanhood has deserted him who knows Brahmanhood as different from Ātman' (Bṛh. Up. II, 4, 6);

'He who thinks he sees manifoldness in this world attains death after death' (Bṛh. Up. IV, 4, 19)—

27. "these *śruti* passages indeed reveal that transmigratory existence results from the understanding that [Ātman] is different [from Brahman].

28. "And thousands [of *śruti* passages] reveal that final release results from the realization of the identity [of Ātman and Brahman]. [For example, through the statement,]

'That is Ātman, That art thou' (Ch. Up. VI, 8, 7, etc.) [the śrutis] establish that [Ātman] is the highest Ātman (= Brahman). Then [they] state,

'One who has a teacher knows' (Ch. Up. VI, 14, 2),

and [they] show final release with the words,

'He is delayed only until [he is freed from bondage of ignorance; then he will arrive at his final goal]' (Ch. Up. VI, 14, 2).

With the simile about the [man] who was not a thief and [therefore] not burned [in the ordeal of the heated axe, the śrutis] teach that he who covers himself with truth does not undergo transmigratory existence since he knows that [Ātman] is identical [with Brahman]; [on the other hand], with the simile about the [man] who was a thief and was [therefore] burned, [the śrutis] teach that he who covers himself with the untruth undergoes transmigratory existence since [he holds] the view that [Ātman] is different [from Brahman].

29. "And with such [similes] as,

'Whatever they are in this world, whether tiger [or lion . . . or mosquito, they become That Existent]' (Ch. Up. VI, 9, 3),

the śrutis [continue to] teach that on account of the contrary view, viz., Brahman]

'[He] rules himself' (Ch. Up. VII, 25, 2).

And with the words,

'But they who know otherwise than this are ruled by another; theirs are perishable worlds' (Ch. Up. VII, 25, 2),

the śrutis [continue to] teach that on account of the contrary view, viz., the view that [Ātman] is different [from Brahman], he undergoes transmigratory existence. This is what is taught in every school of the Veda. So you were indeed wrong in saying, '[I (= Ātman) am] a Brahmin's son belonging to such and such a family; [I (= Ātman) am] a transmigrator, essentially different from the highest Ātman.'

30. "For the above reason it is prohibited [by the śrutis] to hold the view that [Ātman] is different [from Brahman]; use of the rituals is [made] in the sphere of [the view] that [Ātman] is different [from Brahman]; and the sacred thread and the like are requisites for the rituals. Therefore, it should be known that the use of rituals and their requisites is prohibited, if the identity [of Ātman] with the highest Ātman is realized, since [the use of] rituals and their requisites such as the sacred thread is contradictory to the realization of the identity [of Ātman] with the highest Ātman. [The use of] rituals and their requisites such as the sacred thread is indeed enjoined upon a transmigrator [but] not upon one who holds the view of the identity [of Ātman] with the highest Ātman; and the difference [of Ātman] from It is merely due to the view that [Ātman] is different [from Brahman].

31. "If rituals were to be performed and it were not desirable to abandon them, [the śrutis] would not declare in such unambiguous sentences as,

> 'That is Ātman, That art thou' (Ch. Up. VI, 8, 7, etc.),

that the highest Ātman, unrelated to the rituals, their requisites and such factors of the rituals as castes and stages of life, should be realized to be identical with [the inner] Ātman; nor would [the śrutis] condemn the realization that [Ātman] is different [from Brahman], [in passages] such as,

> 'This is the constant greatness of the knower of Brahman; [he does not increase nor decrease by action]' (Bṛh. Up. IV, 4, 23);
> '[He] is unaffected by good, unaffected by evil, [for then he has transcended all sorrows of the heart]' (Bṛh. Up. IV, 3, 22);
> 'In this state a thief is no thief [. . . a mendicant no mendicant, an ascetic no ascetic]' (Bṛh. Up. IV, 3, 22).

32. "[The śrutis] would not declare that [Ātman] is by nature unrelated to the rituals, by nature unconnected with the class and other factors of the rituals, if it were not desirable that the rituals and such requisites of the rituals as the sacred thread be abandoned completely. Therefore the seeker after final release should abandon the ritual together with its requisites since [they] are contradictory to the view of the identity [of Ātman] with the highest Ātman. And [he] should realize that [his] Ātman is the highest [Ātman] as characterized in the śrutis."

33. If [the pupil] says: "Your Holiness, when the body is burned or cut, I evidently perceive pain and I evidently experience suffering from hunger, etc. But in all the śrutis and the smṛtis the highest Ātman is said to be

> 'free from evil, ageless, deathless, sorrowless, hungerless, thirstless' (Ch. Up. VIII, 1, 5),

free from all attributes of transmigratory existence. I am different in essence from It and bound up with many attributes of transmigratory existence. How then can I realize that the highest Ātman is [my] Ātman and that I, a transmigrator, am the highest Ātman?—it is as if I were to hold that fire is cold! Though I am [now] a transmigrator, I am entitled to the means of [attaining] all prosperity and beatitude. How then should I abandon the rituals and their requisites such as the sacred thread which lead [me] to prosperity and beatitude?"—

34. [then the teacher] should answer him: "Your statement, 'When the body is burned or cut, I (= Ātman) evidently perceive pain', is not correct."

"Why?"

"The body, like a tree which is burned [or] cut, is the object which is perceived by the perceiver. The pain of burning or cutting is perceived in the body, which is the object; so the pain has the same locus as the burning [or cutting], since people point out the pain of burning [or cutting] right there where [the body] is burned or cut and not in the perceiver of burning [or cutting]."

"How?"

"When a man is asked, 'Where do you have pain?', he points to the locus where [the body] is burned [or cut] and not to the perceiver, saying, 'I have pain in the head' or 'In the chest' or 'In the stomach'. If pain or the cause of pain such as burning and cutting were located in the perceiver, he would point to [the perceiver] as the locus of pain just as [he points to a part of the body as] the locus of burning and so forth.

35. "And [pain] itself would not be perceived as the form-and-color in the eye [are not perceived by the eye]. Therefore, pain is perceived as having the same locus as burning, cutting and so on; so pain is merely an object like burning and the like.

"As [pain] is of the nature of 'becoming', [it] has its substratum like the cooking of rice. The impression of pain [also] has exactly the same substratum as the pain, since [the impression of pain] is perceived only simultaneously with the recollection [of pain]. The aversion to pain and its causes also has precisely the same substratum as the impression. So it is said,

> 'Passion and aversion have [their] substratum in common with the impression of form-and-color and what is perceived as fear has the intellect as its substratum. Therefore the knower is always pure and free from fear' (*Upadeśasāhasrī* II, 15, 13)."

36. [The student may ask:] "What locus do then the impressions of form-and-color and the like have?"

[Then the teacher] answers: "[The locus] where there are desire and so forth."

"Where are there these desire and the like?"

"Right in the intellect according to such *śruti* passages as,

> 'Desire, volition, doubt, [faith, lack of faith, steadfastness, lack of steadfastness, shame, meditation, fear—all this is truly mind]' (Bṛh. Up. I, 5, 3).

Right there are also the impressions of form-and-color and the like according to the *śruti*,

> 'And on what are the colors and forms based?—On the heart' (Bṛh. Up. III, 9, 20).

Impurity [such as desire and aversion] is in the object and not in Ātman [which is the subject] according to hundreds of *śruti* passages such as,

> 'The desires that are based on heart' (Bṛh. Up. IV, 4, 7; Ka. Up. VI, 14);
> 'For [then] he has passed beyond [all sorrows of the heart]' (Bṛh. Up. IV, 3, 22);
> 'This [person] is without attachments' (Bṛh. Up. IV, 3, 16);

'Even this is His form that is beyond desire' (Bṛh. Up. IV, 3, 21), and according to *smṛti* passages such as,

'He is declared to be unchangeable' (BhG. II, 25);
'Because [He] is beginningless and attributeless' (BhG. XIII, 31); moreover, 'desire, aversion' and so on are the attributes of 'the Field', i.e., the object, and not those of Ātman.

37. "For this reason you (= Ātman) have no relation with the impression of form-and-color and the like; so you (= Ātman) are not different in essence from the highest Ātman. As there is no contradiction to sense-perception and other [means of knowledge], it is reasonable to realize that I (= Ātman) am the highest Ātman according to such *śruti* passages as,

'It knew only itself, ["I am Brahman!"]' (Bṛh. Up. I, 4, 10);
'As a unity only is It to be looked upon' (Bṛh. Up. IV, 4, 20);
'I, indeed, am below. [I am above. . . .]' (Ch. Up. VII, 25, 1);
'Ātman, indeed, is below. [Ātman is behind. . . .]' (Ch. Up. VII, 25, 2);
'One should see everything as Ātman' (Bṛh. Up. IV, 4, 23);
'Where truly everything [has become] one's own Ātman, [then whereby and whom one smell?' (Bṛh. Up. II, 4, 14);
'This all is what this Ātman is' (Bṛh. Up. II, 4, 6);
'That one [is without parts, immortal]' (Pra. Up. VI, 5);
'[This Brahman is . . .] without an inside and without an outside' (Bṛh. Up. II, 5, 19);
'[This is] without and within, unborn' (Mu. Up. II, 1, 2);
'Brahman indeed is this [whole] world' (Mu. Up. II, 1, 2);
'[So, cleaving asunder this very top of the skull,] He entered by that door' (Ait. Up. I, 3, 12);
'[All these, indeed, are] names of intelligence' (Ait. Up. III, 1, 2);
'[He who knows Brahman as the real,] as knowledge, as the infinite' (Taitt. Up. II, 1);
'Space arose indeed from this [Ātman]' (Taitt. Up. II, 1);
'Having created it, It indeed entered into it' (Taitt. Up. II, 6, 1);
'The one God, hidden in all things, [all-pervading]' (Śve. Up. VI, 11);
'[Ātman which is] the bodiless among bodies' (Ka. Up. II, 22);
'[The wise one] is not born, nor dies' (Ka. Up. II, 18);
'[Thinking on the great all-pervading Ātman, by which one contemplates both] the dreaming state and the waking state, [the wise man is not grieved]' (Ka. Up. IV, 4);
'One should know that It is my Ātman' (Kau. Up. III, 8);
'Now, he who on all being [looks as indeed in Ātman and on Ātman as in all beings—he does not shrink away from It]' (Īśā Up. VI);
'It moves. It does not move.' (Īśā Up. V);
'Vena, seeing It, [knowing all creatures, where all have the same nest]' (M.N. Up. II, 3);
'It is, indeed, Agni, [It is Āditya, It is Vāyu . . .]' (Taitt. Ā. X, 1, 2);

'I was Manu and the Sun' (Bṛh. Up. I, 4, 10; *Ṛgveda* IV, 26, 1);
'The Ruler of the creatures entered into [them]' (Taitt. Ā. III, 11, 1);
'[In the beginning,] my dear, [this universe was] the existent only, [one alone, without a second]' (Ch. Up. VI, 2, 1);
'That is the Real, That is Ātman, That art thou' (Ch. Up. VI, 8, 7, etc.).

38. "From *smṛti* passages as well it is established that, being one alone, you, Ātman, are the highest Ātman [and] free from all the attributes of transmigratory existence—for example,

'[All] beings are the bodies of Him who lives in the hearts' (*Āpastamba Dharmasūtra* 1, 8, 22, 4);
'Ātman is indeed [all] gods' (Manu XII, 119);
'[The embodied Ātman,] in the city of nine gates' (BhG. V, 13);
'[The supreme Lord abiding] alike in all beings' (BhG. XIII, 27);
'[The wise see the same thing] in a learned and well-behaved Brahmin, [in a cow, in an elephant, and in a mere dog, and in an outcaste]' (BhG. V, 18);
'Unmanifold in the manifold' (BhG. XVIII, 20; cf. BhG. XIII, 16);
'Vāsudeva (= Kṛṣṇa) is all' (BhG. VII, 19)."

39. If [the pupil] says: "If, your Holiness, Ātman is
'without an inside and without an outside' (Bṛh. Up. IV, 5, 13),
'without and within, unborn' (Mu. Up. II, 1, 2),
'entirely a mass of knowledge' (Bṛh. Up. IV, 5, 13),

like a mass of salt, devoid of all the varieties of forms, and homogeneous like ether, then how is it that the object, means and agent of actions are [either actually] experienced or stated in the śrutis? This is well-known in the śrutis and smṛtis and among common people, and is a matter which causes differences of opinion among hundreds of disputants"—

40. [then] the teacher should reply, "It is the effect of nescience that the object, means and agent of actions are [either actually] experienced or stated in the śrutis; but from the standpoint of the highest truth. Ātman is one alone and [only] appears as many through the vision [affected] by nescience just as the moon [appears] as many to sight [affected] by eye-disease. Duality is the effect of nescience, since it is reasonable [for the śrutis] to condemn the view that [Ātman] is different [from Brahman] by saying,

'Verily, where there seems to be another, [there the one might see the other]' (Bṛh. Up. IV, 3, 31);
'For where there is a duality, as it were, there one sees another' (Bṛh. Up. II, 4, 14);
'Death after death attains he [who thinks he sees manifoldness in this world]' (Bṛh. Up. IV, 4, 19);

> 'But where one sees something else, hears something else, understands something else—that is the small. . . . but the small is the same as the mortal' (Ch. Up. VII, 24, 1);
> '[As, my dear, by one clod of clay everything made of clay may be understood;] the modification is a verbal distinction, a name' (Ch. Up. VI, 1, 4);
> '[So whoever worships another divinity than his Ātman, thinking that] He is one and I another, [he does not know]' (Bṛh. Up. I, 4, 10).

And [the same conclusion is reached] from *śruti* passages which establish oneness, for example,

> '[In the beginning, my dear, this universe was the existent only,] one alone, without a second' (Ch. Up. VI, 2, 1);
> 'Where, verily, [everything has become] one's own [Ātman, then whereby and whom would one smell?]' (Bṛh. Up. II, 4, 14; cf. Bṛh. Up. IV, 5, 15);
> '[Then] what delusion, what sorrow is there [for him who perceives the oneness!]' (Īśā Up. 7)"

41. [The pupil may ask:] "If this be so, your Holiness, for what purpose is difference in object, means, etc., of actions as well as origination and dissolution [of the world] stated in the śrutis?"

42. Then [the teacher] replies, "A man possessed of nescience, being differentiated by the body, etc., thinks that his Ātman is connected with things desirable and undesirable; [and] he does not know how to distinguish the means of attaining things desirable from that of abandoning things undesirable, although he desires to attain things desirable and to abandon things undesirable by some means. The scripture gradually removes his ignorance concerning this matter, but it does not establish the difference in object, means, etc., of actions, since the difference [constitutes] transmigratory existence which is undesirable by nature. Thus [the scripture] uproots nescience which is the view that [Ātman] is different [from Brahman], the root of transmigratory existence, by showing the reasonableness of the oneness of the origination, dissolution, etc. [of the world].

43. "When nescience has been uprooted by means of the śrutis, smṛtis and reasoning, the only knowledge of one who sees the highest truth is established right in this [Ātman] that is described as follows,

> 'Without an inside and without an outside' (Bṛh. Up. II, 5, 19);
> 'Without and within, unborn' (Mu. Up. II, 1, 2);
> like a mass of salt;
>
> '[Entirely] a mass of knowledge' (Bṛh. Up. IV, 5, 13);

and the homogeneous Ātman which is all-pervading like ether. It is not reasonable that [in Ātman] even a trace of impurity should arise from the difference in object and means of actions, origination and dissolution [of the world], and so forth.

44. "A man who wishes to attain this very view of the highest truth should abandon the fivefold form of desire, viz., desires for a son, wealth, and worlds, which result from the misconception that [his] caste, stage of life, etc. [belong to his Ātman]. And as this misconception is contradictory to the right conception, the reasoning for negating the view that [Ātman] is different [from Brahman] is possible; for, when the conception that the sole Ātman is not subject to transmigratory existence has occurred by means of the scripture and reasoning, no contradictory conception persists [any more]; for a conception that fire is cold, or that the body is not subject to old age and death, does not exist. Therefore, since all the rituals and their requisites such as the sacred thread are the effects of nescience, they should be abandoned by him who is established in the view of the highest truth."

Apprehension

45. A certain student, who was tired of transmigratory existence characterized by birth and death and was seeking after final release, approached in the prescribed manner a knower of Brahman who was established in Brahman and who was sitting at his ease, and asked him, "Your Holiness, how can I be released from transmigratory existence? I am aware of the body, the senses and [their] objects; I experience pain in the waking state, and I experience it in the dreaming state after getting relief again and again by entering into the state of deep sleep again and again. Is it indeed my own nature or [is it] due to some cause, my own nature being different? If [this is] my own nature, there is no hope for me to attain final release, since one cannot avoid one's own nature. If [it is] due to some cause, final release is possible after the cause has been removed."

46. The teacher replied to him, "Listen, my child, this is not your own nature but is due to a cause."

47. When he was told this the pupil said, "What is the cause? And what will remove it? And what is my own nature? When the cause is removed, the effect due to the cause no [longer] exists; I will attain to my own nature like a sick person [who recovers his health] when the cause of his disease has been removed."

48. The teacher replied, "The cause is nescience; it is removed by knowledge. When nescience has been removed, you will be released from transmigratory existence which is characterized by birth and death, since its cause will be gone and you will no [longer] experience pain in the dreaming and waking states."

49. The pupil said, "What is that nescience? And what is its object? And what is knowledge, remover of nescience, by which I can realize my own nature?"

50. The teacher replied, "Though you are the highest Ātman and not a transmigrator, you hold the inverted view, 'I am a transmigrator.'

Though you are neither an agent nor an experiencer, and exist [eternally], [you hold the inverted view, 'I am] an agent, an experiencer, and do not exist [eternally]'—this is nescience."

51. The pupil said, "Even though I exist [eternally], still I am not the highest Ātman. My nature is transmigratory existence which is characterized by agency and experiencership, since it is known by sense-perception and other means of knowledge. [Transmigratory existence] has not nesecience as its cause, since nescience cannot have one's own Ātman as its object.

"Nescience is [defined as] the superimposition of the qualities of one [thing] upon another. For example, fully known silver is superimposed upon fully known mother-of-pearl, a fully known person upon a [fully known] tree trunk, or a fully known trunk upon a [fully known] person; but not an unknown [thing] upon [one that is] fully known nor a fully known [thing] upon one that is unknown. Nor is non-Ātman superimposed upon Ātman because Ātman is not fully known, nor Ātman [superimposed] upon non-Ātman, [again] because Ātman is not fully known."

52. The teacher said to him, "That is not right, since there is an exception. My child, it is not possible to make a general rule that a fully known [thing] is superimposed only upon a fully known [thing], since it is a matter of experience that [a fully known thing] is superimposed upon Ātman. [For example,] if one says, 'I am white', 'I am dark', this is [the superimposition] of qualities of the body upon Ātman which is the object of the 'I'-notion. And if one says, 'I am this', this is [the superimposition of Ātman,] which is the object of the 'I'-notion, upon the body."

53. The pupil said, "In that case Ātman is indeed fully known as the object of the 'I'-notion; so is the body as 'this'. If so, [it is only a case of] the mutual superimposition of body and Ātman, both fully known, just like [the mutual superimposition] of tree-trunk and person, and of mother-of-pearl and silver. So, is there a particular reason why Your Holiness said that it is not possible to make a general rule that two fully known [things] are mutually superimposed?"

54. The teacher replied, "Listen. It is true that the body and Ātman are fully known; but they are not fully known to all people as the objects of distinct notions like a tree-trunk and a person."

"How [are they known] then?"

"[They are] always [known] as the objects of constantly non-distinct notions. Since nobody grasps the body and Ātman as two distinct notions, saying, 'This is the body, that is Ātman', people are deluded with regard to Ātman and non-Ātman, thinking, 'Ātman is thus', or 'Ātman is not thus'. This is the particular reason why I said that it is impossible to make a general rule."

55. [The pupil raised another objection:] "Is it not experienced that the thing which is superimposed [upon something] else through nescience does not exist [in the latter]?—for example, silver [does not

exist] in a mother-of-pearl nor a person in a tree-trunk nor a snake in a rope; nor the dark color of the earth's surface in the sky. Likewise, if the body and Ātman are always mutually superimposed in the form of constantly non-distinct notions, then they cannot exist in each other at any time. Silver, etc., which are superimposed through nescience upon mother-of-pearl, etc., do not exist [in the latter] at any time in any way and vice versa; likewise the body and Ātman are mutually superimposed through nescience; this being the case, it would follow as the result that neither the body nor Ātman exists. And it is not acceptable, since it is the theory of the Nihilists.

If, instead of mutual superimposition, [only] the body is superimposed upon Ātman through nescience, it would follow as the result that the body does not exist in Ātman while the latter exists. This is not acceptable either since it is contradictory to sense-perception and other [means of knowledge]. For this reason the body and Ātman are not superimposed upon each other through nescience."

"How then?"

"They are permanently connected with each other like bamboo and pillars [which are interlaced in the structure of a house]."

56. [The teacher said,] "No; because it would follow as the result that [Ātman is] non-eternal and exists for another's sake; since [in your opinion Ātman] is composite, [Ātman exists for another's sake and is non-eternal] just like bamboo, pillars and so forth. Moreover, the Ātman which is assumed by some others to be connected with the body exists for another's sake since it is composite. [Therefore,] it has been first established that the highest [Ātman] is not connected with the body, is different [from it], and is eternal.

57. [The pupil objected,] "Although [the Ātman] is not composite, It is [regarded] merely as the body and superimposed upon the body; from this follow the faults that [the Ātman] does not exist and that [It] is non-eternal and so on. Then there would arise the fault that [you will] arrive at the Nihilists' position that the body has no Ātman."

58. [The teacher replied,] "Not so; because it is accepted that Ātman, like space, is by nature not composite. Although Ātman exists as connected with nothing, it does not follow that the body and other things are without Ātman, just as, although space is connected with nothing, it does not follow that nothing has space. Therefore, there would not arise the fault that [I shall] arrive at the Nihilists' position.

59. "Your further objection,—namely that, if the body does not exist in Ātman [although Ātman exists], this would contradict sense-perception and the other [means of knowledge]: this is not right, because the existence of the body in Ātman is not cognized by sense-perception and the other [means of knowledge]; in Ātman—like a jujube-fruit in a pot, ghee in milk, oil in sesame and a picture on a wall—the body is not cognized by sense-perception and the other [means of knowledge]. Therefore there is no contradiction with sense-perception and the other [means of knowledge]."

60. [The pupil objected,] "How is the body then superimposed upon Ātman which is not established by sense-perception and the other [means of knowledge], and how is Ātman superimposed upon the body?"

61. [The teacher said,] "That is not a fault, because Ātman is established by Its own nature. A general rule cannot be made that superimposition is made only on that which is adventitiously established and not on that which is permanently established, for the dark color and other things on the surface of the earth are seen to be superimposed upon the sky [which is permanently established]."

62. [The pupil asked,] "Your Holiness, is the mutual superimposition of the body and Ātman made by the composite of the body and so on or by Ātman?"

63. The teacher said, "What would happen to you, if [the mutual superimposition] is made by the composite of the body and so on, or if [it] is made by Ātman?"

64. Then the pupil answered, "If I am merely the composite of the body and so on, then I am non-conscious, so I exist for another's sake; consequently, the mutual superimposition of body and Ātman is not effected by me. If I am the highest Ātman different from the composite [of the body and so on], then I am conscious, so I exist for my own sake; consequently, the superimposition [of body] which is the seed of every calamity is effected upon Ātman by me who am conscious."

65. To this the teacher responded, "If you know that the false superimposition is the seed of [every] calamity, then do not make it!"

66. "Your Holiness, I cannot help [it]. I am driven [to do it] by another; I am not independent."

67. [The teacher said,] "Then you are non-conscious, so you do not exist for your own sake. That by which you who are not self-dependent are driven to act is conscious and exists for its own sake; you are only a composite thing [of the body, etc.]"

68. [The pupil objected,] "If I am non-conscious, how do I perceive feelings of pleasure and pain, and [the words] you have spoken?"

69. The teacher said, "Are you different from feelings of pleasure and pain and from [the words] I have spoken, or are you identical [with them]?"

70. The pupil answered, "I am indeed not identical."

"Why?"

"Because I perceive both of them as objects just as [I perceive] a jar and other things [as objects]. If I were identical [with them] I could not perceive either of them; but I do perceive them, so I am different [from both of them]. If [I were] identical [with them] it would follow that the modifications of the feelings of pleasure and pain exist for their own sake and so do [the words] you have spoken; but it is not reasonable that any of them exists for their own sake, for the pleasure and pain produced by sandal and a thorn are not for the sake of the sandal and the thorn, nor is use made of a jar for the sake of the jar.

So, the sandal and other things serve my purpose, i.e., the purpose of their perceiver, since I who am different from them perceive all the objects seated in the intellect."

71. The teacher said to him, "So then, you exist for your own sake since you are conscious. You are not driven [to act] by another. A conscious being is neither dependent on another nor driven [to act] by another, for it is not reasonable that a conscious being should exist for the sake of another conscious being since they are equal like two lights. Nor does a conscious being exist for the sake of a non-conscious being since it is not reasonable that a non-conscious being should have any connection with its own object precisely because it is non-conscious. Nor does experience show that two non-conscious beings exist for each other, as for example a stick of wood and a wall do not fulfill each other's purposes."

72. [The pupil objected,] "Is it not experienced that a servant and his master, though they are equal in the sense of being conscious, exist for each other?"

73. [The teacher said,] "It is not so, for what [I] meant was that you have consciousness just as fire has heat and light. And [in this meaning I] cited the example, 'like two lights'. This being the case, you perceive everything seated in your intellect through your own nature, i.e., the transcendentally changeless, eternal, pure consciousness which is equivalent to heat and light of fire. And if you admit that Ātman is always without distinctions, why did you say, 'After getting relief again and again in the state of deep sleep, I perceive pain in the waking and dreaming states. Is this indeed my own nature or [is it] due to some cause?' Has this delusion left [you now] or not?"

74. To this the pupil replied, "Your Holiness, the delusion has gone thanks to your gracious assistance; but I am in doubt as to how I am transcendentally changeless."

"How?"

"Sound and other [external objects] are not self-established, since they are not conscious. But they [are established] through the rise of notions which take the forms of sound and other [external objects]. It is impossible for notions to be self-established, since they have mutually exclusive attributes and the forms [of external objects] such as blue and yellow. It is, therefore, understood that [notions] are caused by the forms of the external objects; so, [notions] are established as possessing the forms of external objects, i.e., the forms of sound, etc. Likewise, notions, which are the modifications of a thing (= the intellect), the substratum of the 'I'-notion, are also composite, so it is reasonable that they are non-conscious; therefore, as it is impossible that they exist for their own sake, they, like sound and other [external objects], are established as objects to be perceived by a perceiver different in nature [from them]. If I am not composite, I have pure consciousness as my nature; so I exist for my own sake. Nevertheless, I am a perceiver of notions which have the forms [of the external objects] such as blue and yellow [and so] I am indeed subject to change. [For the above reason, I am] in doubt as to how [I am] transcendentally changeless."

75. The teacher said to him, "Your doubt is not reasonable. [Your] perception of those notions is necessary and entire; for this very reason [you] are not subject to transformation. It is, therefore, established that [you] are transcendentally changeless. But you have said that precisely the reason for the above positive conclusion—namely, that [you] perceive the entire movement of the mind—is the reason for [your] doubt [concerning your transcendentally changelessness].—This is why [your doubt is not reasonable].

"If indeed you were subject to transformation, you would not perceive the entire movement of the mind which is your object, just as the mind [does not perceive] its [entire] object and just as the senses [do not perceive] their [entire] objects, and similarly you as Ātman would not perceive even a part of your object. Therefore, you are transcendentally changeless."

76. Then [the pupil] said, "Perception is what is meant by the verbal root, that is, nothing but change; it is contradictory [to this fact] to say that [the nature of] the perceiver is transcendentally changeless."

77. [The teacher said,] "That is not right, for [the term] 'perception' is used figuratively in the sense of a change which is meant by the verbal root; whatever the notion of the intellect may be, that is what is meant by the verbal root; [the notion of the intellect] has change as its nature and end with the result that the perception of Ātman falsely appears [as perceiver]; thus the notion of the intellect is figuratively indicated by the term, 'perception'. For example, the cutting action results [in the static state] that [the object to be cut] is separated in two parts; thus [the term, 'cutting', in the sense of an object to be cut being separated in two parts,] is used figuratively as [the cutting action] which is meant by the verbal root."

78. To this the pupil objected, "Your Holiness, the example cannot explain my transcendental changelessness."

"Why not?"

" 'Cutting' which results in a change in the object to be cut is used figuratively as [the cutting action] which is meant by the verbal root; in the same manner, if the notion of the intellect, which is figuratively indicated by the term 'perception' and is meant by the verbal root, results also in a change in the perception of Ātman, [the example] cannot explain Ātman's transcendental changelessness."

79. The teacher said, "It would be true, if there were a distinction between perception and perceiver. The perceiver is indeed nothing but eternal perception. And it is not [right] that perception and perceiver are different as in the doctrine of the logicians."

80. [The pupil said,] "How does that [action] which is meant by the verbal root result in perception?"

81. [The teacher] answered, "Listen, [I] said that [it] ends with the result that the perception [of Ātman] falsely appears [as perceiver]. Did you not hear? I did not say that [it] results in the production of any change in Ātman."

82. The pupil said, "Why then did you say that if I am transcendentally changeless I am the perceiver of the entire movement of the mind which is my object?"

83. The teacher said to him, "I told [you] only the truth. Precisely because [you are the perceiver of the entire movement of the mind], I said, you are transcendentally changeless."

84. "If so, Your Holiness, I am of the nature of transcendentally changeless and eternal perception whereas the actions of the intellect, which have the forms of [external objects] such as sound, arise and end with the result that my own nature which is perception falsely appears [as perceiver]. Then what is my fault?"

85. [The teacher replied,] "You are right. [You] have no fault. The fault is only nescience as I have said before."

86. [The pupil said,] "If, Your Holiness, as in the state of deep sleep I undergo no change, how [do I experience] the dreaming and waking states?"

87. The teacher said to him, "But do you experience [these states] continuously?"

88. [The pupil answered,] "Certainly I do experience [them], but intermittently and not continuously."

89. The teacher said [to him,] "Both of them are adventitious [and] not your nature. If [they] were your nature [they] would be self-established and continuous like your nature, which is pure consciousness. Moreover, the dreaming and waking states are not your nature, for [they] depart [from you] like clothes and so on. It is certainly not experienced that the nature of anything, whatever it may be, departs from it. But the dreaming and waking states depart from the state of pure consciousness-only. If one's own nature were to depart [from oneself] in the state of deep sleep, it would be negated by saying, 'It has perished', 'It does not exist', since the adventitious attributes which are not one's own nature are seen to consist in both [perishableness and non-existence], for example, wealth, clothes and the like are seen to perish and things which have been obtained in dream or delusion are seen to be non-existent."

90. [The pupil objected,] "[If] so, Your Holiness, it follows [either] that my own nature, i.e., pure consciousness, is also adventitious, since [I] perceive in the dreaming and waking states but not in the state of deep sleep; or that I am not of the nature of pure consciousness."

91. [The teacher replied,] "No. Look. Because that is not reasonable. If you [insist on] looking at your own nature, i.e., pure consciousness, as adventitious, do so! We cannot establish it logically even in a hundred years, nor can any other, i.e., non-conscious, being do so. As [that adventitious consciousness] is composite, nobody can logically

deny that [it] exists for another's sake, is manifold and perishable; for what does not exist for its own sake is not self-established, as we have said before. Nobody can, however, deny that Ātman, which is of the nature of pure consciousness, is self-established; so It does not depend upon anything else, since It does not depart [from anybody]."

92. [The pupil objected,] "Did I not point out that [It] does depart [from me] when I said that in the state of deep sleep I do not see?"

93. [The teacher replied] "That is not right, for it is contradictory."

"How is it a contradiction?"

"Although you are [in truth] seeing, you say, 'I do not see.' This is contradictory."

"But at no time in the state of deep sleep, Your Holiness, have I ever seen pure consciousness or anything else."

"Then you are seeing in the state of deep sleep; for you deny only the seen object, not the seeing. I said that your seeing is pure consciousness. That [eternally] existing one by which you deny [the existence of the seen object] when you say that nothing has been seen, [that precisely] is the seeing, that is pure consciousness. Thus as [It] does not ever depart [from you] [Its] transcendental changelessness and eternity are established solely by Itself without depending upon any means of knowledge. The knower, though self-established, requires means of knowledge for the discernment of an object to be known other [than itself]. And that eternal discernment, which is required for discerning something else (= non-Ātman) which does not have discernment as its nature,—that is certainly eternal, transcendentally changeless and of a self-effulgent nature. The eternal discernment does not require any means of knowledge in order to be itself the means of knowledge or the knower since the eternal discernment is by nature the means of knowledge or the knower. [This is illustrated by the following] example: iron or water requires fire or sun [to obtain] light and heat since light and heat are not their nature; but fire and sun do not require [anything else] for light and heat since [these] are always their nature."

94. "If [you object,] 'There is empirical knowledge in so far as it is not eternal and [there is] no [empirical knowledge], if it is eternal'—

95. "[then I reply,] 'Not so; because it is impossible to make a distinction between eternal apprehension and non-eternal apprehension; when apprehension is empirical knowledge, such distinction is not apprehended that empirical knowledge is non-eternal apprehension and not eternal one.'—

96. "If [you object,] 'When [empirical knowledge] is eternal [apprehension, it] does not require the knower, but when [empirical knowledge] is non-eternal [apprehension], apprehension requires [the knower], since it is mediated by [the knower's] effort.—There would be the above distinction',—

97. "then, it is established that the knower itself is self-established, since [it] does not require any means of knowledge.—

98. "If [you object,] 'Even when [apprehension or empirical knowledge] does not exist, [the knower] does not require [any means of knowledge], since [the knower] is eternal', [my reply is,] 'No; because apprehension exists only in [the knower] itself. Thus your opinion is refuted'.—

99. "If the knower is dependent upon the means of knowledge for its establishment, where does the desire to know belong? It is admitted that that to which the desire to know belongs is indeed the knower. And the object of this desire to know is the object to be known, not the knower, since if the object [of the desire to know] were the knower, a *regressus ad infinitum* with regard to the knower and the desire to know would result; there would be a second knower for the first one, a third knower for the second, and so on. Such would be the case if the desire to know had the knower as its object. And the knower itself cannot be the object to be known, since it is never mediated [by anything]; what in this world is called the object to be known is established, when it is mediated by the rise of desire, remembrance, effort and means of knowledge which belong to the knower. In no other way is apprehension experienced with regard to the object to be known. And it cannot be assumed that the knower itself is mediated by any of the knower's own desire and the like. And remembrance has as its object the object to be remembered and not the subject of remembrance. Likewise, desire has as its object only the object desired and not the one who desires. If remembrance and desire had as their objects the subjects of remembrance and the one who desires respectively, a *regressus ad infinitum* would be inevitable as before.—

100. "If [you say,] 'If apprehension which has the knower as its object is impossible, the knower would not be apprehended'—

101. "Not so; because the apprehension of the apprehender has as its object the object to be apprehended. If [it] were to have the apprehender as its object, a *regressus ad infinitum* would result as before. And it has been proved before that apprehension, i.e., the transcendentally changeless and eternal light of Ātman, is established in Ātman without depending upon anything else as heat and light are in fire, the sun and so on. If apprehension, i.e., the light of Ātman which is pure consciousness were not eternal in one's own Ātman, it would be impossible for Ātman to exist for Its own sake; as It would be composite like the aggregate of the body and senses, It would exist for another's sake and be possessed of faults as we have already said."

"How?"

"If the light of Ātman which is pure consciousness, were not eternal in one's own Ātman, it would be mediated by remembrance and the like and so it would be composite. And as this light of pure consciousness would therefore not exist in Ātman before Its origination and after Its destruction, It would exist for another's sake, since It would be composite like the eye and so on. And if the light of pure consciousness exists in Ātman as something which has arisen, then Ātman does not exist for Its own sake, since it is established according to the existence and absence of that light of pure consciousness that Ātman exists for Its own sake and non-Ātman exists for another's sake. It is therefore established that Ātman is the eternal light of pure consciousness without depending upon anything else."

102. [The pupil objected,] "If so, [and] if the knower is not the subject of empirical knowledge, how is it a knower?"

103. [The teacher] answered, "Because there is no distinction in the nature of empirical knowledge, since empirical knowledge is apprehension. There is no distinction in the nature of this [empirical knowledge] whether it be non-eternal, preceded by remembrance, desire and the like, or transcendentally changeless and eternal, just as there is no distinction in the nature of what is meant by verbal root such as *sthā* (stand), whether it is a non-eternal result preceded by 'going' and other [forms of actions], or an eternal result not preceded [by 'going' or any other forms of actions]; so the same expression is found [in both cases]—'People stand', 'The mountains stand' and so forth. Likewise, although the knower is of the nature of eternal apprehension, it is not contradictory to designate [It] as 'knower', since the result is the same."

104. Here the pupil said, "Ātman, which is of the nature of eternal apprehension, is changeless, so it is impossible for Ātman to be an agent without being connected with the body and the senses, just as a carpenter and other [agents are connected] with an axe and so on. And if that which is by nature not composite were to use the body and the senses, a *regressus ad infinitum* would result. But the carpenter and the other [agents] are constantly connected with the body and the senses; so, when [they] use an axe and the like, no *regressus ad infinitum* occurs."

105. [The teacher said,] "But in that case [Ātman], which is by nature not composite, cannot be an agent when It makes no use of instruments; [It] would have to use an instrument [to be an agent]. [But] the use [of an instrument] would be a change; so in becoming an agent which causes that [change], [It] should use another instrument, [and] in using this instrument, [It] should also use another one. Thus if the knower is independent, a *regressus ad infinitum* is inevitable.

"And no action causes Ātman to act, since [the action] which has not been performed does not have its own nature. If [you object,] 'Something other [than Ātman] approaches Ātman and causes It to perform an action', [I reply,] 'No; because it is impossible for anything other [than Ātman] to be self-established, a non-object, and so forth; it is not experienced that anything else but Ātman, being non-conscious, is self-evident. Sound and all other [objects] are established when they are known by a notion which ends with the result of apprehension.

"If apprehension were to belong to anything else but Ātman, It would also be Ātman, not composite, existing for Its own sake, and not for another. And we cannot apprehend that the body, the senses and their objects exist for their own sake, since it is experienced that they depend for their establishment upon the notions which result in apprehension."

106. [The pupil objected,] "In apprehending the body nobody depends upon any other notions due to sense-perception and other [means of knowledge]."

107. [The teacher said,] "Certainly in the waking state it would be so. But in the states of death and deep sleep the body also depends upon sense-perception and other means of knowledge for its establishment. This is true of the senses. Sound and other [external objects] are indeed transformed into the form of the body and senses; so, [the body and the senses] depend upon sense-perception and other means of knowledge for [their] establishment. And 'establishment' (*siddhi*) is apprehension, i.e., the result of the means of knowledge as we have already said, and this apprehension is transcendentally changeless, self-established, and by nature the light of Ātman."

108. Here [the pupil] objected, saying, "It is contradictory to say that apprehension is the result of the means of knowledge and that it is by nature the transcendentally changeless and eternal light of Ātman."

To this [the teacher] said, "It is not contradictory."

"How then [is it not contradictory]?"

"Although [apprehension] is transcendentally changeless and eternal, [it] appears at the end of the notion [-forming process] due to sense-perception and other [means of knowledge] since [the notion-forming process] aims at it. If the notion due to sense-perception and other [means of knowledge] is non-eternal, [apprehension, though eternal,] appears as if it were non-eternal. Therefore, [apprehension] is figuratively called the result of the means of knowledge."

109. [The pupil said,] "If so, Your Holiness, apprehension is transcendentally changeless, eternal, indeed of the nature of the light of Ātman, and self-established, since it does not depend upon any means of knowledge with regard to itself; everything other than this is non-conscious and exists for another's sake, since it acts together [with others].

"And because of this nature of being apprehended as a notion causing pleasure, pain and delusion, [non-Ātman] exists for another's sake; on account of this very nature non-Ātman exists and not on account of any other nature. It is therefore merely non-existent from the standpoint of the highest truth. Just as it is experienced in this world that a snake [superimposed] upon a rope does not exist nor water in a mirage, and the like, unless they are apprehended [as a notion], so it is reasonable that duality in the waking and dreaming states also does not exist unless it is apprehended [as a notion]. In this manner, Your Holiness, apprehension, i.e., the light of Ātman, is uninterrupted; so it is transcendentally changeless, eternal and non-dual, since it is never absent from any of the various notions. But various notions are absent from apprehension. Just as in the dreaming state the notions in different forms such as blue and yellow, which are absent from that apprehension, are said to be non-existent from the standpoint of the highest truth, so in the waking state also, the various notions such as blue and yellow, which are absent from this very apprehension, must by nature be untrue. And there is no apprehender different from this apprehension to apprehend it; therefore it can itself neither be accepted nor rejected by its own nature, since there is nothing else."

110. [The teacher said,] "Exactly so it is. It is nescience that is the cause of transmigratory existence which is characterized by the waking and dreaming states. The remover of this nescience is knowledge. And so you have reached fearlessness. From now on you will not perceive any pain in the waking and dreaming states. You are released from the sufferings of transmigratory existence."

111. [The pupil said,] "Om."

Parisaṃkhyāna Meditation

112. This *Parisaṃkhyāna* meditation is described for seekers after final release who are devoting themselves to destroying their acquired merit and demerit and do not wish to accumulate any more. Nescience causes faults (= passion and aversion); they cause the activities of speech, mind and body; and from these activities are accumulated karmans of which [in turn] the results are desirable, undesirable, and mixed. For the sake of final release from those karmans [this *Parisaṃkhyāna* meditation is described].

113. Now, sound, touch, form-and-color, taste and odor are the objects of the senses; they are to be perceived by the ear and other [senses]. Therefore, they do not have any knowledge of themselves nor of others, since they are merely things evolved like clay and the like. And they are perceived through the ear and other [senses].

And that by which they are perceived is of a different nature since it is a perceiver. Because they are connected with one another, sound and other [objects of the senses] are possessed of many attributes such as birth, growth, change of state, decay and destruction; connection and separation; appearance and disappearance; effect of change and cause of change; field (= female?) and seed (= male?). They are also commonly possessed of many [other] attributes such as pleasure and pain. Their perceiver is different in its nature from all the attributes of sound and the other [objects of the senses], precisely because it is their perceiver.

114. So the wise man who is tormented by sound and the other [objects of the senses] which are being perceived, should perform *Parisaṃkhyāna* meditation as follows:

115. I (= Ātman) am of the nature of Seeing, non-object (= subject) unconnected [with anything], changeless, motionless, endless, fearless and absolutely subtle. So sound cannot make me its object and touch me, whether as mere noise in general or as [sound] of particular qualities—pleasant [sounds] such as the first note of music or the desirable words of praise and the like, or the undesirable words of un-

truth, disgust, humiliation, abuse, and the like—since I am unconnected [with sound]. For this very reason neither loss nor gain is caused [in me] by sound. Therefore, what can the pleasant sound of praise, the unpleasant sound of blame, and so on do to me? Indeed a pleasant sound may produce gain, and an unpleasant one destruction, for a man lacking in discriminating knowledge, who regards sound as [connected with his] Ātman since he has no discriminating knowledge. But for me who am endowed with discriminating knowledge [sound] cannot produce even a hair's breadth [of gain or loss].

In the very same manner [touch] does not produce for me any change of gain and loss, whether as touch in general or as touch in particular forms—the unpleasant [touch] of cold, heat, softness, hardness, etc., and of fever, stomachache, etc., and any pleasant [touch] either inherent in the body or caused by external and adventitious [objects] —since I am devoid of touch, just as a blow with the fist and the like [does not produce any change] in the sky.

Likewise [form-and-color] produces neither loss nor gain for me, whether as form-and-color in general or as form-and-color in particular, pleasant or unpleasant, such as the female characteristics of a woman and the like, since I am devoid of form-and-color.

Similarly, [taste] produces neither loss nor gain for me who am by nature devoid of taste, whether as taste in general or as taste in particular forms [,pleasant or unpleasant,] such as sweetness, sourness, saltiness, pungency, bitterness, astringency which are perceived by the dull-witted.

In like manner [odor] produces neither loss nor gain for me who am by nature devoid of odor, whether as odor in general or as odor in particular forms, pleasant or unpleasant, such as [the odor] of flowers, etc., and ointment, etc. That is because the *śruti* says:

> "That which is soundless, touchless, formless, imperishable, also tasteless, constant, odorless, . . . [—having perceived that, one is freed from the jaws of death]" (Ka. Up. III, 15).

116. Moreover, whatever sound and the other external [objects of the senses] may be, they are changed into the form of the body, and into the form of the ear and the other [senses] which perceive them, and into the form of the two internal organs and their objects [such as pleasure and pain], since they are mutually connected and composite in all cases of actions. This being the case, to me, a man of knowledge, nobody is foe, friend or neutral.

In this context, if anybody, through a misconception [about Ātman] due to false knowledge, were to wish to connect [me] with [anything], pleasant or unpleasant, which appears as the result of action, he wishes in vain to connect [me] with it, since I am not its object according to the *smṛti* passage:

> "Unmanifest he, unthinkable he, [unchangeable he is declared to be]" (BhG. II, 25).

Likewise, I am not to be changed by [any of] the five elements, since I am not their object according to the *smṛti* passage:

> "Not to be cut is he, not to be burnt is he, [not to be wet nor yet dried]" (BhG. II, 24).

Furthermore, paying attention only to the aggregate of the body and the senses, [people, both] devoted and adverse to me, have the desire to connect [me] with things, pleasant, unpleasant, etc., and therefrom results the acquisition of merit, demerit, and the like. It belongs only to them and does not occur in me who am free from old age, death and fear, since the śrutis and the smṛtis say:

> "Neither what has been done nor what has been left undone affects It" (Bṛh. Up. IV, 4, 22);
> "[This is the constant greatness of knower of Brahman]; he does not increase nor become less by action" (Bṛh. Up. IV, 4, 23);
> "[This is] without and within, unborn" (Mu. Up. II, 1, 2);
> "[So the one inner Ātman of all beings] is not afflicted with the suffering of the world, being outside of it" (Ka. Up. V, 11); etc.

That is because anything other than Ātman does not exist,—this is the highest reason.

As duality does not exist, all the sentences of the *Upaniṣads* concerning non-duality of Ātman should be fully contemplated, should be contemplated.

BRAHMASŪTRABHĀṢYA

Śaṁkara's commentary (*bhāṣya*) on the *Brahmasūtras* is considered by most advaitins, and by most Western and Indian scholars, to be his greatest work. Many commentaries on his commentary have been written by later advaitic thinkers, and it would not be an exaggeration to say that Śaṁkara's *Brahmasūtrabhāṣya* is *the* foundational work of classical Advaita Vedānta. In this work Śaṁkara not only makes systematic sense, as it were, out of the cryptic and laconic sayings of the Sūtras, he also articulates the main philosophical principles of Advaita, offers careful and sometimes persuasive arguments in their support, and—as we have seen —sets forth extensive criticisms of rival "orthodox" and "heterodox" philosophical systems.

The *Brahmasūtras*, as noted previously, is divided into four adhyāyas or parts with four pādas or subsections under each one. The basic philosophical problems which Advaita confronts are not presented in the Sūtras, and consequently in the commentary, according to any very obvious order. We have not, though, imposed any topical headings on the selections or rearranged the materials to conform to some preconceived model of what a logical order of ideas should be. Most of the material which we have selected is taken from adhyāyas I and II, which form the more "philosophical" portion of the work. We have concentrated attention on this material for we are interested here in understanding the philosophy of Vedānta and not in deciding which Vedāntic school is closest, in letter and spirit, to the original Vedāntic texts.

It is necessary, however, to understand something of the exegetical method which Śaṁkara employs in his work, for this method is at times closely intertwined with his style of philosophical reasoning. There is, furthermore, little doubt that Śaṁkara himself sees exegesis and reasoning as necessary to each other, for he rather sharply criticizes the use of "mere reason" in matters which are appropriate to "revelation" alone (e.g., II, 1, 6, and 11). Śaṁkara's general exegetical method is simple and direct. To put it baldly: when *śruti* or *smṛti* make metaphysical statements which, when taken literally, support the general position of Advaita then they are taken in their "primary" meaning; that is to say, their literalness is accepted. When, however, the literal meaning of metaphysical statements found in "scripture" conflict with advaitic principles they are then taken in a "secondary" sense; that is, another fundamental meaning is assigned to them. This arises most often in those cases where *śruti* seems to be upholding the idea of differentiation in the divine nature. Śaṁkara argues here that these statements are put forward only as meditative aids for those who are caught up in "ignorance" (*avidyā*): they are not meant to be true in themselves.

Śaṁkara's justification for this method is set forth in several places and in several different ways. The strongest philosophical case he makes for it is perhaps to be found in the Introduction he wrote for his commentary wherein he describes in detail the process of "superimposition" (*adhyāsa*)—of how we wrongly attribute to one thing the qualities which properly belong to another thing—and how this process leads to the performance of ritual action.

The following selections from the *Brahmasūtrabhāṣya* are from *The Vedānta-Sūtras: with the Commentary by Saṅkarācārya*, translated by George Thibaut, The Sacred Books of the East, vols. 34 and 38, edited by F. Max Müller (Oxford: The Clarendon Press, 1890, 1896).

Śaṁkara's Introduction

It is a matter not requiring any proof that the object and the subject whose respective spheres are the notion of the 'Thou' (the Non-Ego) and the 'Ego,' and which are opposed to each other as much as darkness and light are, cannot be identified. All the less can their respective attributes be identified. Hence it follows that it is wrong to superimpose upon the subject—whose Self is intelligence, and which has for its sphere the notion of the Ego—the object whose sphere is the notion of the Non-Ego, and the attributes of the object, and vice versa to superimpose the subject and the attributes of the subject on the object. In spite of this it is on the part of man a natural procedure—which has its cause in wrong knowledge—not to distinguish the two entities (object and subject) and their respective attributes, although they are absolutely distinct, but to superimpose upon each the characteristic nature and the attributes of the other, and thus, coupling the Real and the Unreal, to make use of expressions such as 'That am I,' 'That is mine.' —But what have we to understand by the term 'superimposition?'—The apparent presentation, in the form of remembrance, to consciousness of something previously observed, in some other thing.

Some indeed define the term 'superimposition' as the superimposition of the attributes of one thing on another thing. Others, again, define superimposition as the error founded on the non-apprehension of the difference of that which is superimposed from that on which it is superimposed. Others, again, define it as the fictitious assumption of attributes contrary to the nature of that thing on which something else is superimposed. But all these definitions agree in so far as they represent superimposition as the apparent presentation of the attributes of one thing in another thing. And therewith agrees also the popular view which is exemplified by expressions such as the following: 'Mother-of-pearl appears like silver,' 'The moon although one only appears as if she were double.' But how is it possible that on the interior Self which itself is not an object there should be superimposed objects and their attributes? For every one superimposes an object only on such other objects as are placed before him (i.e. in contact with his sense-organs), and you have said before that the interior Self which is entirely disconnected from the idea of the Thou (the Non-Ego) is never an object. It is not, we reply, non-object in the absolute sense. For it is the object of the notion of the Ego, and the interior Self is well known to exist on account of its immediate (intuitive) presentation. Nor is it an exceptionless rule that objects can be superimposed only on such other objects as are before us, i.e. in contact with our sense-organs; for non-discerning men superimpose on the ether, which is not the object of sensuous perception, dark-blue colour.

Hence it follows that the assumption of the Non-Self being superimposed on the interior Self is not unreasonable.

This superimposition thus defined, learned men consider to be Nescience (*avidyā*), and the ascertainment of the true nature of that which is (the Self) by means of the discrimination of that (which is superimposed on the Self), they call knowledge (*vidyā*). There being such knowledge (neither the Self nor the Non-Self) are affected in the least by any blemish or (good) quality produced by their mutual superimposition. The mutual superimposition of the Self and the Non-Self, which is termed Nescience, is the presupposition on which there base all the practical distinctions—those made in ordinary life as well as those laid down by the Veda—between means of knowledge, objects of knowledge (and knowing persons), and all scriptual texts, whether they are concerned with injunctions and prohibitions (of meritorious and non-meritorious actions), or with final release.—But how can the means of right knowledge such as perception, inference, &c., and scriptual texts have for their object that which is dependent on Nescience? —Because we reply, the means of right knowledge cannot operate unless there be a knowing personality, and because the existence of the latter depends on the erroneous notion that the body, the sense, and so on, are identical with, or belong to, the Self of the knowing person. For without the employment of the senses, perception and the other means of right knowledge cannot operate. And without a basis (i.e. the body) the senses cannot act. Nor does anybody act by means of a body on which the nature of the Self is not superimposed. Nor can, in the absence of all that, the Self which, in its own nature is free from all contact, become a knowing agent. And if there is no knowing agent, the means of right knowledge cannot operate (as said above). Hence perception and the other means of right knowledge, and the Vedic texts have for their object that which is dependent on Nescience. . . . With reference again to that kind of activity which is founded on the Veda (sacrifices and the like), it is true indeed that the reflecting man who is qualified to enter on it, does so not without knowing that the Self has a relation to another world; yet that qualification does not depend on the knowledge, derivable from the Vedānta texts, of the true nature of the Self as free from all wants, raised above the distinctions of the Brāhmaṇa and Kṣatriya-classes and so on, transcending transmigratory existence. For such knowledge is useless and even contradictory to the claim (on the part of sacrificers, &c. to perform certain actions and enjoy their fruits). And before such knowledge of the Self has arisen, the Vedic texts continue in their operation, to have for their object that which is dependent on Nescience. For such texts as the following, 'A Brāhmaṇa is to sacrifice,' are operative only on the supposition that on the Self are superimposed particular conditions such as caste, state of life, age, outward circumstances, and so on. That by superimposition we have to understand the notion of something in some other thing we have already explained. (The superimposition of the Non-Self will be understood more definitely from the following examples.) Extra-personal attributes are superimposed on the Self, if a man considers himself sound and entire, or the contrary, as long as his wife, children, and so on are sound and entire or not. Attributes of the body are superimposed on the Self, if a man thinks of himself (his Self) as stout, lean, fair, as standing, walking, or jumping. Attributes of the sense-organs, if he thinks 'I am mute, or deaf, or one-eyed, or blind.' Attributes of the internal organ when he considers himself subject to desire, intention, doubt, determination, and so on. Thus the producer of the notion of the Ego (i.e. the internal organ) is superimposed on the interior Self, which, in reality, is the witness of all the modifications of the internal organ, and vice versa the interior Self, which is the witness of everything, is superimposed on the internal organ, the senses, and so on. In this way there goes on this natural beginning—and endless superimposition, which appears in the form of wrong conception, is the cause of individual souls appearing as agents and enjoyers (of the results of their actions), and is observed by every one.

(Sūtra. Then therefore the enquiry into Brahman.)

The word 'then' is here to be taken as denoting immediate consecution; not as indicating the introduction of a new subject to be entered upon; for the enquiry into Brahman (more literally, the desire of knowing Brahman) is not of that nature. Nor has the word 'then' the sense of auspiciousness (or blessing); for a word of that meaning could not be properly construed as a part of the sentence. The word 'then' rather acts as an auspicious term by being pronounced and heard merely, while it denotes at the same time something else, viz. immediate consecution as said above. That the latter is its meaning follows moreover from the circumstance that the relation in which the result stands to the previous topic (viewed as the cause of the result) is non-separate from the relation of immediate consecution.

If, then, the word 'then' intimates immediate consecution it must be explained on what antecedent the enquiry into Brahman specially depends; just as the enquiry into active religious duty (which forms the subject of the Pūrvā Mīmāṁsā) specially depends on the antecedent reading of the Veda. The reading of the Veda indeed is the common antecedent (for those who wish to enter on an enquiry into religious duty as well as for those desirous of knowing Brahman.) The special question with regard to the enquiry into Brahman is whether it presupposes as its antecedent the understanding of the acts of religious duty (which is acquired by means of the Pūrvā Mīmāṁsā.) To this question we reply in the negative, because for a man who has read the Vedānta-parts of the Veda it is possible to enter on the enquiry into Brahman even before engaging in the enquiry into religious duty. . . . The knowledge of active religious duty has for its fruit transitory felicity, and that again depends on the performance of religious acts. The enquiry into Brahman, on the other hand, has for its fruit eternal bliss, and does not depend on the performance of any acts. Acts of religious duty do not yet exist at the time when they are enquired into, but are something to be accomplished (in the future); for they depend on the activity of man. In the *Brahma-mīmāṁsā,* on the other hand, the object of enquiry, i.e. Brahman, is something already accomplished (existent),—for it is eternal,—and does not depend on human energy. The two enquiries differ moreover in so far as the operation of their respective fundamental texts is concerned. For the fundamental texts on which active religious duty depend convey information to man in so far only as they enjoin on him their own particular subjects (sacrifice, &c.); while the fundamental texts about Brahman merely instruct man, without laying on him the injunction of being instructed, instruction being their immediate result. The case is analogous to that of the information regarding objects of sense which ensues as soon as the objects are approximated to the senses. It therefore is requisite that something should be stated subsequent to which the enquiry into Brahman is proposed.—Well, then, we maintain that the antecedent conditions are the discrimination of what is eternal and what is non-eternal; the renunciation of all desire to enjoy the fruit (of one's actions) both here and hereafter; the acquirement of tranquillity, self-restraint, and the other means, and the desire of final release. If these conditions exist, a man may, either before entering on an enquiry into active religious duty or after that, engage in the enquiry into Brahman and come to know it; but not otherwise. The word 'then' therefore intimates that the enquiry into Brahman is subsequent to the acquisition of the above-mentioned (spiritual) means. . . .

But, it may be asked, is Brahman known or not known (previously to the enquiry into its nature)? If it is known we need not enter on an enquiry concerning it; if it is not known we can not enter on such an enquiry.

We reply that Brahman is known. Brahman, which is all-knowing and endowed with all powers, whose essential nature is eternal purity, intelligence, and freedom, exists. For if we consider the derivation of the word 'Brahman,' from the root *bṛh*, 'to be great,' we at once understand that eternal purity, and so on, belong to Brahman. Moreover the existence of Brahman is known on the ground of its being the Self of every one. For every one is conscious of the existence of (his) Self, and never thinks 'I am not.' If the existence of the Self were not known, every one would think 'I am not.' And this Self (of whose existence all are conscious) is Brahman. But if Brahman is generally known as the Self, there is no room for an enquiry into it! Not so, we reply; for there is a conflict of opinions as to its special nature. Unlearned people and the Lokāyatikas are of opinion that the mere body endowed with the quality of intelligence is the Self; others that the organs endowed with intelligence are the Self; others maintain that the internal organ is the Self; others, again, that the Self is a mere momentary idea; others, again, that it is the Void. Others, again (to proceed to the opinion of such as acknowledge the authority of the Veda), maintain that there is a transmigrating being different from the body, and so on, which is both agent and enjoyer (of the fruits of action); others teach that that being is enjoying only, not acting; others believe that in addition to the individual souls, there is an all-knowing, all-powerful Lord. Others, finally, (i.e. the Vedāntins) maintain that the Lord is the Self of the enjoyer (i.e. of the individual soul whose individual existence is apparent only, the product of Nescience).

Thus there are many various opinions, basing part of them on sound arguments and scriptural texts, part of them on fallacious arguments and scriptural texts misunderstood. If therefore a man would embrace some one of these opinions without previous consideration, he would bar himself from the highest beatitude and incur grievous loss. . . . (I, 1, 1)

. . . The full sense of the Sūtra . . . is: That omniscient omnipotent cause from which proceed the origin, subsistence, and dissolution of this world—which world is differentiated by names and forms, contains many agents and enjoyers, is the abode of the fruits of actions, these fruits having their definite places, time, and causes, and the nature of whose arrangement cannot even be conceived by the mind—that cause, we say, is Brahman. . . .

. . . [T]he knowledge of the real nature of a thing does not depend on the notions of man, but only on the thing itself. For to think with regard to a post, 'this is a post or a man, or something else,' is not knowledge of truth; the two ideas, 'it is a man or something else,' being false, and only the third idea, 'it is a post,' which depends on the thing itself, falling under the head of true knowledge. Thus true knowledge of all existing things depends on the things themselves, and hence the knowledge of Brahman all depends altogether on the thing, i.e. Brahman itself.—But, it might be said, as Brahman is an existing substance, it will be the object of the other means of right knowledge also, and from this it follows that a discussion of the Vedānta-texts is purposeless.—This we deny; for as Brahman is not an object of the senses, it has no connection with those other means of knowledge. For the senses have, according to their nature, only external things for their objects, not Brahman. If Brahman were an object of the senses, we might perceive that the world is connected with Brahman as its effect; but as the effect only (i.e. the world) is perceived, it is impossible to decide (through perception) whether it is connected with Brahman or something else. Therefore the Sūtra under discussion is not meant to propound inference (as the means of knowing Brahman), but rather to set forth a Vedānta-text.—Which, then, is the Vedānta-text which the Sūtra points at as having to be considered with reference to the characteristics of Brahman?—It is the passage Taitt. Up. III, 1, 'Bhṛigu Vāruṇi went to his father Varuṇa, saying, Sir, teach me Brahman,' &c., up to 'That from whence these beings are born, that by which, when born, they live, that into which they enter at their death, try to know that. That is Brahman.' The sentence finally determining the sense of this passage is found III, 6: 'From bliss these beings are born; by bliss, when born, they live; into bliss they enter at their death.' Other passages also are to be adduced which declare the cause to be the almighty Being, whose essential nature is eternal purity, intelligence, and freedom. (I, 1, 2)

. . . [F]rom the mere comprehension of Brahman's Self, which is not something either to be avoided or endeavoured after, there results cessation of all pain, and thereby the attainment of man's highest aim. That passages notifying certain divinities, and so on, stand in subordinate relation to acts of devout meditation mentioned in the same chapters may readily be admitted. But it is impossible that Brahman should stand in an analogous relation to injunctions of devout meditation, for if the knowledge of absolute unity has once arisen there exists no longer anything to be desired or avoided, and thereby the conception of duality, according to which we distinguish actions, agents, and the like, is destroyed. If the conception of duality is once uprooted by the conception of absolute unity, it cannot arise again, and so no longer be the cause of Brahman being looked upon as the complementary object of injunction of devotion. Other parts of the Veda may have no authority except in so far as they are connected with injunctions; still it is impossible to impugn on that ground the authoritativeness of passages conveying the knowledge of the Self; for such passages have their own result. Nor, finally, can the authoritativeness of the Veda be proved by inferential reasoning so that it would be dependent on instances observed elsewhere. From all which it follows that the Veda possesses authority as a means of right knowledge of Brahman.

. . . Among eternal things, some indeed may be 'eternal, although changing' (*pariṇāminitya*), viz. those, the idea of whose identity is not destroyed, although they may undergo changes; such, for instance, are earth and the other elements in the opinion of those who maintain the eternity of the world, or the three guṇas in the opinion of the Sāṁkhyas. But this (*mokṣa*) is eternal in the true sense, i.e. eternal without undergoing any changes (*kūṭasthanitya*), omnipresent as ether, free from all modifications, absolutely self-sufficient, not composed of parts, of self-luminous nature. That bodiless entity in fact, to which merit and demerit with their consequences and threefold time do not apply, is called release; a definition agreeing with scriptural passages, such as the following: 'Different from merit and demerit, different from effect and cause, different from past and future' (Ka. Up. I, 2, 14). It (i.e. *mokṣa*) is, therefore, the same as Brahman in the enquiry into which we are at present engaged. If Brahman were represented as supplementary to certain actions, and release were assumed to be the effect of those actions, it would be non-eternal, and would have to be considered merely as something holding a pre-eminent position among the described non-eternal fruits of actions with their various degrees. But that release is something eternal is acknowledged by whoever admits it at all, and the teaching concerning Brahman can therefore not be merely supplementary to actions.

. . . Nor, again, can it be said that there is a dependence on action in consequence of (Brahman or Release) being something which is to be obtained; for as Brahman constitutes a person's Self it is not something to be attained by that person. And even if Brahman were altogether different from a person's Self still it would not be something to be obtained; for as it is omnipresent it is part of its nature that it is ever present to every one, just as the (all-pervading) ether is. Nor, again, can it be maintained that Release is something to be ceremonially purified, and as such depends on an activity. For ceremonial purification (*saṁskāra*) results either from the accretion of some excellence or from the removal of some blemish. The former alternative does not apply to Release as it is of the nature of Brahman, to which no excellence can be added; nor, again, does the latter alternative apply, since Release is of the nature of Brahman, which is eternally pure.—But, it might be said, Release might be a quality of the Self which is merely hidden and becomes manifest on the Self being purified by some action; just as the quality of clearness becomes manifest in a mirror when the mirror is cleaned by means of the action of rubbing.—This objection is invalid, we reply, because the Self cannot be the abode of any action. For an action cannot exist without modifying that in which it abides. But if the Self were modified by an action its non-eternality would result therefrom, and texts such as the following, 'unchangeable he is called,' would thus be stultified; an altogether unacceptable result. Hence it is impossible to assume that any action should abide in the Self. . . .

. . . But how about the objection raised . . . that the information about Brahman cannot be held to have a purpose in the same way as the statement about a rope has one, because a man even after having heard about Brahman continues to belong to this transmigratory world?—We reply as follows: It is impossible to show that a man who has once understood Brahman to be the Self, belongs to the transmigratory world in the same sense as he did before, because that would be contrary to the fact of his being Brahman. For we indeed observe that a person who imagines the body, and so on, to constitute the Self, is subject to fear and pain, but we have no right to assume that the same person after having, by means of the Veda, comprehended Brahman to be the Self, and thus having got over his former imaginings, will still in the same manner be subject to pain and fear whose cause is wrong knowledge. . . . Thus *śruti* also declares, 'When he is free from the body, then neither pleasure nor pain touches him' (Ch. Up. VIII, 12, 1). If it should be objected that the condition of being free from the body follows on death only, we demur, since the cause of man being joined to the body is wrong knowledge. For it is not possible to establish the state of embodiedness upon anything else but wrong knowledge. And that the state of disembodiedness is eternal on account of its not having actions for its cause, we have already explained. The objection again, that embodiedness is caused by the merit and demerit effected by the Self (and therefore real), we refute by remarking that as the (reality of the) conjunction of the Self with the body is itself not established, the circumstance of merit and demerit being due to the action of the Self is likewise not established; for (if we should try to get over this difficulty by representing the Self's embodiedness as caused by merit and demerit) we should commit the logical fault of making embodiedness dependent on merit and demerit, and again merit and demerit on embodiedness.

And the assumption of an endless retrogressive chain (of embodied states and merit and demerit) would be no better than a chain of blind men (who are unable to lead one another)....

... As long as the knowledge of the Self, which Scripture tells us to search after, has not arisen, so long the Self is knowing subject; but that same subject is that which is searched after, viz. (the highest Self) free from all evil and blemish. Just as the idea of the Self being the body is assumed as valid (in ordinary life), so all the ordinary sources of knowledge (perception and the like) are valid only until the one Self is ascertained.' (I, 1, 4)

But, to raise a new objection, there exists no transmigrating soul different from the Lord and obstructed by impediments of knowledge; for *śruti* expressly declares that 'there is no other seer but he; there is no other knower but he' (Bṛh. Up. III, 7, 23). How then can it be said that the origination of knowledge in the transmigrating soul depends on a body, while it does not do so in the case of the Lord?—True, we reply. There is in reality no transmigrating soul different from the Lord. Still the connexion (of the Lord) with limiting adjuncts, consisting of bodies and so on, is assumed, just as we assume the ether to enter into connexion with divers limiting adjuncts such as jars, pots, caves, and the like. And just as in consequence of connexion of the latter kind such conceptions and terms as 'the hollow (space) of a jar,' &c. are generally current, although the space inside a jar is not really different from universal space, and just as in consequence thereof there generally prevails the false notion that there are different spaces such as the space of a jar and so on; so there prevails likewise the false notion that the Lord and the transmigrating soul are different; a notion due to the non-discrimination of the (unreal) connexion of the soul with the limiting conditions, consisting of the body and so on. That the Self, although in reality the only existence, imparts the quality of Selfhood to bodies and the like which are Not-Self is a matter of observation, and is due to mere wrong conception, which depends in its turn on antecedent wrong conception. And the consequence of the soul thus involving itself in the transmigratory state is that its thought depends on a body and the like. (I, 1, 5)

... The individual soul (*jīva*) is called awake as long as being connected with the various external objects by means of the modifications of the mind—which thus constitute limiting adjuncts of the soul—it apprehends those external objects, and identifies itself with the gross body, which is one of those external objects. When, modified by the impressions which the external objects have left, it sees dreams, it is denoted by the term 'mind.' When, on the cessation of the two limiting adjuncts (i.e. the subtle and the gross bodies), and the consequent absence of the modifications due to the adjuncts, it is, in the state of deep sleep, merged in the Self as it were, then it is said to be asleep (resolved into the Self).... (I, 1, 9)

In what precedes we have shown, availing ourselves of appropriate arguments, that the Vedānta-texts exhibited under Sūtras I, 1–11, are capable of proving that the all-knowing, all-powerful Lord is the cause of the origin, subsistence, and dissolution of the world. And we have explained, by pointing to the prevailing uniformity of view (I, 10), that all Vedānta-texts whatever maintain an intelligent cause. The question might therefore be asked, 'What reason is there for the subsequent part of the *Vedāntasūtras*?' (as the chief point is settled already.)

To this question we reply as follows: Brahman is apprehended under two forms; in the first place as qualified by limiting conditions owing to the multiformity of the evolutions of name and form (i.e. the multiformity of the created world[)]; in the second place as being the opposite of this, i.e. free from all limiting conditions whatever. . . .

Although one and the same Self is hidden in all beings movable as well as immovable, yet owing to the gradual rise of excellence of the minds which form the limiting conditions (of the Self), Scripture declares that the Self, although eternally unchanging and uniform, reveals itself in a graduated series of beings, and so appears in forms of various dignity and power; compare, for instance (Ait. Ār. II, 3, 2, 1), 'He who knows the higher manifestation of the Self in him,' &c. . . . (I, 1, 11)

. . . [W]e see that in ordinary life, the Self, which in reality is never anything but the Self, is, owing to non-comprehension of the truth, identified with the Non-Self, i.e. the body and so on; whereby it becomes possible to speak of the Self in so far as it is identified with the body, and so on, as something not searched for but to be searched for, not heard but to be heard, not seized but to be seized, not perceived but to be perceived, not known but to be known, and the like. Scripture, on the other hand, denies, in such passages as 'there is no other seer but he' (Bṛh. Up. III, 7, 23), that there is in reality any seer or hearer different from the all-knowing highest Lord. (Nor can it be said that the Lord is unreal because he is identical with the unreal individual soul; for) the Lord differs from the soul (*vijñānātman*) which is embodied, acts and enjoys, and is the product of Nescience, in the same way as the real juggler who stands on the ground differs from the illusive juggler, who, holding in his hand a shield and a sword, climbs up to the sky by means of a rope; or as the free unlimited ether differs from the ether of a jar, which is determined by its limiting adjunct, (viz. the jar.) . . . (I, 1, 17)

. . . But when he, by means of the cognition of absolute identity, finds absolute rest in the Self consisting of bliss, then he is freed from the fear of transmigratory existence. But this (finding absolute rest) is possible only when we understand by the Self consisting of bliss, the highest Self, and not either the *pradhāna* or the individual soul. Hence it is proved that the Self consisting of bliss is the highest Self.

But, in reality, the following remarks have to be made concerning the true meaning of the word '*ānandamaya*.' On what grounds, we ask, can it be maintained that the affix '*maya*' after having, in the series of compounds beginning with *annamaya* and ending with *vijñānamaya*, denoted mere modifications, should all at once, in the word *ānandamaya*, which belongs to the same series, denote abundance, so that *ānandamaya* would refer to Brahman? If it should be said that the assumption is made on account of the governing influence of the Brahman proclaimed in the *mantra* (which forms the beginning of the chapter, Taitt. Up. II), we reply that therefrom it would follow that also the Selfs consisting of food, breath, &c., denote Brahman (because the governing influence of the *mantra* extends to them also).—The advocate of the former interpretation will here, perhaps, restate an argument already made use of above, viz. as follows: To assume that the Selfs consisting of food, and so on, are not Brahman is quite proper, because after each of them an inner Self is mentioned. After the Self of bliss, on the other hand, no further inner Self is mentioned, and hence it must be considered to be Brahman itself; otherwise we should commit the mistake of dropping the subject-matter in hand (as which Brahman is pointed out by the *mantra*), and taking up a new topic.—But to this we reply that, although unlike the case of the Selfs consisting of food, &c., no inner Self is mentioned after the Self consisting of bliss, still the latter cannot be considered as Brahman, because with reference to the Self consisting of bliss Scripture declares, 'Joy is its head. Satisfaction is its right arm. Great satisfaction is its left arm. Bliss is its trunk. Brahman is its tail, its support.' Now, here the very same Brahman which, in the *mantra*, had been introduced as the subject of the discussion, is called the tail, the support; while the five involucra, extending from the involucrum of food up to the involucrum of bliss, are merely introduced for the purpose of setting forth the knowledge of Brahman. How, then, can it be maintained that our interpretation implies the needless dropping of the general subject-matter and the introduction of a new topic? . . . Nor, again, does Scripture exhibit a frequent repetition of the word '*ānandamaya*;' for merely the radical part of the compound (i.e. the word *ānanda* without the affix *maya*) is repeated in all the following passages; 'It is a flavour, for only after seizing flavour can any one seize bliss. Who could breathe, who could breathe forth, if that bliss existed not in the ether? For he alone causes blessedness;' 'Now this is an examination of bliss;' 'He who knows the bliss of that Brahman fears nothing;' 'He understood that bliss is Brahman.' If it were a settled matter that Brahman is denoted by the term, 'the Self consisting of bliss,' then we could assume that in the subsequent passages, where merely the word 'bliss' is employed, the term 'consisting of bliss' is meant to be repeated; but that the Self consisting of bliss is not Brahman, we have already proved by means of the reason of joy being its head, and so on. (I, 1, 19)

. . . [E]xpressions such as, 'That which is without sound, without touch, without form, without decay,' are made use of where instruction is given about the nature of the highest Lord in so far as he is devoid of all qualities; while passages such as the following one, 'He to whom belong all works, all desires, all sweet odours and tastes' (Ch. Up. III, 14, 2), which represent the highest Lord as the object of devotion, speak of him, who is the cause of everything, as possessing some of the qualities of his effects. Analogously he may be spoken of, in the passage under discussion, as having a beard bright as gold and so on. With reference to the objection that the highest Lord cannot be meant because an abode is spoken of, we remark that, for the purposes of devout meditation, a special abode may be assigned to Brahman, although it abides in its own glory only; for as Brahman is, like ether, all-pervading, it may be viewed as being within the Self of all beings. The statement, finally, about the limitation of Brahman's might, which depends on the distinction of what belongs to the gods and what to the body, has likewise reference to devout meditation only. From all this it follows that the being which Scripture states to be within the eye and the sun is the highest Lord. (I, 1, 20)

... Against the further objection that the omnipresent Brahman cannot be viewed as bounded by heaven we remark that the assignment, to Brahman, of a special locality is not contrary to reason because it subserves the purpose of devout meditation. Nor does it avail anything to say that it is impossible to assign any place to Brahman because Brahman is out of connexion with all place. For it is possible to make such an assumption, because Brahman is connected with certain limiting adjuncts. Accordingly Scripture speaks of different kinds of devout meditation on Brahman as specially connected with certain localities, such as the sun, the eye, the heart. For the same reason it is also possible to attribute to Brahman a multiplicity of abodes, as is done in the clause (quoted above) 'higher than all.'... (I, 1, 24)

... [A]s the passages, 'I am Brahman,' 'That art thou,' and others, prove, there is in reality no such thing as an individual soul absolutely different from Brahman, but Brahman, in so far as it differentiates itself through the mind (*buddhi*) and other limiting conditions, is called individual soul, agent, enjoyer.

... If there were no objects there would be no subjects; and if there were no subjects there would be no objects. For on either side alone nothing could be achieved.... (I, 1, 31)

True, we reply, (there is in reality one universal Self only.) But the highest Self in so far as it is limited by its adjuncts, viz. the body, the senses, and the mind (*mano-buddhi*), is, by the ignorant, spoken of as if it were embodied. Similarly the ether, although in reality unlimited, appears limited owing to certain adjuncts, such as jars and other vessels. With regard to this (unreal limitation of the one Self) the distinction of objects of activity and of agents may be practically assumed, as long as we have not learned—from the passage, 'That art thou'—that the Self is one only. As soon, however, as we grasp the truth that there is only one universal Self, there is an end to the whole practical view of the world with its distinction of bondage, final release, and the like. (I, 2, 6)

... From the circumstance that Brahman is connected with the hearts of all living beings it does not follow that it is, like the embodied Self, subject to fruition. For, between the embodied Self and the highest Self, there is the difference that the former acts and enjoys, acquires merit and demerit, and is affected by pleasure, pain, and so on; while the latter is of the opposite nature, i.e. characterised by being free from all evil and the like. On account of this difference of the two, the fruition of the one does not extend to the other. To assume merely on the ground of the mutual proximity of the two, without considering their essentially different powers, that a connexion with effects exists (in Brahman's case also), would be no better than to suppose that space is on fire (when something in space is on fire).... (I, 2, 8)

... The internal ruler, of whom Scripture speaks with reference to the gods, must be the highest Self, cannot be anything else.—Why so? —Because its qualities are designated in the passage under discussion. The universal rulership implied in the statement that, dwelling within, it rules the entire aggregate of created beings, inclusive of the gods, and so on, is an appropriate attribute of the highest Self, since omnipotence depends on (the omnipotent ruler) being the cause of all created things.—The qualities of Selfhood and immortality also, which are mentioned in the passage, 'He is thy Self, the ruler within, the immortal,' belong in their primary sense to the highest Self.—Further, the passage, 'He whom the earth does not know,' which declares that the internal ruler is not known by the earth-deity, shows him to be different from that deity; for the deity of the earth knows itself to be the earth. —The attributes 'unseen,' 'unheard,' also point to the highest Self, which is devoid of shape and other sensible qualities.—The objection that the highest Self is destitute of the organs of action, and hence cannot be a ruler, is without force, because organs of action may be ascribed to him owing to the organs of action of those whom he rules.— If it should be objected that [if we once admit an internal ruler in addition to the individual soul] we are driven to assume again another and another ruler ad infinitum; we reply that this is not the case, as actually there is no other ruler (but the highest Self). The objection would be valid only in the case of a difference of rulers actually existing.—For all these reasons, the internal ruler is no other but the highest Self. (I, 2, 18)

... The declaration of the difference of the embodied Self and the internal ruler has its reason in the limiting adjunct, consisting of the organs of action, presented by Nescience, and is not absolutely true. For the Self within is one only; two internal Selfs are not possible. But owing to its limiting adjunct the one Self is practically treated as if it were two; just as we make a distinction between the ether of the jar and the universal ether. Hence there is room for those scriptural passages which set forth the distinction of knower and object of knowledge, for perception and the other means of proof, for the intuitive knowledge of the apparent world, and for that part of Scripture which contains injunctions and prohibitions. In accordance with this, the scriptural passage, 'Where there is duality, as it were, there one sees another,' declares that the whole practical world exists only in the sphere of Nescience; while the subsequent passage, 'But when the Self only is all this, how should he see another?' declares that the practical world vanishes in the sphere of true knowledge. (I, 2, 20)

... [T]wo kinds of knowledge are enjoined there (in the Upaniṣad), a lower and a higher one. Of the lower one it is said that it comprises the *Ṛgveda* and so on, and then the text continues, 'The higher knowledge is that by which the Indestructible is apprehended.' Here the Indestructible is declared to be the subject of the higher knowledge. If we now were to assume that the Indestructible distinguished by invisibility and like qualities is something different from the highest Lord, the knowledge referring to it would not be the higher one. For the distinction of lower and higher knowledge is made on account of the diversity of their results, the former leading to mere worldly exaltation, the latter to absolute bliss; and nobody would assume absolute bliss to result from the knowledge of the *pradhāna*.... (I, 2, 21)

... That same highest Brahman constitutes—as we know from passages such as 'that art thou'—the real nature of the individual soul, while its second nature, i.e. that aspect of it which depends on fictitious limiting conditions, is not its real nature. For as long as the individual soul does not free itself from Nescience in the form of duality—which Nescience may be compared to the mistake of him who in the twilight mistakes a post for a man—and does not rise to the knowledge of the Self, whose nature is unchangeable, eternal Cognition—which expresses itself in the form 'I am Brahman'—so long it remains the individual soul. But when, discarding the aggregate of body, sense-organs and mind, it arrives, by means of Scripture, at the knowledge that it is not itself that aggregate, that it does not form part of transmigratory existence, but is the True, the Real, the Self, whose nature is pure intelligence; then knowing itself to be of the nature of unchangeable, eternal Cognition, it lifts itself above the vain conceit of being one with this body, and itself becomes the Self, whose nature is unchanging, eternal Cognition. As is declared in such scriptural passages as 'He who knows the highest Brahman becomes even Brahman' (Mu. Up. III, 2, 9). And this is the real nature of the individual soul by means of which it arises from the body and appears in its own form.

... Before the rise of discriminative knowledge the nature of the individual soul, which is (in reality) pure light, is non-discriminated as it were from its limiting adjuncts consisting of body, senses, mind, sense-objects and feelings, and appears as consisting of the energies of seeing and so on. Similarly—to quote an analogous case from ordinary experience—the true nature of a pure crystal, i.e. its transparency and whiteness, is, before the rise of discriminative knowledge (on the part of the observer,) non-discriminated as it were from any limiting adjuncts of red or blue colour; while, as soon as through some means of true cognition discriminative knowledge has arisen, it is said to have now accomplished its true nature, i.e. transparency and whiteness, although in reality it had already done so before. Thus the discriminative knowledge, effected by *śruti*, on the part of the individual soul which previously is non-discriminated as it were from its limiting adjuncts, is (according to the scriptural passage under discussion) the soul's rising from the body, and the fruit of that discriminative knowledge is its accomplishment in its true nature, i.e. the comprehension that its nature is the pure Self. Thus the embodiedness and the non-embodiedness of the Self are due merely to discrimination and non-discrimination. . . . (I, 3, 19)

. . . [W]hatever is perceived is perceived by the light of Brahman only so that sun, moon, &c. can be said to shine in it; while Brahman as self-luminous is not perceived by means of any other light. Brahman manifests everything else, but is not manifested by anything else; according to such scriptural passages as, 'By the Self alone as his light man sits,' &c. (Bṛh. Up. IV, 3, 6), and 'He is incomprehensible, for he cannot be comprehended' (Bṛh. Up. IV, 2, 4). (I, 3, 22)

. . . [W]e observe the eternity of the connexion between such words as cow, and so on, and the things denoted by them. For, although the individuals of the (species denoted by the word) cow have an origin, their species do not have an origin, since of (the three categories) substances, qualities, and actions the individuals only originate, not the species. Now it is with the species that the words are connected, not with the individuals, which, as being infinite in number, are not capable of entering into that connexion. Hence, although the individuals do not originate, no contradiction arises in the case of words such as cow, and the like, since the species are eternal. Similarly, although individual gods are admitted to originate, there arises no contradiction in the case of such words as Vasu, and the like, since the species denoted by them are eternal. And that the gods, and so on, belong to different species, is to be concluded from the descriptions of their various personal appearance, such as given in the mantras, arthavādas, &c. Terms such as 'Indra' rest on the connexion (of some particular being) with some particular place, analogously to terms such as 'army-leader;' hence, whoever occupies that particular place is called by that particular name.—The origination of the world from the 'word' is not to be understood in that sense, that the word constitutes the material cause of the world, as Brahman does; but while there exist the ever-lasting words, whose essence is the power of denotation in connexion with their eternal sense (i.e. the ākṛtis denoted), the accomplishment of such individual things as are capable of having those words applied to them is called an origination from those words.

How then is it known that the world originates from the word?—'From perception and inference.' Perception here denotes Scripture which, in order to be authoritative, is independent (of anything else). 'Inference' denotes *smṛti* which, in order to be authoritative, depends on something else (viz. Scripture). These two declare that creation is preceded by the word. . . .

Of what nature then is the 'word' with a view to which it is said that the world originates from the 'word?'—It is the *sphoṭa*, the *pūrvapakṣin* says. For on the assumption that the letters are the word, the doctrine that the individual gods, and so on, originates from the eternal words of the Veda could not in any way be proved, since the letters perish as soon as they are produced (i.e. pronounced). These perishable letters are moreover apprehended as differing according to the pronunciation of the individual speaker. For this reason we are able to determine, merely from the sound of the voice of some unseen person whom we hear reading, who is reading, whether Devadatta or Yajñadatta or some other man. And it cannot be maintained that this apprehension of difference regarding the letters is an erroneous one; for we do not apprehend anything else whereby it is refuted. Nor is it reasonable to maintain that the apprehension of the sense of a word results from the letters. For it can neither be maintained that each letter by itself intimates the sense, since that would be too wide an assumption; nor that there takes place a simultaneous apprehension of the whole aggregate of letters; since the letters succeed one another in time. Nor can we admit the explanation that the last letter of the word together with the impressions produced by the perception of the preceding letters is that which makes us apprehend the sense. For the word makes us apprehend the sense only if it is itself apprehended in so far as having reference to the mental grasp of the constant connexion (of the word and the sense), just as smoke makes us infer the existence of fire only when it is itself apprehended; but an apprehension of the last letter combined with the impressions produced by the preceding letters does not actually take place, because those impressions are not objects of perception. Nor, again, can it be maintained that (although those impressions are not objects of perception, yet they may be inferred from their effects, and that thus) the actual perception of the last letter combined with the impressions left by the preceding letters—which impressions are apprehended from their effects—is that which intimates the sense of the word; for that effect of the impressions, viz. the remembrance of the entire word, is itself something consisting of parts which succeed each other in time.—From all this it follows that the *sphoṭa* is the word. After the apprehending agent, i.e. the *buddhi*, has, through the apprehension of the several letters of the word, received rudimentary impressions, and after those impressions have been matured through the apprehension of the last letter, the *sphoṭa* presents itself in the *buddhi* all at once as the object of one mental act of apprehension. —And it must not be maintained that that one act of apprehension is merely an act of remembrance having for its object the letters of the word; for the letters which are more than one cannot form the object of one act of apprehension.—As that *sphoṭa* is recognised as the same as often as the word is pronounced, it is eternal; while the apprehension of difference referred to above has for its object the letters merely. From this eternal word, which is of the nature of the *sphoṭa* and possesses denotative power, there is produced the object denoted, i.e. this world which consists of actions, agents, and results of action.

Against this doctrine the reverend Upavarṣa maintains that the letters only are the word.—But—an objection is raised—it has been said above that the letters no sooner produced pass away!—That assertion is not true, we reply; for they are recognised as the same letters (each time they are produced anew).—Nor can it be maintained that the recognition is due to similarity only, as in the case of hairs, for instance; for the fact of the recognition being a recognition in the strict sense of the word is not contradicted by any other means of proof.—Nor, again, can it be said that the recognition has its cause in the species (so that not the same individual letter would be recognised, but only a letter belonging to the same species as other letters heard before); for, as a matter of fact, the same individual letters are recognised. That the recognition of the letters rests on the species could be maintained only if whenever the letters are pronounced different individual letters were apprehended, just as several cows are apprehended as different individuals belonging to the same species. But this is actually not the case; for the (same) individual letters are recognised as often as they are pronounced. If, for instance, the word 'cow' is pronounced twice, we think not that two different words have been pronounced, but that the same individual word has been repeated.—But, our opponent reminds us, it has been shown above, that the letters are apprehended as different owing to differences of pronunciation, as appears from the fact that we apprehend a difference when merely hearing the sound of Devadatta or Yajñadatta reading.—Although, we reply, it is a settled matter that the letters are recognised as the same, yet we admit that there are differences in the apprehension of the letters; but as the letters are articulated by means of conjunction and disjunction (of the breath with the palate, the teeth, &c.), those differences are rightly ascribed to the various character of the articulating agents and not to the intrinsic nature of the letters themselves. Those, moreover, who maintain that the individual letters are different have, in order to account for the fact of recognition, to assume species of letters, and further to admit that the apprehension of difference is conditioned by external factors. Is it then not much simpler to assume, as we do, that the apprehension of difference is conditioned by external factors while the recognition is due to the intrinsic nature of the letters? And this very fact of recognition is that mental process which prevents us from looking on the apprehension of difference as having the letters for its object (so that the opponent was wrong in denying the existence of such a process). For how should, for instance, the one syllable *ga*, when it is pronounced in the same moment by several persons, be at the same time of different nature, viz. accented with the *udātta*, the *anudātta*, and the *svarita* and nasal as well as non-nasal? Or else—and this is the preferable explanation—we assume that the difference of apprehension is caused not by the letters but by the tone (*dhvani*). By this tone we have to understand that which enters the ear of a person who is listening from a distance and not able to distinguish the separate letters, and which, for a person standing near, affects the letters with its own distinctions, such as high or low pitch and so on. It is on this tone that all the distinctions of *udātta*, *anudātta*, and so on depend, and not on the intrinsic nature of the letters; for they are recognised as the same whenever they are pronounced. On this theory only we gain a basis for the distinctive apprehension of the *udātta*, the *anudātta*, and the like. For on the theory first propounded (but now rejected), we should have to assume that the distinctions of *udātta* and so on are due to the processes of conjunction and disjunction described above, since the letters themselves, which are even recognised as the same, are not different. But as those processes of conjunction and disjunction are not matter of perception, we cannot definitely ascertain in the letters any differences based on those processes, and hence the apprehension of the *udātta* and so on remains without a basis.—Nor should it be urged that from the difference of the *udātta* and so on there results also a difference of the letters recognised. For a difference in one matter does not involve a difference in some other matter which in itself is free from difference. Nobody, for instance, thinks that because the individuals are different from each other the species also contains a difference in itself.

The assumption of the *sphoṭa* is further gratuitous, because the sense of the word may be apprehended from the letters.—But—our opponent here objects—I do not assume the existence of the *sphoṭa*. I, on the contrary, actually perceive it; for after the *buddhi* has been impressed by the successive apprehension of the letters of the word, the *sphoṭa* all at once presents itself as the object of cognition.—You are mistaken, we reply. The object of the cognitional act of which you speak is simply the letters of the word. That one comprehensive cognition which follows upon the apprehension of the successive letters of the word has for its object the entire aggregate of the letters constituting the word, and not anything else. We conclude this from the circumstance that in that final comprehensive cognition there are included those letters only of which a definite given word consists, and not any other letters. If that cognitional act had for its object the *sphoṭa*—i.e. something different from the letters of a given word—then those letters would be excluded from it just as much as the letters of any other word. But as this is not the case, it follows that that final comprehensive act of cognition is nothing but an act of remembrance which has the letters of the word for its object.—Our opponent has asserted above that the letters of a word being several cannot form the object of one mental act. But there he is wrong again. The ideas which we have of a row, for instance, or a wood or an army, or of the numbers ten, hundred, thousand, and so on, show that also such things as comprise several unities can become the objects of one and the same cognitional act. The idea which has for its object the word as one whole is a derived one, in so far as it depends on the determination of one sense in many letters; in the same way as the idea of a wood, an army, and so on.—But—our opponent may here object—if the word were nothing else but the letters which in their aggregate become the object of one mental act, such couples of words as *jārā* and *rājā* or *pika* and *kapi* would not be cognised as different words; for here the same letters are presented to consciousness in each of the words constituting one couple.—There is indeed, we reply, in both cases a comprehensive consciousness of the same totality of letters; but just as ants constitute the idea of a row only if they march one after the other, so the letters also constitute the idea of a certain word only if they follow each other in a certain order. Hence it is not contrary to reason that the same letters are cognised as different words, in consequence of the different order in which they are arranged.

The hypothesis of him who maintains that the letters are the word may therefore be finally formulated as follows. The letters of which a word consists—assisted by a certain order and number—have, through traditional use, entered into a connexion with a definite sense. At the time when they are employed they present themselves as such (i.e. in their definite order and number) to the *buddhi*, which, after having apprehended the several letters in succession, finally comprehends the entire aggregate, and they thus unerringly intimate to the *buddhi* their definite sense. This hypothesis is certainly simpler than the complicated hypothesis of the grammarians who teach that the *sphoṭa* is the word. For they have to disregard what is given by perception, and to assume something which is never perceived; the letters apprehended in a definite order are said to manifest the *sphoṭa*, and the *sphoṭa* in its turn is said to manifest the sense.

Or let it even be admitted that the letters are different ones each time they are pronounced; yet, as in that case we necessarily must assume species of letters as the basis of the recognition of the individual letters, the function of conveying the sense which we have demonstrated in the case of the (individual) letters has then to be attributed to the species.

From all this it follows that the theory according to which the individual gods and so on originate from the eternal words is unobjectionable. (I, 3, 28)

Moreover, this world when being dissolved (in a *mahāpralaya*) is dissolved to that extent only that the potentiality (*śakti*) of the world remains, and (when it is produced again) it is produced from the root of that potentiality; otherwise we should have to admit an effect without a cause. Nor have we the right to assume potentialities of different kind (for the different periods of the world). Hence, although the series of worlds from the earth upwards, and the series of different classes of animate beings such as gods, animals, and men, and the different conditions based on caste, *āśrama*, religious duty and fruit (of works), although all these we say are again and again interrupted and thereupon produced anew; we yet have to understand that they are, in the beginningless *saṁsāra*, subject to a certain determinateness analogous to the determinateness governing the connexion between the senses and their objects. For it is impossible to imagine that the relation of senses and sense-objects should be a different one in different creations, so that, for instance, in some new creation a sixth sense and a corresponding sixth sense-object should manifest themselves. As, therefore, the phenomenal world is the same in all *kalpas* and as the Lords are able to continue their previous forms of existence, there manifest themselves, in each new creation, individuals bearing the same names and forms as the individuals of the preceding creations, and, owing to this equality of names and forms, the admitted periodical renovations of the world in the form of general *pralayas* and general creations do not conflict with the authoritativeness of the word of the Veda. . . . (I, 3, 30)

. . . [T]he Śūdras have no such claim, on account of their not studying the Veda. A person who has studied the Veda and understood its sense is indeed qualified for Vedic matters; but a Śūdra does not study the Veda, for such study demands as its antecedent the *upanāyana*-ceremony, and that ceremony belongs to the three (higher) castes only. The mere circumstances of being in a condition of desire does not furnish a reason for qualification, if capability is absent. Mere temporal capability again does not constitute a reason for qualification, spiritual capability being required in spiritual matters. And spiritual capability is (in the case of the Śūdras) excluded by their being excluded from the study of the Veda.—The Vedic statement, moreover, that the Śūdra is unfit for sacrifices intimates, because founded on reasoning, that he is unfit for knowledge also; for the argumentation is the same in both cases. . . . (I, 3, 34)

It is not possible—our opponent says—to prove either that Brahman is the cause of the origin, &c. of the world, or that all Vedānta-texts refer to Brahman; because we observe that the Vedānta-texts contradict one another. All the Vedānta-passages which treat of the creation enumerate its successive steps in different order, and so in reality speak of different creations. In one place it is said that from the Self there sprang the ether (Taitt. Up. II, 1); in another place that the creation began with fire (Ch. Up. VI, 2, 3); in another place, again, that the Person created breath and from breath faith (Pra. Up. VI, 4); in another place, again, that the Self created these worlds, the water (above the heaven), light, the mortal (earth), and the water (below the earth) (Ait. Ār. II, 4, 1, 2; 3). There no order is stated at all. Somewhere else it is said that the creation originated from the Non-existent. 'In the beginning this was non-existent; from it was born what exists' (Taitt. Up. II, 7); and, 'In the beginning this was non-existent; it became existent; it grew' (Ch. Up. III, 19, 1). In another place, again, the doctrine of the Non-existent being the antecedent of the creation is impugned, and the Existent mentioned in its stead. 'Others say, in the beginning there was that only which is not; but how could it be thus, my dear? How could that which is be born of that which is not?' (Ch. Up. VI, 2, 1; 2.) And in another place, again, the development of the world is spoken of as having taken place spontaneously, 'Now all this was then undeveloped. It became developed by form and name' (Bṛh. Up. I, 4, 7).—As therefore manifold discrepancies are observed, and as no option is possible in the case of an accomplished matter, the Vedānta-passages cannot be accepted as authorities for determining the cause of the world, but we must rather accept some other cause of the world resting on the authority of *smṛti* and Reasoning.

To this we make the following reply.—Although the Vedānta-passages may be conflicting with regard to the order of the things created, such as ether and so on, they do not conflict with regard to the creator, 'on account of his being represented as described.' That means: such as the creator is described in any one Vedānta-passage, viz. as all-knowing, the Lord of all, the Self of all, without a second, so he is represented in all other Vedānta-passages also. Let us consider, for instance, the description of Brahman (given in Taitt. Up. II, 1 ff.). There it is said at first, 'Truth, knowledge, infinite is Brahman.' Here the word 'knowledge,' and so likewise the statement, made later on, that Brahman desired (II, 6), intimate that Brahman is of the nature of intelligence. Further, the text declares that the cause of the world is the general Lord, by representing it as not dependent on anything else. It further applies to the cause of the world the term 'Self' (II, 1), and it represents it as abiding within the series of sheaths beginning with the gross body; whereby it affirms it to be the internal Self within all beings. Again—in the passage, 'May I be many, may I grow forth'—it tells how the Self became many, and thereby declares that the creator is non-different from the created effects. And—in the passage, 'He created all this whatever there is'—it represents the creator as the Cause of the entire world, and thereby declares him to have been without a second previously to the creation. The same characteristics which in the above passages are predicated of Brahman, viewed as the Cause of the world, we find to be predicated of it in other passages also, so, for instance, 'Being only, my dear, was this in the beginning, one only, without a second. It thought, may I be many, may I grow forth. It sent forth fire' (Ch. Up. VI, 2, 1; 3), and 'In the beginning all this was Self, one only; there was nothing else blinking whatsoever. He thought, shall I send forth worlds?' (Ait. Ār. II, 4, 1, 1; 2.) The Vedānta-passages which are concerned with setting forth the cause of the world are thus in harmony throughout.—On the other hand, there are found conflicting statements concerning the world, the creation being in some places said to begin with ether, in other places with fire, and so on. But, in the first place, it cannot be said that the conflict of statements concerning the world affects the statements concerning the cause, i.e. Brahman, in which all the Vedānta-texts are seen to agree—for that would be an altogether unfounded generalization;—and in the second place, the teacher will reconcile later on (II, 3) those conflicting passages also which refer to the world. And, to consider the matter more thoroughly, a conflict of statements regarding the world would not even matter greatly, since the creation of the world and similar topics are not at all what Scripture wishes to teach. For we neither observe nor are told by Scripture that the welfare of man depends on those matters in any way; nor have we the right to assume such a thing; because we conclude from the introductory and concluding clauses that the passages about the creation and the like form only subordinate members of passages treating of Brahman. . . . (I, 4, 14)

. . . We, moreover, must assume that the world was evolved at the beginning of the creation in the same way as it is at present seen to develop itself by names and forms, viz. under the rulership of an intelligent creator; for we have no right to make assumptions contrary to what is at present actually observed. . . . (I, 4, 15)

As therefore the individual soul and the highest Self differ in name only, it being a settled matter that perfect knowledge has for its object the absolute oneness of the two; it is senseless to insist (as some do) on a plurality of Selfs, and to maintain that the individual soul is different from the highest Self, and the highest Self from the individual soul. For the Self is indeed called by many different names, but it is one only. Nor does the passage, 'He who knows Brahman which is real, knowledge, infinite, as hidden in the cave' (Taitt. Up. II, 1), refer to some one cave (different from the abode of the individual soul). And that nobody else but Brahman is hidden in the cave we know from a subsequent passage, viz. 'Having sent forth he entered into it' (Taitt. Up. II, 6), according to which the creator only entered into the created beings.—Those who insist on the distinction of the individual and the highest Self oppose themselves to the true sense of the Vedānta-texts, stand thereby in the way of perfect knowledge, which is the door to perfect beatitude, and groundlessly assume release to be something effected, and therefore non-eternal. (And if they attempt to show that *mokṣa*, although effected, is eternal) they involve themselves in a conflict with sound logic. (I, 4, 22)

It has been said that, as practical religious duty has to be enquired into because it is the cause of an increase of happiness, so Brahman has to be inquired into because it is the cause of absolute beatitude. And Brahman has been defined as that from which there proceed the origination, sustentation, and retractation of this world. Now as this definition comprises alike the relation of substantial causality in which clay and gold, for instance, stand to golden ornaments and earthen pots, and the relation of operative causality in which the potter and the goldsmith stand to the things mentioned; a doubt arises to which of these two kinds the causality of Brahman belongs.

The *pūrvapakṣin* maintains that Brahman evidently is the operative cause of the world only, because Scripture declares his creative energy to be preceded by reflection. Compare, for instance, Pra. Up. VI, 3; 4: 'He reflected, he created *prāṇa*.' For observation shows that the action of operative causes only, such as potters and the like, is preceded by reflection, and moreover that the result of some activity is brought about by the concurrence of several factors. It is therefore appropriate that we should view the prime creator in the same light. The circumstance of his being known as 'the Lord' furnishes another argument. For lords such as kings and the son of Vivasvat are known only as operative causes, and the highest Lord also must on that account be viewed as an operative cause only.—Further, the effect of the creator's activity, viz. this world, is seen to consist of parts, to be non-intelligent and impure; we therefore must assume that its cause also is of the same nature; for it is a matter of general observation that cause and effect are alike in kind. But that Brahman does not resemble the world in nature, we know from many scriptural passages, such as 'It is without parts, without actions, tranquil, without fault, without taint' [(]Śve. Up. VI, 19). Hence there remains no other alternative but to admit that in addition to Brahman there exists a material cause of the world of impure nature, such as is known from *smṛti,* and to limit the causality of Brahman, as declared by Scripture, to operative causality.

To this we make the following reply.—Brahman is to be acknowledged as the material cause as well as the operative cause; because this latter view does not conflict with the promissory statements and the illustrative instances. The promissory statement chiefly meant is the following one, 'Have you ever asked for that instruction by which that which is not heard becomes heard; that which is not perceived, perceived; that which is not known, known?' (Ch. Up. VI, 1, 3.) This passage intimates that through the cognition of one thing everything else, even if (previously) unknown, becomes known. Now the knowledge of everything is possible through the cognition of the material cause, since the effect is non-different from the material cause. On the other hand, effects are not non-different from their operative cause; for we know from ordinary experience that the carpenter, for instance, is different from the house he has built.—The illustrative example referred to is the one mentioned (Ch. Up. VI, 1, 4), 'My dear, as by one clod of clay all that is made of clay is known, the modification (i.e. the effect) being a name merely which has its origin in speech, while the truth is that it is clay merely;' which passage again has reference to the material cause. . . . The Self is thus the operative cause, because there is no other ruling principle, and the material cause because there is no other substance from which the world could originate. (I, 4, 23)

. . . Now it has been shown already that the *śruti*-texts aim at conveying the doctrine that the Lord is the universal cause, and as wherever different smṛtis conflict those maintaining one view must be accepted, while those which maintain the opposite view must be set aside, those smṛtis which follow *śruti* are to be considered as authoritative, while all others are to be disregarded. . . . (II, 1, 1)

Your assertion that this world cannot have originated from Brahman on account of the difference of its character is not founded on an absolutely true tenet. For we see that from man, who is acknowledged to be intelligent, non-intelligent things such as hair and nails originate, and that, on the other hand, from avowedly non-intelligent matter, such as cow-dung, scorpions and similar animals are produced.—But—to state an objection—the real cause of the non-intelligent hair and nails is the human body which is itself non-intelligent, and the non-intelligent bodies only of scorpions are the effects of non-intelligent dung.—Even thus, we reply, there remains a difference in character (between the cause, for instance, the dung, and the effect, for instance, the body of the scorpion), in so far as some non-intelligent matter (the body) is the abode of an intelligent principle (the scorpion's soul), while other non-intelligent matter (the dung) is not. Moreover, the difference of nature—due to the cause passing over into the effect—between the bodies of men on the one side and hair and nails on the other side, is, on account of the divergence of colour, form, &c., very considerable after all. The same remark holds good with regard to cow-dung and the bodies of scorpions, &c. If absolute equality were insisted on (in the case of one thing being the effect of another), the relation of material cause and effect (which after all requires a distinction of the two) would be annihilated. If, again, it be remarked that in the case of men and hair as well as in that of scorpions and cow-dung there is one characteristic feature, at least, which is found in the effect as well as in the cause, viz. the quality of being of an earthy nature; we reply that in the case of Brahman and the world also one characteristic feature, viz. that of existence (*sattā*), is found in ether, &c. (which are the effects) as well as in Brahman (which is the cause).—He, moreover, who on the ground of the difference of the attributes tries to invalidate the doctrine of Brahman being the cause of the world, must assert that he understands by difference of attributes either the non-occurrence (in the world) of the entire complex of the characteristics of Brahman, or the non-occurrence of any (some or other) characteristic, or the non-occurrence of the characteristic of intelligence. The first assertion would lead to the negation of the relation of cause and effect in general, which relation is based on the fact of there being in the effect something over and above the cause (for if the two were absolutely identical they could not be distinguished). The second assertion is open to the charge of running counter to what is well known; for, as we have already remarked, the characteristic quality of existence which belongs to Brahman is found likewise in ether and so on. For the third assertion the requisite proving instances are wanting; for what instances could be brought forward against the upholder of Brahman, in order to prove the general assertion that whatever is devoid of intelligence is seen not to be an effect of Brahman? (The upholder of Brahman would simply not admit any such instances) because he maintains that this entire complex of things has Brahman for its material cause. And that all such assertions are contrary to Scripture, is clear, as we have already shown it to be the purport of Scripture that Brahman is the cause and substance of the world. It has indeed been maintained by *pūrvapakṣin* that the other means of proof also (and not merely sacred tradition) apply to Brahman, on account of its being an accomplished entity (not something to be accomplished as religious duties are); but such an assertion is entirely gratuitous. For Brahman, as being devoid of form and so on, cannot become an object of perception; and as there are in its case no characteristic marks (on which conclusions, &c. might be based), inference also and the other means of proof do not apply to it; but, like religious duty, it is to be known solely on the ground of holy tradition. . . . And if it has been maintained above that the scriptural passage enjoining thought (on Brahman) in addition to mere hearing (of the sacred texts treating of Brahman) shows that reasoning also is to be allowed its place, we reply that the passage must not deceitfully be taken as enjoining bare independent ratiocination, but must be understood to represent reasoning as a subordinate auxiliary of intuitional knowledge. By reasoning of the latter type we may, for instance, arrive at the following conclusions; that because the state of dream and the waking state exclude each other the Self is not connected with those states; that, as the soul in the state of deep sleep leaves the phenomenal world behind and becomes one with that whose Self is pure Being, it has for its Self pure Being apart from the phenomenal world; that as the world springs from Brahman it cannot be separate from Brahman, according to the principle of the non-difference of cause and effect, &c. The fallaciousness of mere reasoning will moreover be demonstrated later on (II, 1, 11). . . . (II, 1, 6)

There is nothing objectionable in our system.—The objection that the effect when being reabsorbed into its cause would inquinate the latter with its qualities does not damage our position 'because there are parallel instances,' i.e. because there are instances of effects not inquinating with their qualities the causes into which they are reabsorbed. Things, for instance, made of clay, such as pots, &c., which in their state of separate existence are of various descriptions, do not, when they are reabsorbed into their original matter (i.e. clay), impart to the latter their individual qualities; nor do golden ornaments impart their individual qualities to their elementary material, i.e. gold, into which they may finally be reabsorbed. Nor does the fourfold complex of organic beings which springs from earth impart its qualities to the latter at the time of reabsorption. You (i.e. the *pūrvapakṣin*), on the other hand, have not any instances to quote in your favour. For reabsorption could not take place at all if the effect when passing back into its causal substance continued to subsist there with all its individual properties. And that in spite of the non-difference of cause and effect the effect has its Self in the cause, but not the cause in the effect, is a point which we shall render clear later on, under II, 1, 14.

. . . We can quote other examples in favour of our doctrine. As the magician is not at any time affected by the magical illusion produced by himself, because it is unreal, so the highest Self is not affected by the world-illusion. And as one dreaming person is not affected by the illusory visions of his dream because they do not accompany the waking state and the state of dreamless sleep; so the one permanent witness of the three states (viz. the highest Self which is the one unchanging witness of the creation, subsistence, and reabsorption of the world) is not touched by the mutually exclusive three states. For that the highest Self appears in those three states, is a mere illusion, not more substantial than the snake for which the rope is mistaken in the twilight. With reference to this point teachers knowing the true tradition of the Vedānta have made the following declaration, 'When the individual soul which is held in the bonds of slumber by the beginningless *māyā* awakes, then it knows the eternal, sleepless, dreamless non-duality' (Gauḍap. Kār. I, 16).

So far we have shown that—on our doctrine—there is no danger of the cause being affected at the time of reabsorption by the qualities of the effect, such as grossness and the like.—With regard to the second objection, viz. that if we assume all distinctions to pass (at the time of reabsorption) into the state of non-distinction there would be no special reason for the origin of a new world affected with distinctions, we likewise refer to the 'existence of parallel instances.' For the case is parallel to that of deep sleep and trance. In those states also the soul enters into an essential condition of non-distinction; nevertheless, wrong knowledge being not yet finally overcome, the old state of distinction re-established itself as soon as the soul awakes from its sleep or trance. . . . For just as during the subsistence of the world the phenomenon of multifarious distinct existence, based on wrong knowledge, proceeds unimpeded like the vision of a dream, although there is only one highest Self devoid of all distinction; so, we conclude, there remains, even after reabsorption, the power of distinction (potential distinction) founded on wrong knowledge.—Herewith the objection that—according to our doctrine—even the finally released souls would be born again is already disposed of. They will not be born again because in their case wrong knowledge has been entirely discarded by perfect knowledge.—The last alternative finally (which the *pūrvapakṣin* had represented as open to the Vedāntin), viz. that even at the time of reabsorption the world should remain distinct from Brahman, precludes itself because it is not admitted by the Vedāntins themselves.—Hence the system founded on the Upaniṣads is in every way unobjectionable. (II, 1, 9)

In matters to be known from Scripture mere reasoning is not to be relied on for the following reason also. As the thoughts of man are altogether unfettered, reasoning which disregards the holy texts and rests on individual opinion only has no proper foundation. We see how arguments, which some clever men had excogitated with great pains, are shown, by people still more ingenious, to be fallacious, and how the arguments of the latter again are refuted in their turn by other men; so that, on account of the diversity of men's opinions, it is impossible to accept mere reasoning as having a sure foundation. Nor can we get over this difficulty by accepting as well-founded the reasoning of some person of recognised mental eminence, may he now be Kapila or anybody else; since we observe that even men of the most undoubted mental eminence, such as Kapila, Kaṇāda, and other founders of philosophical schools, have contradicted one another. (II, 1, 11)

Another objection, based on reasoning, is raised against the doctrine of Brahman being the cause of the world.—Although Scripture is authoritative with regard to its own special subject-matter (as, for instance, the causality of Brahman), still it may have to be taken in a secondary sense in those cases where the subject-matter is taken out of its grasp by other means of right knowledge; just as *mantras* and *arthavādas* have occasionally to be explained in the secondary sense (when the primary, literal sense is rendered impossible by other means of right knowledge). Analogously reasoning is to be considered invalid outside its legitimate sphere; so, for instance, in the case of religious duty and its opposite.—Hence Scripture cannot be acknowledged to refute what is settled by other means of right knowledge. And if you ask, 'Where does Scripture oppose itself to what is thus established?' we give you the following instance. The distinction of enjoyers and objects of enjoyment is well known from ordinary experience, the enjoyers being intelligent, embodied souls, while sound and the like are the objects of enjoyment. Devadatta, for instance, is an enjoyer, the dish (which he eats) an object of enjoyment. The distinction of the two would be reduced to non-existence if the enjoyer passed over into the object of enjoyment, and vice versa. Now this passing over of one thing into another would actually result from the doctrine of the world being non-different from Brahman. But the sublation of a well-established distinction is objectionable, not only with regard to the present time when that distinction is observed to exist, but also with regard to the past and the future, for which it is inferred. The doctrine of Brahman's causality must therefore be abandoned, as it would lead to the sublation of the well-established distinction of enjoyers and objects of enjoyment.

To the preceding objection we reply, 'It may exist as in ordinary experience.' Even on our philosophic view the distinction may exist, as ordinary experience furnishes us with analogous instances. We see, for instance, that waves, foam, bubbles, and other modifications of the sea, although they really are not different from the sea-water, exist, sometimes in the state of mutual separation, sometimes in the state of conjunction, &c. From the fact of their being non-different from the sea-water, it does not follow that they pass over into each other; and, again, although they do not pass over into each other, still they are not different from the sea. So it is in the case under discussion also. The enjoyers and the objects of enjoyment do not pass over into each other, and yet they are not different from the highest Brahman. And although the enjoyer is not really an effect of Brahman, since the unmodified creator himself, in so far as he enters into the effect, is called the enjoyer (according to the passage, 'Having created he entered into it,' Taitt. Up. II, 6), still after Brahman has entered into its effects it passes into a state of distinction, in consequence of the effect acting as a limiting adjunct; just as the universal ether is divided by its contact with jars and other limiting adjuncts. The conclusion is, that the distinction of enjoyers and objects of enjoyment is possible, although both are non-different from Brahman, their highest cause, as the analogous instance of the sea and its waves demonstrates. (II, 1, 13)

The refutation contained in the preceding Sūtra was set forth on the condition of the practical distinction of enjoyers and objects of enjoyment being acknowledged. In reality, however, that distinction does not exist because there is understood to be non-difference (identity) of cause and effect. The effect is this manifold world consisting of ether and so on; the cause is the highest Brahman. Of the effect it is understood that in reality it is non-different from the cause, i.e. has no existence apart from the cause.—How so?—'On account of the scriptural word "origin" and others.' The word 'origin' is used in connexion with a simile, in a passage undertaking to show how through the knowledge of one thing everything is known; viz. Ch. Up. VI, 1, 4, 'As, my dear, by one clod of clay all that is made of clay is known, the modification (i.e. the effect; the thing made of clay) being a name merely which has its origin in speech, while the truth is that it is clay merely; thus,' &c.—The meaning of this passage is that, if there is known a lump of clay which really and truly is nothing but clay, there are known thereby likewise all things made of clay, such as jars, dishes, pails, and so on, all of which agree in having clay for their true nature. For these modifications or effects are names only, exist through or originate from speech only, while in reality there exists no such thing as a modification. In so far as they are names (individual effects distinguished by names) they are untrue; in so far as they are clay they are true.—This parallel instance is given with reference to Brahman; applying the phrase 'having its origin in speech' to the case illustrated by the instance quoted we understand that the entire body of effects has no existence apart from

Brahman. . . . We therefore must adopt the following view. In the same way as those parts of ethereal space which are limited by jars and waterpots are not really different from the universal ethereal space, and as the water of a mirage is not really different from the surface of the salty steppe—for the nature of that water is that it is seen in one moment and has vanished in the next, and moreover, it is not to be perceived by its own nature (i.e. apart from the surface of the desert)—; so this manifold world with its objects of enjoyment, enjoyers and so on has no existence apart from Brahman.—But—it might be objected—Brahman has in itself elements of manifoldness. As the tree has many branches, so Brahman possesses many powers and energies dependent on those powers. Unity and manifoldness are therefore both true. Thus, a tree considered in itself is one, but it is manifold if viewed as having branches; so the sea in itself is one, but manifold as having waves and foam; so the clay in itself is one, but manifold if viewed with regard to the jars and dishes made of it. On this assumption the process of final release resulting from right knowledge may be established in connexion with the element of unity (in Brahman), while the two processes of common worldly activity and of activity according to the Veda—which depend on the *karmakāṇḍa*—may be established in connexion with the element of manifoldness. And with this view the parallel instances of clay &c. agree very well.

This theory, we reply, is untenable because in the instance (quoted in the Upaniṣad) the phrase 'as clay they are true' asserts the cause only to be true while the phrase 'having its origin in speech' declares the unreality of all effects. And with reference to the matter illustrated by the instance given (viz. the highest cause, Brahman) we read, 'In that all this has its Self;' and, again, 'That is true,' whereby it is asserted that only the one highest cause is true. The following passage again, 'That is the Self; thou art that, O Śvetaketu!' teaches that the embodied soul (the individual soul) also is Brahman. (And we must note that) the passage distinctly teaches that the fact of the embodied soul having its Self in Brahman is self-established, not to be accomplished by endeavour. This doctrine of the individual soul having its Self in Brahman, if once accepted as the doctrine of the Veda, does away with the independent existence of the individual soul, just as the idea of the rope does away with the idea of the snake (for which the rope had been mistaken). And if the doctrine of the independent existence of the individual soul has to be set aside, then the opinion of the entire phenomenal world—which is based on the individual soul—having an independent existence is likewise to be set aside. But only for the establishment of the latter an element of manifoldness would have to be assumed in Brahman, in addition to the element of unity.—Scriptural passages also (such as 'When the Self only is all this, how should he see another?' Bṛh. Up. II, 4, 13) declare that for him who sees that everything has its Self in Brahman the whole phenomenal world with its actions, agents, and results of actions is non-existent.

Nor can it be said that this non-existence of the phenomenal world is declared (by Scripture) to be limited to certain states; for the passage 'Thou art that' shows that the general fact of Brahman being the Self of all is not limited by any particular state. Moreover, Scripture, showing by the instance of the thief (Ch. Up. VI, 16) that the false-minded is bound while the true-minded is released, declares thereby that unity is the one true existence while manifoldness is evolved out of wrong knowledge. For if both were true how could the man who acquiesces in the reality of this phenomenal world be called false-minded? Another scriptural passage ('from death to death goes he who perceives therein any diversity,' Bṛh. Up. IV, 4, 19) declares the same, by blaming those who perceive any distinction.—Moreover, on the doctrine, which we are at present impugning, release cannot result from knowledge, because the doctrine does not acknowledge that some kind of wrong knowledge, to be removed by perfect knowledge, is the cause of the phenomenal world. For how can the cognition of unity remove the cognition of manifoldness if both are true?

Other objections are started.—If we acquiesce in the doctrine of absolute unity, the ordinary means of right knowledge, perception, &c., become invalid because the absence of manifoldness deprives them of their objects; just as the idea of a man becomes invalid after the right idea of the post (which at first had been mistaken for a man) has presented itself. Moreover, all the texts embodying injunctions and prohibitions will lose their purport if the distinction on which their validity depends does not really exist. And further, the entire body of doctrine which refers to final release will collapse, if the distinction of teacher and pupil on which it depends is not real. And if the doctrine of release is untrue, how can we maintain the truth of the absolute unity of the Self, which forms an item of that doctrine?

These objections, we reply, do not damage our position because the entire complex of phenomenal existence is considered as true as long as the knowledge of Brahman being the Self of all has not arisen; just as the phantoms of a dream are considered to be true until the sleeper wakes. For as long as a person has not reached the true knowledge of the unity of the Self, so long it does not enter his mind that the world of effects with its means and objects of right knowledge and its results of actions is untrue; he rather, in consequence of his ignorance, looks on mere effects (such as body, offspring, wealth, &c.) as forming part of and belonging to his Self, forgetful of Brahman being in reality the Self of all. Hence, as long as true knowledge does not present itself, there is no reason why the ordinary course of secular and religious activity should not hold on undisturbed. The case is analogous to that of a dreaming man who in his dream sees manifold things, and, up to the moment of waking, is convinced that his ideas are produced by real perception without suspecting the perception to be a merely apparent one.—But how (to restate an objection raised above) can the Vedānta-texts if untrue convey information about the true being of

Brahman? We certainly do not observe that a man bitten by a rope-snake (i.e. a snake falsely imagined in a rope) dies, nor is the water appearing in a mirage used for drinking or bathing.—This objection, we reply, is without force (because as a matter of fact we do see real effects to result from unreal causes), for we observe that death sometimes takes place from imaginary venom, (when a man imagines himself to have been bitten by a venomous snake,) and effects (of what is perceived in a dream) such as the bite of a snake or bathing in a river take place with regard to a dreaming person.—But, it will be said, these effects themselves are unreal!—These effects themselves, we reply, are unreal indeed; but not so the consciousness which the dreaming person has of them. This consciousness is a real result; for it is not sublated by the waking consciousness. The man who has risen from sleep does indeed consider the effects perceived by him in his dream such as being bitten by a snake, bathing in a river, &c. to be unreal, but he does not on that account consider the consciousness he had of them to be unreal likewise.—(We remark in passing that) by this fact of the consciousness of the dreaming person not being sublated (by the waking consciousness) the doctrine of the body being our true Self is to be considered as refuted.—Scripture also (in the passage, 'If a man who is engaged in some sacrifice undertaken for some special wish sees in his dream a woman, he is to infer therefrom success in his work') declares that by the unreal phantom of a dream a real result such as prosperity may be obtained. And, again, another scriptural passage, after having declared that from the observation of certain unfavourable omens a man is to conclude that he will not live long, continues 'if somebody sees in his dream a black man with black teeth and that man kills him,' intimating thereby that by the unreal dream-phantom a real fact, viz. death, is notified.—It is, moreover, known from the experience of persons who carefully observe positive and negative instances that such and such dreams are auspicious omens, others the reverse. And (to quote another example that something true can result from or be known through something untrue) we see that the knowledge of the real sounds A. &c. is reached by means of the unreal written letters. Moreover, the reasons which establish the unity of the Self are altogether final, so that subsequently to them nothing more is required for full satisfaction. An injunction as, for instance, 'He is to sacrifice' at once renders us desirous of knowing what is to be effected, and by what means and in what manner it is to be effected; but passages such as, 'Thou art that,' 'I am Brahman,' leave nothing to be desired because the state of consciousness produced by them has for its object the unity of the universal Self. For as long as something else remains a desire is possible; but there is nothing else which could be desired in addition to the absolute unity of Brahman. . . . Nor, again, can such consciousness be objected to on the ground either of uselessness or of erroneousness, because, firstly, it is seen to have for its result the cessation of ignorance, and because, secondly, there is no other kind of knowledge by which it could be sublated. And that before the knowledge of the unity of the Self has been reached the whole real-unreal course of ordinary life, worldly as well as religious, goes on unimpeded, we have already explained. When, however, final authority having intimated the unity of the Self, the entire course of the world which was founded on the previous distinction is sublated, then there is no longer any opportunity for assuming a Brahman comprising in itself various elements.

... Thus the Lord depends (as Lord) upon the limiting adjuncts of name and form, the products of Nescience; just as the universal ether depends (as limited ether, such as the ether of a jar, &c.) upon the limiting adjuncts in the shape of jars, pots, &c. He (the Lord) stands in the realm of the phenomenal in the relation of a ruler to the so-called jīvas (individual souls) or cognitional Selfs (*vijñānātman*), which indeed are one with his own Self—just as the portions of ether enclosed in jars and the like are one with the universal ether—but are limited by aggregates of instruments of action (i.e. bodies) produced from name and form, the presentations of Nescience. Hence the Lord's being a Lord, his omniscience, his omnipotence, &c. all depend on the limitation due to the adjuncts whose Self is Nescience; while in reality none of these qualities belong to the Self whose true nature is cleared, by right knowledge, from all adjuncts whatever. . . . (II, 1, 14)

For the following reason also the effect is non-different from the cause, because only when the cause exists the effect is observed to exist, not when it does not exist. For instance, only when the clay exists the jar is observed to exist, and the cloth only when the threads exist. That it is not a general rule that when one thing exists another is also observed to exist, appears, for instance, from the fact, that a horse which is other (different) from a cow is not observed to exist only when a cow exists. Nor is the jar observed to exist only when the potter exists; for in that case non-difference does not exist, although the relation between the two is that of an operative cause and its effect.—But—it may be objected—even in the case of things other (i.e. non-identical) we find that the observation of one thing regularly depends on the existence of another; smoke, for instance, is observed only when fire exists.—We reply that this is untrue, because sometimes smoke is observed even after the fire has been extinguished; as, for instance, in the case of smoke being kept by herdsmen in jars.—Well, then—the objector will say—let us add to smoke a certain qualification enabling us to say that smoke of such and such a kind does not exist unless fire exists.—Even thus, we reply, your objection is not valid, because we declare that the reason for assuming the non-difference of cause and effect is the fact of the internal organ (*buddhi*) being affected (impressed) by cause and effect jointly. And that does not take place in the case of fire and smoke. . . . The non-difference of cause and effect results not only from Scripture but also from the existence of perception. For the non-difference of the two is perceived, for instance, in an aggregate of threads, where we do not perceive a thing called 'cloth,' in addition to the threads, but merely threads running lengthways and crossways. So again, in the threads we perceive finer threads (the aggregate of which is identical with the grosser threads), in them again finer threads, and so on. On the ground of this our perception we conclude that the finest parts which we can perceive are ultimately identical with their causes, viz. red, white, and black (the colours of fire, water, and earth, according to Ch. Up. VI, 4); those, again, with air, the latter with ether, and ether with Brahman, which is one and without a second. . . . (II, 1, 15)

For the following reason also the effect is to be considered as non-different (from the cause). That which is posterior in time, i.e. the effect, is declared by Scripture to have, previous to its actual beginning, its Being in the cause, by the Self of the cause merely. For in passages like, 'In the beginning, my dear, this was that only which is' (Ch. Up. VI, 2, 1); and, 'Verily, in the beginning this was Self, one only' (Ait. Ār. II, 4, 1, 1), the effect which is denoted by the word 'this' appears in grammatical co-ordination with (the word denoting) the cause (from which it appears that both inhere in the same substratum). A thing, on the other hand, which does not exist in another thing by the Self of the latter is not produced from that other thing; for instance, oil is not produced from sand. Hence as there is non-difference before the production (of the effect), we understand that the effect even after having been produced continues to be non-different from the cause. As the cause, i.e. Brahman, is in all time neither more nor less than that which is, so the effect also, viz. the world, is in all time only that which is. But that which is is one only; therefore the effect is non-different from the cause. (II, 1, 16)

That the effect exists before its origination and is non-different from the cause, follows from reasoning as well as from a further scriptural passage.

We at first set forth the argumentation.—Ordinary experience teaches us that those who wish to produce certain effects, such as curds, or earthen jars, or golden ornaments, employ for their purpose certain determined causal substances such as milk, clay, and gold; those who wish to produce sour milk do not employ clay, nor do those who intend to make jars employ milk and so on. But, according to that doctrine which teaches that the effect is non-existent (before its actual production), all this should be possible. For if before their actual origination all effects are equally non-existent in any causal substance, why then should curds be produced from milk only and not from clay also, and jars from clay only and not from milk as well?—Let us then maintain, the *asatkāryavādin* rejoins, that there is indeed an equal non-existence of any effect in any cause, but that at the same time each causal substance has a certain capacity reaching beyond itself (*atiśaya*) for some particular effect only and not for other effects; that, for instance, milk only, and not clay, has a certain capacity for curds; and clay only, and not milk, an analogous capacity for jars.—What, we ask in return, do you understand by that '*atiśaya*?' If you understand by it the antecedent condition of the effect (before its actual origination), you abandon your doctrine that the effect does not exist in the cause, and prove our doctrine according to which it does so exist. If, on the other hand, you understand by the *atiśaya* a certain power of the cause assumed to the end of accounting for the fact that only one determined effect springs from the cause, you must admit that the power can determine the particular effect only if it neither is other (than cause and effect) nor non-existent; for if it were either, it would not be different from anything else which is either non-existent or other than cause and effect, (and how then should it alone be able to produce the particular effect?) Hence it follows that that power is identical with the Self of the cause, and that the effect is identical with the Self of that power.—Moreover, as the ideas of cause and effect on the one hand and of substance and qualities on the other hand are not separate ones, as, for instance, the ideas of a horse and a buffalo, it follows that the identity of the cause and the effect as well as of the substance and its qualities has to be admitted. (Let it then be assumed, the opponent rejoins, that the cause and the effect, although really different, are not apprehended as such, because they are connected by the so-called *samavāya* connexion.)—If, we reply, you assume the *samavāya* connexion between cause and effect, you have either to admit that the *samavāya* itself is joined by a certain connexion to the two terms which are connected by *samavāya*, and then that connexion will again require a new connexion (joining it to the two terms which it binds together), and you will thus be compelled to postulate an infinite series of connexions; or else you will have to maintain that the *samavāya* is not joined by any connexion to the terms which it binds together, and from that will result the dissolution of the bond which connects the two terms of the *samavāya* relation.—Well then, the opponent rejoins, let us assume that the *samavāya* connexion as itself being a connexion may be connected with the terms which it joins without the help of any further connexion.—Then, we reply, conjunction (*saṁyoga*) also must be connected with the two terms which it joins without the help of the *samavāya* connexion; for conjunction also is a kind of connexion.—Moreover, as substances, qualities, and so on are apprehended as standing in the relation of identity, the assumption of the *samavāya* relation has really no purport.

In what manner again do you—who maintain that the cause and the effect are joined by the *samavāya* relation—assume a substance consisting of parts which is an effect to abide in its causes, i.e. in the material parts of which it consists? Does it abide in all the parts taken together or in each particular part?—If you say that it abides in all parts together, it follows that the whole as such cannot be perceived, as it is impossible that all the parts should be in contact with the organs of perception. (And let it not be objected that the whole may be apprehended through some of the parts only), for manyness which abides in all its substrates together (i.e. in all the many things), is not apprehended so long as only some of those substrates are apprehended.—Let it then be assumed that the whole abides in all the parts by the mediation of intervening aggregates of parts.—In that case, we reply, we should have to assume other parts in addition to the primary originative parts of the whole, in order that by means of those other parts the whole could abide in the primary parts in the manner indicated by you. For we see (that one thing which abides in another abides there by means of parts different from those of that other thing), that the sword, for instance, pervades the sheath by means of parts different from the parts of the sheath. But an assumption of that kind would lead us into a regressus in infinitum, because in order to explain how the whole abides in certain given parts we should always have to assume further parts.—Well, then, let us maintain the second alternative, viz. that the whole abides in each particular part.—That also cannot be admitted; for if the whole is present in one part it cannot be present in other parts also; not any more than Devadatta can be present in Śrughna and in Pāṭaliputra on one and the same day. If the whole were present in more than one part, several wholes would result, comparable to Devadatta and Yajñadatta, who, as being two different persons, may live one of them at Śrughna and the other at Pāṭaliputra.—If the opponent should rejoin that the whole may be fully present in each part, just as the generic character of the cow is fully present in each individual cow; we point out that the generic attributes of the cow are visibly perceived in each individual cow, but that the whole is not thus perceived in each particular part. If the whole were fully present in each part, the consequence would be that the whole would produce its effects indifferently with any of its parts; a cow, for instance, would give milk from her horns or her tail. But such things are not seen to take place.

We proceed to consider some further arguments opposed to the doctrine that the effect does not exist in the cause.—That doctrine involves the conclusion that the actual origination of an effect is without an agent and thus devoid of substantial being. For origination is an action, and as such requires an agent; just as the action of walking does. To speak of an action without an agent would be a contradiction. But if you deny the pre-existence of the effect in the cause, it would have to be assumed that whenever the origination of a jar, for instance, is spoken of the agent is not the jar (which before its origination did not exist) but something else, and again that when the origination of the two halves of the jar is spoken of the agent is not the two halves but something else. From this it would follow that the sentence, 'the jar is originated,' means as much as 'the potter and the other (operative) causes are originated.' But as a matter of fact the former sentence is never understood to mean the latter; and it is, moreover, known that at the time when the jar originates, the potter, &c. are already in existence.—Let us then say, the opponent resumes, that origination is the connexion of the effect with the existence of its cause and its obtaining existence as a Self.—How, we ask in reply, can something which has not yet obtained existence enter into connexion with something else? A connexion is possible of two existing things only, not of one existing and one non-existing thing or of two non-existing things. To something non-existing which on that account is indefinable, it is moreover not possible to assign a limit as the opponent does when maintaining that the effect is non-existing before its origination; for experience teaches us that existing things only such as fields and houses have limits, but not non-existing things. If somebody should use, for instance, a phrase such as the following one, 'The son of a barren woman was king previously to the coronation of Pūrṇavarman,' the declaration of a limit in time implied in that phrase does not in reality determine that the son of the barren woman, i.e. a mere non-entity, either was or is or will be king. If the son of a barren woman could become an existing thing subsequently to the activity of some causal agent, in that case it would be possible also that the non-existing effect should be something existing, subsequently to the activity of some causal agent. But we know that the one thing can take place no more than the other thing; the non-existing effect and the son of the barren woman are both equally non-entities and can never be.—But, the *asatkāryavādin* here objects, from your doctrine there follows the result that the activity of causal agents is altogether purposeless. For if the effect were lying already fully accomplished in the cause and were non-different from it, nobody would endeavour to bring it about, no more than anybody endeavours to bring about the cause which is already fully accomplished previously to all endeavour. But as a matter of fact causal agents do endeavour to bring about effects, and it is in order not to have to condemn their efforts as altogether useless that we assume the non-existence of the effect previously to its origination.—Your objection is refuted, we reply, by the consideration that the endeavour of the causal agent may be looked upon as having a purpose in so far as it arranges the causal substance in the form of the effect. That, however, even the form of the effect (is not something previously non-existing, but) belongs to the Self of the cause already because what is devoid of Selfhood cannot be begun at all, we have already shown above.—Nor does a substance become another substance merely by appearing under a different aspect. Devadatta may at one time be seen with his arms and legs closely drawn up to his body, and another time with his arms and legs stretched out, and yet he remains the same substantial being, for he is recognised as such. Thus the persons also by whom we are surrounded, such as fathers, mothers, brothers, &c., remain the same, although we see them in continually changing states and attitudes; for they are always recognised as fathers, mothers, brothers, and so on. If our opponent objects to this last illustrative example on the ground that fathers, mothers, and so on remain the same substantial beings, because the different states in which they appear are not separated from each other by birth or death, while the effect, for instance a jar, appears only after the cause, for instance the clay, has undergone destruction as it were (so that the effect may be looked upon as something altogether different from the cause); we rebut this objection by remarking that causal substances also such as milk, for instance, are perceived to exist even after they have entered into the condition of effects such as curds and the like (so that we have no right to say that the cause undergoes destruction). And even in those cases where the continued existence of the cause is not perceived, as, for instance, in the case of seeds of the fig-tree from which there spring sprouts and trees, the term 'birth' (when applied to the sprout) only means that the causal substance, viz. the seed, becomes visible by becoming a sprout through the continual accretion of similar particles of matter; and the term 'death' only means that, through the secession of those particles, the cause again passes beyond the sphere of visibility. Nor can it be said that from such separation by birth and death as described just now it follows that the non-existing becomes existing, and the existing non-existing; for if that were so, it would also follow that the unborn child in the mother's womb and the new-born babe stretched out on the bed are altogether different beings.

The doctrine that the effect is non-existent previously to its actual origination, moreover, leads to the conclusion that the activity of the causal agent has no object; for what does not exist cannot possibly be an object; not any more than the ether can be cleft by swords and other weapons for striking or cutting. The object can certainly not be the inherent cause; for that would lead to the erroneous conclusion that from the activity of the causal agent, which has for its object the inherent cause, there results something else (viz. the effect). And if (in order to preclude this erroneous conclusion) the opponent should say that the effect is (not something different from the cause, but) a certain relative power (*atiśaya*) of the inherent cause; he thereby would simply concede our doctrine, according to which the effect exists in the cause already.

We maintain, therefore, as our final conclusion, that milk and other substances are called effects when they are in the state of curds and so on, and that it is impossible, even within hundreds of years, even to bring about an effect which is different from its cause. The fundamental cause of all appears in the form of this and that effect, up to the last effect of all, just as an actor appears in various robes and costumes, and thereby becomes the basis for all the current notions and terms concerning the phenomenal world. (II, 1, 18)

Another objection is raised against the doctrine of an intelligent cause of the world.—If that doctrine is accepted, certain faults, as, for instance, doing what is not beneficial, will attach (to the intelligent cause, i.e. Brahman), 'on account of the other being designated.' For Scripture declares the other, i.e. the embodied soul, to be one with Brahman, as is shown by the passage, 'That is the Self; that art thou, O Śvetaketu!' (Ch. Up. VI, 8, 7).—Or else (if we interpret 'the other' of the Sūtra in a different way) Scripture declares the other, i.e. Brahman, to be the Self of the embodied soul. For the passage, 'Having created that he entered into it,' declares the creator, i.e. the unmodified Brahman, to constitute the Self of the embodied soul, in consequence of his entering into his products. The following passage also, 'Entering (into them) with this living Self I will evolve names and forms' (Ch. Up. VI, 3, 2), in which the highest divinity designates the living (soul) by the word 'Self,' shows that the embodied Self is not different from Brahman. Therefore the creative power of Brahman belongs to the embodied Self also, and the latter, being thus an independent agent, might be expected to produce only what is beneficial to itself, and not things of a contrary nature, such as birth, death, old age, disease, and whatever may be the other meshes of the net of suffering. For we know that no free person will build a prison for himself, taking up his abode in it. Nor would a being, itself absolutely stainless, look on this altogether unclean body as forming part of its Self. It would, moreover, free itself, according to its liking, of the consequences of those of its former actions which result in pain, and would enjoy the consequences of those actions only which are rewarded by pleasure. Further, it would remember that it had created this manifold world; for every person who has produced some clearly appearing effect remembers that he has been the cause of it. And as the magician easily retracts, whenever he likes, the magical illusion which he had emitted, so the embodied soul also would be able to reabsorb this world into itself. The fact is, however, that the embodied soul cannot reabsorb its own body even. As we therefore see that 'what would be beneficial is not done,' the hypothesis of the world having proceeded from an intelligent cause is unacceptable. (II, 1, 21)

. . . We rather declare that that omniscient, omnipotent Brahman, whose essence is eternal pure cognition and freedom, and which is additional to, i.e. different from the embodied Self, is the creative principle of the world. The faults specified above, such as doing what is not beneficial, and the like, do not attach to that Brahman; for as eternal freedom is its characteristic nature, there is nothing either beneficial to be done by it or non-beneficial to be avoided by it. Nor is there any impediment to its knowledge and power; for it is omniscient and omnipotent. The embodied Self, on the other hand, is of a different nature, and to it the mentioned faults adhere. . . . Moreover, as soon as, in consequence of the declaration of non-difference contained in such passages as 'that art thou,' the consciousness of non-difference arises in us, the transmigratory state of the individual soul and the creative quality of Brahman vanish at once, the whole phenomenon of plurality, which springs from wrong knowledge, being sublated by perfect knowledge, and what becomes then of the creation and the faults of not doing what is beneficial, and the like? For that this entire apparent world, in which good and evil actions are done, &c., is a mere illusion, owing to the non-discrimination of (the Self's) limiting adjuncts, viz. a body, and so on, which spring from name and form the presentations of Nescience, and does in reality not exist at all, we have explained more than once. The illusion is analogous to the mistaken notion we entertain as to the dying, being born, being hurt, &c. of ourselves (our Selfs; while in reality the body only dies, is born, &c.). And with regard to the state in which the appearance of plurality is not yet sublated, it follows from passages declaratory of such difference (as, for instance, 'That we must search for,' &c.) that Brahman is superior to the individual soul; whereby the possibility of faults adhering to it is excluded. (II, 1, 22)

As among minerals, which are all mere modifications of earth, nevertheless great variety is observed, some being precious gems, such as diamonds, lapis lazuli, &c., others, such as crystals and the like, being of medium value, and others again stones only fit to be flung at dogs or crows; and as from seeds which are placed in one and the same ground various plants are seen to spring, such as sandalwood and cucumbers, which show the greatest difference in their leaves, blossoms, fruits, fragrancy, juice, &c.; and as one and the same food produces various effects, such as blood and hair; so the one Brahman also may contain in itself the distinction of the individual Selfs and the highest Self, and may produce various effects. Hence the objections imagined by others (against the doctrine of Brahman being the cause of the world) cannot be maintained.—Further arguments are furnished by the fact of all effects having, as Scripture declares, their origin in speech only, and by the analogous instance of the variety of dream phantoms (while the dreaming person remains one). (II, 1, 23)

Your assertion that the intelligent Brahman alone, without a second, is the cause of the world cannot be maintained, on account of the observation of employment (of instruments). For in ordinary life we see that potters, weavers, and other handicraftsmen produce jars, cloth, and the like, after having put themselves in possession of the means thereto by providing themselves with various implements, such as clay, staffs, wheels, string, &c.; Brahman, on the other hand, you conceive to be without any help; how then can it act as a creator without providing itself with instruments to work with?—We therefore maintain that Brahman is not the cause of the world.

This objection is not valid, because causation is possible in consequence of a peculiar constitution of the causal substance, as in the case of milk. Just as milk and water turn into curds and ice respectively, without any extraneous means, so it is in the case of Brahman also. And if you object to this analogy for the reason that milk, in order to turn into curds, does require an extraneous agent, viz. heat, we reply that milk by itself also undergoes a certain amount of definite change, and that its turning is merely accelerated by heat. If milk did not possess that capability of itself, heat coud not compel it to turn; for we see that air or ether, for instance, is not compelled by the action of heat to turn into sour milk. By the co-operation of auxiliary means the milk's capability of turning into sour milk is merely completed. The absolutely complete power of Brahman, on the other hand, does not require to be supplemented by any extraneous help. . . . (II, 1, 24)

. . . [W]e maintain that the (alleged) break in Brahman's nature is a mere figment of Nescience. By a break of that nature a thing is not really broken up into parts, not any more than the moon is really multiplied by appearing double to a person of defective vision. By that element of plurality which is the fiction of Nescience, which is characterised by name and form, which is evolved as well as non-evolved, which is not to be defined either as the Existing or the Non-existing, Brahman becomes the basis of this entire apparent world with its changes, and so on, while in its true and real nature it at the same time remains unchanged, lifted above the phenomenal universe. And as the distinction of names and forms, the fiction of Nescience, originates entirely from speech only, it does not militate against the fact of Brahman being without parts.—Nor have the scriptural passages which speak of Brahman as undergoing change the purpose of teaching the fact of change; for such instruction would have no fruit. They rather aim at imparting instruction about Brahman's Self as raised above this apparent world; that being an instruction which we know to have a result of its own. . . . (II, 1, 27)

Another objection is raised against the doctrine of an intelligent cause of the world.—The intelligent highest Self cannot be the creator of the sphere of this world, 'on account of actions having a purpose.'—We known from ordinary experience that man, who is an intelligent being, begins to act after due consideration only, and does not engage even in an unimportant undertaking unless it serves some purpose of his own; much less so in important business. There is also a scriptural passage confirming this result of common experience, 'Verily everything is not dear that you may love everything; but that you may love the Self therefore everything is dear' (Bṛh. Up. II, 4, 5). Now the undertaking of creating the sphere of this world, with all its various contents, is certainly a weighty one. If, then, on the one hand, you assume it to serve some purpose of the intelligent highest Self, you thereby sublate its self-sufficiency vouched for by Scripture; if, on the other hand, you affirm absence of motive on its part, you must affirm absence of activity also.—Let us then assume that just as sometimes an intelligent person when in a state of frenzy proceeds, owing to his mental aberration, to action without a motive, so the highest Self also created this world without any motive.—That, we reply, would contradict the omniscience of the highest Self, which is vouched for by Scripture.—Hence the doctrine of the creation proceeding from an intelligent Being is untenable. (II, 1, 32)

... We see in every-day life that certain doings of princes or other men of high position who have no unfulfilled desires left have no reference to any extraneous purpose, but proceed from mere sportfulness, as, for instance, their recreations in places of amusement. We further see that the process of inhalation and exhalation is going on without reference to any extraneous purpose, merely following the law of its own nature. Analogously, the activity of the Lord also may be supposed to be mere sport, proceeding from his own nature, without reference to any purpose. For on the ground neither of reason nor of Scripture can we construe any other purpose of the Lord. Nor can his nature be questioned.—Although the creation of this world appears to us a weighty and difficult undertaking, it is mere play to the Lord, whose power is unlimited. And if in ordinary life we might possibly, by close scrutiny, detect some subtle motive, even for sportful action, we cannot do so with regard to the actions of the Lord, all whose wishes are fulfilled, as Scripture says.—Nor can it be said that he either does not act or acts like a senseless person; for Scripture affirms the fact of the creation on the one hand, and the Lord's omniscience on the other hand. And, finally, we must remember that the scriptural doctrine of creation does not refer to the highest reality; it refers to the apparent world only, which is characterised by name and form, the figments of Nescience, and it, moreover, aims at intimating that Brahman is the Self of everything. (II, 1, 33)

In order to strengthen the tenet which we are at present defending, we follow the procedure of him who shakes a pole planted in the ground (in order to test whether it is firmly planted), and raise another objection against the doctrine of the Lord being the cause of the world.—The Lord, it is said, cannot be the cause of the world, because, on that hypothesis, the reproach of inequality of dispensation and cruelty would attach to him. Some beings, viz. the gods and others, he renders eminently happy; others, as for instance the animals, eminently unhappy; to some again, as for instance men, he allots an intermediate position. To a Lord bringing about such an unequal condition of things, passion and malice would have to be ascribed, just as to any common person acting similarly; while attributes would be contrary to the essential goodness of the Lord affirmed by *śruti* and *smṛti*. Moreover, as the infliction of pain and the final destruction of all creatures would form part of his dispensation, he would have to be taxed with great cruelty, a quality abhorred by low people even. For these two reasons Brahman cannot be the cause of the world.

The Lord, we reply, cannot be reproached with inequality of dispensation and cruelty, 'because he is bound by regards.' If the Lord on his own account, without any extraneous regards, produced this unequal creation, he would expose himself to blame; but the fact is, that in creating he is bound by certain regards, i.e. he has to look to merit and demerit. Hence the circumstance of the creation being unequal is due to the merit and demerit of the living creatures created, and is not a fault for which the Lord is to blame. The position of the Lord is to be looked on as analogous to that of Parjanya, the Giver of rain. For as Parjanya is the common cause of the production of rice, barley, and other plants, while the difference between the various species is due to the various potentialities lying hidden in the respective seeds, so the Lord is the common cause of the creation of gods, men, &c., while the differences between these classes of beings are due to the different merit belonging to the individual souls. Hence the Lord, being bound by regards, cannot be reproached with inequality of dispensation and cruelty. . . . (II, 1, 34)

But—an objection is raised—the passage, 'Being only this was in the beginning, one, without a second,' affirms that before the creation there was no distinction and consequently no merit on account of which the creation might have become unequal. And if we assume the Lord to have been guided in his dispensations by the actions of living beings subsequent to the creation, we involve ourselves in the circular reasoning that work depends on diversity of condition of life, and diversity of condition again on work. The Lord may be considered as acting with regard to religious merit after distinction had once arisen; but as before that the cause of inequality, viz. merit, did not exist, it follows that the first creation must have been free from inequalities.

This objection we meet by the remark, that the transmigratory world is without beginning.—The objection would be valid if the world had a beginning; but as it is without beginning, merit and inequality are, like seed and sprout, caused as well as causes, and there is therefore no logical objection to their operation. . . . (II, 1, 35)

The beginninglessness of the world recommends itself to reason. For if it had a beginning it would follow that, the world springing into existence without a cause, the released souls also would again enter into the circle of transmigratory existence; and further, as then there would exist no determining cause of the unequal dispensation of pleasure and pain, we should have to acquiesce in the doctrine of rewards and punishments being allotted, without reference to previous good or bad actions. That the Lord is not the cause of the inequality, has already been remarked. Nor can Nescience by itself be the cause, as it is of a uniform nature. On the other hand, Nescience may be the cause of inequality, if it be considered as having regard to merit accruing from action produced by the mental impressions of wrath, hatred, and other afflicting passions. Without merit and demerit nobody can enter into existence, and again, without a body merit and demerit cannot be formed; so that—on the doctrine of the world having a beginning—we are led into a logical see-saw. The opposite doctrine, on the other hand, explains all matters in a manner analogous to the case of the seed and sprout, so that no difficulty remains. . . . (II, 1, 36)

Owing to the conflicting views of the philosophical schools there arises a doubt whether, as the followers of Kaṇāda think, the soul is in itself non-intelligent, so that its intelligence is merely adventitious; or if, as the Sāṁkhyas think, eternal intelligence constitutes its very nature.

The *pūrvapakṣin* maintains that the intelligence of the Self is adventitious, and is produced by the conjunction of the Self with the mind (*manas*), just as, for instance, the quality of redness is produced in a jar by the conjunction of the jar with fire. For if the soul were of eternal (essential) intelligence, it would remain intelligent in the states of deep sleep, swoon, and possession, while as a matter of fact, men when waking from sleep and so on declare in reply to questions addressed to them that they were not conscious of anything. Men in their ordinary state, on the other hand, are seen to be (actively) intelligent. Hence, as intelligence is clearly intermittent, we conclude that the Self's intelligence is adventitious only.

To this we reply that the soul is of eternal intelligence, for that very reason that it is not a product but nothing else but the unmodified highest Brahman which, owing to the contact with its limiting adjuncts, appears as individual soul. That intelligence constitutes the essential nature of the highest Brahman, we know from scriptural passages such as 'Brahman is knowledge and bliss' (Bṛh. Up. III, 9, 28, 7); 'Brahman is true, knowledge, infinite' (Taitt. Up. II, 1); 'Having neither inside nor outside, but being altogether a mass of knowledge' (Bṛh. Up. IV, 5, 13). Now, if the individual soul is nothing but that highest Brahman, then eternal intelligence constitutes the soul's essential nature also, just as light and heat constitute the nature of fire. . . . (II, 3, 18)

The internal organ which constitutes the limiting adjunct of the soul is called in different places by different names, such as *manas* (mind), *buddhi* (intelligence), *vijñāna* (knowledge), *citta* (thought). This difference of nomenclature is something made dependent on the difference of the modifications of the internal organ which is called *manas* when it is in the state of doubt, &c., *buddhi* when it is in the state of determination and the like.—Now we must necessarily acknowledge the existence of such an internal organ; because otherwise there would result either perpetual perception or perpetual non-perception. There would result perpetual perception whenever there is a conjunction of the soul, the senses and the objects of sense—the three together constituting the instruments of perception; or else, if on the conjunction of the three causes the effect did not follow, there would take place perpetual non-perception. But neither of these two alternatives is actually observed.—Or else we should have to assume that there are obstacles in the way of the energy either of the Self or the sense-organs. But the former is not possible, as the Self is not capable of any modification; nor the latter, as we cannot assume that the energy of the sense-organ which is non-obstructed in the preceding and the following moment should, without any cause, be obstructed (in the intervening moment). Hence we have to acknowledge the existence of an internal organ through whose attention and non-attention perception and non-perception take place. . . . (II, 3, 32)

The Lord makes the soul act, having regard to the efforts made by it, whether meritorious or non-meritorious. . . . Having regard to the inequality of the virtuous and vicious actions of the souls, the Lord, acting as a mere occasional cause, allots to them corresponding unequal results. An analogous case is furnished by rain. As rain constitutes the common occasional cause for shrubs, bushes, corn, and so on, which belong to different species and spring each from its particular seed—for the inequality of their sap, flowers, fruits, and leaves results neither when rain is absent nor when the special seeds are absent—; so we also must assume that the Lord arranges favourable or unfavourable circumstances for the souls with a view to their former efforts.—But if the activity of the soul is dependent on something else, this having regard (on the part of the Lord) to former effort is inappropriate.—By no means, we reply; for although the activity of the soul is not independent, yet the soul does act. The Lord indeed causes it to act, but it acts itself. Moreover, the Lord in causing it to act now has regard to its former efforts, and he caused it to act in a former existence, having regard to its efforts previous to that existence; a regressus against which, considering the eternity of the *saṁsāra*, no objections can be raised. . . . (II, 3, 42)

We maintain that the highest Lord does not feel the pain of the *saṁsāra*-state in the same way as the soul does. The soul being engrossed by Nescience identifies itself as it were with the body and so on, and imagines itself to be affected by the experience of pain which is due to Nescience, 'I am afflicted by the pain due to the body;' the highest Lord, on the other hand, neither identifies himself with a body, nor imagines himself to be afflicted by pain. The pain of the individual soul also is not real, but imaginary only, caused by the error consisting in the non-discrimination of (the Self from) the body, senses, and other limiting adjuncts which are due to name and form, the effects of Nescience. And as a person feels the pain of a burn or cut which affects his body by erroneously identifying himself with the latter, so he feels also the pain affecting others, such as sons or friends, by erroneously identifying himself with them, entering as it were into them through love, and imagining 'I am the son, I am the friend.' Wherefrom we infer with certainty that the feeling of pain is due merely to the error of false imagination. At the same conclusion we arrive on the ground of negative instances. Let us consider the case of many men, each of whom possesses sons, friends, &c., sitting together, some of them erroneously imagining that they are connected with their sons, friends, &c., while others do not. If then somebody calls out 'the son has died,' 'the friend has died,' grief is produced in the minds of those who are under the imagination of being connected with sons and friends, but not in the minds of religious mendicants who have freed themselves from that imagination. From this it appears that perfect knowledge is of use even to an ordinary man; of how much greater use then will it be to him (i.e. the Lord) whose nature is eternal pure intelligence, who sees nothing beside the Self for which there are no objects. Hence it follows that perfect knowledge is not purposeless. . . . (II, 3, 46)

. . . [A]lthough the Self must be admitted to be one only, injunctions and prohibitions are possible owing to the difference effected by its connexion with bodies and other limiting adjuncts, the products of Nescience.—It then follows that for him who has obtained perfect knowledge, injunctions and prohibitions are purportless.—No, we reply, (they are not purportless for him, but they do not refer to him), since to him who has obtained the highest aim no obligation can apply. For obligations are imposed with reference to things to be avoided or desired; how then should he, who sees nothing, either to be wished or avoided, beyond the universal Self, stand under any obligation? The Self certainly cannot be enjoined on the Self.—Should it be said that injunctions and prohibitions apply to all those who discern that the soul is something different from the body (and therefore also to him who possesses perfect knowledge), we reply that (such an assertion is too wide, since) obligation depends on a man's imagining his Self to be (actually) connected with the body. It is true that obligation exists for him only who views the soul as something different from the body; but fundamentally all obligation is an erroneous imagination existing in the case of him only who does not see that his Self is no more connected with a body than the ether is with jars and the like. For him, on the other hand, who does not see that connexion no obligation exists, much less, therefore, for him who discerns the unity of the Self.—Nor does it result from the absence of obligation, that he who has arrived at perfect knowledge can act as he likes; for in all cases it is only the wrong imagination (as to the Self's connexion with a body) that impels to action, and that imagination is absent in the case of him who has reached perfect knowledge.—From all this it follows that injunctions and prohibitions are based on the Self's connexion with the body. . . . (II, 3, 48)

And that individual soul is to be considered a mere appearance of the highest Self, like the reflection of the sun in the water; it is neither directly that (i.e. the highest Self), nor a different thing. Hence just as, when one reflected image of the sun trembles, another reflected image does not on that account tremble also; so, when one soul is connected with actions and results of actions, another soul is not on that account connected likewise. There is therefore no confusion of actions and results. And as that 'appearance' is the effect of Nescience, it follows that the *saṁsāra* which is based on it (the appearance) is also the effect of Nescience, so that from the removal of the latter there results the cognition of the soul being in reality nothing but Brahman. (II, 3, 50)

...It is not true that the world of dreams is real; it is mere illusion and there is not a particle of reality in it.—Why?—'On account of its nature not manifesting itself with the totality,' i.e. because the nature of the dream world does not manifest itself with the totality of the attributes of real things.—What then do you mean by the 'totality'?—The fulfilment of the conditions of place, time, and cause, and the circumstance of non-refutation. All these have their sphere in real things, but cannot be applied to dreams. In the first place there is, in a dream, no space for chariots and the like; for those cannot possibly find room in the limited confines of the body.... In the second place we see that dreams are in conflict with the conditions of time. One person lying asleep at night dreams that it is day in the Bhārata Varṣa; another lives, during a dream which lasts one *muhūrta* only, through many crowds of years.—In the third place there do not exist in the state of dreaming the requisite efficient causes for either thought or action; for as, in sleep, the organs are drawn inward, the dreaming person has no eyes, &c. for perceiving chariots and other things; and whence should he, in the space of the twinkling of an eye, have the power of—or procure the material for—making chariots and the like?—In the fourth place the chariots, horses, &c., which the dream creates, are refuted, i.e. shown not to exist by the waking state. And apart from this, the dream itself refutes what it creates, as its end often contradicts its beginning; what at first was considered to be a chariot turns, in a moment, into a man, and what was conceived to be a man has all at once become a tree.... (III, 2, 3)

...We only maintain that the world connected with the intermediate state (i.e. the world of dreams) is not real in the same sense as the world consisting of ether and so on is real. On the other hand we must remember that also the so-called real creation with its ether, air, &c., is not absolutely real; for as we have proved before (II, 1, 14) the entire expanse of things is mere illusion. The world consisting of ether, &c. remains fixed and distinct up to the moment when the soul cognizes that Brahman is the Self of all; the world of dreams on the other hand is daily sublated by the waking state. That the latter is mere illusion has, therefore, to be understood with a distinction. (III, 2, 4)

We now attempt to ascertain, on the ground of *śruti*, the nature of that Brahman with which the individual soul becomes united in the state of deep sleep and so on, in consequence of the cessation of the limiting adjuncts.—The scriptural passages which refer to Brahman are of a double character; some indicate that Brahman is affected by difference, so, e.g. 'He to whom belong all works, all desires, all sweet odours and tastes' (Ch. Up. III, 14, 2); others, that it is without difference, so, e.g. 'It is neither coarse nor fine, neither short no long,' &c.

(Bṛh. Up. III, 8, 8). Have we, on the ground of these passages, to assume that Brahman has a double nature, or either nature, and, if either, that it is affected with difference, or without difference? This is the point to be discussed.

The *pūrvapakṣin* maintains that, in conformity with the scriptural passages which indicate a double nature, a double nature is to be ascribed to Brahman.

To this we reply as follows.—At any rate the highest Brahman cannot, by itself, possess double characteristics; for on account of the contradiction implied therein, it is impossible to admit that one and the same thing should by itself possess certain qualities, such as colour, &c., and should not possess them.—Nor is it possible that Brahman should possess double characteristics 'on account of place,' i.e. on account of its conjunction with its limiting adjuncts, such as earth, &c. For the connexion with limiting adjuncts is unavailing to impart to a thing of a certain nature an altogether different nature. The crystal, e.g. which is in itself clear, does not become dim through its conjunction with a limiting adjunct in the form of red colour; for that it is pervaded by the quality of dimness is an altogether erroneous notion. In the case of Brahman the limiting adjuncts are, moreover, presented by Nescience merely. Hence (as the upādhis are the product of Nescience) if we embrace either of the two alternatives, we must decide in favour of that according to which Brahma is absolutely devoid of all difference, not in favour of the opposite one. For all passages whose aim it is to represent the nature of Brahman (such as, 'It is without sound, without touch, without form, without decay,' Ka. Up. I, 3, 15) teach that it is free from all difference. (III, 2, 11)

Brahman, we must definitively assert, is devoid of all form, colour, and so on, and does not in any way possess form, and so on.—Why?—'On account of this being the main purport (of scripture).'—'It is neither coarse nor fine, neither short nor long' (Bṛh. Up. III, 8, 8); 'That which is without sound, without touch, without form, without decay' (Ka. Up. I, 3, 15); 'He who is called ether is the revealer of all forms and names. That within which forms and names are, that is Brahman' (Ch. Up. VIII, 14, 1); 'That heavenly person is without body, he is both without and within, not produced' (Mu. Up. II, 1, 2); 'That Brahman is without cause and without effect, without anything inside or outside, this Self is Brahman, omnipresent and omniscient' (Bṛh. Up. II, 5, 19). These and similar passages have for their purport the true nature of Brahman as non-connected with any world, and have not any other purport, as we have proved under I, 1, 4. On the ground of such passages we therefore must definitively conclude that Brahman is devoid of form. Those other passages, on the other hand, which refer to a Brahman qualified by form do not aim at setting forth the nature of Brahman, but rather at enjoining the worship of Brahman. . . . (III, 2, 14)

Just as the light of the sun or the moon after having passed through space enters into contact with a finger or some other limiting adjunct, and, according as the latter is straight or bent, itself becomes straight or bent as it were; so Brahman also assumes, as it were, the form of the earth and the other limiting adjuncts with which it enters into connexion. Hence there is no reason why certain texts should not teach, with a view to meditative worship, that Brahman has that and that form. . . . (III, 2, 15)

Because that Self is of the nature of intelligence, devoid of all difference, transcending speech and mind, to be described only by denying of it all other characteristics, therefore the Mokṣa Śāstras compare it to the images of the sun reflected in the water and the like, meaning thereby that all difference in Brahman is unreal, only due to its limiting conditions. Compare, e.g. out of many, the two following passages: 'As the one luminous sun when entering into relation to many different waters is himself rendered multiform by his limiting adjuncts; so also the one divine unborn Self;' and 'The one Self of all beings separately abides in all the individual beings; hence it appears one and many at the same time, just as the one moon is multiplied by its reflections in the water.' (III, 2, 18)

The parallel instance (of the sun's reflection in the water) is unobjectionable, since a common feature—with reference to which alone the comparison is instituted—does exist. Whenever two things are compared, they are so only with reference to some particular point they have in common. Entire equality of the two can never be demonstrated; indeed if it could be demonstrated there would be an end of that particular relation which gives rise to the comparison. Nor does the *sūtrakāra* institute the comparison objected to on his own account; he merely sets forth the purport of a comparison actually met with in scripture.—Now, the special feature on which the comparison rests is 'the participation in increase and decrease.' The reflected image of the sun dilates when the surface of the water expands; it contracts when the water shrinks; it trembles when the water is agitated; it divides itself when the water is divided. It thus participates in all the attributes and conditions of the water; while the real sun remains all the time the same.—Similarly Brahman, although in reality uniform and never changing, participates as it were in the attributes and states of the body and the other limiting adjuncts within which it abides; it grows with them as it were, decreases with them as it were, and so on. As thus the two things compared possess certain common features no objection can be made to the comparison. (III, 2, 20)

What then, it may be asked, is the meaning of those Vedic passages which speak of the highest Brahman as something to be seen, to be heard, and so on?—They aim, we reply, not at enjoining the knowledge of truth, but merely at directing our attention to it. Similarly in ordinary life imperative phrases such as 'Listen to this!' 'Look at this!' are frequently meant to express not that we are immediately to cognize this or that, but only that we are to direct our attention to it. Even when a person is face to face with some object of knowledge, knowledge may either arise or not; all that another person wishing to inform him about the object can do is to point it out to him; knowledge will thereupon spring up in his mind of itself, according to the object of knowledge and according to the means of knowledge employed. . . . (III, 2, 21)

We read, Bṛh. Up. II, 3, 'Two forms of Brahman there are indeed, the material and the immaterial, the mortal and the immortal, the solid and the fluid, *sat* and *tya*'. . . .

. . . It is impossible that the phrase, 'Not so, not so!' should negative both, since that would imply the doctrine of a general Void. Whenever we deny something unreal, we do so with reference to something real; the unreal snake, e.g. is negatived with reference to the real rope. But this (denial of something unreal with inference to something real) is possible only if some entity is left. If everything is denied, no entity is left, and if no entity is left, the denial of some other entity which we may wish to undertake, becomes impossible, i.e. that latter entity becomes real and as such cannot be negatived. . . .

The passage of the Bṛh. Up. under discussion has, therefore, to be understood as follows. Brahman is that whose nature is permanent purity, intelligence, and freedom; it transcends speech and mind, does not fall within the category of 'object,' and constitutes the inward Self of all. Of this Brahman our text denies all plurality of forms; but Brahman itself it leaves untouched. . . . Now, after the two forms have been set forth, there arises the desire of knowing that to which the two forms belong, and hence the text continues, 'Now then the teaching by means of "Not so, not so." ' This passage, we conclude, conveys information regarding the nature of Brahman by denying the reality of the forms fictitiously attributed to it; for the phrase, 'Not so, not so!' negatives the whole aggregate of effects superimposed on Brahman. Effects we know to have no real existence, and they can therefore be negatived; not so, however, Brahman, which constitutes the necessary basis for all fictitious superimposition. . . . (III, 2, 22)

. . . There can exist nothing different from Brahman, since we are unable to observe a proof for such existence. That all existences which have a beginning spring from, subsist through, and return into Brahman we have already ascertained, and have shown that the effect is non-different from the cause.—Nor can there exist, apart from Brahman, something which has no beginning, since scripture affirms that 'Being only this was in the beginning, one, without a second.' The promise moreover that through the cognition of one thing everything will be known, renders it impossible that there should exist anything different from Brahman. . . . (III, 2, 32)

. . . *Adhyāsa* takes place when the idea of one of two things not being dismissed from the mind, the idea of the second thing is superimposed on that of the first thing; so that together with the superimposed idea the former idea remains attached to the thing on which the second idea is superimposed. When e.g. the idea of (the entity) Brahman superimposes itself upon the idea of the name, the latter idea continues in the mind and is not driven out by the former. A similar instance is furnished by the superimposition of the idea of the god Viṣṇu on a statue of Viṣṇu. . . . We, in the second place, have *apavāda* when an idea previously attached to some object is recognised as false and driven out by the true idea springing up after the false one. So e.g. when the false idea of the body, the senses, and so on being the Self is driven out by the true idea springing up later—and expressed by judgments such as 'Thou art that'—that the idea of the Self is to be attached to the Self only. . . . (III, 3, 9)

Here now some materialists (*lokāyatika*), who see the Self in the body only, are of opinion that a Self separate from the body does not exist; assume that consciousness (*caitanya*), although not observed in earth and the other external elements—either single or combined—may yet appear in them when transformed into the shape of a body, so that consciousness springs from them; and thus maintain that knowledge is analogous to intoxicating quality (which arises when certain materials are mixed in certain proportions), and that man is only a body qualified by consciousness. There is thus, according to them, no Self separate from the body and capable of going to the heavenly world or obtaining release, through which consciousness is in the body; but the body alone is what is conscious, is the Self. For this assertion they allege the reason stated in the Sūtra, 'On account of its existence where a body is.' For wherever something exists if some other thing exists, and does not exist if that other thing does not exist, we determine the former thing to be a mere quality of the latter; light and heat, e.g. we determine to be qualities of fire. And as life, movement, consciousness, remembrance and so on—which by the upholders of an independent Self are considered qualities of that Self—are observed only within bodies and not outside bodies, and as an abode of those qualities, different from the body, cannot be proved, it follows that they must be qualities of the body only. The Self therefore is not different from the body. . . . (III, 3, 53)

The assertion that the Self is not separate from the body cannot be maintained. The Self rather must be something separate from the body, 'because the existence (of the Self) does not depend on the existence of that (i.e. the body).' For if from the circumstance that they are where the body is you conclude that the qualities of the Self are qualities of the body, you also must conclude from the fact that they are not where the body is that they are not qualities of the body, because thereby they show themselves to be different in character from the qualities of the body. Now the (real) qualities of the body, such as form and so on, may be viewed as existing as long as the body exists; life, movement, &c., on the other hand, do not exist even when the body exists, viz. in the state of death. The qualities of the body, again, such as form and so on, are perceived by others; not so the qualities of the Self, such as consciousness, remembrance, and so on. Moreover, we can indeed ascertain the presence of those latter qualities as long as the body exists in the state of life, but we cannot ascertain their non-existence when the body does not exist; for it is possible that even after this body has died the qualities of the Self should continue to exist by passing over into another body. The opposite opinion is thus precluded also for the reason of its being a mere hypothesis.—We further must question our opponent as to the nature of that consciousness which he assumes to spring from the elements; for the materialists do not admit the existence of anything but the four elements. Should he say that consciousness is the perception of the elements and what springs from the elements, we remark that in that case the elements and their products are objects of consciousness and that hence the latter cannot be a quality of them, as it is contradictory that anything should act on itself. Fire is hot indeed but does not burn itself, and the acrobat, well trained as he may be, cannot mount on his own shoulders. As little could consciousness, if it were a mere quality of the elements and their products, render them objects of itself. For form and other (undoubted) qualities do not make their own colour or the colour of something else their objects; the elements and their products, on the other hand, whether external or belonging to the Self (the organism) are rendered objects by consciousness. Hence in the same way as we admit the existence of that perceptive consciousness which has the material elements and their products for its objects, we also must admit the separateness of that consciousness from the elements. And as consciousness constitutes the character of our Self, the Self must be distinct from the body. That consciousness is permanent, follows from the uniformity of its character (and we therefore may conclude that the conscious Self is permanent also; as also follows) from the fact that the Self, although connected with a different state, recognises itself as the conscious agent—a recognition expressed in judgments such as 'I saw this,'—and from the fact of remembrance and so on being possible.

The argumentation that consciousness is an attribute of the body because it is where a body is, is already refuted by the reasons stated above. Moreover, perceptive consciousness takes place where there are certain auxiliaries such as lamps and the like, and does not take place where those are absent, without its following therefrom that perception is an attribute of the lamp or the like. Analogously the fact that perception takes place where there is a body, and does not take place where there is none, does not imply that it is an attribute of the body; for like lamps and so on the body may be used (by the Self) as a mere auxiliary. Nor is it even true that the body is absolutely required as an auxiliary of perception; for in the state of dream we have manifold perceptions while the body lies motionless.—The view of the Self being something separate from the body is therefore free from all objections. (III, 3, 54)

... [T]he sentence 'Thou art that' teaches that what is denoted by the term 'thou' is identical with what is denoted by 'that'. Now the latter term denotes the subject of the entire section, viz. the thinking Brahman which is the cause of the origin and so on of the world.... The entity thus described—which is free from all the qualities of transmigratory existence, has consciousness for its Self and is called Brahman—is known, by all students of the Vedānta, as what is denoted by the term 'that.' They likewise know that what is denoted by the term 'thou' is the inward Self (*pratyagātman*); which is the agent in seeing and hearing, is (successively) apprehended as the inward Self of all the outward involucra beginning with the gross body (cp. Taitt. Up.), and finally ascertained as of the nature of intelligence.... (IV, 1, 2)

... [W]here scripture intends the contemplation of something in a symbol, it conveys its meaning through a single enunciation such as 'Brahman is Mind' (Ch. Up. III, 18, 1), or 'Brahman is Āditya' (Ch. Up. III, 19, 1). But in the passage quoted above, scripture says, 'I am Thou and thou art I.' As here the form of expression differs from that of texts teaching the contemplation of symbols, the passage must be understood as teaching non-difference.... (IV, 1, 3)

The supplement to the third *adhyāya* is finished herewith, and an inquiry now begins concerning the fruit of the knowledge of Brahman.—The doubt here presents itself whether, on the attainment of Brahman, sins the results of which are opposed in nature to such attainment are extinguished or not....

... On the obtainment of Brahman there take place the non-clinging (to the agent) of the posterior sins and the annihilation of anterior ones.—'On account of this being declared.' For in a chapter treating of the knowledge of Brahman scripture expressly declares that future sins which might be presumed to cling to the agent do not cling to him who knows: 'As water does not cling to a lotus-leaf, so no evil deed clings to him who knows this' (Ch. Up. IV, 14, 3). Similarly scripture declares the destruction of previously accumulated evil deeds: 'As the fibres of the Iṣīkā reed when thrown into the fire are burned, thus all his sins are burned' (Ch. Up. V, 24, 3).... Nor is there any force in the averment that the assumption of works being extinguished without their fruits having been enjoyed would render scripture futile. For we by no means deny the fruit-producing power of works; this power actually exists; but we maintain that it is counteracted by other causes such as knowledge.... (IV, 1, 13)

In the two preceding *adhikaraṇas* it has been proved that good as well as evil works are annihilated through knowledge. We now have to consider the question whether this annihilation extends, without distinction, to those works whose effects have already begun to operate as well as to those whose effects have not yet begun; or only to works of the latter kind.

Here the *pūrvapakṣin* maintains that on the ground of scriptural passages such as 'He thereby overcomes both,' which refer to all works without any distinction, all works whatever must be considered to undergo destruction.

To this we reply, 'But only those whose effects have not begun.' Former works, i.e. works, whether good or evil, which have been accumulated in previous forms of existence as well as in the current form of existence before the origination of knowledge, are destroyed by the attainment of knowledge only if their fruit has not yet begun to operate. Those works, on the other hand, whose effects have begun and whose results have been half enjoyed—i.e. those very works to which there is due the present state of existence in which the knowledge of Brahman arises—are not destroyed by that knowledge. . . . Were it otherwise, i.e. were all works whatever extinguished by knowledge, there would be no reason for the continuance of the current form of existence, and the rise of knowledge would therefore be immediately followed by the state of final release; in which case scripture would not teach that one has to wait for the death of the body.—But, an objection is raised, the knowledge of the Self being essentially non-active does by its intrinsic power destroy (all) works; how then should it destroy some only and leave others unaffected? We certainly have no right to assume that when fire and seeds come into contact the germinative power of some seeds only is destroyed while that of others remains unimpaired!—The origination of knowledge, we reply, cannot take place without dependence on an aggregate of works whose effects have already begun to operate, and when this dependence has once been entered into, we must—as in the case of the potter's wheel—wait until the motion of that which once has begun to move comes to an end, there being nothing to obstruct it in the interim. The knowledge of our Self being essentially non-active destroys all works by means of refuting wrong knowledge; but wrong knowledge—comparable to the appearance of a double moon—lasts for some time even after it has been refuted, owing to the impression it has made.—Moreover it is not a matter for dispute at all whether the body of him who knows Brahman continues to exist for some time or not. For how can one man contest the fact of another possessing the knowledge of Brahman—vouched for by his heart's conviction—and at the same time continuing to enjoy bodily existence? This same point is explained in scripture and *smṛti,* where they describe him who stands firm in the highest knowledge.—The final decision therefore is that knowledge effects the destruction of those works only—whether good or evil—whose effects have not yet begun to operate. (IV, 1, 15)

BHĀṢYA ON BṚHADĀRAṆYAKA UPANIṢAD

We noted before that some of the commentaries on the Upaniṣads attributed to Śaṁkara are probably spurious. But there is no doubt that the commentary on the *Bṛhadāraṇyaka Upaniṣad* (the longest and one of the oldest and most important of the Upaniṣads) which is attributed to him is authentic. In this work Śaṁkara once again combines exegesis and dialectic into a powerful method for interpreting *śruti* and for combating rival philosophical schools.

In the first brief section selected (I, 4, 7), Śaṁkara analyzes what it means "to attain" Brahman, and in the longer section (IV, 3, 7), Śaṁkara discusses the nature of the self and the "illuminating" quality of consciousness, and criticizes further certain Buddhist teachings. The selection is from *The Bṛhadāraṇyaka Upaniṣad: with the Commentary of Śankarācārya*, translated by Swāmī Mādhavānanda (Mayavati, Almora, Himalayas: Advaita Ashrama, 1950).

. . . The non-attainment of the Self is but the ignorance of It. Hence the knowledge of the Self is Its attainment. The attainment of the Self cannot be, as in the case of things other than It, the obtaining of something not obtained before, for here there is no difference between the person attaining and the object attained. Where the Self has to attain something other than Itself, the Self is the attainer and the non-Self is the object attained. This, not being already attained, is separated by acts such as producing, and is to be attained by the initiation of a particular action with the help of particular auxiliaries. And that attainment of something new is transitory, being due to desire and action that are themselves the product of a false notion, like the birth of a son etc. in a dream. But this Self is the very opposite of that. By the very fact of Its being the Self, It is not separated by acts such as producing. But although It is always attained, It is separated by ignorance only. Just as when a mother-of-pearl appears through mistake as a piece of silver, the non-apprehension of the former, although it is being perceived all the while, is merely due to the obstruction of the false impression, and its (subsequent) apprehension is but knowledge, for this is what removes the obstruction of false impression, similarly here also the non-attainment of the Self is merely due to the obstruction of ignorance. Therefore the attainment of It is simply the removal of that obstruction by knowledge. . . . (I, 4, 7)

Text: *'Which is the self?' 'This infinite entity* (puruṣa) *that is identified with the intellect and is in the midst of the organs, the (self-effulgent) light within the heart (intellect). Assuming the likeness (of the intellect), it moves between the two worlds; it thinks, as it were, and shakes, as it were. Being identified with dreams, it transcends this world—the forms of death (ignorance etc.).'*

Śaṁkara's Commentary:

Though the self has been proved to be other than the body and organs, yet, owing to a misconception caused by the observation that things which help others are of the same class as they, Janaka cannot decide whether the self is just one of the organs or something different, and therefore asks: *Which is the self?* The misconception is quite natural, for the logic involved is too subtle to grasp easily. Or, although the self has been proved to be other than the body, yet all the organs appear to be intelligent, since the self is not perceived as distinct from them; so I ask you: Which is the self? Among the body, organs, vital force and mind, which is the self you have spoken of—through which light, you said, a man sits and does other kinds of work? Or, which of these organs is 'this self identified with the intellect' that you have meant, for all the organs appear to be intelligent? . . . In the first explanation, 'Which is the self?' is the question, and 'This infinite entity that is identified with the intellect,' etc., is the answer; in the second, 'Which of the organs is the self that is identified with the intellect?' is the question. Or the whole sentence, 'Which is this self that is identified with the intellect and is in the midst of the organs, the light within the heart?' is the question. The words, 'That is identified with the intellect,' etc. give the precise description of the self that has been known only in a general way. But the word 'iti' in, 'Which is the self,' ought to mark the end of the question, without its being connected with a remote word. Hence we conclude that the expression, 'Which is the self,' is really the question, and all the rest of the sentence, beginning with, 'This infinite entity that is identified with the intellect,' etc., is the answer.

The word *this* has been used with reference to the self, since it is directly known to us. *Vijñānamaya* means *identified with the intellect*; the self is so called because of our failure to discriminate its association with its limiting adjunct, the intellect, for it is perceived as associated with the intellect. . . . The intellect is the instrument that helps us in everything, like a lamp set in front amidst darkness. . . . Every object is perceived only as associated with the light of the intellect, as objects in the dark are lighted up by a lamp placed in front; the other organs are but the channels for the intellect. Therefore the Self is described in terms of that, as 'identified with the intellect'. . . .

. . . The self is called light, because it is self-effulgent, for through this light, the self-effulgent Ātman, this aggregate of body and organs sits, goes out and works, as if it were sentient, as a jar placed in the sun (shines). Or as an emerald or any other gem, dropped for testing into milk etc., imparts its lustre to them, so does this luminous self, being finer than even the heart or intellect, unify and impart its lustre to the body and organs, including the intellect etc., although it is within the intellect; for these have varying degrees of fineness or grossness in a certain order, and the self is the innermost of them all.

The intellect, being transparent and next to the self, easily catches the reflection of the intelligence of the self. Therefore even wise men happen to identify themselves with it first; next comes the *manas*, which catches the reflection of the self through the intellect; then the organs, through contact with the *manas*; and lastly the body, through the organs. Thus the self successively illumines with its own intelligence the entire aggregate of body and organs. It is therefore that all people identify themselves with the body and organs and their modifications indefinitely according to their discrimination. . . .

It has been said that when the external lights that help the different organs have ceased to work, the self, the infinite entity that is the light within the intellect, helps the organs through the mind. Even when the external aids of the organs, viz. the sun and other lights, exist, since these latter (being compounds) subserve the purpose of some other agency, and the body and organs, being insentient, cannot exist for themselves, this aggregate of body and organs cannot function without the help of the self, the light that lives for itself. It is always through the help of the light of the self that all our activities take place. . . .

Though it is so, yet during the waking state that light called the self, being beyond the organs and being particularly mixed up in the diversity of functions of the body and the organs, internal and external, such as the intellect, cannot be shown extricated from them, like a stalk of grass from its sheath; hence, in order to show it in the dream state. Yājñavalkya begins: *Assuming the likeness . . . it moves between the two worlds.* The infinite entity that is the self-effulgent Ātman, assuming the likeness—of what?—of the intellect, which is the topic, and is also contiguous. In the phrase, 'within the heart' there occurs the word 'heart,' meaning the intellect, and it is quite close; therefore that is meant. And what is meant by 'likeness'? The failure to distinguish (between the intellect and the self) as between a horse and a buffalo. The intellect is that which is illumined, and the light of the self is that which illumines, like light; and it is well known that we cannot distinguish the two. It is because light is pure that it assumes the likeness of that which it illumines. When it illumines something coloured, it assumes the likeness of that colour. When, for instance, it illumines something green, blue or red, it is coloured like them. Similarly the self, illumining the intellect, illumines through it the entire body and organs, as we have already stated through the illustration of the emerald. Therefore through the similarity of the intellect, the self assumes the likeness of everything. Hence, it will be described later on as 'Identified with everything' (IV. iv. 5).

Therefore it cannot be taken apart from anything else, like a stalk of grass from its sheath, and shown in its self-effulgent form. It is for this reason that the whole world, to its utter delusion, superimposes all activities peculiar to name and form on the self, and all attributes of this self-effulgent light on name and form, and also superimposes name and form on the light of the self, and thinks, 'This is the self, or is not the self; it has such and such attributes, or has not such and such attributes; it is the agent, or is not the agent; it is pure, or impure; it is bound, or free; it is fixed, or gone, or come; it exists, or does not exist,' and so on. Therefore 'assuming the likeness (of the intellect) it moves' alternately 'between the two worlds'—this one and the next, the one that has been attained and the one that is to be attained—by successively discarding the body and organs already possessed, and taking new ones, hundreds of them, in an unbroken series. This movement between the two worlds is merely due to its resembling the intellect—not natural to it. That it is attributable to its resembling the limiting adjuncts of name and form created by a confusion, and is not natural to it, is being stated: Because, assuming the likeness (of the intellect), it moves alternately between the two worlds. The text goes on to show that this is a fact of experience. *It thinks, as it were*: By illumining the intellect, which does the thinking, through its own self-effulgent light that pervades the intellect, the self assumes the likeness of the latter and seems to think, just as light (looks coloured). Hence people mistake that the self thinks; but really it does not. Likewise it *shakes, as it were*: When the intellect and other organs as well as the prāṇas move, the self, which illumines them, becomes like them, and therefore seems to move rapidly; but really the light of the self has no motion.

How are we to know that it is owing to the delusive likeness of the intellect that the self moves between the two worlds and does other activities, and not by itself? This is being answered by a statement of reason: *Being identified with dreams*, etc. The self seems to become whatever the intellect, which it resembles, becomes. Therefore when the intellect turns into a dream, i.e. taken on the modification called a dream, the self also assumes that form; when the intellect wants to wake up, it too does that. Hence the text says: *Being identified with dreams*, revealing the modification known as dreams assumed by the intellect, and thereby resembling them, *it transcends this world*, i.e. the body and organs, functioning in the waking state, round which our secular and scriptural activities are centered. Because the self stands revealing by its own distinct light the modification known as dreams assumed by the intellect, therefore it must really be self-effulgent, pure and devoid of agent and action with its factors and results. It is only the likeness of the intellect that gives rise to the delusion that the self moves between the two worlds and has other such activities. *The forms of death*, i.e. work, ignorance, etc. Death has no other forms of its own; the body and organs are its forms. Hence the self transcends those forms of death, on which actions and their results depend.

Buddhist objection: We say there is no such thing as the light of the self similar to the intellect and revealing it, for we experience nothing but the intellect either through perception or through inference, just as we do not experience a second intellect at the same time. You say that since the light that reveals and the jar, for instance, that is revealed are not distinguishable in spite of their difference, they resemble each other. We reply that in that particular case, the light being perceived as different from the jar, there may well be similarity between them, because they are merely joined together, remaining all the while different. But in this case we do not similarly experience either through perception or through inference any other light revealing the intellect, just as the light reveals the jar. It is the intellect which, as the consciousness that reveals, assumes its own form as well as those of the objects. Therefore neither through perception nor through inference is it possible to establish a separate light which reveals the intellect.

What has been said above by way of example, viz. that there may be similarity between the light that reveals and the jar, for instance, that is revealed, because they are merely joined together, remaining all the while different, has been said only tentatively; it is not that the jar that is revealed is different from the light that reveals it. In reality it is the self-luminous jar that reveals itself; for (each moment) a new jar is produced, and it is consciousness that takes the form of the self-luminous jar or any other object. Such being the case, there is no instance of an external object, for everything is mere consciousness.

Thus the Buddhists, after conceiving the intellect as tainted by assuming a double form, the revealer and the revealed (subject and object), desire to purify it. Some of them, for instance, maintain that consciousness is untrammelled by the dualism of subject and object, is pure and momentary; others want to deny that even. For instance, the Mādhyamikas hold that consciousness is free from the dual aspect of subject and object, hidden and simply void, like the external objects such as a jar.

All these assumptions are contradictory to this Vedic path of well-being that we are discussing, since they deny the light of the self as distinct from the body and illumining the consciousness of the intellect. Now to those who believe in an objective world we reply: Objects such as a jar are not self-luminous: a jar in darkness never reveals itself, but is noticed as being regularly revealed by coming in contact with the light of a lamp etc. Then we say that the jar is in contact with light. Even though the jar and the light are in contact, they are distinct from each other, for we see their difference, as between a rope and a jar, when they repeatedly come in contact and are disjoined. This distinction means that the jar is revealed by something else; it certainly does not reveal itself.

Objection: But do we not see that a lamp reveals itself? People do not use another light to see a lamp, as they do in the case of a jar etc. Therefore a lamp reveals itself.

Reply: No, for there is no difference as regards its being revealed by something else (the self). Although a lamp, being luminous, reveals other things, yet it is, just like a jar etc., invariably revealed by an intelligence other than itself. Since this is so, the lamp cannot but be revealed by something other than itself.

Objection: But there is a difference. A jar, even though revealed by an intelligence, requires a light different from itself (to manifest it), while the lamp does not require another lamp. Therefore the lamp, although revealed by something else, reveals itself as well as the jar.

Reply: Not so, for there is no difference, directly or indirectly (between a jar and a lamp). As the jar is revealed by an intelligence, so is equally the lamp. Your statement that the lamp reveals both itself and the jar is wrong. Why? Because what can its condition be when it does not reveal itself? As a matter of fact, we notice no difference in it, either directly or indirectly. A thing is said to be revealed only when we notice some difference in it through the presence or absence of the revealing agent. But there can be no question of a lamp being present before or absent from itself; and when no difference is caused by the presence or absence, it is idle to say that the lamp reveals itself.

But as regards being revealed by an intelligence the lamp is on a par with the jar etc. Therefore the lamp is not an illustration in point to show that consciousness (of the intellect) reveals itself; it is revealed by an intelligence just as much as the external objects are. Now, if consciousness is revealed by an intelligence, which consciousness is it?—the one that is revealed (the consciousness of the intellect), or the one that reveals (i.e. the consciousness of the self)? Since there is a doubt on the point, we should infer on the analogy of observed facts, not contrary to them. Such being the case, just as we see that external objects such as a lamp are revealed by something different from them (the self), so also should consciousness—although it reveals other things like a lamp—be inferred, on the ground of its being revealed by an intelligence, to be revealed not by itself, but by an intelligence different from it. And that other entity which reveals consciousness is the self—the intelligence which is different from that consciousness.

Objection: But that would lead to a *regressus in infinitum.*

Reply: No; it has only been stated on logical grounds that because consciousness is an object revealed by something, the latter must be distinct from that consciousness. Obviously there cannot be any infallible ground for inferring that the self literally reveals the consciousness in question, or that, as the witness, it requires another agency to reveal it. Therefore there is no question of a *regressus in infinitum.*

Objection: If consciousness is revealed by something else, some means of revelation is required, and this would again lead to a *regressus in infinitum.*

Reply: No, for there is no such restriction; it is not a universal rule. We cannot lay down an absolute condition that whenever something is revealed by another, there must be some means of revelation besides the two—that which reveals and that which is revealed, for we observe diversity of conditions. For instance, a jar is perceived by something different from itself, viz. the self; here light such as that of a lamp, which is other than the perceiving subject and the perceived object, is a means. The light of the lamp etc. is neither a part of the jar nor of the eye. But though the lamp, like the jar, is perceived by the eye, the latter does not require any external means corresponding to the light, over and above the lamp (which is the object). Hence we can never lay down the rule that wherever a thing is perceived by something else, there must be some means besides the two. Therefore, if consciousness is admitted to be revealed by a subject different from it, the charge of a *regressus in infinitum*, either through the means or through the perceiving subject (the self), is altogether untenable. Hence it is proved that there is another light, viz. the light of the self, which is different from consciousness.

Objection (by the idealist): We say there is no external object like the jar etc., or the lamp, apart from consciousness and it is commonly observed that a thing which is not perceived apart from something else is nothing but the latter; as for instance things such as the jar and cloth seen in dream consciousness. Because we do not perceive the jar, lamp and so forth seen in a dream, apart from the dream consciousness, we take it for granted that they are nothing but the latter. Similarly in the waking state, the jar, lamp and so forth, not being perceived apart from the consciousness of that state, should be taken merely as that consciousness and nothing more. Therefore there is no external object such as the jar or lamp, and everything is but consciousness. Hence your statement that since consciousness is revealed, like the jar etc., by something else, there is another light besides consciousness, is groundless; for everything being but consciousness, there is no illustration to support you.

Reply: No, for you admit the existence of the external world to a certain extent. You do not altogether deny it.

Objection: We deny it absolutely.

Reply: No. Since the words 'consciousness,' 'jar' and 'lamp' are different and have different meanings, you cannot help admitting to a certain extent the existence of external objects. If you do not admit the existence of objects different from consciousness, words such as 'consciousness,' 'jar' and 'cloth,' having the same meaning, would be synonymous. Similarly, the means being identical with the result, your scriptures inculcating a difference between them would be useless, and their author (Buddha) would be charged with ignorance.

Moreover, you yourself admit that a debate between rivals as well as its defects are different from consciousness. You certainly do not consider the debate and its defects to be identical with one's consciousness, for the opponent, for instance, has to be refuted. Nobody admits that it is either his own consciousness or his own self that is meant to be refuted; were it so, all human activities would stop. Nor do you assume that the opponent perceives himself; rather you take it for granted that he is perceived by others. Therefore we conclude that the whole objective world is perceived by something other than itself, because it is an object of our perception in the waking state, just like other objects perceived in that state, such as the opponent—which is an easy enough illustration; or as one series of (momentary) consciousness, or any single one of them, is perceived by another of the same kind. Therefore not even the idealist can deny the existence of another light different from consciousness.

Objection: You are wrong to say that there is an external world, since in dreams we perceive nothing but consciousness.

Reply: No, for even for this absence of external objects we can demonstrate their difference from consciousness. You yourself have admitted that in dreams the consciousness of a jar or the like is real; but in the same breath you say that there is no jar apart from that consciousness! The point is, whether the jar which forms the object of that consciousness is unreal or real, in either case you have admitted that the consciousness of the jar is real, and it cannot be denied, for there is no reason to support the denial. By this the theory of the voidness of everything is also refuted; as also the Mīmāṁsaka view that the Self is perceived by the individual self as the 'I.'

Your statement that every moment a different jar in contact with light is produced, is wrong, for even at a subsequent moment we recognise it to be the same jar.

Objection: The recognition may be due to similarity, as in the case of hair, nails, etc. that have been cut and have grown anew.

Reply: No, for even in that case the momentariness is disproved. Besides, the recognition is due merely to an identity of species. When the hair, nails, etc. have been cut and have grown again, there being an identity of species as hair, nails, etc., their recognition as such due to that identity is unquestionable. But when we see the hair, nails, etc. that have grown again after being cut, we never have the idea that they are, individually, those identical hairs or nails. When after a great lapse of time we see on a person hair, nails, etc. of the same size as before, we perceive that the hair, nails, etc. we see at that particular moment are like those seen on the previous occasion, but never that they are the same ones. But in the case of a jar etc. we perceive that they are identical. Therefore the two cases are not parallel.

When a thing is directly recognised as identical, it is improper to infer that it is something else, for when an inference contradicts perception, the ground of such inference becomes fallacious. Moreover, the perception of similarity is impossible because of the momentariness of knowledge (held by you). The perception of similarity takes place when one and the same person sees two things at different times. But according to you the person who sees a thing does not exist till the next moment to see another thing, for consciousness, being momentary, ceases to be as soon as it has seen some one thing. To explain: The perception of similarity takes the form of 'This is like that.' 'That' refers to the remembrance of something seen; 'this' to the perception of something present. If after remembering the past experience denoted by 'that,' consciousness should linger till the present moment referred to by 'this,' then the doctrine of momentariness would be gone. If, however, the remembrance terminates with the notion of 'that,' and a different perception relating to the present (arises and) dies with the notion of 'this,' then no perception of similarity expressed by, 'This is like that,' will result, as there will be no single consciousness perceiving more than one thing (so as to draw the comparison). Moreover, it will be impossible to describe our experiences. Since consciousness ceases to be just after seeing what was to be seen, we cannot use such expressions as, 'I see this,' or 'I saw that,' for the person who has seen them will not exist till the moment of making these utterances. Or, if he does, the doctrine of momentariness will be contradicted. If, on the other hand, the person who makes these utterances and perceives the similarity is other than the one who saw those things, then, like the remarks of a man born blind about particular colours and his perception of their similarity, the writing of scriptural books by the omniscient Buddha and other such things will all become an instance of the blind following the blind. But this is contrary to your views. Moreover, the charges of obtaining results of actions not done and not obtaining those of actions already done, are quite patent in the doctrine of momentariness.

Objection: It is possible to describe a past experience by means of a single chain-like perception that takes place so as to include both the preceding and the succeeding perception, and this also accounts for the comparison, 'This is like that.'

Reply: Not so, for the past and the present perceptions belong to different times. The present perception is one link of the chain and the past perception another, and these two perceptions belong to different times. If the chain-like perception touches the objects of both these perceptions, then the same consciousness extending over two moments, the doctrine of momentariness again falls to the ground. And such distinctions as 'mine' and 'yours' being impossible all our dealings in the world will come to naught.

Moreover, since you hold everything to be but consciousness perceptible only to itself, and at the same time say that consciousness is by nature but the reflection of pellucid knowledge, and since there is no other witness to it, it is impossible to regard it as various such as transitory, painful, void and unreal. Nor can consciousness be treated as having many contradictory parts, like a pomegranate etc., for according to you it is of the nature of pellucid knowledge. Moreover, if the transitoriness, painfulness, etc. are parts of consciousness, the very fact that they are perceived will throw them into the category of objects, different from the subject. If, on the other hand, consciousness is essentially transitory, painful and so on, then it is impossible to conceive that it will become pure by getting rid of those characteristics, for a thing becomes pure by getting rid of the impurities that are connected with it, as in the case of a mirror etc., but it can never divest itself of its natural property. Fire, for instance, is never seen to part with its natural light or heat. Although the redness and other qualities of a flower are seen to be removed by the addition of other substances, yet even there we infer that those features were the result of previous combinations, for we observe that by subjecting the seeds to a particular process, a different quality is imparted to flowers, fruits, etc. Hence consciousness cannot be conceived to be purified.

Besides you conceive consciousness to be impure when it appears in the dual character of subject and object. That too is impossible, since it does not come in contact with anything else. A thing cannot surely come in contact with something that does not exist; and when there is no contact with anything else, the properties that are observed in a thing belong naturally to it, and cannot be separated from it, as the heat of fire, or the light of the sun. Therefore we conclude that your assumption that consciousness becomes impure by coming temporarily in contact with something else, and is again free from this impurity, is merely an instance of the blind following the blind, and is unsupported by any evidence.

Lastly, the Buddhistic assumption that the extinction of that consciousness is the highest end of human life, is untenable, for there is no recipient of results. For a person who has got a thorn stuck into him, the relief of the pain caused by it is the result (he seeks); but if he dies, we do not find any recipient of the resulting cessation of pain. Similarly, if consciousness is altogether extinct and there is nobody to reap that benefit, to talk of it as the highest end of human life is meaningless. If that very entity or self, designated by the word 'person'—consciousness, according to you—whose well-being is meant, is extinct, for whose sake will the highest end be? But those who (with us) believe in a self different from consciousness and witnessing many objects, will find it easy to explain all phenomena such as the remembrance of things previously seen and the contact and cessation of pain—the impurity, for instance, being ascribed to contact with extraneous things, and the purification to dissociation from them. As for the view of the nihilist, since it is contradicted by all the evidences of knowledge, no attempt is being made to refute it. (IV, 3, 7)

BHAGAVADGĪTĀBHĀṢYA

The *Bhagavadgītā* is somewhat of an embarrassment for Advaita Vedānta. As we have seen, the *Gītā* exhibits a strong if not dominant "theistic" dimension: it emphasizes a *karma-yoga*, or way of action, and *bhakti,* devotion to a "personal" deity. Śaṁkara, accordingly, must strain the text rather considerably in order to bring it into harmony with his advaitic principles.

The following short selections from Śaṁkara's commentary on the *Gītā* may illustrate further his methods of interpretation and his steadfast holding to the superiority of *jñāna-yoga*, the discipline of knowledge, in providing enlightenment to man. The selections are from *The Bhagavad-Gîtâ: with the Commentary of Śrî Śankaracharyâ,* translated by A. Mahâdeva Śâstri (Madras: V. Ramaswamy Sastrulu & Sons, 1961).

III, 3. The superiority of knowledge to action, referred to by Arjuna (iii. 1), must be true, because there is no denial of it. And it must also be true that the path of knowledge is intended for saṁnyāsins only. Since it has been stated that the two paths are intended for two distinct classes of aspirants, such is evidently the opinion of the Lord. . . .

III, 5. *None, verily even for an instant, ever remains doing no action; for every one is driven helpless to action by the energies born of Nature.*

The energies (guṇas) are three, *sattva, rajas* and *tamas.* 'Every one' means every living being that is ignorant, (*ajña*), who knows not (the

Self); for, it is said of a wise man (that he is one) "who is unshaken by the energies" (xiv 23).

Since the Sāṁkhyas have been distinguished from the yogins (iii. 3), the *karma-yoga,* devotion to action, is indeed meant for the ignorant only, not for the wise. As for the wise who are unshaken by the guṇas, and who in themselves are devoid of any change whatever, the *karma-yoga* is out of place. . . .

III, 8. *Do thou perform (thy) bounden duty; for action is superior to inaction. And even the maintenance of the body would not be possible for thee by inaction.*

Thy bounden duty is the obligatory (*nitya*) act, that which one is bound to perform, and which is not prescribed (in the scriptures) as a means to a specific end. Action is superior to inaction in point of result. By inaction you cannot attain success in the life's journey. The distinction between action and inaction is thus seen in our own experience.

It is also wrong to suppose that actions lead to bondage and that they should not therefore be performed.—Why?

III, 9. *Except in the case of action for Sacrifice's sake, this world is action-bound. Action for the sake Thereof, do thou, O son of Kunti, perform, free from attachment.*

Sacrifice (*yajña*) here means Īśvara, the Supreme Lord. So, the *śruti* says '*Yajña,* verily, is Viṣṇu.' 'This world' means those persons who, as qualified for action only, are bound to do it and who accordingly perform it. The world is not bound by action done for the Lord's sake. Perform action without attachment.

IV, 18. *He who can see inaction in action, who can also see action in inaction, he is wise among men, he is devout, he is the performer of all action.*

'Action' means what is done, an act in general. Inaction can be seen in action and action in inaction, since both inaction (*nivṛtti*) and action (*pravṛtti*) presuppose an agent. In fact, all our experience of such things as action and agent is possible only in a state of *avidyā,* only when we have not yet attained to the Real (*vastu*). He who sees inaction in action and who sees action in inaction,—he is wise among men, he is devout (*yukta, yogin*), he has done all action—Thus is he extolled who sees action in inaction and *vice versa.*

(*Objection*):—What means this incongruity, "who can see inaction in action and action in inaction"? Surely action can never realize such an incongruity?

(*Answer*):—This objection does not apply to our interpretation. To an ignorant man of the world, what in reality is inaction appears as action, and what in reality is action appears as inaction. With a view to teach what their real nature is, the Lord says "He who can see inaction in action," &c. Hence no incongruity. It must be a bare truth that the Lord means to teach here, inasmuch as He has said that he who realizes this view of action and inaction is *wise,* and has introduced the subject by saying that there is much to be *learnt* about action and inaction, (iv. 17). It has also been said that 'by knowing which thou shalt be liberated from evil' (iv. 1); and certainly freedom from evil cannot be achieved by means of *false* knowledge. Wherefore, we should understand that action and inaction are misunderstood by all living beings and that the Lord, wishing to remove this false view of them teaches "He who can see inaction in action" &c. Moreover, inaction cannot be said to be *located in* action or contained in it, as jujube (badara) fruits in a vessel, nor can action be said to be located in inaction: for, inaction is but the absence of action. Wherefore (the meaning of the Lord must be that) action and inaction are not rightly understood by people and that the one is mistaken for the other, as the mirage is mistaken for water, or as the mother-of-pearl is mistaken for silver.

(*Objection*):—Action is ever action to all; it never appears to be anything else?

(*Answer*):—Not so. When a ship is in motion, the motionless trees on the shore appear to a man on board the ship, to move in the opposite direction; distant and moving bodies which are far away from our eye appear to be motionless. Similarly, here, (in the case of the Self) inaction is mistaken for action, and action for inaction. Wherefore, to remove this false impression, the Lord says "He who can see inaction in action" &c.

Though such an objection has been more than once answered, people who have long been subject to great misconceptions are deluded often and often, forget the truth though often and often taught, and often and often raise objections based on false premises. Wherefore, seeing how difficult the Real is for us to know, the Lord often answers such objections.

The truth that the Self is actionless, so clearly taught by *śruti*, *smṛti*, and reason has been taught here also in ii. 20–24; and it will also be taught hereafter. It is, however a deep-rooted habit of the mind to connect action with the actionless Self, though it is contrary to His real nature wherefore, "even the wise are deluded as to what is action and what is inaction" (v. 16). Action pertains to the physical body (*deha*) etc., but man falsely attributes action to the Self and imagines "I am the agent, mine is action, by me shall the fruit of action be reaped." Similarly, he falsely imputes to the Self the cessation (of activity) which really pertains to the body and the senses, as also the happiness which results from that cessation (of activity): he imagines 'I shall be quiet, so that I may be happy, without worry and without action; and I do nothing now, I am quiet and happy." To remove this false impression, the Lord says "He who can see inaction in action," &c.

Now, action which belongs to the body and the senses, while yet retaining its own nature as action, is falsely imputed by all to the Self who is actionless and immutable; whence even a learned man thinks "I act." Hence the passage means:—He who sees inaction in action, *i.e.*, he who has the right knowledge that action which is commonly supposed by all to pertain to the Self, does not really belong to the Self, just as motion does not really pertain to the trees (on the shore of the river) which appear (to a man on board the ship) to move in the opposite direction; and he who sees action in inaction, *i.e.*, he who knows that even inaction is action—for, inaction is but a cessation of bodily and mental activities, and like *action* it is falsely attributed to the Self and causes the feeling of egoism as expressed in the words "quiet and doing nothing, I sit happy;"—he who can realize the nature of action and inaction as now explained is wise among men; he is devout (*yogin*), he is the performer of all actions. He is released from evil; he has achieved all.

This verse has been interpreted in a different way by some commentators.—How?—The obligatory duties (*nitya-karma*), performed for the sake of Īśvara, do not produce any effect and may therefore, be figuratively termed inaction *i.e.*, they are equivalent to inaction; and neglect of those duties produces evil and may therefore, only figuratively, be termed action *i.e.*, it is equivalent to action. Accordingly they have interpreted the verse thus:—He who regards the obligatory duties (*nitya-karma*) as inaction, since they do not produce any effect—just as a cow may be said to be no cow when she does not serve the purpose of yielding milk,—and he who regards the neglect of obligatory duties as an action, since it produces evil such as hell (*naraka*), he is wise among men, &c.

This interpretation cannot hold good. As such knowledge cannot lead to liberation from evil, the Lord's statement that "by knowing which thou shalt be liberated from evil" (iv. 16) would prove false. Even though it be granted (for mere argument's sake) that liberation from evil accrues from the performance of obligatory duties (*nitya-karma*) it can never be granted that it will accrue from the mere *knowledge* that they do not produce any effect. Certainly it is nowhere taught (in *śruti*) that liberation from evil accrues from the knowledge that obligatory duties do not produce effects or from a knowledge of those obligatory duties themselves. It cannot be urged that it has been taught here by the Lord. The same argument holds good also against their view as to seeing action in inaction. Indeed, this precept enjoins, (they hold), not that neglect of obligatory duties (*nitya-karma*) should be regarded as action, but only that obligatory duties should be performed. Moreover, no good can result from the knowledge that non-performance of obligatory duties leads to evil. Neither can non-performance (which is non-existent in itself) of obligatory duties be enjoined as an object on which to fix our thought. Nor by a false knowledge which regards inaction as action can a man be released from evil, or said to be wise and devout and to have performed all actions: and such a knowledge deserves no praise. False knowledge is itself *the* evil; how can it release us from another evil? Darkness does not expel darkness.

(*Objection*):—The knowledge that inaction is action or that action is inaction is not an illusion, but a figurative idea based upon the fact of productiveness or unproductiveness of effects.

(*Answer*):—No. For, nowhere is it taught that even such a figurative idea regarding action and inaction is of any good. Neither is any purpose served by thus ignoring the immediate subject of discourse and speaking of something else. It is, moreover, possible to express more directly the fact that obligatory duties do not produce effects and that their omission leads to hell. What, then, might be the purpose served by such an ambiguous circumlocution as "he who can see inaction in action" &c.? Such an explanation is tantamount to saying that the Lord wanted to confound others by these utterances. It is not necessary to mystify the doctrine (of obligatory duties) by means of symbolic language, nor is it possible to maintain that it can be easily understood if expressed often and often and in more ways than one. For, the same doctrine is more clearly expressed in ii. 47, and needs no reiteration. It is only what is high, and worthy of our effort that is worth knowing, but not the worthless. No false knowledge is worth acquiring: nor is its object—which is unreal—worth knowing. No evil can arise from non-performance; no existence can arise from non-existence. It has been said here, "Of the unreal no being that is," (ii. 16) and in the *śruti* "How can the existent arise from the non existent?" (Ch. Up. 6–2–2). To say that an existent object arises from the non-existent is tantamount to saying that non-existence itself becomes existence and *vice versa*, which cannot be maintained as it is against all evidence. The scripture (*śāstra*) cannot enjoin an act which is productive of no good; for, such an act [is] painful in its performance and no pain would ever be deliberately incurred. Since it is admitted that omission of such duties leads to hell, it would simply amount to this, that Revelation (*śāstra*) is of no good, since performance as well as omission of duties therein enjoined alike result in pain. Moreover, he who admits that obligatory duties produce no effects and at the same time holds that they lead to salvation, lands himself in a self-contradiction.

Wherefore, this verse admits only of a literal interpretation, and we have interpreted it accordingly.

The realization of inaction in action and *vice versa* is extolled as follows:

IV, 19. *He whose engagements are all devoid of desires and purposes, and whose actions have been burnt by the fire of wisdom, him the wise call a sage.*

The man who has realized the truth described above, whose works are all free from desires and from purposes (*saṁkalpa*) which cause those desires, who performs mere deeds without any immediate purpose,—if he be engaged in worldly action, he does so with a view to set an example to the masses; if he has renounced worldly life, he performs deeds only for bodily maintenance,—whose actions, good and bad, are consumed in the fire of wisdom which consists in the realization of inaction and *vice versa*: him the wise who know Brahman call a real sage (*paṇḍita*).

He who can see action in inaction and *vice versa*, (*i.e.*, who has realized the true nature of action and inaction), is by virtue of that very realization, free from action; he renounces (the world) and engages in no action,—only doing what is required for the bare existence of his body,—even though he had been engaged in action before realizing the truth. On the other hand, there may be a person who, having started with action and having since obtained the right knowledge of the Self, really abandons action with all its accessories, as he finds action of no use; but who, finding that for some reason he cannot abandon action, may continue doing action as before with a view to set an example to the world at large, devoid of attachment to action and its result, and therefore having no selfish end in view; such a man really does nothing. His action is equivalent to inaction, since all his actions are consumed in the fire of knowledge. . . .

V (Introduction). In iv. 18, 19, 21, 22, 24, 32, 33, 37 and 41, the Lord has spoken of the renunciation of all actions; and in iv. 42 He has exhorted Arjuna to engage in Yoga, in performance of action. Owing to the mutual opposition between performance of action and renunciation thereof as between motion and rest, the two cannot be accomplished by an individual at one and the same time. Neither have two distinct periods of time been prescribed for their respective observance. By inference, therefore, only one of them forms Arjuna's duty; so that thinking that, of the two,—performance of action and renunciation thereof,—he should resort to the better of the two to the exclusion of the other. Arjuna asks (v. 1) of the Lord with a desire to know which is the better of the two.

(*Objection*):—As going to speak of entire devotion to *jñāna-yoga* on the part of him who has realised the Self, the Lord has taught, in the passages quoted above, that such a man has to renounce action, but not he who has not realised the Self. Since performance of action and renunciation of action thus pertain to two distinct classes of people respectively, Arjuna's question with a view to know which of the two is better than the other is irrelevant.

(*Answer*):—Yes; from your standpoint the question is irrelevant. But from the questioner's (Arjuna's) own standpoint, the question, we say is quite relevant—How?—In the passages quoted above, the Lord enjoins renunciation as a duty (in the form "Let the wise man renounce"); and it cannot be enjoined as a duty unless it (the term 'renounce'), is more important than the agent (*i.e.*, the term 'wise'); so that this injunction of renunciation should be extended so as to apply to that man also who has not realised the Self, because renunciation is elsewhere enjoined on him also. It cannot be made out that renunciation of action is here intended for that man only who has realised the Self. Thus arguing, Arjuna thinks, that an ignorant man may either perform action or renounce it. But, owing to the mutual opposition of the two courses as shown above, only one of them can form the duty (of an individual at a time). And inasmuch as it is the better one of the two that should be followed, but not the other, the question with a view to know which of the two is the better is not irrelevant.

That this is the meaning of Arjuna's question is also evident from an examination of the meaning of the words in reply.—How?—The reply runs as follows: "*Saṁnyāsa* and *karma-yoga* both lead to the highest bliss; but *karma-yoga* is the better of the two" (v. 2). We should now ascertain: Is it in reference to the *karma-yoga* and the *karma-saṁnyāsa* resorted to by a man who has realised the Self that it is said that they lead to the highest bliss as their result, and that the *karma-yoga* is for some reason the better of the two? Or is it in reference to those resorted to by a man who has not realised the Self that the statement is made? —What then?—Listen: As a man who has realised the Self resorts to neither *karma-yoga* nor *saṁnyāsa*, it is not right to speak of them as alike leading to the highest bliss or of the superiority of his *karma-yoga* over his *karma-saṁnyāsa*. If for a man who has realised the Self, *karma-saṁnyāsa* and its opposite—*karma-yoga* (performance of action) —were possible, then it would have been right to speak of them as alike leading to the highest bliss or to speak of the superiority of his *karma-yoga* over his *karma-saṁnyāsa*. Inasmuch as, however, neither *karma-saṁnyāsa* nor *karma-yoga* is possible for a man who has realised the Self, it is not right to speak of them as alike leading to the highest bliss, or to say that *karma-yoga* is better than *karma-saṁnyāsa*.

(*Question*):—Are both *karma-yoga* and *karma-saṁnyāsa* impossible, or is only one of them impossible, for a man who has realised the Self? If only one of them, is it *karma-yoga* or *karma-saṁnyāsa*? What is the reason for the impossibility?

(*Answer*):—Since the man who has realised the Self is free from illusory knowledge, *karma-yoga* which is based upon illusion must be impossible for him. Here, in the *Gītā-śāstra*, in the sections treating of the real nature of the Self, it is said that a man who knows the Self, who knows himself to be the Self that is devoid of all changes of birth, etc., and is actionless, and whose illusory knowledge has been replaced by right knowledge,—that such a man has to renounce all actions, ever dwelling in the true actionless Self; and it is further said that, owing to the opposition between right knowledge and illusory knowledge as well as between their effects, he has nothing to do with *karma-yoga*, the reverse of *karma-saṁnyāsa*, presupposing an active Self and based on the idea of agency caused by illusory knowledge. Wherefore it is but right to say that, for him who has realised the Self and who is free from illusory knowledge, *karma-yoga* which is based upon the illusory knowledge is impossible.

XIII, 2. *And do thou also know Me as* kṣetrajña *in all kṣetras, O Bharata. The knowledge of* kṣetra *and* kṣetrajña *is deemed by Me as* the *knowledge.*

Do thou also know the *kṣetrajña*, described above, to be Myself, to be the Supreme Lord, not a being of the world (*saṁsāra*). The meaning is this:—the *kṣetrajña* who is in all kṣetras, and who is differentiated by the manifold upādhis or kṣetras, from Brahma down to a clump of grass, is, you should understand, really devoid of all the various upādhis (conditions) and is inaccessible to any such word or thought as '*sat*' or '*asat*,' existent or non-existent. As nothing else remains to be known apart from the true nature of *kṣetra*, *kṣetrajña* and the Īśvara, that knowledge by which the two objects of knowledge, *kṣetra* and *kṣetrajña*, are known is considered by Me—the Lord, Viṣṇu—to be the right knowledge.

(*Objection*):—If only one Being, namely, Īśvara, exists in all kṣetras, if there exists no being, no other enjoyer, distinct from Him, it would follow either that the Īśvara is a *saṁsārin*; or that there is no *saṁsāra* because there is no *saṁsārin*—none else apart from the Īśvara. Neither conclusion is acceptable; for, then, it would follow that the scriptures which treat of bondage and liberation and their respective causes would have no purpose to serve. Moreover, the conclusion is opposed to all evidence, including sensuous perception (*pratyakṣa*). In the first place, pleasure and pain and their causes, which together constitute the *saṁsāra*, are known to us by immediate perception. And from our perception of variety in the world may also be inferred the existence of *saṁsāra* arising from *dharma* and *adharma*. All this would be inexplicable if the Ātman and the Īśvara, the Self and the Lord, be identical.

(*Answer*):—No, for, that can be explained as due to a distinction between *jñāna*, and *ajñāna*, between knowledge and ignorance. It has been said:

"These, what is known as wisdom and what is known as unwisdom, are quite distinct and lead to different goals."—(Ka. Up. ii. 4.)

And so also a distinction through effect between *vidyā* and *avidyā*, wisdom and unwisdom, as producing quite opposite results,—the right and the sweet—is pointed out (in the same Upaniṣad and in the same context), wisdom leading to the right, while the sweet is the effect of unwisdom. . . .

So also we see that an ignorant man regards the physical body, etc., as the Self, is impelled by attachment and hatred and the like, performs righteous and unrighteous deeds (*dharma* and *adharma*), and is born and dead, while those are liberated who, knowing the Self to be distinct from the body and the like give up attachment and hatred, and no longer engage in righteous or unrighteous deeds to which those passions may lead. This nobody can deny by argument. Such being the case, the *kṣetrajña*, who is the Īśvara Himself, appears to be a *saṁsārin* owing to a distinction in the upādhis set up by *avidyā*, in the same way that the Ātman or individual Self appears (by *avidyā*) to be identical with the physical body, etc. It is a well-ascertained truth that that notion of identity of the individual Self with the not-Self,—with the physical body and the like—which is common to all mortal creatures is caused by *avidyā*, just as a pillar (in darkness) is mistaken (through *avidyā*) for a human being. But thereby no essential quality of the man is actually transferred to the pillar, nor is any essential quality of the pillar actually transferred to the man. Similarly consciousness never actually pertains to the body; neither can it be that any attributes of the body—such as pleasure, pain and dulness—actually pertain to Consciousness, to the Self; for, like decay and death, such attributes are ascribed to the Self through *avidyā*.

(*Objection*):—No, the two cases are dissimilar. The pillar and the man are *both objects* of cognition (*i.e.*, external to the Self) and are as such mistaken one for the other by the cognizer through *avidyā*, whereas you say that the body and the Self, which are respectively the cognized and the cognizer, are mistaken one for the other. Thus the illustration differs from what has to be illustrated. Wherefore the attribute of the body, though an object of cognition, actually pertains to the Self, the cognizer.

(*Answer*):—No; for, then the Self would also become unconscious, etc. If the attributes—such as pleasure, pain, delusion, desire, hatred—of the body, etc., *i.e.*, of *kṣetra* (Matter) which is an object of cognition, could ever pertain to the Self the cognizer, then it would be necessary to state a reason for the difference,—*i.e.*, to explain why a few attributes only of *kṣetra* (an object of cognition) which are ascribed to the Self by *avidyā* actually pertain to the Self while others such as decay and death do not. On the other hand, we are led to infer that those qualities of *kṣetra* do not actually pertain to the Self, because, like decay and death, they also are attributed to the Self, by *avidyā*; also because they are objects shunned or sought for, and so on. Such being the case, inasmuch as *saṁsāra* which consists in doing and enjoying, and which has its root in the cognized, is only attributed to the cognizer by *avidyā*,—the cognizer is not thereby affected, just as the *ākāśa* or ether is not affected by the attributes of dirtiness and concavity which are ascribed to it by children through ignorance. . . .

(*Objection*):—Then, in the absence of *saṁsāra* and saṁsārins, the conclusion is inevitable that the *śāstra* or scripture serves no purpose, and so on.

(*Answer*):—No; for, it is admitted by all. The burden of explaining an objectionable point admitted into their systems by all those philosophers who argue the existence of Ātman does not lie on only one of them.—In what way do all classes of philosophers admit into their systems this objectionable point?—All philosophers who admit the existence of a Self agree that liberated Selfs are not conscious of *saṁsāra* or of the state of being bound to *saṁsāra*; still, it is not believed that their systems are open to the objection that the *śāstra* serves no purpose. So, according to our view, when the kṣetrajñas become one with the Lord, then let the *śāstra* serve no purpose. It has, however, a purpose to serve where there is *avidyā*. . . .

In point of fact, the objection that the *śāstra* would have no purpose to serve cannot be brought against non-dualism; for, the *śāstra* is concerned with the ignorant who view things as they present themselves to their consciousness.—It is, indeed, the ignorant who identify themselves with the cause and the effect, with the not-Self. But not the wise; for, these latter do not identify themselves with the cause and the effect since they know that the Self is distinct from the cause and the effect. Not even the dullest or the most insane person regards water and fire, or light and darkness, as identical: how much less a wise man. Wherefore, the injunctions and prohibitions of the *śāstra* do not apply to him who knows the Self to be distinct from the cause and the effect. . . .

(*Objection*):—Notwithstanding his knowledge that the Self is unconnected with the cause and the effect, it is quite possible for a wise man to regard himself—in reference to the connection (between the Self and the body, etc.) once set up by *avidyā* (*prakṛti*)—as still bound by the injunctions of the *śāstra,* thinking that he has been enjoined to adopt a certain course of action by which to attain a desirable end, and to avoid a certain other course of action which leads to an evil; just as a father and his sons regard every one among themselves as bound by the injunctions and prohibitions addressed to every other, notwithstanding their knowledge that they are all-persons distinct from each other.

(*Answer*):—No; it is only prior to the knowledge of the Self unconnected with causes and effects that it is possible for one to identify the Self with them; for, it is only after having duly observed the injunctions and prohibitions of the *śāstra*—but not before—that a person attains to the knowledge that the Self is quite unconnected with causes and effects. Hence the conclusion that the injunctions and prohibitions of the *śāstra* concern only the ignorant. . . .

Therefore, *saṁsāra* is only based on *avidyā* and exists only for the ignorant man who sees the world as it appears to him. Neither *avidyā* nor its effect pertains to *kṣetrajña* pure and simple. Nor is illusory knowledge able to affect the Real Thing. The water of the mirage, for instance, can by no means render the saline soil miry with moisture. So, too, *avidyā* can do nothing to *kṣetrajña*. . . .

CHAPTER 9

Sureśvara

We turn now to post-Śaṁkara Advaita. Once Śaṁkara had succeeded in demolishing or absorbing rival philosophies, a school of Advaita Vedānta could be formed with its members having the opportunities to quarrel among themselves. And out of these quarrels many of the ideas of Śaṁkara were refined and given greater precision. At times, to be sure, the reader feels somewhat oppressed by the scholastic nature of the commentaries upon commentaries, but nevertheless there is a good deal of exciting philosophical analysis to be found in them.

The very first phase of post-Śaṁkara Advaita presents an historical problem. Until rather recently Vedāntins maintained that two of the most important thinkers who followed Śaṁkara were actually one person. Maṇḍana Miśra, the spiritual father of the Bhāmatī school, and Sureśvara, one of Śaṁkara's pupils, were identified as one. Maṇḍana, it is now believed, was closer in spirit than Sureśvara to the pre-Śaṁkara Vedānta tradition in holding to the necessity for ritual action and meditation (*upāsanā*) as prerequisites to the attainment of *mokṣa,* and in claiming that real freedom takes place only upon the death of the body (*videhamukti*). Conversely, Sureśvara, it is now believed, was closer to Śaṁkara in insisting upon knowledge (*jñāna*) as the sole means to *mokṣa* and to the real freedom which it is possible to attain while living (*jīvanmukti*). Maṇḍana, in his *Brahmasiddhi,* also shows preference for the idea that the locus (*āśraya*) of *avidyā* is the individual self, the *jīva,* while Sureśvara favors the idea that Brahman, the Self, is at once the object (*viṣaya*) and the locus (*āśraya*) of all ignorance.

This dispute about the locus of ignorance is central to the doctrinal divisions between the two main sub-schools of Advaita—the Bhāmatī (represented by thinkers such as Vācaspati Miśra, Amalānanda, etc.) and the Vivaraṇa (represented by thinkers such as Padmapāda, Sarvajñātman, Prakāśātman, etc.). According to the Bhāmatī (following Maṇḍana), the individual self must be the locus of *avidyā,* because such "ignorance" cannot intelligibly be assigned to Brahman; and there must be a plurality of individuals each with his own *avidyā*, for if one person is released from the bondage of ignorance it does not mean that everyone is released. There may be a primal or public ignorance (*mūlāvidyā*), but there assuredly is an individual or private one (*tulāvidyā*). The Vivaraṇa school criticizes the Bhāmatī position on the grounds that it is unintelligible for the *jīva* to be both a product of *avidyā* and its source. It argues that Brahman, the Self, must be the locus of *avidyā*. Many individuals may be said to exist as different reflections of Brahman on the mirror of ignorance.

In the latter development of Advaita, a doctrine known as *ekajīvavāda*, the theory that there is only one individual, was also put forward (namely by Prakāśānanda in *Vedāntasiddhāntamuktāvalī*) which tended towards a kind of solipsism and "subjective idealism" (*dṛṣṭi-sṛṣṭi-vāda*—the theory that perception is or precedes creation), but this extreme doctrine is not really part of the classical Vivaraṇa school and it would clearly have been rejected by Śaṁkara.

The following selections, from Sureśvara's *Naiṣkarmyasiddhi*, exhibit, among other things, his treatment of this problem of "Whose is *avidyā*?" and indicates the line of thought that the Vivaraṇa school later develops. A good translation of the *Naiṣkarmyasiddhi* has been made by A. J. Alston, *The Naiṣkarmya Siddhi of Śrī Sureśvara* (London: Shanti Sadan, 1959) and the selections are from this text. The commentary which accompanies the selections is that of Sureśvara.

NAIṢKARMYA SIDDHI OF ŚRĪ SUREŚVARA

Criticisms of *bhedābheda*

I, 68. The doctrine that Brahman is known through a conjunction of knowledge and *karman* is difficult to maintain even in the case of those whose Brahman permanently retains differentiations.

Comm. Now we state two varieties of *bhedābhedavāda* and refute the doctrine of conjunction in relation to both.

I, 69. The doctrine of conjunction can be maintained neither by those bhedābhedavādins who hold that *jīva* and Brahman are identical even in *saṁsāra*, nor by those who hold they are different. For on the view that they are identical, failure to "attain" Brahman can be due to ignorance alone; and on the view that they are different liberation is impossible.

Comm. Here, on the view that *jīva* is ever fundamentally Brahman by his very nature, it is only satanic ignorance that can prevent God-realisation. In regard to this view we say:

I, 70. Actions are not the means to destroy ignorance. Since this is achieved by knowledge and knowledge only, actions are useless in this regard.

Comm. And on the view that Brahman is different from *jīva*, neither can action lead to realisation of Brahman, nor knowledge, nor can knowledge and action conjoined. For if Brahman shows itself to be different from *jīva*, such difference must be self-revealed by Brahman alone.

I, 71. Where two things are essentially different, neither can become identical with the other. Even supposing they could, as between *jīva* and Brahman we should have not liberation and God-realisation but the total destruction of the *jīva*.

Comm. Now we mention another school of bhedābhedavādins, who speak of liberation through knowledge, but base the doctrine on a Vedic command.

I, 72. Even the miserable dualists would attain liberation if they practised intellectual and spiritual discipline such as accords with the highest Self. But the bhedābhedavādins fail because they attempt to attain liberation through action, which contradicts the highest Self by its mere presence.

I, 73. And tell me, O bhedābhedavādins, how any command could be a cause of action in him who is established in Brahman alone, who has discarded all else, and who sees no variety anywhere?

I, 74. Further, the *bhedābhedavādin* who admits identity with Brahman in *saṁsāra* admits the identity of the *jīva* with all castes. This nullifies, for him, the impelling power of the Vedic injunctions addressed as all of them are to men of specific castes.

Comm. Suppose the *bhedābhedavādin* in question says "Injunctions can have force even for the *jīva* who knows his identity with Brahman, since he may continue to identify himself with his physical body", we reply "not so".

I, 75. Nor can the *jñānī* identify himself with the physical body, since such identification is due to satanic nescience. If the latter had power to afflict even the *jñānī*, God-realisation would be useless.

Comm. The opponent has now been thoroughly refuted, since we have shown that action is an effect of nescience, and that therefore there can be no association either simultaneous or even successive between knowledge and *karman*, based on the real and the unreal respectively as they are. Still, in case he should still go on clutching at straws, we remark further:

I, 76. If the *jñānī* should once again identify himself with the individual body and mind he merely shows that he was not a *jñānī* but deluded. Let him perform actions—who can restrain the ignorant?

Comm. Moreover, since all action is already achieved, action cannot be something *commanded*.

I, 77. *Karman* in both its particular and universal aspects is the very self of such a yogī (as the doctrine under discussion has in mind). It can no more be the subject of an injunction than breathing.

Comm. Suppose the (still *bhedābhedavādin*) opponent retracts the doctrine of the identity of *jīva* with Brahman in a (real) *saṁsāra*; suppose he says, "well, at any rate Brahman is both differentiated and undifferentiated. Hence a conjunction of knowledge and action *is* possible—the knowledge having reference to His undifferentiated, the action to His differentiated aspect."

But this view will not stand either. For the notion of difference cannot rise in relation to any object without contradicting the previous notion that it was not different. Unless this be admitted, neither identical nor different things can exist in the world.

If the opponent persists in maintaining his defenceless position, then, since his position accepts both difference and non-difference as characteristic of Brahman, we select for discussion the position that non-difference is characteristic of Him, and remark that in that case Brahman must be afflicted with pain (which is absurd).

I, 78. If Brahman be both identical with and different from all things both particular and general, then (in His aspect as identical with them) He is certainly subject to pain. Indeed all the pain that exists anywhere falls to His lot. Such is the wisdom of these exalted metaphysicians.

Comm. Now we sum up our theme that knowledge and action cannot be conjoined.

I, 79. To say that knowledge can coalesce with action is like saying that darkness coalesces with the sun, coolness with fire, or heat with water.

The Self as Witness; *sākṣin*

II, 107. Of the three factors of empirical cognition, the "known" is the external object having visible form, "knowledge" is the succession of modifications in the mind (doubt, memory, certainty etc.) and the knower is the "I" which constantly accompanies these two; but the witness is the Self which is constant and eternal.

II, 108. That witness of all acts of acquiring and rejecting, itself beyond acquiring and rejecting, is the one that is—*in the empirical sense*—neither knower, knowledge nor known.

II, 109. Each of the three factors of empirical cognition is transitory. None can witness its own rise or destruction. Hence none can establish its own reality, and hence none in reality exists to witness the rise and destruction of the others. Hence they are witnessed by something different from any of them.

Comm. Objection. The theory of a witness leaves us in infinite regress, for any given witness requires a further witness to witness his existence.

Answer. No. Unlike the instruments of empirical knowledge, which are inert, objective, subject to modification, and transient, the witness requires no external support to establish its own existence.

II, 110. The unchangeable Self does not require proof from outside as the intellect does. All else is proved to exist in reference to that independent One. But He himself requires no proof.

The Locus of Ignorance

III, *Comm.* Now ignorance (*ajñāna*) cannot exist in the void. It must always be ignorance of someone about something, must always have a conscious 'locus' or 'support' in which it exists (*āśraya*) and an object which it conceals from view (*viṣaya*). Further we have already established that two categories exist and two only, the Self and the not-Self. From this it follows that the *āśraya* (support or locus) of *ajñāna* cannot be the not-Self. For the very nature of the not-Self is *ajñāna*, and ignorance existing in mere ignorance is unthinkable (since the existence of ignorance implies a knower or at least knowledge). Even if it could so exist, what difference would the rise of ignorance in pure ignorance effect that we could say it was an event having any significance whatever? Again, on the view that the locus of ignorance were the not-Self there could be no attainment of knowledge, and knowledge would not exist. But ignorance depends on knowledge for its own existence, since it exists only by virtue of negating it. Further, the not-Self is born of ignorance. It is absurd to suppose that that which is logically and causally prior can only exist supported by and dependent on its own effect. Nor, again, has the not-Self any form independent of and different from ignorance whereby it could serve as its locus and support. These arguments refute the possibility of the not-Self serving as the support of ignorance, and if duly reflected on, they show it cannot be the object concealed by ignorance either. Therefore the not-Self is neither the one in ignorance (*āśraya* of *avidyā*) nor the object concealed by ignorance (*viṣaya* of *avidyā*).

Hence we conclude, as the only remaining alternative, that it is the Self alone which is both *āśraya* and *viṣaya* of *avidyā*. All of us have the experience "I do not know", and in *śruti* Śrī Nārada says "I am only a knower of the mantras, my lord; I do not know the Self" (Ch. Up. VII. 1. 3). Nor do the arguments which tell against the not-Self as *āśraya* of *avidyā* apply to the Self. The Self, indeed, is not identical with ignorance, since its nature is pure consciousness. Again, on the hypothesis that the Self is the locus of ignorance, a difference is introduced into the locus in the form of a break in knowledge, whereby the existence of ignorance as supported in the locus can be established and regarded as a significant event. And again, on this view the attainment of knowledge is possible, since the Self, through its reflection in the mind, produced knowledge. Nor has the Self the disqualifying characteristic of being born of ignorance, since it is the eternal rock-firm changeless Self by nature. And finally the conscious Self has a form and existence independent of those of ignorance whereby it can serve as the latter's support. From all this we conclude that it is the Self alone which is ignorant (i.e. which is the locus or support of ignorance).

"What then is the object concealed by this ignorance sustained by the Self?" "The Self is that object", we reply. "Well then, is it not a fact that ignorance is incompatible with the Self, since the latter is of the very nature of knowledge, is non-relational, is instrumental in the production of the very opposite of ignorance (viz. knowledge), and is contradictory to knowledge in other ways too?"

To this objection we reply that ignorance *is* compatible with the Self. For in reality the Self remains undifferentiated. It becomes differentiated into knower, knowledge and the known through mere ignorance alone, just as it is through mere ignorance that the rope becomes a snake—the Self and the rope remaining in reality quite unaffected. Hence when ignorance is shaken off there is complete absence of all the evils of duality. . . .

Enlightenment

IV, 49. For him who knows the Self thus there is no more "I" and "mine" any more than there is darkness in front of one who carries in his hand a lighted lamp.

IV, 50. Just as before enlightenment the existence of anything other than the world of duality remained unproved, so after enlightenment the existence of the intellect etc. is completely negated because the viewpoint is now that of the inner Self.

IV, 51. The enlightened man knows and accepts everything in the empirical world and at the same time denies everything. The acceptance is but a deliberate and artificial acceptance of distinctions; the denial is the natural reaction based on the real state of affairs.

IV, 56. Through knowledge of reality he brings *saṃsāra* to a halt. Right-knowledge destroys the path of renunciation as surely as it destroys the path of action.

IV, 57. Through merely becoming aware of the Self once one destroys the whole of *saṁsāra*, through negation of ignorance once and for all. There is no more wrong knowledge afterwards.

IV, 58. Time and space etc. are the effects of delusion, and do not inhere in the Self. Once the Self is known, there is no more knowledge to gain and no ignorance left unconsumed.

CHAPTER 10

Maṇḍana Miśra

Maṇḍana Miśra, probably an elder contemporary of Śaṁkara, is one of the most important thinkers in post-Śaṁkara Advaita. Besides his major work, the *Brahmasiddhi,* he wrote several works on Mīmāṁsā and conducted studies in the philosophy of language (*Sphoṭasiddhi*) and theory of error (*Vibhramaviveka*). In the *Brahmasiddhi,* Maṇḍana argues persuasively for the view that *ānanda,* the bliss of Brahman, is a positive state, and for the view that Brahman, being pure consciousness, cannot be known as an object of consciousness. Maṇḍana was especially concerned with the problem of what the proper relation is between *karman* or ritual action and *jñāna,* the highest knowledge of Brahman. This theme exhibits once again the subtle dependence of advaitic thinkers on the main-line Brahmanic tradition and the various efforts that were made to uphold at the same time the advaitic position that knowledge alone is the means to *mokṣa.*

The following section from the first chapter of the *Brahmasiddhi* deals with this problem of relating *karman* to *jñāna.* The translation is from an unpublished manuscript by Dr. R. Balasubramanian, reader in philosophy at the University of Madras.

BRAHMASIDDHI

This is to be inquired now. Does the entire Veda establish Brahman by negating the world of diversity or only a part of it? With regard to this, some hold the following view. Everywhere in the Veda the negation of some difference in a particular place is conveyed as, for example, the denial of the notion that the body is the Self is conveyed by the injunction "One who desires heaven should perform a sacrifice." What is conveyed here is that the eligible person is one who, being different from the body, is competent to enjoy heaven; by this there is the denial of the view which treats the body as the Self. In the same way, since the person (who performs the *darśapūrṇamāsa*) is the one eligible (for sprinkling), the injunction "One who desires cattle should sprinkle with the milk-pail" (*Āpastaṁbaśrautasūtra* 1. 16. 3) negates the notion that the person eligible (for sprinkling with the milk-pail) is different. Likewise, injunctions and prohibitions, too, seek to negate the natural activities which are caused by passion, etc.; while prohibitions do that directly, injunctions do so by enjoining other actions; and in the world, too, people are diverted from the undesirable path either directly or (indirectly) by the advice to follow a different path. Thus, the injunctions which enjoin rites are directly conducive to the attainment of the knowledge of the Self by negating the various natural activities caused by passion, etc. This can be explained as follows: a person who has controlled the mind and the senses and who is calm is eligible for the knowledge of the Self; and also he can attain it. Indeed, a person who is attracted by the objects of desire and is engrossed in the activities which are conducive to them cannot concentrate his mind on the Self; on the contrary, a person who is free from natural activities and who has controlled his mind is eligible for the knowledge of the Self, because of his competence.

Some others think like this: a person who has not fulfilled his desires and whose mind is polluted by desire is not eligible for the knowledge of the supreme non-dual reality; but a person who has destroyed his desires (through fulfillment) by means of rites spread over one thousand years attains the non-dual Self which is superior to the status of Prajāpati. According to these two views, the entire Veda has its purport only in one result, viz., the knowledge of the Self.

The view of some others is as follows: Having separate fruits of their own (different from the knowledge of the Self), the injunctions which enjoin rites make a person fit for the knowledge of the Self, since one who has not liquidated the three debts is not eligible therefor, as stated in the text, "Having liquidated the three debts, one has to set one's mind on release" (*Manu* 6. 35).

But there are others who argue that all rites are conducive to the attainment of the knowledge of the Self in accordance with the principle of two-in-oneness as stated in the *śruti* text, "The *Brāhmaṇas* seek to know It through sacrifice" (Bṛh. Up. 4. 4. 22), and also in the text, "Through the performance of any sacrifice, even like *darvīhoma*, one attains a mind which is free from distractions."

Others hold the view that rites make a person eligible for knowledge of the Self through purification as stated in the text, "One becomes fit for the knowledge of Brahman through the *mahāyajñas* and also through sacrifices" (*Manu* 2. 28); there is also the text, "He who has these forty purificatory ceremonies and eight virtues" (*Gautama-dharmasūtra*, 8. 22).

There are others who, reversing the relation (between rite and knowledge) as mentioned above, argue that it is the knowledge of the Self which makes a person eligible for the performance of a rite by causing purification in the agent.

Some others think that rite and the knowledge of the Self which are mutually opposed have no relation whatsoever, for the one involves duality, while the other non-duality.

Of these, the first view is not tenable. The injunctions which enjoin rites do not really need some other fruit than the fruits like heaven, etc., mentioned in those texts themselves. Nor does the injunction about the knowledge of the Self, whose scope is fulfilled by celibacy and other means as stated, need the injunctions which enjoin rites. If so, how could they have one result? If it be said that the injunctions which enjoin rites do not have fruits as mentioned therein, since heaven, etc., are mentioned as subsidiary to something else, the section which discusses about the desire for heaven must be explained to this person. Further, if all injunctions and prohibitions have their purport in negating the world of name and form, the rise and fall of all creatures are not due to previous deeds, and thereby they will be without any cause; in the same way release, too, will be without any cause, and this will result in the futility of Scripture also.

Objection: The injunctions which enjoin rites are related to knowledge by (giving instruction about) results like heaven, etc., in the same way as the instruction about passing through certain villages on the way is related to the instruction about reaching the desired town.

Reply: This argument is wrong. It is proper to say that, since reaching the villages on the way is not what is desired, the instruction about them is related to the instruction about reaching the desired place. The end which is desired is not really attained through the instructions about the villages on the way. It follows that insofar as the scope (of these instructions) is not fulfilled, they come to be related to that (instruction) by which the desired end is attained. But in the case of the injunctions which enjoin rites, there is no absence of the desired end, since heaven, etc., are desired by the person. Since their scope thus comes to be fulfilled, how can they come into relation with the other (viz., knowledge)?

Objection: When a person is persuaded to reach the desired place by informing him about the advantages of going to the villages situated one after another on the way, the earlier instructions about the villages come to be related to the other instruction about attaining the desired result.

Reply: It is proper; but what happens there is that the intention of the speaker is known through some other means of knowledge; indeed, through some other means of knowledge this is what is known: when reaching this particular place, this object desired by the speaker is attained; hence, this is the intention of the speaker. But this cannot be known merely by following the verbal statement. This must be so for the following reason also. When there is the realization of the desired ends in every village, and when the intention of the speaker and that of the hearer in respect of reaching some other place is not known through some other means of knowledge, those who are nearby and hear the verbal statement understand the earlier instructions as having their import only in those ends; they also understand that the instruction about the other place is for the sake of its own end. Though, in truth, the objects intimated by the earlier instructions are useful to the attainment of the other object, the import of the verbal statement is not understood in that way, just as the injunction which enjoins the acquisition of wealth, though useful to the injunction which enjoins a sacrifice, does not have its purport therein. Hence (in respect of the Vedic injunctions) the purport must be understood by following the verbal statement, because of the absence of other means of knowledge (in this regard). Further, since the instructions about the villages on the way are understood to have their import only in what they say, the person who listens to them goes to those places and attains the desired objects; but if the instructions have their purport in reaching the other place, he will not necessarily go to the villages. Since reaching the other place is what is intended, he will go there through some other route also. . . .

Moreover, it must be explained how the injunctions which enjoin rites are conducive to the attainment of knowledge in a perceptible way. If it be said that they do so by preventing the perceptible natural activities caused by passion, etc., let it be in the case of prohibitions. But it must be explained how the injunctions which enjoin rites prevent them. They are not, indeed, exclusive injunctions; nor are they restrictive injunctions, for what they convey is utterly unknown. In respect of what is already known, an injunction can, indeed, be understood as intending the elimination of something. It cannot be said that there is elimination (of the natural activities) due to the conflict (between Scripture-ordained rites and natural activities) insofar as they lead to the same result. The activities enjoined by the Veda which do not yield their fruits at a specified time have imperceptible results; but the natural activities which are caused by passion, etc., have perceptible results. There is no conflict between doing a sacrifice called *sāṅgrahaṇī* and doing service, in respect of their being a means to the attainment of a village; Scripture has validity only to this extent (i.e., as enjoining a means to an end). This being the case, what is the conflict when a person who is desirous of abundant fruit does service and also performs *sāṅgrahaṇī* either simultaneously or one after another? Further, if all activities which yield perceptible results are prevented, even the activities which are based on the Vedic injunction will be prevented, because those (Scripture-ordained) activities are not possible for one who has not acquired wealth, and who is, therefore, without the means for performing them. Moreover, there is no difference between the activities which yield perceptible results and those which yield imperceptible results, if both of them being prompted by desire are conducive to the desired end. This can be explained as follows: Assuming an activity caused by desire in the case of one who desires heaven, the injunction enjoins a special means (for attaining the end); since there is similarity (between them) in respect of attachment to the world, by which reason does the one become useful to the attainment of the knowledge of the Self, while the other is opposed to it? The attraction of desire is, indeed, the same for the mind. If it be argued that Scripture-ordained rites are not the means to the desired end, then the rise and fall of all creatures, it has already been said, will be without a cause; and also the principle enunciated (by Jaimini) will be thrown down. Since the two kinds of activities are opposed as giving rise to the same result, it was argued that the one (viz., natural activity) will get removed; this argument stands refuted far away.

It is argued that the injunctions which enjoin rites are useful to the attainment of knowledge insofar as they lead to the dissolution of desires through fulfilling them, as stated in the text, "When all desires that cling to one's heart fall off, then a mortal becomes immortal, (and) one attains Brahman here" (Ka. Up. 2. 3. 14). This is also wrong, for desires are not dissolved by fulfilling them, but only by the discrimination arising as a result of the reflection on their defects. If the mind is touched even very little by desires, it is stolen by the captivating desires; it has been said, "Desires can never be extinguished by their enjoyment" *Manu* 2. 94); there is again the saying, "Desires as well as the abilities of the senses grow keeping pace with enjoyment" (*Yogasūtrabhāṣya* 2. 15). If at least the Vedic injunctions are not known as enjoining means (to attain the desired ends), a person will be free from desires and take refuge in the knowledge of the Self which by its very nature stills all sufferings; but a person who knows the means as indicated by the injunctions which enjoin rites will be drawn towards the enjoyment of pleasures which by their very nature captivate the mind; and he will dislike the knowledge of the Self which by its very nature quiets down all desires. Though the bliss of the Self is known through Scripture, it is not experienced, and so it is not competent even to slacken the longing for pleasure caused by objects, which has been experienced, much less to destroy it. Hence, discrimination alone is the only means for destroying desire; but the injunctions which enjoin rites do the opposite.

It was argued that everywhere in the Veda the negation of some difference in a particular place is conveyed, as for example the denial of the notion that the body is the Self is conveyed by the injunction, "One who desires heaven should perform a sacrifice." This argument, too, is wrong, because the injunction (given above as example) does not have its purport therein; indeed, this text does not have its purport in intimating the reality of the Self as different from the body. If it be said that by implication it purports to intimate it, even though it may have its purport in something else, it is like inferring the existence of an elephant from its foot-print when it is directly seen. Indeed, the negation of the notions that the body, senses, etc., are the Self is directly stated by the text beginning with "It is neither gross" (Bṛh. Up. 3. 8. 8). It will follow by implication that the hardness of the knot of desire (due to the pursuit of the different means as enjoined in the Vedic injunctions) is because of the Veda.

Since desires, as stated earlier, can never be killed by their enjoyment, since the injunctions which enjoin rites have their scope fulfilled through fruits mentioned therein, and since there is no valid reason for considering the injunctions as connected with the other (viz., the knowledge of the Self), the second view also is untenable. If there is one end (for both the injunctions which enjoin rites and the injunction which enjoins knowledge), there will be combination of all rites with knowledge; and this is impossible.

Those who, by reversing the relation (i.e., by making knowledge subsidiary to rite), maintain that there is one end for knowledge and rite must state the evidence in respect of the (subsidiary) relation of knowledge to rite. There is no authority for connecting knowledge with rites in the same way as there is the textual authority, "One sprinkles the rice-grains," for connecting the rice-grains with rites. In this case, since it is futile to sprinkle the rice-grains which are not used in rites, the word "rice-grain" conveys, because of the context (*prakaraṇa*), that rice-grains when sprinkled are connected with the unseen potency of the rite mentioned in the context by being conducive to it. . . . But the knowledge of the Self is not stated in the context (of *karmakāṇḍa*); nor is the Self invariably related to rite; so it is wrong to speak about its connection with rite. Thus, since the knowledge of the Self is not for the sake of something else, the *śruti* text which speaks about the fruit that accures is not a commendatory one, and so (having a fruit of its own), the person eligible for that is a different one.

Objection: It may be argued in this way. Since the *śruti* text, "He does not return hither again" (Ch. Up. 8. 15. 1), is in the present tense, and since it does not show any connection with desire, the fruit that will accrue must be stated by changing the wording of the text; and that is possible only if there is expectancy of fruit in the text; but there is no such expectancy when it has a perceptible fruit. To be engaged in activities which will give rise to fruits to be enjoyed in some other body is the perceptible fruit of the injunction which enjoins knowledge. Hence the injunction which enjoins knowledge is like the injunction which enjoins the study of one's own Veda. The injunction which enjoins the study of one's own Veda has no expectancy, for understanding the meaning of rite is its perceptible fruit; and so it does not seek a fruit from a commendatory text; since this is also true in the case of the injunction which enjoins knowledge, the latter does not have a separate fruit.

Reply: This view also is wrong, for this person who is different (from the agent and the enjoyer) and who is taught in the *Upaniṣads* is known from the *Vedānta*. The knowledge of this person does not cause the performance of rite; he is not really an agent and an enjoyer. Thus has it been said, "It does not eat anything" (Ch. Up. 8. 15. 1), "The other looks on without eating" (Mu. Up. 3. 1. 1). But the one who is the agent and the enjoyer of rites, that person alone is directly known in our day-to-day experience, and so he is not to be known through Scripture.

Objection: The individual soul (*jīva*) and the supreme Self (*Ātman*) are only the same. Indeed, it has been said thus, "By this *jīva*, by this *Ātman*" (Ch. Up. 6. 3. 2)

Reply: It is true; but only the individual soul which is in association with *avidyā* is what is known directly (in our day-to-day experience). And this knowledge (of the individual soul) is the cause of the performance of rite; and for this, Scripture is not required. But the supreme Self which is self-luminous and which is free from all distinctions is to be known through Scripture; and this (knowledge of the Self) is opposed to the performance of rite. How can it be that the performance of rite is the perceptible fruit of this knowledge? This can be explained as follows: What for should a person who knows the Self which is the highest bliss, which is one and non-dual, undertake any action? And how could he undertake any action? For, he has all his desires fulfilled, and there is the absence of the means of action. . . .

There are those who think that there is no relation at all between rite and knowledge as they are opposed to each other, for while rite is concerned with duality, knowledge is concerned with non-duality. But this is wrong; if that were the case, there will not be the possibility at all of the rise of the knowledge of non-duality to them, since (according to them) there is conflict between the cognition involving distinctions like means of knowledge, etc., and the cognition of non-duality.

Objection: Since the means and the end do not exist simultaneously, there is no conflict between them; all distinctions do disappear when there is the cognition of non-duality. There is no conflict between them; nor does the one cease to be the means to the other; this is because of the fact that the means is chronologically earlier, and at that time the distinctions (like *pramāṇa*, etc.,) have not disappeared. Further, difference alone is the means for the rise of the cognition of non-duality.

Reply: If so, (for knowledge) there is no conflict even with rites, since they, too, are the means.

Objection[1]: Let this be so. There is no use of rites in respect of Brahman, since it is not something to be accomplished; and this is stated in the *śruti* text "What is not the result (viz., Brahman) cannot be brought into being by what is done (by rites)" (Mu. Up. 1. 2. 12). Nor are they useful in respect of the origination of knowledge, for knowledge is dependent on the means of knowledge. Rites cannot even be an auxiliary to knowledge, for there is not anything to be accomplished by knowledge. Release is not what is accomplished by knowledge, for in that case it would cease to be eternal. It may be argued that the destruction of the cause of bondage is something which can be accomplished; and so when the cause of bondage is destroyed, that being absent, a person attains release. If so, what is the cause of bondage? If the answer is that the beginningless ignorance is the cause of bondage, then its destruction is not something different from knowledge to be accomplished by it, for the rise of knowledge itself is the destruction of ignorance.

Let it be, it may be argued, that the rise of knowledge is the destruction of ignorance which is of the nature of non-apprehension, for the origination of what is positive alone is the destruction of its prior non-existence. But the rise of knowledge itself is not the destruction of erroneous cognition. Indeed, a positive entity cannot bring about the destruction of another positive entity, for positive entities are not of the nature of mutual non-existence; if that were the case, it would result in the void. It may be replied that erroneous cognition which is due to the non-apprehension of truth gets itself removed when its cause (viz., non-apprehension) is removed. But this is wrong. Non-apprehension which is negative cannot really be the cause of anything, for otherwise in the state of swoon, etc., there would be the possibility of it (erroneous cognition). What, then, is the cause of it? It has been said, "Ignorance which is beginningless and also purposeless." And there is no room for the question about the cause of ignorance. Since both erroneous cognition and its impressions are explained through the relation of cause and effect reciprocally, there is no defect. So, since the removal of erroneous cognition can be accomplished by knowledge, for the latter, there is the need of the auxiliary thereto.

The above argument, too, is untenable. It is well known that the valid cognitions which arise subsequent to the erroneous cognition of shell, etc., do not endeavor separately for their removal; nor do they seek the help of the auxiliary; for, the mere origination of another positive entity which is its opposite is the destruction of the earlier (erroneous cognition); and this (destruction) is not the void; for otherwise the destruction will not have a cause. Knowledge is the opposite of the erroneous cognition. When it arises, there is certainly the destruction of the erroneous cognition.

It may be said that rites are the cause of bondage, and that their destruction is caused by knowledge through the help of the auxiliary. But this is wrong. As long as there is ignorance, there is empirical experience involving distinctions of rite and fruit. How can this take place when there arises the pure knowledge which is free from the entire plurality? It is in this way that rites are said to be on a par with erroneous cognition and doubt in the following text, "The knot of the heart is cut, all doubts are dispelled, and his deeds terminate, when the Self is seen, the higher and the lower" (Mu. Up. 2. 2. 8). It may be argued that there is the need of the other in order to make knowledge pure; but this argument, too, is futile, for doubt and erroneous cognition which are the impurities of knowledge are not possible in the case of knowledge which has arisen from a means of valid knowledge.

It may be argued that what is desired is the direct knowledge which is different from the verbal cognition and which is free from all distinctions consequent on the destruction of the perception of diversity. Brahman can, indeed, be comprehended by this knowledge; it cannot be comprehended by the verbal cognition arising from the mutual relation among the different word-senses. There is the need of rite, meditation, etc., in respect of its origination.

Even this view is wrong. What is the speciality of this knowledge for the sake of which it is sought after? If it is said that owing to its clarity (it is sought after), there is no use of it. Knowledge, indeed, is needed for the sake of knowing the object. When there arises the verbal cognition, the object is known. If it be argued that, since cognition finally leads to direct perceptual knowledge wherein the expectancy (of the knower) comes to an end, it is sought after, then what is that other thing that is needed when the object is known? If it be said that another means of knowledge is needed, it is not so, for it is needed for knowing an object. If it be said that it is needed for knowing the object once again, then that object can be known through the earlier means of knowledge many a time. Further, there is no reason for knowing once again what is already known. If it be said that there is another means of knowledge (by which the same object can be known), then the other means may be sought after; but in respect of the object (which is already known), there is no expectancy (in the knower). If it be said that the exceptional satisfaction (which one attains) is the cause for knowing it again, then though the satisfaction has taken place through the previous means of knowledge, by knowing it again (through the same means) the exceptional satisfaction takes place; and another means of knowledge is not required for attaining that. Though an object is known through perception, it has to be known through other means of knowledge (like inference), since that exceptional satisfaction takes place there also, and since there is no difference among them (in this regard). They, too, determine the nature of the object, since they are means of knowledge. If it be argued that perception has for its object something which is capable of being rejected, etc., since the object is in proximity, but the other means of knowledge is not so, then the cause of proximity may be sought after, but not the means of knowledge, since the knowledge of the object has already been attained. In the case of the Self which is the object of knowledge in the present context, this distinction does not exist. If it be argued that verbal testimony, etc., makes known general features, while perception makes known the specific feature, then the content of perception is not at all known through verbal testimony. Assuredly, it may be replied, it is so; and it has already been said that Brahman is not the content of the knowledge arising from the verbal testimony. (But this will lead to some other difficulty). If the specific nature of Brahman is not known through verbal testimony, how is meditation on that (Brahman) possible? When one thing is meditated upon, another thing is not directly known. Further, what is that nature of Brahman for the direct realization of which sacrifice, etc., are enjoined? The injunction which enjoins the performance of sacrifice, etc., is intelligible (as providing the means) for directly realizing the Self which is Brahman by nature, which is of the nature of the unsurpassable bliss, and which is free from evil, etc., as shown by the verbal testimony. If that nature of Brahman which is the highest end desired by man is not known (through verbal testimony), or if that Brahman is known differently, then that injunction is futile. So when the Self which is of the nature of Brahman and which is free from evil, etc., is clearly known through the verbal testimony which is free from doubt, there is no need of the other means. It may be argued that, even though the non-difference of Brahman and the Self is known through the *śruti* text "That thou art" (Ch. Up. 6. 8. 7), there is the experience of the attributes of bondage as before and that, therefore, here is the need of the other means for its removal. But this argument is untenable. How is it, indeed, possible for one who has realized Brahman as the Self and who has known the true nature of the Self to have the attributes of bondage, which are due to erroneous cognition? And also, there is the *śruti* text which says, "One who knows Brahman becomes Brahman indeed" (Mu. Up. 3. 2. 9). There is no room for these attributes in Brahman which is free from evil, etc., as shown in the text, "If a man knows the Self as 'I am this,' then desiring what and for whose sake will he suffer in the wake of the body?" (Bṛh. Up. 4. 4. 12). And also, there is the text which says, "Verily, pleasure and pain do not touch one who is bodiless (Ch. Up. 8. 12. 1). Relation with the body is due to the wrong notion (which considers the body as the Self); when that relation is removed by the knowledge of the true nature of the Self, the person (though living) is bodiless; that pleasure and pain have no relation with the Self is declared (by the *śruti* text). Therefore, one who has realized the non-difference of Brahman and the Self does not have the attributes of bondage as before; but one who has them as before has not realized the non-difference of Brahman and the Self.

Reply: Even though the truth is known through the means of knowledge, illusory cognitions do not disappear in all cases; due to some specific reason, they also continue like the illusion of two-moon and the illusion of direction, though the truth about the moon and the direction is decidedly known through the utterance of a trustworthy person. In the same way, there is the continuance of the illusion due to the capacity of the powerful impressions which have accumulated on account of the repetition of the beginningless erroneous cognition for one who has known the reality of the Self through Scripture which is free from doubt; in order to remove that, there is the need of something else; and that something is the well-known repeated contemplation on the knowledge of the truth; sacrifice, etc., (which are useful) are based on the Scriptural authority. Indeed, repeated contemplation continues the work by strengthening the impressions (of the knowledge of the truth) and by preventing the earlier impressions (of the erroneous cognition); sacrifice, etc., also do their work through some imperceptible way. According to some others, they do their work by destroying the impurities of evil which are opposed to the good, for the performance of obligatory rites causes the destruction of evil.

Let this be so, it may be argued; let the illusions continue; but there is the ascertainment of the truth through the means of knowledge; as a person ascertains the truth as it is, so he conducts himself; and so the pursuit of any activity, whether good or bad, is untenable for one who has known the truth of the Self. To all this we reply as follows. Even though the knowledge of the truth has taken place, so long as its impression has not grown strong, while the impression generated by the erroneous cognition is strong, even the valid cognitions do not begin their work in the same way as the cognitions that the objects are illusory do not; in the same way as one who has the illusion of direction and who (though told about the direction) does not constantly keep in mind the utterance of the trustworthy person is seen to behave as before. Likewise, when there is no contemplation on the valid cognition of the rope, even though the truth of the rope is known, there is fear due to the illusion of snake. Therefore, even though the knowledge of the truth has arisen from the means of valid knowledge, for the purpose of mitigating or destroying the strong impression arising from the repetition of the beginningless erroneous cognition, repeated contemplation on the knowledge of the truth is thought of. That is why it is said, "The Self should be reflected on and meditated upon" (Bṛh. Up. 2. 4. 5). Other means like control of the mind, control of the senses, celibacy, sacrifice, etc., are also prescribed; otherwise, what are they advised for? It may be argued that the knowledge of the truth arises from the verbal testimony only on account of the means like celibacy, etc. But this argument is wrong, for knowledge originates from the verbal testimony alone. Indeed, the verbal testimony which intends to convey the knowledge of the truth does not fail to convey it without the special means (like control of the mind); nor does it lack certainty, for it is free from all doubts; otherwise the knowledge of those means which are prescribed therein will be impossible. Further, the actors who are seen on the stage are the cause of sorrow, fear, etc., (to the spectators) through illusory appearance, although it is otherwise known for certain (that they are on the stage); similarly even though there is certainty about the sweetness of sugar, its bitterness which is illusory causes sorrow (to a person whose taste is affected by bile) as if it is real, for he spits it out as if it is real. So even a person who has known with certainty the non-difference of Brahman and the Self is in need of other aids in order to remove that (continuance of illusion). Just as release does not become an effect which is accomplished when the nature of its reality is manifested by the means of knowledge, so also is it the case when it is manifested in a special way by aids (like sacrifice). Scriptural texts (which declare that release is attained through knowledge) have for their content that final stage of direct knowledge which arises from the consummation of contemplation; or let them be explained as pointing to the knowledge from the verbal testimony, since it is the cause of the subsequent (direct knowledge). What has elaborately been said so far will do.

It was said that the injunctions which enjoin rites, having separate fruits of their own, make a person fit for knowledge, since one who has liquidated the three debts is eligible therefor. But this is not true as a general principle, for different orders of life are stated in texts like, "To him there are many orders of life, according to some" (*Gautamadharmasūtra* 1. 3. 1), "He should dwell in that order of life which he likes." There is also the *śruti* text which says: "Otherwise (if a suitable occasion arises) let one renounce from the life of studentship" (*Jābāla Upaniṣad* 4). There are other texts like "Knowing this very thing, verily, the ancients did not offer the *agnihotra* sacrifice" (Kau. Up. 2. 4) "What shall we achieve through children?" (Bṛh. Up. 4. 4. 22), "What for shall we study the Veda? What for shall we do sacrifice?" in which the abandonment of rite (etc.) is stated. The text, "Having liquidated the three debts" (*Manu* 6. 35), states that a person who has accepted the life of a householder, and who, thinking that only through the knowledge of the Self his aim will be fulfilled, remains indifferent towards the liquidation of his debts, incurs sin as a result of not performing the prescribed rites, which is a hindrance to the rise of knowledge.

This view (unlike the previous ones) is acceptable—this view which maintains the rites, whose scope has been fulfilled by results (like heaven), are subsidiary to knowledge because of the principle of two-in-oneness, as shown in the text, "The *Brāhmaṇas* seek to know It through the study of the Vedas, through sacrifice" (Bṛh. Up. 4. 4. 22). But they are subsidiary (to knowledge) by being useful to the manifestation (of knowledge), and not by helping in the production of the result like *prayāja*, for there is no other result than knowledge. And also, the view about purification (i.e., the view which holds that rites make a person eligible for knowledge through purification) is acceptable, because of the *smṛti* text; indeed, knowledge arises to one who is purified. It has been said, "And the rites belonging to the stages also should be performed, since they are enjoined (by Scripture)" (*Brahmasūtra* 3. 4. 32).

Objection: Knowledge originates from the means which are perceptible; so what is to be practiced in a perceptible way like control of the mind, control of the senses, etc., which are exceptional means and which put an end to the disturbed state of the mind may be sought after, for only to a person who practices contemplation with a tranquil mind, knowledge which is pure arises; but sacrifice, etc., are not required, for even without them, it takes place through contemplation.

Reply: It is true; it is in this way that those who practice life-long celibacy wish to attain the pure knowledge, even without them (sacrifice, etc.). But there is difference in respect of the time (taken for reaching the goal); for knowledge is manifested quickly or very quickly because of the exceptional means, and in their absence, it is manifested slowly or very slowly. It has been said, "And there is need of all works, on account of the *śruti* text enjoining sacrifices, etc., as in the case of the horse" (*Brahmasūtra* 3. 4. 26). This is the meaning: even though knowledge may be attained through contemplation, there is the need of all rites, since there is the *śruti* text which says, "By sacrifice, by charity" (Bṛh. Up. 4. 4. 22); though the village may be reached even without a horse, yet a horse is sought after for reaching the place quickly or for being free from suffering.

It may be argued that Brahman is of the nature of knowledge itself; knowledge is not different from Brahman; and that (Brahman) is eternal, and so is not something which is brought into being. That being the case, how can something be required thereto? To the above argument the reply is: Just as a jewel whose colour is concealed by the adjunct which is nearby seeks the removal of the adjunct for the manifestation of its nature, in the same way it must be understood here. Indeed, the previous colour of the jewel has not been lost because of the presence of the adjunct; nor is another one originated when that is removed. The origination (of a momentary white colour) similar to the earlier one after being separated by many dissimilar (red-colour) moments cannot take place without any cause. Indeed, when fire is put out, the wood does not once again come into being from the pieces of charcoal. So, just as the colour of the jewel which is not at all produced requires the removal of the adjunct, even so the nature of the Self.

Objection: Let it be so; but the knowledge (of the nature of the jewel which a person wants to attain) requires something; and that knowledge which is different from the jewel is what is to be accomplished; in this case, the endeavour of the person is really for the sake of knowledge.

Reply: If so, is knowledge sought after for its own sake or for the sake of determining the nature of an object? It is not sought after for its own sake, for all our activity is connected with the object; it is not the case that activity is dependent only on cognition; it is also based on erroneous cognition. If it is said that knowledge is sought after for knowing the nature of an object, our search for knowledge is for the sake of the object. Knowledge does not bring about any change whatsoever in the object, for there is no connection between them; connection in terms of proximate co-existence obtains everywhere (and so it is no connection at all); further, (if it is said that knowledge causes some change in the object known) then, it should have been known to all; and also, it is not possible in the case of objects which are no more, and objects which are yet to come. Therefore, just as the jewel, though not really veiled, appears to be veiled as it were and seeks the removal of the adjunct as though it is to be revealed, even so the reality of the Self is not veiled, but appears as though it is veiled and as though it is to be revealed through effort.

CHAPTER 11

Padmapāda

According to tradition Padmapāda (ca. 820 A.D.), the founder of the Vivaraṇa school of Advaita, was, along with Sureśvara, a direct pupil of Śaṁkara. Tradition has it that after completing a commentary on Śaṁkara's *Brahmasūtrabhāṣya* Padmapāda traveled on a pilgrimage to Rāmeśvaram in the South. On the way he stopped at the house of an uncle who was an ardent supporter of Prabhākara—one of the leaders of an important school of Mīmāṁsā. The uncle was entrusted with the safety of the manuscript while Padmapāda continued on his journey, but the uncle, upon reading Padmapāda's attack upon Prabhākara, set fire to his own house in order to destroy the manuscript. Padmapāda later related to Śaṁkara how the manuscript had been destroyed whereupon Śaṁkara dictated to him from memory Padmapāda's commentary on the first five parts of his own work, hence the title *Pañcapādikā* for Padmapāda's work. (Portions of this work, however, were probably lost, as the present text covers only the gloss on I. i. 1–4 of Śaṁkara's *Brahmasūtrabhāṣya*).

The Vivaraṇa school, as founded by Padmapāda, refined a number of important doctrines of Advaita (e.g., the notion of *mithyā*, falsehood) and elaborated a few themes in somewhat new directions (e.g., the theory of perception). As indicated previously, the question of the locus or support of *avidyā* became an important problem for post-Śaṁkara Advaita, with the Vivaraṇa school arguing quite clearly that Brahman must be the locus. In connection with this, it elaborated a theory of "reflexionism" for working out the relation that obtains between the individual self (*jīva*) and Brahman, arguing that the *jīva* is a mere reflection (*pratibimba*) of its prototype (*bimba*) and that hence, in essence, the individual is identical with Brahman. The Vivaraṇa school also held that an encounter with any of the "great sayings" (*mahāvākyas*) of Advaita such as *tat tvam asi* ("thou art that") is sufficient for the attainment of enlightenment, of the realization of the identity between the self and Reality.

The following selections from the *Pañcapādikā* are from *The*

Pañcapādikā of Padmapāda, translated by D. Venkataramiah (Baroda: Oriental Institute, 1948), and deal with the topic of superimposition (*adhyāsa*).

PAÑCAPĀDIKĀ OF PADMAPĀDA

I, 2. . . . "With the object of getting rid of this (erroneous idea) which is the cause of misery, and thereby arriving at the knowledge of the oneness of the self with the Absolute, the study of the whole of the Vedānta is begun". There, by the phrase, "with the object of getting rid of this which is the cause of misery" the fruit (*prayojana*) is indicated, and by the phrase, "for arriving at the knowledge of the oneness of the self with the Absolute" the subject-matter (*viṣaya*) is rendered explicit. As that is so, what is the purpose of the Bhāṣya beginning with '*yuṣmad-asmat*' (and ending with '*sarvalokapratyakṣaḥ*') by which it is intended to show the error-begotten nature of men's doings (*i.e.*, their modes of thought and conduct) characterized by egoity as evidenced in the expression '*aham manuṣyaḥ*'—'I am man', where the self is identified with the body or the senses, '*ahamidam*'—I am this (*i.e.*, the body, etc.), '*mamedam*'—mine is this (children, wealth, etc., belonging to me and so on).

I, 3. This will be said in answer: The knowledge of Brahman as the solvent of the root-cause of the ills of life (*anartha*) is suggested in the *sūtra*, and *anartha* is constituted by (the notion that one is) an agent and an enjoyer which again presupposes (the belief that one is) a cogniser. If that (*anartha*) be genuinely real, it cannot be annihilated by *jñāna* (knowledge), for *jñāna* can remove only *ajñāna* (nescience). If on the other hand agency and enjoyment are grounded in nescience, then what is going to be stated (by the Sūtrakāra, *viz.*, that the knowledge of Brahman is the solvent of the cause of *anartha*) would be appropriate. Hence (*i.e.*, since knowledge is powerless to destroy the notions of *kartṛtva*, etc., unless the latter are rooted in nescience), it comes to this—that agency and enjoyment as the outcome of nescience have been clearly indicated by the aphorist himself, when he suggests that *Brahmajñāna* is the solvent of *anartha*.

Hence, in order that it may serve to establish the meaning conveyed by the *sūtra*, (the explanation of the nature of illusion has to be undertaken) by pointing out the error-begotten character of bondage, and as such this prefatory commentary has the purpose of serving as the introduction to the entire *śāstra* (*viz.*, Vedānta).

I, 4. And therefore, what this *śāstra* in substance expounds is that all the Vedānta texts culminate in showing that the ultimate nature of the individual soul (*ātman*) alleged to be *saṁsārin* (transmigratory being) is one uniform bliss, the very essence of existence, non-mutable and consciousness entire. . . .

III, 8. (Now follows the *bhāṣya* text)—["It is evident that the mutual identity of the object (*viṣaya*) and the subject (*viṣayī*), which are as opposite in character as darkness and light, is what is impossible to support"]. (Here these questions appear pertinent:) Which is this opposition? Of what nature is the mutual identity (indistinguishability) held to be? On account of the untenability of which is the comparison —'like darkness and light' adduced? If opposition (*virodha*) is defined as mutual exclusion (lit. non-residence in the same locus), then the presence of light would not warrant the presence of darkness. But this is not true. It is common knowledge that in a dimly-lit room objects (lit. colour or shape) are perceived not clearly but elsewhere (*i.e.*, where well-lit) clearly. From this it is obvious that in a room having a dim light, darkness also exists in some degree. Similarly, even in shade, warmth experienced in varying degrees indicates the presence of sunshine therein. From this it must be understood that com-presence of heat and cold may be taken to have been established.

III, 9. We say (in answer) that opposition is characterized by the absence of mutual identity (*tādātmya*). This means that no actual relation is possible as in the case of the universal and the particular (*jāti* and *vyakti*). Hence the identity of the one with the other, that is, their mutual identification is indefensible.

How (is that there can be no identity)? In so far as its nature is concerned (*i.e.*, in itself—*svatastāvat*), the *viṣayī* or the self can have (in reality) no identity of being with the *viṣaya* or the non-self, because it (the self) is wholly of the essence of consciousness (*cidekarasa*); nor through the other (*viṣaya*) because it is incapable of transformation (*pariṇāma*) and is unattached. The object also cannot by its own nature attain identity of being with the self by transforming itself into consciousness (*cit*), for then it will lose its characteristic as object by attaining equal status with consciousness. Nor through the other (the self by drawing the non-self into itself) can the non-self partake of the nature of the self, for the self is actionless (*niṣkriya*).

IV, 12. Superimposition (*adhyāsa*) means the manifestation of the nature of something in another which is not of that nature. That (manifestation), it is reasonable to hold, is false (*mithyā*). The word '*mithyā*' is of double signification—it is denotative of negation as well as of inexpressibility (*anirvacanīyatā*). Here it is an expression of negation. . . .

V, 13. Though it is so (*i.e.*, though superimposition is not warranted), yet it is seen to be congenital, or a constant accompaniment of the mere being (*mātra*) of the inner self. This means the mutual superimposition of the 'thou' and the 'I' as exemplified in the worlds (*loka*) usage (*vyavahāra*)—['I am this' and 'mine is this'].

Hence (because it is established by experience), just as the existence of the 'I' notion cannot be negated (being indubitable), even so that of superimposition; (the ego-concept necessarily involves the notion of superimposition). By the word '*loka*' is meant the whole class of beings permeated by the conceit, 'I am a man' (*i.e.*, ego-conscious). *Vyavahāra* is usage. (How)? Superimposition as is evident in 'I' and 'mine' means egoity in the form of 'I am a man'. (Hence the sentence means that the conceit 'I am a man,' is a matter of common experience and is beginningless.

VI, 16. When superimposition is proved to be the product of (*mithyājñāna*), how could it be said to be beginningless (*naisargika*)? Here is the answer:—It cannot but be admitted that there exists this potency of nescience in things external, as well as internal, its existence being a constant accompaniment of their inner nature. Otherwise (*i.e.*, if nescience is not admitted) the appearance of illusory objects becomes inexplicable. And that nescience does not cause any impediment to the manifestation of the real nature of insentient objects since their non-cognition is caused merely by the absence of the (necessary) means of valid knowledge. Prior to the manifestation of 'silver' and after (its manifestation also), even though it (*avidyā*) exists, its real nature (i.e., of silver) is apprehended. Hence it (*avidyā*) is but the cause of the manifestation of something different (from the original, the real; e.g., appearance of silver in shell—*rūpāntara*. This is due to the *vikṣepaśakti* of *avidyā*). In the inner self however which is of the nature of (pure) intelligence and as such self-lucent, since the non-manifestation of Brahman cannot be accounted for by anything else, its non-manifestation (it must be admitted) is due to the obstruction caused by the potency of nescience which is existent therein (in Brahman) and is beginningless. Hence it (primal nescience) obstructs the manifestation of the real nature of Brahman in the inner self (*jīva*) and it becomes the cause of the appearance of something other than its nature, like the ego notion, etc.; and in deep slumber, etc., having remained in the residual state of mere impressions of ego-notion, etc., which are the outcome of its projective power, it revives again (on waking). Hence though the superimposition as evidenced in the notions of men such as 'I' and 'mine' is beginningless (because the *hetu*, *viz*., *avidyā* is beginningless) it is spoken of as having *mithyājñāna* as its cause, but not as adventitious. Therefore its beginninglessness is not in conflict with its coming into existence as the result of a cause.

VII, 17. ["And (erroneously transferring the attributes) of the one with those of the other—*anyonyadharmāmśca*".] The reason why the attributes are taken separately is to show that in some cases superimposition of mere attributes (without reference to the substance) is perceived (as in 'I am deaf'. Deafness is the property of the organ of hearing and not of the self). . . . Again, where is the superimposition of attributes perceived? These (questions) the Bhāṣyakāra himself answers. He points to the form that superimposition takes in "This am I" and "This is mine". The ego notion so far is the first *adhyāsa*.

Is it not that the integral (partless) *cit* alone manifests itself in the '*aham*—ego' and that there is no additional part (seen in the ego-notion) either superimposed or not superimposed?

We will show; (when explicating the 'ego') how the superimposed part (*viz*., the insentient) is involved therein.

VII, 18. Well, in the notion—'this' (referring to one's body), the body—the aggregate of cause and effect which is the means of the enjoyment (of the agent denoted by the ego—'*aham kartā*') is manifest to view (*i.e.*, is seen as the object of perception); and in 'this is mine', (the body) is related to the agent as his property (*i.e.*, as a thing distinct from him). There (in consequence) nothing appears to be superimposed.

Here is the answer: When the notion of ego as agent is (admitted to be) a cause of superimposition, then alone is it evident that its auxiliary also is an erroneous notion; (when the notion of self—*jīva* as manifested in the 'I' is error-ridden, the body which is intended for its service is likewise an erroneous notion, *i.e.*, of like nature, when spoken of as 'this is mine'). Of one who has been crowned king in a dream, or a king who is a creation of mighty magic, the paraphernalia of royalty cannot have any real existence. It is thus that all worldly activities beginning with the ego-agency (I am doer, etc.), and embracing action, means and results (*phala*) are superimposed on Ātman which is by nature eternal, pure, enlightened and free. Hence it is by such knowledge as culminates in the experience of the identity of Ātman with Brahman, thus characterised, that freedom from the evil-causing *adhyāsa* (superimposition) results, so that the beginning of a study of the Vedānta philosophy having such (knowledge) as its content becomes appropriate.

IX, 24. [It (superimposition) is "the manifestation, in some other object, of that which is of the nature of recollection of what had been observed before]—thus is enunciated the definition of the term 'superimposition' (*adhyāsa*) found in the question (*viz.*, 'what is it that is meant by *adhyāsa*?'). Here, when it is said '*paratra*' ('in some other object') it becomes evident by implication that the manifestation is of something other (than the presented object). (The phrase) 'being of the nature of recollection' is its (manifested object—*parasya*) attribute. What is recollected—that is 'recollection'. This construction is justified on the ground of usage, for the termination '*ghañ*', etc., is sometimes used in *kāraka* which is not denotative of subject though its sense is derivative. The manifested object only resembles the object remembered (*i.e.*, the appearance, *i.e.*, *rūpa* of the superimposed object, is only similar to the appearance of the recollected object), but is not the thing (actually) recollected; and this is clear from the fact that what is presented to the sense (and not what is remembered) is (what is) manifested. That it (*adhyāsa*) resembles recollection is corroborated by the explanation that it is the manifestation of what was perceived in the past. There can be no manifestation of silver to one in direct sense-contact with the shell, who has not seen silver before.

XXI, 70. Well, was it not said that *jīva* is non-distinct from Brahman?

True, it is for that very reason that *avidyā*, which conceals in *jīva* the luminous nature of Brahman, is posited by implication (*arthāt*). Otherwise (if the individual soul is admitted to be, distinct from the

Absolute, insentient, or of finite intelligence, *avidyā*, a positive entity having the capacity of concealment cannot be maintained), when the *jīva* is in reality (of the nature of) Brahman, if the knowledge of identity also were eternally established, then the teaching of identity (*tādātmyopadeśa*) would be purposeless. As such it must be admitted by those learned in the *śruti*, *smṛti* and Nyāya that Brahman which is homogeneous consciousness is the substratum of the illusion of the endless souls which are conditioned by the beginningless nescience.

XXIX, 107. Here (the opponent of the doctrine that the object and the image are identical) says—let it be conceded that there is no distinct object, but the assertion, 'that alone is that' (*i.e.*, that *pratibimba* is nothing but *bimba*) cannot be tolerated, for it is perceived that the silver (appearing) in the nacre though unreal, manifests itself as identical in nature with the real silver.

It is not so. There (in the shell-silver cognition) because of the sublation it is regarded as illusory. Here no sublation of the image as such is in evidence. The disappearance of that (*i.e.*, the image on the removal of the mirror) is not a case of sublation; for then it (sublation) would overtake the mirror also.

XXIX, 108. *Pūrvapakṣin*.—Well, is not sublation evident from the sentence 'That thou art'?

Siddhāntin.—Not so; there (in the sentence) 'that thou (art)' what is intimated is that the individual soul (*jīva*) which is in the position of the image (*pratibimba*) is of the nature of Brahman occupying the position of the object (*bimba*). Otherwise the sentence would not be (of the form)—'that thou art' but would be 'thou art not' like 'silver is not'.

XXIX, 109. Moreover the śāstraic usage also confirms the view that the reflection is in reality identical with the object. "At no time, should one see the sun when he is just rising, when he is setting, when he is eclipsed, when he is reflected in water, and when he has reached the mid-sky."

XXIX, 110. He who thinks that it is not the original (*bimba*) alone, that as existing outside itself is revealed by the visual rays which have turned back from the reflector but that the original remaining in its own place (*viz.*, the neck) is revealed by the rays which having impinged upon the mirror turn back and proceed in the opposite direction —him, experience itself condemns; as such his view is not controverted.

XXIX, 111. *Prābhākara*.—How could, that which is circumscribed, singles, of the nature of being one (*ekasvabhāva*) and which manifests itself in its wholeness in two separate regions, be absolutely in both?

Siddhāntin.—We do not say that the manifestation (of a single object) in separate spots (at the same time) is absolutely real, but (we maintain) *ekatva* (oneness). The appearance (of the object) as distinct is the display of *māyā* and as is well-known there is nothing incongruous to *māyā*. . . .

XXX, 112. *Pūrvapakṣin.*—Even when the identity of the reflection with the original is cognised there (still) exists the erroneous manifestation of separateness, etc., pertaining to it (*i.e.*, the reflection); similarly even when the identity of the individual soul with Brahman is cognised (through study and reflection), there does exist the erroneous manifestation of separation, etc. (between the *jīva* and Brahman) which cannot be got rid of (*i.e.*, even though one is cognizant of the oneness with the Absolute one cannot get rid of the notion of one's separation from the Absolute).

Siddhāntin.—This is how it is met. The reason is that what is reflected is only Devadatta's insentient part. Even admitting that what is reflected is insentient (we say) that just as the duskiness of the mirror—the cause of reflection—(affects the reflected image) even so being pervaded (lit. assailed) by the inertness of the mirror that reflection (of Devadatta's face) does not cognise its identity with the prototype (*bimba*). Because it is inert (it is not sentient as held by the Cārvāka). And such is experience (*i.e.*, experience corroborates that reflection is insentient); without the movement of the *bimba* the *pratibimba* does not move.

XXX, 113. Indeed when illusion arises in a person whether in relation to himself (*e.g.*, as in 'I am enjoyer', etc.) or in something extrinsic (as in 'shell-silver') that illusion is sublated by the right knowledge appertaining only to him. Devadatta who understands his identity (lit. non-separateness) with the reflection is untouched by the defects belonging to it. And neither is the reflection sublated merely by the right knowledge, because the cause of reflection, *viz.*, mirror is real (*i.e.*, in a relative sense—*laukikapāramārthika*).

The *jīva* on the other hand which may be likened to reflection is of the nature of *cit* (sentience) as is within the cognizance of us all and is not pervaded by the inertness pertaining to the inner sense. And that (*jīva*) entertains the notion of self-agency (*i.e.*, of itself as of the nature of active agent) but not of its oneness with Brahman which resembles the original (*bimba*). Hence it is reasonable that the illusion should disappear with the knowledge of its nature (as Brahman, because of the disappearance of *upādhi*, *viz.*, the inner sense, etc.).

XXX, 114. *Pūrvapakṣin.*—Is it not a fact that there (*i.e.*, in the cognition of reflection and crystal-red) a real thing which constitutes the cause of illusion, such as the mirror or the China-rose, is in close proximity of the person who is deluded? Here (in Ātman) in every case of the superimposition of non-sentience (including egoity, etc.), when a person is attracted by illusory diversions no such real object exists in the vicinity?

Siddhāntin.—That such a doubt may not arise they (Scriptures) give the rope-serpent example.

XXXI, 115. *Pūrvapakṣin.*—Well, even there (*i.e.*, in the rope-serpent) if indeed the serpent is not in the vicinity now (at the present moment) still the *saṁskāra* (impression) of the experience which must have arisen in the past certainly does exist; (this *saṁskāra* is itself the *upādhi*).

Siddhāntin.—It is true (that there exists the cause afforded by the persistent impressions). Even here the notion of the agency of the Self and its residual impression are beginningless like the seed-sprout (series) and since their relation as cause and effect will be later demonstrated there exists the *saṁskāra* as the ground of illusion.

XXXI, 116. There (in the red-crystal) the non-relation of the red colour with the crystal becomes evident on the basis of *anirvacanīyatā* (the principle of inexplicability, or on that of sublation by *jñāna*) though the crystal, etc., possessing parts are fit to be so related; still (the person under delusion) imagines as if (the redness which is) reflected in the crystal is related to it (crystal). In the rope on the other hand there arises only the serpent-notion and neither the idea of relation nor of non-relation. From (examples such as) these, the non-relational character of Ātman as vouched for in the Scriptural texts, *viz.*, "Ātman is unattached, for it does not attach itself", *Bṛh. Up.*, 4, 4, 22; "This person is unattached", etc., is not clearly brought out. With this in view the example of ether-in-the-pot (is adduced). There (in the pot-ether) indeed, apart from reminding it (*viz.*, the limitation constituted by the 'pot'), difference, form, serviceability and name are not perceived as belonging to itself.

XXXI, 117. And all this aggregate of examples is for the purpose of removing the doubt that may arise regarding what has been established by the Scriptures, conformatory logic and experience, and also for mental concord; it is not for directly stabilising the thing itself (*viz.*, Ātman).

XLII, 159. Thus having established the existence of superimposition, the Bhāṣyakāra, with the statement "we have explained that all that superimposition means is the apprehension of something in what is not that something" reminds us that, what has already been defined in the commentary beginning with 'of the nature of recollection', etc., and ending with '*adhyāsa*, however understood, does not depart from the definition that it is the apparent manifestation of the attributes of one thing in another', is literally the superimposition of 'what is not that.' (And this statement is made) in order to specifically point out, which thing, as denoted by the 'thou (object)', is superimposed on which thing, as denoted by the 'ego' (subject) and again in the reverse order. What it means is the apparent presentation of the notion of what is denoted by the 'thou' (*i.e.*, 'the this') in what is denoted by the 'not this'-ego; (again) in what is the 'not-this', (*i.e.*, in what is denoted by the 'not-thou'). Hence says (the commentator—'As when sons and wife, etc.')

XLII, 160. *Pūrvapakṣin*: Well, it is not literally (*i.e.*, in the primary sense) that the soundness or the unsoundness (of health) of one's children, etc., that one attributes through ignorance to one's own self and indeed it was undertaken by you to show the superimposition of what is not the 'that' in a primary sense (and not in a figurative sense).

Siddhāntin: Yes, it is true (that superimposition is literal and not figurative). That only is illustrated. How? It is thus—when a baby-son is decorated with clothes and ornaments by someone who is in no way related (to the child) except as a neighbour, the father thinks in no figurative sense that he has honoured the father only, because of the fact that he himself is honoured; and the person honouring also thinks that he honoured the father only, because of the fact that the sense of pride at being honoured has not developed in the child. Similarly, with the object of vanquishing a king a neighbouring king who is desirous of victory, having destroyed only a single town in his kingdom thinks that he has vanquished him only; and he also (*i.e.*, the pillaged king) grieves (saying) 'I am vanquished'. Hence in this wise, superimposition in a real sense is perceived in the self which is patently distinct (from children, wife, etc.). Where then is the need to state that superimposition is real (not figurative) in the case of one who imagines thus—'I am lean, I am stout', etc.? To point this out (the Bhāṣya) says, ["myself alone am unsound or sound; thus he superimposes on the self qualities which do not pertain to him"]. The superimposition of what is denoted by the 'Thou' (*yuṣmat*) is only that of the attributes (*dharma*) belonging to external objects as (when one appropriates to oneself) the honour, etc., done to the sons and so on. The meaning of the word '*asmat*' is in fact that which is interrelated to the ground of the ego-notion (*i.e.*, the inner sense or *antaḥkaraṇa*), which is the sentient part as distinguished from the 'this' (*i.e.*, the nonsentient world), and which is the object; but it is not pure consciousness only, as in the case of the superimposition of the inner sense (on Ātman) where there is no interposition of an additional superimposition (except *ajñāna*); even so 'the attributes of the body such as leaness, etc.,' (are superimposed on the self); alike the superimposition of the thing possessing attributes.... The use of the word '*dharma*' is to indicate that the superimposition is of the body, only as associated with attributes like 'manhood' (being a man), etc., and not to denote (association with others as illustrated in) 'I am body'. And based on that (*viz.*, the superimposition of attributes —*dharmādhyāsa*) distinct (lit. such and such) rules relating to distinct actions are enjoined by the Scripture....

XLVII, 180. What is it that is meant by the term '*tarka*'?

It is reasoning.

Well, this is only a synonym. Its nature had better be explained.

This is its explanation:—It is of the nature of discriminating cognition by which the probability (or improbability) of *pramāṇa, śakti* and *viṣaya* (*viz.*, the identity of Brahman and the individual soul) is ascertained.

XLVII, 181. *Pūrvapakṣin*: Well, if so (the Vedānta) since it requires *tarka* to establish the certitude of what it imports becomes invalid having lost its character of non-dependence (on extraneous aid).

Siddhāntin: It does not (become non-valid merely because it requires *tarka*); for by its own potency it is productive of the indubitable knowledge of what it denotes (*svaviṣaya*, which here is the identity of Ātman and the absolute).

Pūrvapakṣin: Then what is the purpose served by *tarka*? (If the *mahāvākya* itself is competent to bring home the knowledge of identity, what is the function of *tarka*)?

Siddhāntin: When there is improbability regarding the *viṣaya* (*viz.*, the unity of the individual soul with Brahman) and the fruition of that kind of experience (which brings about the destruction of *anartha* or the evils of life) has not arisen (*tarka* is useful) in removing the obstacles to the *phala* (fruition) through pointing to its probability (*sambhava*). As such in the *mahāvākhya* (*tat tvam asi*) the meaning of '*tvam*' is the *jīva* (or individual soul) and this *jīva* presuming the improbability of his being identical with Brahman which the word '*tat*' denotes, (nay), further, thinking that he is of an opposite nature, fails to arrive at the truth, though the knowledge (identity) has arisen, so long as he does not recognise the probability of his own self being identical with Brahman, having (first) through the aid of *tarka* removed the impediments.

CHAPTER 12

Vācaspati Miśra

Vācaspati Miśra (ca. 850 A.D.) is considered by many scholars to be one of the most important contributors to Advaita in its post-Śaṁkara phase. He is the author of a famous commentary on a portion of Śaṁkara's *Brahmasūtrabhāṣya* and of several other works, among them works on other Indian philosophical systems such as the Nyāya and Sāṁkhya. Vācaspati, following Maṇḍana, argues for the position that ignorance resides in many different selves, with the locus of *avidyā* being not Brahman but the empirical self (*jīva*). Brahman or Ātman is the object (*viṣaya*) of ignorance, but the individual is its locus. He also argues for a "limitation" theory (*avaccheda-vāda*) to account for the appearance of the individual *jīva*.

Although the Vivaraṇa school later attracted many more important thinkers to it, the Bhāmatī school has enjoyed a considerable influence in Indian thought. For a full statement on the contributions of this school S. S. Hasurkar's *Vācaspati Miśra on Advaita Vedānta* (Darbhanga: Mithila Institute, 1958) is recommended.

The following selections from the *Bhāmatī* on the topic of superimposition are from S. S. Suryanarayana Sastri and C. Kunhan Raja's translation published by the Theosophical Publishing House, Adyar, Madras, India, 1933 (pp. 4–59), and on the topic of the unchangeableness of Brahman from the unpublished translation of P. K. Sundaram, University of Madras.

BHĀMATĪ

... [S]alvation which consists in the cessation of transmigration is the profit here desired to be set forth. Transmigration has for its cause the non-experience of the true nature of the self, and is to be got rid of by knowledge of the true nature of the self. If that (transmigration) which is beginningless persists alongside the beginningless knowledge of the true nature of the self, how can there be the riddance of the former, there being no opposition (between the two)? And how can there be non-experience of the true nature of the self? Other than the experience of "I," there is indeed no knowledge of the true nature of the self. Nor can this self, which is other than the body, the organ etc., and which is established by the very patent experience of "I" common to all men, be negatived even by a thousand Upaniṣads, that being opposed to experience. A thousand Scriptures, verily, cannot convert a pot into a cloth. Therefore, because of opposition to experience, we see fit to hold that the Upaniṣads have but a figurative sense. Raising a doubt, with these ideas in mind (the commentator) answers it (thus):

... The self of the nature of intelligence is the subject (*viṣayin*), the non-intelligent intellect, organs, body and objects, are the objects of cognition (viṣayas). For, these bind the intelligent self, that is to say, make it determinable through their own form. As an example of absolute difference, which is the ground of the impossibility of reciprocal super-imposition, (there is mentioned) "like darkness and light". Never indeed, can one understand such utterly different things as light and darkness each to be of the nature of the other. This is stated thus: "when it is established that one cannot intelligibly be of the nature of the other." The one being the other means the one having the nature of the other, that is to say, the identity of the one with the other; this is unintelligible.

Be this so. Let there be no reciprocal identity between different substrates (*i.e.*, the self and the not-self); there may occur yet the reciprocal super-imposition of their attributes, such as inertness and intelligence, eternality and non-eternality etc. Even where substrates are distinguished, there is indeed seen to occur super-imposition of their attributes, *e.g.*, in the crystal though apprehended as different from the flower, yet because of its absolute transparency, there arises the illusion of redness, in the experience "red crystal", generated by the reflection of the hibiscus flower. To this it is said: "for their attributes too." The existence of the attributes of one substrate in the other, *i.e.*, their mutual transfer; this is unintelligible. This is the idea: it is indeed a substance with colour, which, on account of its absolute transparency takes on the reflection of another substance with colour, though apprehended as different from itself; the intelligent self, however, is the colourless subject and cannot take on the reflection of the object. As they (the Bhāṭṭas) say: "Of sound, smell, taste etc., in what way can there be reflection?" Hence it follows by elimination that mutual transfer of the constantly associated attributes of the object and the subject is possible only on the basis of the reciprocal connection of these two. If these two substrates being apprehended as absolutely distinct are unrelated, their attributes are even more clearly unrelated, they being further removed from each other by the interposition of their respective substrates. This is stated thus: "the more," etc. "Through an error in respect of that" means through an error in respect of the object. The word "illusion" signifies concealment. This is what is said: super-imposition is pervaded by non-apprehension of difference; the opposite thereof, *i.e.*, the apprehension of difference, is present here, which, getting rid of that non-apprehension of difference, gets rid also of the super-imposition pervaded thereby. "Though they can properly be only illusion, yet": this is the construction.

This is the underlying idea.—(All) this might be so, if the true nature of the self were manifest in the experience of the "I". This, however, is not so. It is thus: the true nature of the self is declared in Scripture, traditional codes (*smṛti*), epics (itihāsas), and mythologies (purāṇas) as undefined by any limiting conditions, as of the one consistency of endless bliss and intelligence, as indifferent, as one and without a second. Nor can those (statements) which have the purport of teaching the self as of this nature, through their introductory, intermediate and concluding passages, and through purportful repetition, be made figurative even by Indra. For, from repetition results the eminence of the object, as in "Lo, beautiful, lo, beautiful!", not its littleness; nor even figurativeness (that being) remote indeed. The experience of the "I," exhibiting as it does the self as finite and as confounded by a multitude of griefs and sorrows, how can it have the true nature of the self for its sphere? Or how can it be undeluded (experience)? Nor can it be said that since Scripture is opposed to perception, which is the elder means of valid knowledge (*pramāṇa*), the former alone as dependent on the latter should be declared invalid or figurative; for, since that (Scripture) is not of human origin and is free from even the suspicion of any defect, and since its validity is self-revealed by the very fact of its conveying knowledge, it is independent (of any other means of knowledge) in respect of its effect, *i.e.*, valid knowledge. If it be said that though independent in respect of the knowledge (it generates), yet since it is dependent on perception in respect of its origin, and since there is opposition to that (perception), there will be the non-validity of Scriptural teaching, consisting in its non-production,—no (we reply); for, there is no opposition to its origination (by perception). Scriptural knowledge does not indeed annul the empirical validity of perception, whereby it would itself cease to be, because of the non-existence of its cause; rather (does it annul) the absolute (validity of perception). Nor is its cause the absolutely true (perception), since true knowledge is seen to arise from means of knowledge which are empirically though not absolutely valid. Thus, the qualities of short and long, though foreign to letters (belonging as they do to sound: *dhvani*), being super-imposed thereon, are causes of true apprehension; those who in the world understand by *nāga* and *naga* different objects such as elephant and tree are not, verily, deluded people.

Having thus stated the nature of superimposition and its fruit, *viz.*, empirical usage, he states its cause in the words "through non-discrimination of each from the other," *i.e.*, through non-apprehension of (their) distinctness. Now, why should it not be that there is no difference at all? And thus, (if there were none), there would be no superimposition. To this he says: "of the attribute and the substrate which are absolutely distinct." Distinctness from the absolute standpoint means non-identity in the case of substrates, and non-confusion in the case of attributes.

Be this so. The delusion as to identity conditioned by non-apprehension of the difference between two real entities is intelligible, like the delusion of the identity with silver in the case of nacre, because of non-apprehension of their difference. Here, however, there is no real entity like the body, other than the intelligent self, which is the absolute reality. Whence then the non-apprehension of the distinctness of the intelligent self? Whence the delusion of identity? To this he replies: "by coupling the true with the untrue." The construction is: after superimposing because of non-apprehension of distinctness (through coupling the true etc.) The true is the intelligent self; the untrue are the intellect, the organs, the body etc.; coupling these two substrates; coupling means yoking. Because there cannot be any real coupling of the phenomenal with the absolutely real, there is used the *cvi* suffix (*mithunī-* instead of *mithunam-*), which signifies *what is not that becoming that as it were*. This is what is said: the imposition of what does not appear being impossible, what is required is the *cognition* of what is imposed, not its *real existence.*

Be this so. When there is cognition of what is superimposed, there is the superimposition of what was formerly seen, while that cognition itself is conditioned by superimposition; thus, (the defect of) reciprocal dependence seems difficult to avoid. To this he says: "natural". This empirical usage is natural, beginningless. Through the beginninglessness of the usage, there is declared the beginninglessness of its cause—superimposition. Hence, of the intellect, organs, body etc., appearing in every prior illusory cognition, there is use in every subsequent instance of superimposition. This (process) being beginningless, like (the succession of) the seed and the sprout, there is no reciprocal dependence; this is the meaning.

Be this so. Certainly, it is only the prior appearance that counts in imposition, not the absolute reality of what appears. But even appearance is unintelligible in the case of the body, the organs etc., which are wholly unreal, and are comparable to the lotus-pond in the sky. The reality even of the intelligent self is but manifestation, and nothing other than that, like the inherence of the class-Being (*sattā-sāmānya-samavāya*) or practical efficiency (*artha-kriyā-kāritā*), as (the admission of) these would lead to duality. Further, with the postulation of another Being and another practical efficiency (to determine the reality) of this *Being* and this *practically efficient*, we shall have an infinite regress. Hence, manifestation alone has to be admitted as constituting reality. Thus, the body etc., since they are manifest, are not unreal, being like the intelligent self; or else, if unreal, they cannot be manifest; how then can there be the coupling of the true with the untrue? In the absence of this (coupling) whose difference is it that is not apprehended? and from what? That (non-apprehension of difference) failing, whence the superimposition? With this in mind, the objector says: "What is this thing called superimposition?" The (pronoun) "what" has the sense of an objection. The respondent meets the objection by simply giving the definition of superimposition well-known to the world: "The reply is—the appearance elsewhere, with a nature like to that of recollection, of what was seen before." *Avabhāsa* is that appearance which is terminated or depreciated. Termination or depreciation is sublation by another cognition; by this, it (*avabhāsa*) is said to be an illusory cognition.

This is the further commentary on that (definition): "what was seen before" etc. *Pūrva-dṛṣṭā-'vabhāsaḥ* means the appearance of what was seen before. The illusory appearance cannot come about without the coupling of the imposed element with that on which it is imposed; hence what is untrue and superimposed is understood by the words "what was seen before". The word "seen" is used to indicate that it (the superimposed element) counts only as *phenomenal* not as *absolutely real.* Even thus, what is now seen is not capable of being imposed; hence the use of the word "before". What was seen before, though real in its own nature, is yet, as superimposed, indeterminable and hence unreal. The locus of imposition, which is real, is stated in: "elsewhere." Elsewhere, in nacre etc., which are absolutely real. Thus is declared the coupling of the true with the untrue.

This is what is said: it is not that manifestation alone constitutes reality, in which case, bodies, organs, etc., by the very fact of manifestation, would be real. It is not as if ropes etc., do not appear as snakes etc., or crystals etc., as endowed with red colour and so on; nor, as thus appearing, do they really become those objects or endowed with those attributes. If that were so, one would conclude in the case of a mirage that it is the Mandākinī which has come down close by, with her garlands of constantly agitated waves high and low, and proceeding (thereto) should be able to quench one's thirst by drinking of that water. Hence, of what is superimposed, even though manifest, absolute reality cannot be admitted, even though this (conclusion) be not desired.

Nor is it admissible to ask thus: "in the mirage, the water is unreal, but in its own nature (as mirage) it is absolutely real; whereas, the body, organs etc., are unreal even in their own nature, and as such cannot be the sphere of any experience; how then can they be superimposed?" For, if what is unreal cannot be the object of any experience, how then do the mirage etc., which are unreal, become the sphere of experience as water etc.? Though real in their own nature, they (the mirage etc.) cannot become real as water, etc., as well.

It may be said: there is nothing called non-existence (*abhāva*) as distinct from existence (*bhāva*). An existent considered as of the nature of another existent becomes non-existence; but in its own nature it is but existence. As is said: "Non-existence is but another existent considered in relation to something else." Hence, this, which may be explained as another mode of existence, may well be in the sphere of experience. The world, which is absolutely unreal, devoid of any capacity, devoid of any (true) essence, how can it be an object of experience? How, again, can it be superimposed on the intelligent self? Nor is it admissible that, though the objects (of experience) are wholly devoid of any capacity (to appear), the respective cognitions, through the capacity residing in them as cognitions, of themselves give rise to the appearance of the unreal, as a product of a unique nature, and that this capacity (of the cognitions) to make the unreal appear is Nescience. What is this faculty of cognition whereby it makes the unreal appear? What is it that it is capable of? If it is the unreal, is it effected or only made known by it? It cannot be effected, since that is unintelligible in the case of the unreal. Nor is it what is made known, since there is no other cognition known (other than that which makes manifest); further, (what is thus manifested being unreal and requiring its relation to the new cognition to be explained), infinite regress would result. If now, it be said that it is the very essence of cognition to manifest the unreal, what is this relation between the real and the unreal? If it be said that the relation of cognition, which is real, to that which is unreal is that the former is made determinate under the control of what is unreal, lo! how very fortunate is this poor cognition that attains to determination even through the unreal. Nor does cognition do anything thereto, since being the support (of any such thing) is inappropriate in the case of what is unreal. If it be said that the cognition is not controlled by the unreal, but that it is of the very nature of cognition not to appear apart from the unreal, lo! unfortunate indeed is this partiality for the unreal, whereby cognition is invariably linked to the unreal, though neither originating therefrom nor of the same nature as that. Hence, body, organs, etc., which are wholly unreal and have no (true) essence, cannot become objects of experience.

To this we reply: if what has no (true) essence be not within the sphere of experience, are these rays real *as water*, in such wise that they may come within the sphere of experience? (The *pūrvapakṣin* says): They have no (true) essence (in the nature of water), since the rays are not of the nature of water. The essence of things is of two kinds, real or unreal, the former in respect of themselves, the latter in respect of things other than themselves. As is said: "The essence of things is grasped by some at some time or other either as real or as unreal in respect of (those things) themselves or in respect of others." (We reply): Is the cognition of water in the rays in the sphere of the true? Then, being valid, it would not be delusive; nor would it be sublated. (The *pūrvapakṣin* rejoins): certainly, it would not be sublated, if it apprehended the rays, which truly are not of the nature of water, as not of the nature of water. When apprehended as of the nature of water, however, how can it be non-delusive or non-sublated? Lo! then (we reply) of the rays whose nature is non-waterness, their nature as waterness is not real, since they, being non-different from non-waterness, cannot intelligibly be of the nature of waterness; nor is it unreal; for, it is recognized by you, in the words "Non-existence is existence in another form, not anything else, since no (such thing) is proved," that the unreality of one thing is but another thing. Nor is the imposed form another thing; if it were, it should be either the rays or the water in the Ganges. On the first alternative, the cognition would be of the form "rays," not of the form "water"; on the latter (alternative), it would be of the form "water in the Ganges," not "(water) here". (Further) if the particular place be not recollected, it should be (of the form) "water" (merely), not "here". Nor is it admissible that this is something wholly unreal, a mere falsehood devoid of all existence, since that cannot intelligibly be within the sphere of experience; this has been said earlier. Hence, the water superimposed on the rays has to be recognised to be indeterminable, being neither real nor unreal nor yet real and unreal, this (last) being self-contradictory. Thus, in this way, the superimposed water is like absolutely real water, and for that reason is like what was formerly seen; but really that is not water, nor what was formerly seen; but it is untrue, indeterminable. In the same way, even the universe of bodies, organs etc. is indeterminable; though novel, yet they are superimposed on something other, *i.e.*, the intelligent self, in the same way as what was presented in prior erroneous cognitions. This is intelligible, since the definition of superimposition applies. The sublation of the universe of bodies, organs etc. will be explained later. As for the intelligent self, it is in the sphere of Scripture, traditional codes, epics and purāṇas; as ascertained by reasoning based on and not in conflict with these, it is of the nature of purity, intelligence and freedom, and is determinable as certainly real. Unsublated self-luminosity is its reality; that is of the very nature of the intelligent self, not something other (than this), such as inherence of the class-Being, or practical efficiency. Thus, everything is clear.

. . . The delusion that one thing is of the nature of another is established in experience; but there is not seen the delusion of difference in the case of what is one and non-different; whence the delusion of difference for the jīvas who are not different from the intelligent self? To this he says: "the moon, though one, appears as if having a second."

In the words "Again, how," etc., the superimposition on the intelligent self is again objected to. This is the meaning: is this intelligent self manifest or not? If it be not manifest, how can there be the superimposition of objects and their attributes thereon? There is not, verily, the superimposition of silver or its attributes on a non-manifest substance in front (of us). If this self is manifest, it does not stand to reason that it is inert, and manifested in dependence on another, like a pot etc. (The self that is manifest should be either self-manifest or manifested by another; it is not the latter; nor can it be the former.) Verily, the same thing cannot be both agent and object, because of contradiction. The object is, indeed, that which can bear the fruit of activity inherent in another; the knowing activity is not inherent in another (than the self); how, then, can that (self) be the object thereof? Nor can the same be both self- and other- (dependent), because of contradiction. But if inherence (of the knowing activity) in another self be admitted, the known self would become a not-self (not being the subject of that activity). Further, for that (another knowing self would be required, and) for that (another), so that there is infinite regress.

(He who holds that consciousness is self-manifest, but not the self, may say:) be this so. The self, though inert, though manifest in the cognitions of all things, is agent alone, not object, being, like Caitra, not characterised by bearing the fruit of activity inherent in another. In Caitra's reaching a city through activity inherent in himself, though the product inheres in both Caitra and the city, the object-ness belongs to the city alone, since to that belongs the property of bearing the fruit of activity inherent in another, and not to Caitra, though he too bears the fruit of activity, as the act of going is inherent in Caitra (alone).

This is not (sound), because of opposition to Scripture. Scripture, indeed, says: "Truth, knowledge, infinitude *is* Brahman."

This is intelligible too. It is thus: that fruit, which is the manifestation of the object, that in which the object and the self manifest themselves, is that inert or self-manifest? If that were inert, both the object and the self would be inert; which, then, would be manifest in which, there being no distinction (among the three)? Thus would result non-manifestation for the whole universe. (Nor can the reciprocal dependence of these three be of any avail); and thus the proverb: "As the blind holding on to the blind falls at every step." Nor may it be said that cognition, being itself hidden, (yet) makes known both the object and the self, like the sense of sight etc. (which, themselves unperceived, yet cause perception); for, to make known is to produce cognition, and the cognition that is produced, being inert, would not surmount the above-mentioned defect (of the blind leading the blind). Thus, the subsequent cognition too being inert, there would be infinite regress. Therefore, consciousness should be acknowledged to be manifested without dependence on another.

Even thus, what is gained (by you) for the object and the self, which (you hold) are both inert by nature? This is the gain, (you may say), that the consciousness of them is not inert. (But it does not follow that the object and the self, the causes of consciousness, are not inert); in that case, because the son is a scholar, should the father be a scholar too? It is of the very nature of the self-luminous consciousness to be related to the object and the self: if this be said, alas! then, it is equally the nature of the scholarly son to be related to his father. (You may define the relation thus): the manifestation of consciousness is along with the manifestation of the object and the self, never without the manifestation of the object and the self; this is its nature. If this be said, is consciousness, then, different from the manifestation of consciousness (on the one hand), and the manifestation of the object and the self (on the other)? If that were so, then, consciousness would no longer be self-manifest, nor would consciousness be the manifestation of the object and the self. Then, (you may say), the two manifestations, of consciousness and of the object and self, are not different from consciousness; these two are but consciousness. If this be said, then, what is said in "conciousness (goes) along with the object and the self," that (alone) is what is said in "(the manifestation of) consciousness (goes) along with the manifestation of the object and the self" (so that there is no advance in your position). (Hence), what is desired to be stated by you (that the self, itself inert, is the locus of the self-manifest consciousness) does not result.

Nor is there concomitance with the object in the case of that consciousness which has objects past and future for its sphere (though such concomitance has been assumed in the argument so far). Since there is generated the cognition of rejection, acceptance or indifference relating to that as content, there is concomitance with the object: if this be said, no (we reply); because the cognition of rejection etc., like the consciousness of the object itself, cannot intelligibly have that (past or future object) as content. Because of giving rise to rejection etc., the cognition of rejection etc. too have the object as content; and because of giving rise to the cognition of rejection etc., which have the object as content, the consciousness of the object too has that (object) as content: if this be said, since the conjunction of the body with the self that puts forth effort is the cause of the setting up and cessation of bodily activity in respect of an object, is that (conjunction) too (we ask) a manifestation of the object? Because of its inertness, (you may say), the conjunction of the body and the self is not a manifestation of the object. Now, though this (consciousness) is self-manifest (unlike the afore-said conjunction), its luminosity, like that of a glow-worm, is only in respect itself; in respect of objects, however, it is inert; this has been explained (by the analogy of the scholarly son's father).

Nor are objects of the very nature of light (*i.e.*, of consciousness, as the Vijñānavādins say); they are experienced as finite, as long or gross, while light manifests itself as internal, neither gross nor subtle, neither short nor long. Therefore, we see fit to hold that the object, which is other than the self-manifest, is certainly indeterminable, like the second moon experienced along with the moon. And no natural differentiation is experienced in this light as such (so that there is no obstacle to its identity with the self, which is one). Nor can differences among objects, which are indeterminable, introduce differences into light, which is determinate, as that would prove too much. It will also be shown later that reciprocal difference does not come in the line of valid knowledge. Therefore, this very light, which is self-luminous, one, immutable, eternal, without parts, is the inner self, *i.e.*, the self that knows the determinate self to be other than the body, organs etc., which are indeterminable.

That self, not being other-dependent for its manifestation, and being without parts, cannot be an object (of cognition). How, then, can there be the superimposition thereon of the attributes of objects, *i.e.*, of bodies, organs etc.? The word "how" (in the commentary) is in the sense of an objection. This superimposition does not stand to reason;

this is the objection. Why does it not stand to reason? To this he says: "For, every one superimposes an object upon another object that is present before one." This is what is said: that, whose manifestation is other-dependent and which has parts, appears other than what it is, being apprehended in its general nature, but not apprehended in its specific nature, because of defect in the organs (of cognition). The inner self, however, not being other-dependent for its manifestation, does not require for the knowledge of itself any organs, by defects in which it would itself become defective. Nor has it any parts, in which case, it could be apprehended in some part, but not in others. It cannot, verily, happen that the same (thing) is at the same time and by itself both apprehended and not apprehended; hence on the view of the self-luminosity (of the self) there can be no superimposition. (And) even if it be never manifest, there can be no superimposition, since it is not before us, *i.e.*, is not immediately experienced. Silver is not, verily, superimposed in the form "this is silver", when nacre is not present before us. Hence it follows that there can be no superimposition both when there is complete apprehension and when there is total non-apprehension.

Be this so. If the intelligent self were not an object, then indeed, there could be no superimposition thereon; but it is the object of the concept "I". Why then can there be no superimposition? To this he says: "which is ever outside the concept of 'Thou'." For, if the intelligent self were the object, the subject (*viṣayin*) would be other than that. And thus, he who is the subject is himself the intelligent self; the object, however, should be admitted to be other than that, and in the sphere of the concept of "Thou". Hence, "being outside the concept of 'Thou' " is (stated) for the purpose of remedying the possibility of non-selfhood (for the self) and of infinite regress; hence it is that not being an object has to be predicated of the self; and thus, there is no superimposition: this is the meaning.

He answers this: "The reply is—now, this is not invariably a non-object." Why (not)? "Because it is the object of the concept 'I'." This is the meaning: true, the inner self being self-manifest is not an object and is without parts; but yet, having attained to the state of the *jīva*, though not really defined by the particular defining conditions posited by indeterminable beginningless Nescience, such as the intellect, the mind, bodies subtle and gross, and the organs, he appears as if defined; though not different, he appears as if different; though not an agent, he appears as agent; though not an enjoyer, he appears as enjoyer; and though not an object, he appears as the object of the concept "I"; just as the ether because of differences defined by adjuncts such as pot, ewer, basin etc., appears as different and possessing diverse attributes. Of the self that is but of the one essence of intelligence, there is not, verily, anything unapprehended, when the element of intelligence is apprehended. Bliss, eternality, pervasiveness etc. are not, indeed, different from its nature as intelligence, such that they are not apprehended along with the apprehension of that element. While being certainly apprehended, yet, because of posited difference, they appear as if not discriminated, and hence not apprehended. Nor is the difference of the self from the intellect etc. real, so that that (difference) too is apprehended, when the intelligent self is apprehended; for, the intellect etc., being indeterminable, their difference (from the self) too is indeterminable (and unreal). Thus, it is for the intelligent self itself, which is self-manifest and undefined, that there is the condition of the *jīva*, through non-apprehension of the difference from the defined intellect etc., and the (consequent) superimposition of these. Of this, which partakes of the nature of the "not-this (non-object: the intelligent self)" and the "this (the inert object)," being the object of the concept "I" is intelligible. It is thus: the intelligent self appears, in the concept "I," as agent and enjoyer. And for that (self) which is indifferent there cannot occur the capacity either to act or to enjoy. And for that aggregate of the effect (the body) and the organs, *i.e.*, the intellect etc., to which belong the capacities to act and enjoy, there is no intelligence. Hence, it is the intelligent self that, linked to the aggregate of the effect (the body) and the organs, gains the capacity to act and enjoy; though self-manifest, yet by intermixture with objects like the intellect etc., it somehow becomes the object of the concept "I," the substrate of "I-ness," and is (variously) designated *jīva*, creature (*jantu*), or knower of the field (*kṣetrajña*). The *jīva* indeed is not different from the intelligent self. For, thus runs Scripture: "in its own nature, as that *jīva*" etc. Thus, the *jīva* though self-manifest, because of being non-different from the intelligent self, is yet made by the concept "I" fit for empirical usage as agent and enjoyer; hence it is said to be the basis of the concept "I." Nor is it admissible (to say) that there is reciprocal dependence in that (the *jīva*) becomes an object if there is superimposition, and there is superimposition if (he) becomes an object; for, the (process) is beginningless, like the (dependence of) seed and sprout, and there is no inconsistency in every subsequent superimposition having for its object that which has been made the content of each earlier superimposition and its impressions; this has been said in the text of the commentary: "this natural empirical usage." Hence it has been well-said: "now, this is not invariably a non-object." The *jīva* though not an object, as (non-different from) the intelligent self and as self-manifest, is yet an object in his conditioned form: this is the idea.

. . . This is what is said: it is of the very nature of the repetition of the ascertainment of truth that it removes illusory cognition, though beginningless and having deep-rooted and dense impressions. It is, indeed, of the nature of the intellect to be partial to truth. As even outsiders say: "Of the essential nature of things unaffected by error, there is no sublation; for, the intellect, even though making no effort, has a partiality for it." More particularly (there is the question): "Whence can there be sublation of the wholly internal (intimate) knowledge of the truth, which is of the nature of the intelligent self, by Nescience, which is indeterminable?"

In the statement "coupling the true with the untrue, there is, through non-discrimination of each from the other, the empirical usage 'I am this,' 'this is mine,' " empirical usage in the nature of verbal designation is expressly mentioned. Ordinary empirical usage, indicated by the word *iti* is shown in the words: "It is in the wake of the afore-mentioned mutual superimposition of the self and the not-self, designated Nescience" etc.; this is self-explanatory. . . .

An objection is raised: "How, again, is it that perception and other means of valid knowledge have reference to one characterised by Nescience?" Valid knowledge or *vidyā* is, verily, determination of the truth; how can the means of valid knowledge which are instruments thereto have for their locus what is characterised by Nescience? Means of valid knowledge cannot find a locus in what is characterised by Nescience, since their effect, *viz.*, knowledge, is opposed to Nescience: this is the idea. Or let perception etc. be as you say empirically (valid); but sacred teachings, whose purport is to teach what is beneficial to man, being opposed to Nescience, cannot have reference to what is characterised by Nescience; hence he says: "and sacred teachings." He answers: "The reply is." "When one devoid of the conceit of 'I' and 'mine' in the body, senses etc.," devoid of the superimposition of the nature and attributes of the self, "cannot intelligibly be a knower, the functioning of the means of valid knowledge is unintelligible." This is the meaning: to be a knower is to be an agent in respect of knowledge; and that is independence (in respect of the cognitive act). Independence consists in inciting all causal conditions other than the knower, without being incited by them. By him, therefore, is to be incited the *pramāṇa*, the means of valid knowledge. Nor can an instrument be incited without activity on one's part. Nor can the immutable, eternal, intelligent self, which is incapable of transformation, be active of itself. Hence, being active by the superimposition of the nature of the intellect etc., which are active, it can control the means of valid knowledge; therefore, the means of valid knowledge have reference to, *i.e.*, are located in the person characterised by Nescience.

. . . Valid knowledge is a variety of the modification of the internal organ, directed towards the object known, and is of the nature of the intelligence residing in the agent. And how could a modification of the inert internal organ be of the nature of intelligence, if the intelligent self were not superimposed thereon? How, again, could this have the intelligent self as agent, if the functioning internal organ were not superimposed on the intelligent self? Hence, from reciprocal superimposition, there results the fruit called valid knowledge, which resides in the intelligent self as agent; when that results, there results knowership. With this same valid knowledge as content, there ensues the activity of the means of valid knowledge. By the use of the word "knowership," valid knowledge is also implied. If the fruit, valid knowledge, were non-existent, the means of valid knowledge would not be active; and thus the means of valid knowledge would cease to be such: this is the meaning. He concludes: "Therefore, perception and other means of valid knowledge have reference only to what is characterised by Nescience." . . .

Having thus expounded through objection and answer the reciprocal superimposition of the self and the not-self, and strengthened it by the discourse on the means and objects of valid knowledge, he reminds us of its already declared nature, in order to expound elaborately its being the cause of evil: "We have already said that what is called superimposition is the cognition as something of what is not that." This is a summary way of stating what was said earlier, that it is "the appearance elsewhere, with a nature like to that of recollection, of what was seen before". Here, "I," which is the superimposition of the nature of the substrate alone, cannot be the cause of evil without generating the "mine," the superimposition of attributes; hence the superimposition of attributes, the notion of "mine," is alone the direct cause of the entire evil of the migratory cycle; this is elaborately explained in: "It is thus: when the son, wife" etc. Superimposing identity with the body on the self, and superimposing thereon the bodily attribute of the ownership of son, wife etc., in the same way as leanness etc., one says "I am myself unsound or sound." The sense of ownership being complete, when there is a fullness of wealth, the owner (in this case) becomes complete, perfect; similarly, from the lack of wealth, ownership too becoming incomplete, the owner becomes incomplete, imperfect. The external attributes, like unsoundness which attach to the body through the channel of ownership, these one superimposes on the self: this is the meaning. When this is the case in respect of bodily attributes, like ownership, dependent on external adjuncts, what need be said about bodily attributes, like leanness etc., which do not depend on external adjuncts? In this view, he says: "Similarly, the attributes of the body" etc. He superimposes on the self the attributes of deafness etc., which are the attributes of the senses, which are more intimate than the body, and on which the nature of the self has been superimposed, (he also superimposes on the self) desire, resolve, etc., which are attributes of the internal organ, which is even more intimate, and on which the nature of the self has been superimposed: this is the construction.

Having in this exposition stated the superimposition of attributes, he states its basis, the superimposition of the substrate: "In this way, after superimposing the denotation of the concept 'I' " etc. That in which the psychosis, the concept "I," occurs, *i.e.*, the internal organ, that is the denotation of the concept "I" (*ahaṁpratyayin*); that is superimposed on the inner self, which, on account of its intelligence and indifference, is the witness of the processes of the internal organ. Thus are explained agency and enjoyership. Intelligence is explained: "by the reverse of that," by the reverse of the internal organ etc.,—the internal organ etc. are inert, the reverse of that is intelligence; by that;

the instrumental case is used to imply "in this wise"—"one superimposes that inner self, the witness of all, on the internal organ etc." This is what is said hereby: the inner self defined by the internal organ etc., the intelligent being compounded of the "this" and the "not-this," is the *jīva*, the agent, the enjoyer, the support of the two kinds of Nescience—the result and the cause—the substrate of "I-ness," the transmigrator, the vessel of the entire host of woes, the material cause of reciprocal superimposition; the material cause of that again is superimposition; hence, this being beginningless, like the seed and the sprout, there is not (the defect of) reciprocal dependence.

THE UNCHANGEABLENESS OF BRAHMAN

II, 1.22. *Adhikaṁ tu bhedanirdeśāt* (But Brahman) is something more (than the individual soul) on account of the indication of difference.

Bhāmatī on this: True; Just as the Supreme Self, being omniscient, sees the individual souls who are really non-different from Itself, (and) makes manifest (the fact) that for these (souls) there is *really* no attachment to the experience of pleasure, pain etc., but that, for these (souls), there is the (false) notion that they have that (experience of pleasure, pain etc.), due to the power of nescience (*avidyā*), similarly It sees also as: "I am unaffected in their (soul's) experience of pleasure, pain etc.; there is no harm to me even when there is the entry into bondage for them (i.e. the souls)."

II, 1.26. If Brahman be the material cause of the world, there will result either (the change of) the entire (Brahman) or the violation of the texts (declaring Brahman) to be without parts.

II, 1.27. But (it is not so) on account of Vedic testimony (since Brahman's causality) has its ground in scripture. (An objection is stated) there is no modification of Brahman whereby it will become an object of change either wholly or in part. But the nature of being the basis for the empirical usage of modification etc., for Brahman in the form of the evolved and the non-evolved, is apprehended through the diversity of form characterized by name and form, indeterminable either as real or unreal, (all) projected by nescience. Surely, the illusory form does not affect Reality. Indeed, the imagination of duality of the moon, in a person suffering from a diseased vision, does not bring about duality in the moon (which in reality is only one). Nor is there the unintelligibility or absurdity (of duality) in the moon by dint of the unintelligibility in that (i.e., imaginary duality). Therefore, though the imagination of illusory modification is unintelligible, it does not carry (this) unintelligibility (or absurdity of being plural) into Brahman, which is absolutely real.

Hence, (the objection concludes) since the objection is absent, this *adhikaraṇa* (section) need not be commenced. (In answer to this objection), he (the commentator) says: Non-dual Intelligence-self is the cause of the world. Though the modification has been refuted as unreal by hundreds of Śruti texts, which express the absolute non-duality (of Brahman), even though, as the reality of modification seems to be introduced by another objection by the illustration of milk, curds etc. (used by Śaṁkara himself in his answer to the first objection), by way of refuting this second objection, by maintaining that this (opposite) view cannot be held by any means, by both the Sūtras (which follow) *viz., śrutestu śabdamūlatvāt* (i.e., But (it is not so) on account of Vedic testimony since (Brahman's causality) has its ground in Scripture) and *ātmani caivaṁ vicitrāś ca hi* (i.e., For thus it is even within the Self and wondrous), the definition of absolute non-duality which is the meaning of Scripture is examined (by the said *sūtras*) through strengthening the view of transfiguration or illusory manifestation, *vivarta*. This is the meaning. "Brahman is unmodified," means that (Brahman is) really unmodified.

CHAPTER 13

Sarvajñātman

Sarvajñātman (ca. 900 A.D.), a disciple of Sureśvara, is associated primarily with the Vivaraṇa school. He argued for "reflexionism" in understanding the relations that obtain between the individual self (*jīva*), the world, and Brahman, and favored the view that ignorance resides in Brahman. Sarvajñātman was a very able thinker. He drew a sharp distinction between *adhiṣṭhāna* (the ground of appearances; the true Brahman) and *ādhāra* (the object to which false appearances refer; Brahman as modified by ignorance). He also set forth rather clearly the relationship between the *pariṇāmavāda* (the transformation theory of causality) and the *vivartavāda* (appearance-only theory of causality), showing how the former is preliminary to the latter.

The following selections are taken from Sarvajñātman's *Saṁkṣepaśārīraka*, as translated by T. Mahadevan in an unpublished manuscript submitted to the University of Madras in fulfillment of the thesis requirement for the degree of master of literature.

SAṀKṢEPAŚĀRĪRAKA

Nescience, on the strength of the self, which alone is its content and locus, and with the assistance of the capacities of obscuration and projection, after obscuring the luminous self, illusorily manifests (it) in the form of the *jīva*, Īśvara, and the universe.

That nescience, on the strength of the inner self which alone is its content and locus, stands obscuring the non-dual and absolutely attributeless inner nature, and projecting as external figurations what is within.

Perception, inference and vedic texts show the painless, eternal and blissful nature of the self; the aforesaid finitude is not possible in this plenitude whose nature is painlessness, eternality, and blissfulness.

After enjoying the bliss of the *prajñā*-self (during the state of deep sleep) which is devoid of all kinds of objective cognition, and waking thereafter, every *jīva* is aware of the bliss of that (state), in the recollection, "I was asleep; in that (state) there was bliss."

The knowers of the definition of bliss describe bliss as that for the sake of which all things exist, and which, by its own nature, abandons the state of existing for others. This (definition) is apt in the inner self; hence, its blissfulness. (I, 20–24)

The word, *adhiṣṭhāna* (real substratum), is prevalent (only) in the entity which is the object of nescience with its figurations, and not in the entity which is the *ādhāra* (apparent support) of superimposition. Hence, the view of some great people of cloudy vision who assert obstinately that, if reciprocal superimposition be admitted, the universe would have no substratum, and would become a void, is a baseless delusion.

This question would certainly arise, if the *adhiṣṭhāna* were identical with the *ādhāra*; it is not so. The word, *adhiṣṭhāna*, is universally established as representing the entity which is the object of nescience with its figurations.

Moreover, if two unreal objects were intended to be superimposed here, then, your objection would be pertinent. But, the couple of a real and an unreal object is mutually superimposed. Then, where is the room for the argument of voidness?

The object indicated by the term, 'this', is also superimposed on silver, and the silver-object on the 'this', because of its being manifested in the delusion of silver. If not, it would not have manifested itself in the delusion just as nacre (is not manifest).

Indeed, there is the cognition of 'this' in silver, as there is the cognition of silver in 'this'. Such being the case, how can there not be the ascertainment of reciprocal superimposition?

The superimposed alone is, indeed, manifested in delusions, and, nothing else is even manifested in delusions. (This is so) because of the non-cognition of the natures of the rope, nacre, desert-land, single moon, etc. (which are not superimposed).

Consequently, reciprocal superimposition alone is proper with regard to the conscious and the non-conscious, because of its being known to be thus in silver-delusions, etc., more elaborate assumption is, in fact, unwarranted. (I, 31–37)

The non-differentiated and the pure consciousness alone forms the locus as well as the content (of nescience); for, what is subsequent (the *jīva* and Īśvara) can be neither the locus nor the content of the nescience that is antecedent (to this direction).

The state of non-existence for this (nescience) is not intelligible, because of the obscuring nature; the champions of non-existence do not tell (us) that non-existence can obscure. The son of Vāsudeva (Kṛṣṇa) has told (us) that nescience is an obscurer (of knowledge). Consequently, we understand that it (nescience) is of the nature of an existent.

O King! Man has only one enemy; and not a second one on a par with nescience; veiled by which, completely deluded he performs acts which are fraught with fear and evil.

In fact, the inertness constant (invariably) in the universe is of the nature of an existent; so, too, the ignorance invariable in man appears as an entity. And, this nescience well known through experience as inertness and as ignorance is, they say, capable of concealing the final beatitude.

The wise declare that the non-dual consciousness depending upon this phenomenal (nescience) is the cause of transmigration. And this (nescience), because it is phenomenal, is only of the channel in respect of the cause of transmigration. But causality belongs only to consciousness.

What is held by others (the Sāṁkhyas, the Naiyāyikas, etc.), that something other than consciousness is the cause of the worldly illusion, is not admitted by the advocates of the Vedānta system because of (its) inertness. For, concerning this, the author of the aphorisms (Bādarāyaṇa) tells (us) clearly that whatever is inert cannot be the cause of transmigration.

All inert things are the means in respect of the causality of the non-inert (i.e., non-dual, consciousness); but (they themselves) are not the causes. Thus have the Upaniṣadic scholars told (us) while refuting Kapila's (the Sāṁkhya) system.

The qualified (consciousness) is declared by the word "the self (Ātman)". And there is a *śruti* (text) that "all are the products of the self". Consequently the qualified self is the material cause of the world; thus some other scholars have declared.

(Just as) it is only the reflection of the conscious (and not the qualified) self in the internal organ which comes to have the agency in respect of good and bad deeds, similarly it is only the reflection in nescience of the Supreme Self (and not that as qualified by nescience) which comes to have (the agency) in respect of the universe.

Just as the qualified conscious Self is the material cause in respect of good and bad deeds, similarly, the material cause in respect of the manifestation of ether, air (etc.) is the Supreme consciousness in its qualified form.

By the word, "Ātman" (and its synonyms), the qualified is not expressed, but only the Pure Consciousness. The qualified adjunct is (only) to impose expressibility in respect of the self, because of the latter being encompassed by the qualification.

The Pure consciousness is denoted by the word, the Self, because of its wearing the garb of qualifications. Hence proceeds this delusion of people that the qualified (alone, and not the pure consciousness) is denoted by the word, the Self. (I, 319–330)

And this Brahman-knowledge can be known (only) when Brahman is known; and, not otherwise. If this Brahman-reality has been known, (then), release is attained; there is nothing to be done by the injunctions (thereafter).

Those established in the Vedānta declare that for consciousness, reciprocal superimposition which has for its sphere the macrocosmic and the microcosmic body, and which is a product of nescience, is an evil. Hence, release is contemporaneous with knowledge.

The cognition which is caused by the Vedānta, which is firm, and which has the self for its content, controls with its very origination the beginningless nescience, which is like the cloth-bandage for the eye, and thoroughly burns it so that the root of *saṁsāra* is destroyed (with the *vāsanās*), thus, verily, (says) the *śruti.* (I, 452–454)

It is thus: the *saguṇa* Brahman is of a combined nature as consisting of the real and the non-real; similar is the knowledge thereof. Similarly, the purport of the Vedic text having that (*saguṇa* Brahman) as content is of this nature. Hence, it is stated on the basis of a distinction (of content) that the secondary purport of the Vedic text is of one kind and the other (primary purport) having for its content the real *nirguṇa* entity (is of a different kind).

A single silver-cognition arising in the form, "This is silver" manifests the real and the non-real objects as identical. Similarly, it is beyond doubt that this single *pramāṇa* which has the *saguṇa* for its content, and, which is a presentation of the real and illusory, manifests two objects related to each other. (I, 464–465)

"That One consciousness which is made probable (by inference) as the material cause of this (universe), understand That to be Brahman"; this text syntactically relating to the text, "That thou art" unequivocally states the definition of the Supreme Brahman established (by inference) in right earnest, differentiating the nature of Brahman, (from *pradhāna,* etc.) implied in the word, "That."

It is well-known in this world that the definition of the defined is three-fold; viz., one's own nature, attribute *per proprium,* and attribute *per accidens.* I shall explain these distinctly with definitions. Know that.

That (characteristic) which inheres in the *lakṣya* object and which, when apprehended, makes known the real entity thoroughly different from other objects, this, they say, is the definition. This is the general definition for (all) the three definitions.

Svarūpalakṣaṇa:—That which while itself being the nature of the *lakṣya* directly differentiates it from other objects—this definition they declare to be the *svarūpalakṣaṇa* of that (*lakṣya*) the object which is to be defined. "The sky is hollow," "the water is liquid," are of this group in worldly usage.

Viśeṣaṇa: On the other hand, that which is the cause of the generation of a cognition of its relation with the *lakṣya*-entity is its definition *per proprium,* just like mane, etc., for objects like horse, etc.

Upalakṣaṇa: That which, while abandoning the causality of the generation of a cognition of its relations with the *lakṣya,* becomes its definition in spite of its being not of its nature—that, they say, is the qualification *per accidens,* like the crow (for Devadatta's house).

(That nature of) being the material cause of the origination, sustentation and dissolution of the universe, of this conscious-reality which accepts no accessories,—that (nature) should be termed as the qualification *per accidens.* Why? In order that there may be no contradiction in the significant capacity of the word which indicates the secondary sense, viz., "Brahman."

If the definition of the single (the non-dual impartite) stated here (in the Veda), viz., being the material cause of the origination, sustentation, and dissolution of the universe, be admitted as the qualification of Brahman *per proprium,* then, there would be the diminution of the word denoting *lakṣya,* viz., "Brahman."

They say that the word expressing the *lakṣya*-object is primary here in the text aiming at the *lakṣaṇa* and the rest are secondary. And, the word, Brahman, denoting the *lakṣya* is capable of stating only the infinite, and not the mortal finite.

Hence, because of the fear of the principal word being injured it is reasonable to take the secondary words in the sense of attribute *per accidens*; and, this (word) Brahman to supply the *upalakṣya.* Thus, in this (sentence) this collocation of words is appropriate.

The (texts setting forth) definitions are not (intended) to mention the nature of the *lakṣya*; nor only (to make known that) this word is expressive of this. Indeed, the definitions are to tell (us) only this—that this is different from all other objects.

For, it is recognised that this person cognising the nature of *lakṣya* (by the sense of sight) and seeing the definition as existent in that alone, is capable of teaching by this definition the same *lakṣya* as different from other objects.

Nowhere is it admitted that the definition is for the sake of the cognition of the relationship between the word and its sense. It is but the cause of the apprehension of difference from anything else in respect of the *lakṣya*; for, the disputants in the world collect the various definitions in right earnest and differentiate the *lakṣya* from others by means of these definitions.

Hence, the *śruti* did not state the definition of Brahman, namely, "(whence) the origination, etc., of the visible world" for the establishment in respect of Brahman, the relation between the word and its sense; nor even is it stated with the intention of making known Brahman's own nature, but, for the establishment of its difference from all non-Brahman elements. (I, 513–526)

All pramāṇas, exclusive of the Vedāntic texts, have for their content only the external world; and, from the example of light manifesting colour, it is well-known that whatever manifestor is elemental is itself elemental.

Whatever manifestor is seen in the world is observed to be similar in generic nature to the object manifested; for lamp-light known in the world as manifestor (of colour) is well-known to be similar to colour in respect of light-nature.

The intellect bent upon the cognition of all objects is also of the same generic nature as the object manifested. It is well-known in the śrutis that intellect is elemental. Hence, let that, too, have elemental contents.

Thus, all the pramāṇas, excluding the Vedāntic texts, relate for the above-said reasoning, to the objects (alone) and they do not have the inner self for content. The *śruti*, too, has clearly told us the same above-stated sense in the text, "*parāñci,*" etc. (Ka. Up. IV, 1.1).

The self-born forced the senses outwards. Hence (the person) cognises the external and not the inner self. A wise man desirous of immortality and with his senses turned back sees (directly) the inner self.

The *pramāṇa* which is well-known in the world as the means of a cognition in respect of its object not divested of its objectivity should be accepted here, as having only inert objects for its content and not the inner self for content, because of the aforesaid reason.

The *pramāṇa* which endeavours to make known its object divested of its objectivity is competent to have the inner self as its content. Such a *pramāṇa* is texts like "That thou (art)" and not any other *pramāṇa.* (II, 9–15)

Now, it seems that this view of the revered (Śaṁkara) is similar to that of the Śākya mendicant. If the external object be unreal, how, indeed, could these two views be not similar?

If the cognition alone be accepted as real, and not the cognised, surely, the view of the sage, Buddha, alone has been wholly adopted by the Vaidic saṁnyāsins (the followers of Śaṁkara).

Answer: How can this Vedic sage accepting the cogniser, the *pramāṇa,* the object, and the cognition as different from one another's be similar to the Buddhist sage?

In our system, we certainly recognise the cogniser, the *pramāṇa,* the object, etc., as permanent, reciprocally distinct products of darkness (nescience) located in the Supreme self.

The Supreme self, immutable, consciousness, and non-dual, perceives as a witness, and without the aid of instruments, the four-fold universe created by nescience.

The *puruṣa* encompassed by his own *māyā* which is non-autonomous, becomes the witness by seeing the entire illusory universe by his own light (consciousness).

If that valid recognition making known the permanence of the apprehended and the apprehender were not intelligible, then, there would have resulted the similarity between our final views. But, since it (recognition) can be intelligible, there results the permanence which is the nature of the universe as also of consciousness in my view, just as momentariness is the nature of everything in your view.

Now, if the waking state be an imposition, tell (us) what kind of difference you have admitted to distinguish it from a dream. (For, superimposedness is common to both).

So long as the cogniser exists, (the objects) of the waking state are not sublated like the objects seen in a dream; for, the darkness (nescience) is negated only together with the cogniser, the *pramāṇa*, the object and the cognition.

Indeed, the darkness (nescience) causing the waking state is destroyed simultaneously by the knowledge of the self generated by the Vedic text together with (its products, viz.) place, time, finite self and state (intervening time).

The object seen in a dream is sublated, like a rope-serpent, when place, time, and cogniser exist. But, the object of the waking state does not find such a sublator, because it is not so seen.

Consequently, people understand that the waking state with attributes opposed to those of dream and delusion is real till the realisation of the real, Supreme self. What is sublated by it (knowledge) is not real anywhere.

The intellectual psychosis related to the Supreme self-reality, being steady, destroys what is superimposed there (on consciousness) in different forms as real and unreal, by the darkness (nescience) located in the inner self.

Just as Arjuna kills the line of the Kauravas (already) killed by Vāsudeva, so also, the psychosis generated by the (Vedāntic) texts destroys the world-delusion (already) annihilated by consciousness (which, though) eternal, (is reflected in and manifested by psychosis).

Outside the system of the Brahmavādin, it is difficult to conceive of the real and the unreal. If the unreal be something distinct from the real, then, there is the contingence of that, too, becoming real.

If the unreal be not different from the real, then, all the more would it have to be accepted as real. The unreal cannot be held to be of the nature of both (different and non-different from the real) because of the aforesaid refutations on the two views. (II, 25–40)

After climbing the lower step, it is possible to climb the higher step; thus, the *śāstra*, too, at first sets forth the relationship between the cause and the effect through the declaration of transformation (by the aphorism, "*Bhoktrāpatteḥ*") and, now (in the *ārambhaṇa* section) denies (it) to establish the illusoriness of change.

In the Vedāntic view, the transformation theory is indeed the preliminary step to the transfiguration theory. When this transformation theory is established, the transfiguration theory follows of its own accord (without any difficulty).

Just as people first resort to the means to successfully secure the fruit, so too, the *śruti* and the eminent sage propound the transformation theory to establish transfiguration.

The origination theory is Kaṇāda's position; while the aggregation theory is the Buddha's position. The position of the Sāṁkhyas, etc., (the Yogas) is the transformation theory; while the position of the Vedāntins is the transfiguration theory.

Assuming for discussion the transformation theory of Kapila, etc., the Sūtrakāra and the *śruti* standing on the previous step declare (this) in order to expound (the theory of) transfiguration.

The wise say that transformation is the capacity in the case of what is non-different, and has parts, to exhibit real diversity of form, just like the earth's (capacity) to create crops.

The meaning of the word, transfiguration, is well-known here (in the world) as the capacity of what is non-different and changeless to exhibit many illusory forms just like a diversity of moons caused by a diversity of waves.

Stating transformation at first (by the text) "I shall myself be born (as the universe, and, consequently) become many" and, then, stating the illusoriness of the change the *śruti* brings in the transfiguration theory.

And, thus, in the light of transfiguration there is intelligibility for all *śruti* and *smṛti* texts which declare *māyā* and have for purport the denial of reality in the case of everything analyzable into cause or effect and formerly held to be absolutely real, because of being cognised. (II, 60–68)

The nescience of the jīvas which are reflections, as it were, of Brahman which is the prototype, as it were, is like the generic nature in particulars, the originator of all delusions; it abandons the man of knowledge, (but) resorts to the man devoid of knowledge, just as the generic nature (abandons) the particular object which has perished, (but, resorts to the particular object) which has not perished. (Thus), have said some. (II, 132)

Just as there is a bird in the sky, and, (at the same time) there is no (bird in the sky), similarly, there can and there cannot be nescience in the Supreme Brahman which is pure, of the nature of consciousness, spotless by nature, devoid of association, devoid of qualities, eternal, differenceless, birthless, deathless and partless; and, thus, (this argument) is faultless, say (some) others eager to establish (their) position.

Though darkness (nescience) penetrates (only) into the pure entity, still, it will enter into Brahman only after taking another causal condition in the shape of the mind. And, this internal organ (mind) while persisting even in the sleep-state in an extremely subtle form always regulates nescience in relation to consciousness externally (i.e., as an *accidens*).

The nescience-associated Brahman is reflected in the intellects, and, then, becoming the movable and the immovable through its own nescience (it) at one place is released through knowledge, and, at another (place) is bound (through the absence of knowledge). And that nescience has perished (through knowledge); but, still, the same (nescience) persists, because of the intelligibility of the difference of aspects. Thus (through the perishing and the non-perishing of nescience) in relation to the different aspects all (these) distinctions in relation to the Supreme Being greatly stands to reason; thus (say) some.

Māyā, the binding capacity of Hari, and the generator of things external and internal, spreads out like the net of the fisherman, in respect of ignorant jīvas, and contracts (in the case of jīvas with knowledge) through the will of the Lord. Be this *māyā* real or illusory, (but) contraction and the opposite (expansion) are natural (therefor); and, thus, too (say some).

Some have accepted that in respect of the Supreme Brahman as content, there is nescience beginningless like a stream consisting in a succession of residual impressions and delusions different from each human being. Uprooting this through the combination (of knowledge and rites) a person can attain to release; in the absence of that (combination) a person transmigrates. And, that (nescience) has *jīva* for (its) locus.

Because of self-luminosity, the inner self is established for us as ignorant, (in the experience) "I am ignorant." But, how can the unknown Brahman be established for you? (Is it) from valid knowledge, or from delusion, or from self-luminosity? (II, 134–139)

That Supreme Īśvara devoid of the bondage, viz., egoity, is really omniscience being free from nescience; for, His knowledge is admitted to be without any obscuration; the jīva's being with obscuration, it is ignorant.

The supreme *puruṣa*, and not the *jīva*, supports the entire galaxy of cognitions (reality to all objects), the fruit of all pramāṇas, whatsoever. Hence, the knowledge of Īśvara is without obscuration; and, the jīva's is with obscuration, because of its distinction (from that of Īśvara).

The (Supreme) self of the nature of reality permanently illumines nescience, and the product thereof, viz., the entire universe, being proximate thereto, because of its luminosity; while, the *jīva* is not thus; hence, its knowledge is with obscuration. (But) Īśvara's, indeed, is said to be without obscuration.

What is there which is uncognised in this world for Him (Īśvara), who is of the nature of knowledge, who is the free embodiment of pure *sattva*, wherefrom all defects are removed, who is ever immediately manifest, and who resides in the hearts of all human beings?

This omnipresent (Īśvara) stretches out *māyā* thus (in the form of the universe). The Supreme Īśvara (controller) controls this (*māyā*) permanently. These statements in the *purāṇa* are highly intelligible. Nescience (too) is dependent on Him, because of its being dependent on consciousness (Īśvara). (II, 183–187)

"Except myself, there was, there will be, and there is no other person to experience bondage or release, etc.," this aforesaid statement I am not at all able to apprehend, because of its conflict with one's own experience.

What is it that is said to conflict? Is it experience of duality, or, is it the (experience), viz., "I am the Supreme (Brahman)?" Or else, is there any other experience here which will, in your view, import conflict? "The experience of non-duality brings about conflict:", this statement does not stand to reason; nor does the experience having duality for content (cause the conflict), for, there is sublation of this latter by the former.

If it is said that there is rise of sublation for this (singleness of the *jīva*), because of the experience having duality-cum-non-duality for content, then, (we say) there is no such experience for anybody in all the three states (of waking, dream, and deep sleep). Indeed, in this world, none is seen as having the experience whose content is the sun as well as darkness. If this (dual non-dual experience) were possible, why should not that (the sun-darkness experience) be possible? (II, 218–220)

The *māyā* which is well-known here, in the waking state is determined, indeed, to be nescience alone. It alone should be known from the Veda and from inference, because of the establishment in respect of that, of the cognitions of the significant capacity and invariable concomitance.

In the dream, too, as here, there is established no other *māyā* except the sole nescience (located) in the dream-consciousness. Consequently, in respect of that alone, and nowhere else, does this word, *māyā*, of the Sūtrakāra apply.

The Sūtrakāra standing on (resorting to) dream which is but the nescience (located) in the inner self, and causing to cognise the significant capacity and invariable concomitance, began, as in the world, to bring in, by the word, *māyā*, the Veda and inference (in respect of the illusoriness of the waking world).

It was formerly stated by Hari, the Supreme Īśvara, that nescience is the obscurer of the conscious-reality, and, that *māyā* is the obscurer (of the conscious-reality). Knowing this, we understand unequivocally that the reality (of *māyā* and nescience) is one. By ignorance is knowledge obscured; thereby are creatures deluded.

The Lord has said out of compassion in the *Gītā* that knowledge is the remover of these both (*māyā* and nescience). Thereby, too, there comes in the cognition that this reality (of these) is (only) one, because of the aforesaid similarity between the definitions. (III, 105–109)

What is in the waking state does not exist during dream; because of the illusoriness of dream. They declare that what exists during waking is real. Unreality is declared in regard to dream on the strength of sublation (by the waking state). Consequently, consciousness alone is your nature; anything other than this is perishable. (III, 115)

"For a man in deep sleep, there is no nescience." "This man in deep sleep was in dense darkness (nescience)." What is thus stated should be apprehended by you as being without conflict after reflection and through experience and reasoning.

Thus, during deep sleep, there was no nescience at all. In other words, the *jīva*, indeed, has become the supreme *puruṣa*. Because of the absence of relationship (with the causal condition) it (the *jīva*) has attained to the state of being devoid of the seed (of transmigration); for, here, there is not the clear experience of nescience.

During deep sleep, because of the absence of nescience and its product, viz., the mind, you are the Pure, Supreme, eternally released Lord. At that time, how can desire, activity, and all (their products) be in you who are an ocean of consciousness, who are limitless, and who are perfect?

There was the egoity produced by your own nescience. It brings in and shows to you extreme misery (and pleasure), while you are awake and while you are in dream. It does not exist during deep sleep, because of the destruction of its seed. Hence it is that you were very pure (during deep sleep).

The wise declare thus:

This nescience, like the darkness of the night, is admitted to be of the nature of an existent, because of its being experienced as what obscures self-consciousness. Like the sun, knowledge which is of the nature of an inert luminary, is the remover of it (nescience).

By the disputants, too, it should be admitted only thus—(by them) who admit previously non-manifestation in regard to consciousness. Indeed, in regard to consciousness, nescience which is of the nature of the absence of consciousness is not admitted; nor is the absence of *buddhi*.

Consequently, the Upaniṣadic texts and the great sages have stated in various places that it is not conflicting that nescience has the self for its content, nescience which is the single primary cause of the entire world. Hence, there is no conflict. (III, 125–131)

That consciousness of the self which persists in the changing states, viz., waking, dream, deep sleep, swoon, and the extinction of the body—that, indeed, is real. Whatever is changing, is, indeed, illusory, like garland, serpent, stick, etc. It is impossible to say that the persistent conscious reality, like the rope, is illusory.

This *citta*, whose qualities are waking, dream and deep sleep, has arisen from your nescience; hence, it is always you alone. It does not differ from you. Your nescience is established on the strength of your experience (and) it is, in fact, illusory. Since it did not, does not, and will not exist (in consciousness), your perfect consciousness (alone) remains. (III, 139–140)

CHAPTER 14

Vimuktātman

Vimuktātman, an eleventh- or twelfth-century advaitin, was the author of a well-known work in Vedāntic philosophy called the *Iṣṭa Siddhi.* The main contribution of this work lies in its subtle analysis of the problem of error or illusion (*khyāti*) as this is worked out in various non-Vedāntic and Vedāntic schools of thought. In order to illustrate this type of analysis in post-Śaṁkara Advaita we have selected a few short sections from an unpublished translation of the *Iṣṭa Siddhi* by P. K. Sundaram of the Centre for the Advanced Study of Philosophy, University of Madras.

IṢṬA SIDDHI

III, 22. If apprehension of an object which is not in contact with the senses is accepted, then, the function of the senses being unnecessary, men of defective vision will always be omniscient. If illusion is due to the apprehension of similar objects, even then, there will be no illusion since it is cognized. If the knowledge of an object not in contact with the senses is accepted through the favour of defects, then, the knowledge of that not requiring the function of the senses, a man of defective vision should see everything always, since there is no distinction. If it be maintained that since similarity also is a defect, the apprehension of an object through defect requires the knowledge of a similar object, not when there is no apprehension at all; nor even when there is the apprehension of something else; and the correct knowledge is not from defect; error alone arises. Therefore, even a person of defective vision would not see everything always; to this,

We reply: when the object is apprehended, there cannot be any illusion, because of apprehension itself. And since, otherwise, there is undue extension.

Now: in your view also illusion is only in respect of what is apprehended. Indeed, when the substrate does not appear, there is no illusion.

(Reply): True, there is illusion only when the substrate appears. And not what is apprehended is the object of illusory knowledge; since it is accepted that illusion and its object are of the nature of *māyā.* And the substrate is not the object of illusion, since being sublated by silver, it loses its capacity of being the substrate. And, the Ātman, not cognized, is the substrate because of self-luminosity. Therefore, in my view, there is no illusion in respect of what is apprehended.

III, 23. If it is maintained that illusion results when the object is not cognized in all its aspects, then, let illusion be always, since no object is cognized in all its aspects. If it results when some special feature is not cognized, then, let illusion be always, since nobody realises all the special features at any time.

If it is said: even when some aspect is cognized, there can be illusion as shell, etc., are not cognized in all their aspects, no; because of the contingence of illusion always. Indeed, by no knowledge, one is capable of cognizing an object in all its aspects. It is said (as a general rule): "An object is not cognized by any knowledge in all its aspects." If it be said that even when it is cognized, illusion is through the non-apprehension of special features, even then, let illusion be always. Indeed, all special features are not possible to be cognized by any knowledge.

III, 24. And here, there is non-apprehension of any one of the specific quality. Is not the white colour a speciality? The knowledge of the object (*dravya*) as white is not the knowledge of mere general features.

If it be said: all special features are not to be cognized; even when one specific qualities is cognized there is no illusion, it is replied: When an object similar to the shell is perceived, the speciality, viz., white colour, is cognized and hence it need not be an illusion. Indeed, the knowledge of similarities like white colour is not the knowledge of mere general features, since a particular substance similar to the shell and associated with white colour is perceived. Indeed, mere general feature is not similarity.

Criticism of the *Prābhākara* Theory of Illusion

IV, 17. If it be asked: how the remembrance of an existent object be said to have an object, and how its remembrance can be without it, it is replied that it is so because of having that form. And the form also is possible because of latent impression even without the object-sense relationship.

If it be said: since the remembrance is observed even when the object is extinct, remembrance cannot be said to have an object; how can remembrance of that object arise without it?, (it is replied): because of being of that form. If it be asked: How can it have that form without sense-object contact, (it is replied), because of mere latent impression.

IV, 18. The object in the remembrance is only the form of knowledge and it is experienced by *sākṣin*, witness-intelligence, and not by empirical knowledge. Since the witness is not perceptible like empirical knowledge (mental mode), there is no infinite regress, nor self-dependence.

If it be said: the extinct object, too, appears in the remembrance, (it is replied) that object is only a form of cognition born of the latent impression of the (earlier) cognition of the object, like the impression formed by a seal, and not an external object, since it is already extinct.

The same line of reasoning is to be adopted even in respect of what is not extinct, since remembrance is invalid. If it is the form of intellect, how can it be cognized by it? Not at all. It is to be apprehended only by the Witness. *Sākṣin* or Witness being imperceptible, there is no infinite regress if it is aprehended by it as in the case of a mental mode, being perceptible by another mental mode.

Criticism of the Vijñānavādin's Theory of Illusion

The author gives another objection in respect of *Ātmakhyāti*.

IV, 19. For the Buddhist, there being no Witness, the mental mode is not witnessed by it; nor even by another mode because of the defects of infinite regress, etc., already mentioned. Nor even by itself.

IV, 20. If mental mode is not apprehended, there can be no apprehension of the object. If both are not apprehended, there can be no latent impression. Without it, there can be no form of silver for the cognition, because of momentariness.

IV, 21. There is no illusion, nor correct knowledge, and the whole world will thus become blind and dumb. Scripture, etc., will be baseless. Hence illusion is not *Ātmakhyāti*.

CHAPTER 15

Vidyāraṇya

One of the most popular thinkers in the post-Śaṁkara advaitic tradition is Vidyāraṇya (also known as Bhāratītīrtha), who lived in the fourteenth century. He is associated mainly with the Vivaraṇa school and is credited with presenting Advaita in a clear, systematic manner and of refining many of its concepts. His most widely read work is a kind of convenient handbook of Advaita and is entitled *Pañcadaśī.* In it Vidyāraṇya presents rather precise definitions of the most important terms in Advaita, and the following sections from this work have been selected in order to give an example of this attempt at exact definition. Vidyāraṇya was mainly concerned with cosmological or metaphysical themes rather than with psychological or epistemological analysis and his definitions exhibit this concern as does his explication of *māyā* as a creative power. Vidyāraṇya also tries to synthesize Vedānta with certain basic Sāṁkhyan principles (e.g., the doctrine of the guṇas) and he rather clearly shows the way in which Sāṁkhya was absorbed, or made use of, by Vedānta.

The material presented here is from *Panchadasi: A Treatise on Advaita Metaphysics*, translated by Hari Prasad Shastri (London: Shanti Sadan, 1956).

PAÑCADAŚĪ

The primordial substance is called *prakṛti* when the three elements of which it is composed, *sattva, rajas* and *tamas*, are in a state of homogeneity. Brahman is always reflected in it. The nature of Brahman, pure consciousness and bliss, is diametrically opposed to the nature of *prakṛti.*

When *sattva,* one of the component parts of *prakṛti,* predominates, *prakṛti* is known as *māyā.* Brahman, pure consciousness and bliss reflected in *māyā,* is known as Īśvara, the Lord of the Universe. *Māyā* functions under his command, and he is called omniscient.

When the element of *sattva* (light, balance) is over-powered by *rajas* and *tamas, prakṛti* is called *avidyā* (nescience). The admixture of *rajas* and *tamas* with *sattva,* in which Brahman casts its reflection, gives rise to the different grades of jīvas, such as devas, men and the lower animals. This nescience is also known as the causal body (*kāraṇa-śarīra*). Knowledge of Brahman negates nescience. The *jīva*, identifying himself with the causal body, develops separative individualism (*ahaṁkāra*). The technical name of this state of the *jīva* is *prajñā*.

At the command of Īśvara the part of *prakṛti* in which *tamas* predominates produced the five subtle elements, ether, air, fire, water and earth, for *prajñā* to experience as pleasure and pain.

The *sattva* (refined) part of the five subtle elements of *prakṛti* gave rise to the five subtle sensory organs, those of hearing, touch, sight taste and smell.

The *sattva* portion of the five subtle elements in combination produced the organ of inner (psychic) conception called *antaḥkaraṇa*. *Manas* (mind) is that aspect of it which functions as the faculty of doubt, and *buddhi* (intellect) is that which functions as the faculty of decision and discrimination.

The *rajas* portion of the five subtle elements gave rise respectively to the organ of speech, the hands, the feet, and the organs of excretion and generation.

The *rajas* portion of all the five subtle elements in combination gave rise to the vital air (*prāṇa*) with its five-fold function known as *prāṇa*, *apāna*, *samāna*, *udāna* and *vyāna*.

The subtle body, which is called the *sūkṣma* or *liṅga-śarīra*, comprises the five sensory organs, the five organs of action, the five vital airs, mind (*manas*) and intellect (*buddhi*), making seventeen parts in all. (I, 15–23)

The five sheaths, enveloped in which the Self forgets its real nature and becomes subject to the cycle of births and deaths, are the food sheath, the vital sheath, the mind sheath, the intellect sheath and the bliss sheath.

The product of the quintuplicated elements called the gross body is known as the food sheath (*annamayakośa*). That portion of the subtle body which is composed of the five vital airs and the five organs of action, and which is the effect of the *rajas* aspect of *prakṛti*, is called the vital sheath (*prāṇamayakośa*).

The mind with its faculty of doubt (*vimarśa*) and the five sensory organs, products of the sattvic principle make up the mind sheath (*manomayakośa*). The intellect with its faculty of determination and the same sensory organs make up the intellect sheath (*vijñānamayakośa*).

The bliss sheath (*ānandamayakośa*) is composed of the causal substance which manifests joy by the vṛttis (mental movements) of joy and its latent faculties. As the Self identifies itself with the sheaths, it assumes their natures.

By applying the method of distinguishing between the variable and the invariable the Self can realise its disidentification from the five sheaths and its identity with the transcendent Brahman. (I, 33–37)

Brahman becomes the material and instrumental cause of the world when associated with those aspects of *māyā* in which there is a predominance of *tamas* and *sattva* respectively. This Brahman is referred to as 'That' in the text 'That thou art'.

'Thou' in the text 'That thou art' refers to that condition of Brahman which results from His superimposing on Himself *avidyā*, that is *sattva* mixed with *rajas* and *tamas*. Thus desires and activities are created in him. (I, 44–45)

As the power to burn exists in fire, so *māyā*, which has no existence independent of Brahman and which is inferred by its effect (the world), existed in a potential form in Brahman before creation. Before the effect appears, the power behind the effect is not directly experienced by anyone anywhere.

The power of a substance is not the substance itself, as for instance, the power to burn is not the fire itself. Similarly, *māyā*, which is a power of Brahman, is not Brahman. "If *māyā* is something other than Brahman, then define its nature", says the opponent.

"If *māyā* is really nothing, then the effects of nothing cannot be something." To this objection the Vedāntin gives the following answer: "*Māyā* is not non-existence (*asat*) like the son of a barren woman, nor is it existence (*sat*) like Brahman. It is something the nature of which is not determinable in terms of either existence or non-existence." (II, 47–49)

With Brahman (*sat*) as its basis *māyā* creates the various objects of the world, just as a variety of pictures are drawn on a wall by the use of different colours. (II, 59)

As the Self is self-evident, and experience, in a certain sense, takes place in the Self, the Self cannot be an object of experience. Further, since no knower nor knowledge exists apart from it, there is no second entity by which the Self can be known; and for this reason again the Self cannot be an object of experience; but it should not be inferred from this that it does not exist. (III, 13)

That by which the whole universe is known cannot be known by anything else. By what can the knower be known? The mind is the instrument of knowledge, and its function is limited to the field of its percepts.

The Self knows all that is knowable. There is no knower other than the Self. The Self is of the nature of consciousness, and is therefore other than the known and the unknown. (III, 17, 18)

If you ask what sort of thing the Self is, we reply that the Self cannot be described as being of this or that sort. You must understand that it cannot be conceived as being 'like this' or 'like that'.

An object which the senses can perceive can be perceived to be 'like this'; an object which is beyond the range of sense perception can be conceived to be 'like that'. That which is the very Self of everyone is subject neither to perception nor conception.

Ātman is self-luminous, though the intellect cannot grasp it. The Veda declares it to be existence, consciousness and infinity.

Existence is undeniable; it cannot be negated, whereas the world can be, as is experienced in dreamless sleep and *samādhi*. The Self as witness of the perishable world cannot be perishable, for who could there be to witness the fact of its perishability? It is absurd to postulate the possibility of its destruction without also postulating a witness of it.

When all forms have been destroyed, the formless space still remains. So, when all the names and forms are negated, what remains is the imperishable Brahman. (III, 26–30)

Brahman is existence, consciousness and infinity. Īśvara, the omniscient Lord of the world, and *jīva*, the individual soul, are superimposed on Brahman by the two illusory adjuncts *māyā* and *avidyā*, respectively.

There is a divine power (*māyā*) which controls everything in the universe. It exists in all objects from the bliss sheath to the physical body.

It is this power which determines the particular attributes of all objects; but for it there would be nothing to distinguish the properties of one object from those of another, and chaos would result.

This power becomes active only when it is associated with the reflection of Brahman; when He is associated with this power, Brahman is called the omniscient Lord (Īśvara).

Brahman is called the individual soul (*jīva*) when He is considered in association with the five sheaths. In the same way a man is called a father and a grandfather when considered in relation to his son and his grandson.

A man is neither a father nor a grandfather when considered apart from his son and his grandson; Brahman is neither Īśvara nor *jīva* when considered apart from *māyā* and the five sheaths. (III, 37–42)

Māyā associated with Īśvara has the power of creating illusion as well as the projecting power which creates the world. Thus it is that *māyā* deludes the *jīva*.

The *jīva*, through delusion believing himself to be powerless and identifying himself with the sheaths, becomes subject to grief. This in brief is the duality created by Īśvara. (IV, 12–13)

By mere thought Īśvara creates all these objects through His innate power, *māyā*; and by mere thought *jīva* enjoys them through the modifications (vṛttis) of his mind.

Objects created by Īśvara do not alter. For instance, the nature of a gem created by Īśvara does not alter, but the gem may affect different people differently according to their mental state.

One man may feel happy on obtaining a gem, whereas another may feel disappointed at failing to obtain it. A third man, who is uninterested in it, will feel neither happiness nor disappointment on either obtaining or failing to obtain it.

The *jīva* creates the feelings of happiness, disappointment or indifference with regard to the gem, but the nature of the gem as created by Īśvara remains the same throughout. (IV, 19–22)

The mind, which is the illuminator of all objects, assumes the forms of the objects which it perceives just as sunlight assumes the forms of the objects which it illumines.

Śri Sureśvara holds that the means of cognition (*pramāṇa*) arises from the knower; having arisen, it embraces the object of cognition and assumes its form; being united with the object it becomes the illuminator of it.

This being so, in the perception of something such as a pot there are two objects, one material and the other mental. The one made of matter is known through perception, and the mental one is perceived by the witness (*sākṣi*). (IV, 29–31)

A liar told a man whose son had gone to a foreign country that the boy was dead, although he was still alive. The father believed him and was grieved.

If, on the other hand, his son had really died abroad but no news had reached him, he would have felt no grief. This shows that the real cause of a man's bondage is his own mental world.

An opponent may object that this amounts to pure idealism and that it deprives external objects of all significance. We reply that our position is not one of mere idealism, because we accept the fact that external objects give rise to the mental world.

We admit that external objects serve little useful purpose, yet we cannot dispense with them altogether. In any case, cognition is concerned with the existence of objects and not with their utility. (IV, 34–37)

There are four stages in the painting of a picture before it is completed. Similarly there are four stages in the modification of the Supreme Self.

In a picture there is first the canvas which is the background, second the application of starch upon the canvas, third the drawing of the outlines and finally the application of colour. In the case of the supreme Self first there is *cit*, pure consciousness, second there is the Inner Ruler, *antaryāmin*, third the totality of all the subtle bodies, *sūtrātman*, and finally the totality of all the physical bodies, *virāṭ*.

The white canvas is the basis of the picture; by the application of starch it is stiffened; the outlines are drafted in with a black pencil; and when the appropriate colours are applied to it, the picture is complete.

Brahman by virtue of His own nature is pure consciousness; when associated with *māyā* He is called the Inner Ruler (*antaryāmin*); when spoken of in relation to the subtle bodies He is given the name *sūtrātman*; and when He is considered as the totality of gross bodies, He is given the name of *virāṭ*.

As in a picture on a canvas there are major, minor and insignificant objects, so in the supreme Lord there are all beings from the four-headed God Brahmā down to the animate and inanimate objects.

The men in a picture are painted wearing clothes of different kinds, and the clothes are so painted that they appear as real as the canvas of the picture.

On consciousness are superimposed various forms. In each of them there is a reflection of consciousness. They are known as the jīvas and are subject to the process of *saṁsāra*, that is, birth and death.

Ignorant people imagine that the colours representing the clothes of the figures are real and attribute to them the reality of the canvas on which the picture is superimposed. Similarly the ignorant imagine that the transformations of the jīvas are undergone by *paramātman*, the substratum on which the jīvas are superimposed.

Just as the hills and the landscape in a picture are not painted as if dressed in clothes, so the inert objects of the world, such as earth, are not endowed with the reflection of consciousness.

Owing to the primal nescience people consider *saṁsāra* with its pleasures and pain as *paramātman*. It is by the knowledge of reality that this ignorance is overcome. (VI, 1–10)

The Mādhyamika Buddhists hold that the intellect is passing like the flashes of lightning in the clouds, and that because we know of no other Self beyond the intellect the Self is nothing.

In support of their position the Mādhyamikas quote the *śruti*: "In the beginning all this was non-existent (*asat*)." They say that perception and the objects of perception are the creations of illusion.

The Vedāntin refutes their doctrine by saying that there can be no illusion without a substratum which is not an illusion. The existence of the Self (Ātman) must be admitted. Even the void has a witness; if not, it would be impossible to say: "There is a void". (VI, 74–76)

All people admit in their experience the existence of *māyā*. From the logical point of view *māyā* is unaccountable because, as declared by the *Śruti*, it is neither existence nor non-existence.

The effects of *māyā* are undeniably manifest; hence its existence cannot be denied. Being destroyed by illumination, it cannot really be said to exist. From the point of view of empirical knowledge it constantly suffers negation in its details and hence must be considered an illusory appearance.

From the point of view of the ignorant it is assumed to exist; for the illumined it is insignificant and empirical reason establishes its indefinability.

Its existence and non-existence are seen in the phenomena of the world, which appear in the waking state and disappear in dreamless sleep. The process is comparable to the rolling and unrolling of the scroll of a picture.

Māyā has no independent existence, as in the absence of the cognising faculty the effects of *māyā* cannot be experienced. All the same there is one sense in which *māyā* enjoys an astonishing independence and it is in that it can make the ever-free Ātman appear to be attached.

Māyā transforms the immutable Kuṭastha, the ever-associationless Ātman, phenomenally into the form of the universe. Casting the reflection of Ātman in itself, *māyā* creates *jīva* and Īśvara.

Without in any way affecting the real nature of Ātman, *māyā* creates the world. It makes the impossible look possible. How powerful *māyā* is!

As fluidity is the nature of water, heat of fire and hardness of stone, so the making of the impossible possible is the nature of *māyā*. It is unique in this respect.

The magic show looks inexplicable as long as the magician is not perceived: but when the spectators perceive the magician, the magic show is no longer wonderful.

Those who believe in the reality of the world regard the effects of *māyā* as wonderful. But since the nature of *māyā* itself is a wonder, it is only to be expected that its power too is marvellous.

By raising objections to the wonderfulness of *māyā* we do not solve the mystery. Besides, the Vedāntin can raise serious counter-objections. What is essential is that we should eradicate *māyā* by systematic enquiry. Dialectics will lead to no good result.

Māyā is materialized marvellousness; the wise must make efforts to abolish it.

If you want to know the nature of *māyā* before trying to eradicate it, allright—do so! *Māyā* being undefinable does not lend itself to any logical definition. But do you know the popular definition of *māyā*?

The popular definition of *māyā* is that it is something which though apprehensible is at the same time beyond all determination. What is true of magic is true also of *māyā*.

Though without a doubt the world appears, yet its nature defies definition. Be impartial, and regard the universe as nothing but a projection of *māyā*. (VI, 128–142)

CHAPTER 16

Madhusūdana Sarasvatī

Madhusūdana, a sixteenth-century advaitin, was the author of many works in Advaita philosophy. His most important work is perhaps the *Advaitasiddhi* wherein he refutes the doctrines and criticisms of *Vyāsarājasvāmin*, a thinker of the Dvaita (dualistic) school of Vedānta. Madhusūdana is often credited with being the first to reconcile fully the metaphysical principles of Advaita with the path of *bhakti*, of devotion to a personal diety.

The earliest work believed to have been written by Madhusūdana is a short treatise entitled *Vedāntakalpalatikā.* It offers critiques of rival philosophical schools and is concerned especially with showing that Brahman (being the basis of all knowledge) is not an object of knowledge and that *mokṣa* (being an eternal state) is not a product of experience.

The following selections are from *Vedāntakalpalatikā*, translated by R. D. Karmarkar (Poona: Bhandarkar Oriental Research Institute, 1962).

VEDĀNTAKALPALATIKĀ

19. . . . What is the use of the refutations of the (so-called) threatening (arguments) of the various disputants and their howlings jarring upon the ear, in the case of those who have fixed their thoughts and are wedded to non-duality?—After this, now would be convincingly proved by right reasoning, what again is this matter in hand—the Entity constituted of the one knowledge, without a second, the highest bliss, not different from the inmost (Ātman).

20. (I say, says the objector)—The impropriety is the same even in the view of the followers of the Upaniṣads. To explain the same—As desire cannot rise in respect of something unknown, the desire must be spoken of there in respect of what is known. And so, how can it arise in respect of the Ātman always existent, which has nothing to be abandoned and nothing to be taken? If the Ātman is (already) established, there cannot be any desire (for the same) and there would be the undesirable result of salvation even in the *saṁsāra*-state. As has been said—

> And further, salvation not known by any means of proof—is it longed for or not? If it is known, as the Ātman is eternal, there cannot be any desire for the same whatsoever. (Bṛh. Vā. Kā. 289)

Nor again should it be argued by you—In the *saṁsāra*-state, because it is screened by *avidyā*, the bliss due to the realisation of non-duality although existing, does not appear on the scene; but when the *avidyā* is removed by *vidyā*, it by itself spreads on in the form of bliss owing to its self-illumining nature—thus arises the desire characterised by the removal of *avidyā*—because the removal of *avidyā* is difficult to point out. (We ask you)—Is that *avidyā* different from Ātman, or his own nature? Apropos the first (alternative), there would arise the undesirable admission of duality, and also the wrath of the *śruti* advocating his being one without a second; apropos the second (alternative) there would be the fault pointed out before.

21. In this connection, we reply (as follows)—There is not the absence of longing in respect of the Ātman, merely on the ground of his being established. Is being established, existence or being known or being the object of unobstructed realisation? Not the first (alternative can stand). Because it is vitiated in respect of the finding of the necklace that is forgotten and in respect of the disappearance of the snake on the rope. For the same reason, the second (alternative) also (cannot stand), because it points out to the desire. The third (alternative), however, can stand in the way of desire. But that exists not in the present case, on account of the obstacles, wrong conception etc. For this very reason, in the case of a person whose tongue is spoiled by the bile, in eating sugar although knowing it to be possessed of sweetness, there is no rise of the special contentment due to the sweetness, on account of the absence of the realisation of sweetness, due to the blemish of the bile. Thus there are two things desirable—(1) the village etc., which is not really reached, (2) the golden necklace etc., although already secured, screened by illusion. Similarly things fit to be discarded are also two-fold—(1) ditch etc., which cannot actually be discarded, (2) the serpent on the rope etc., always given up, are as good as not discarded on account of there being only illusion. There, in the case of the first two, the impediments for the action are (respectively) the attainment (already) and the discarding. In the case of the second two, they are to be attained by realisation (realistic attitude) alone. Here, verily, one understands the highest human purpose owing to action not being the intervening (or screening) factor. Similarly, even in the case of the attainment of the Highest bliss and the removal of *avidyā*, there does exist rightly the nature of being the object of longing, owing to the conclusion that they stand as unestablished, as they are screened by illusion. As has been said in the *Vārttika*—

> It is not right to say that longing does not exist in men on being released; because there is seen the longing for happiness etc., not circumscribed by space and time. (Bṛh. Saṁ. Vā. 290)

The sense is—Even though the state of being the Ātman is established, the state of having unlimited happiness, not being established, the desire (or, longing) rightly persists in that form. . . .

22. As to what has been stated (by you)—the removal of *avidyā* is difficult to point out (our reply is)—That (is) not (so), on account of

our admitting a fifth mode. Just as the fourth mode, the 'indescribable nature' itself, was admitted, as (1) existence, (2) non-existence, or (3) existence and non-existence, are not possible in the case of *avidyā* and its effects; so, as the *anirvacanīya* is invariably identical with *avidyā*, and because its removal and counter-entity cannot have identity with it, even something different from *anirvacanīya* is established, in the case of the removal of *avidyā*; everywhere (the argument) 'the impossibility otherwise' being the strongest. Again, as the *śruti* advocating non-duality, is concerned merely with 'Sat-Advaita', there is no conflict with it. Such being the position, the passages (describing the Ātman) as 'not gross' etc., would also be rightly given their due, as the negations of being gross etc., can be cognised in the Ātman, and the cognition of the absence of a second, by the expression 'without a second' also. Otherwise, if there is the knowledge only of the Ātman, in the absence of comprehension of the absence of homogenous and heterogenous distinctions, what is being opposed by the *śruti* advocating non-duality? Therefore, the admission of 'negation' (as a means of proof), verily, establishes the nature of being without a second—thus there is no impropriety whatsoever (in concluding thus)—so hold the author of *Iṣṭasiddhi* and others.

In reality, however, as negation is constituted of sentiency, its apprehension ought to be taken as being connected with the self-illumining sentiency itself; if its imaginary nature has to be necessarily spoken of owing to the impossibility of connection with reality of something absolutely unchanging and of contactless nature, then as the whole fancy is based upon *avidyā*, the fancy about negation is also based upon *avidyā*—and so, there exists not the unique indescribable nature about it. So has been spoken of by the author of the *Vārttika*—

> There is no other existence apart from Ajñāna like that of a second other than Ātman. Its removal is, verily, that (comprehension) itself; and no other (removal) by the comprehension of Ātman is there. (Bṛh. Vā. III, 8, 122)

As for the passages (describing the qualities) 'not gross etc.,—they only convey the nature of the Ātman as being quite different from the 'gross' etc.; they do not convey the negation of them; because the presence and the absence of fancied entities have only the nature of their basis (*adhiṣṭhāna*). As the conch-shell substance itself, when unknown is constituted of the nature of silver; that same when comprehended is constituted of the negation of silver, on account of its unique nature itself being constituted of the negation of silver.—Thus here also the Ātman, unknown, is constituted of the nature of all duality; but when known he is constituted of its negation, on account of the nature of the negation of duality of that unusual form itself. . . .

46. . . . If it is argued that its knowledge, verily, possibly referring to its object would be the remover of that *ajñāna*—(our reply is)—no. Because only something having a common object is characterised by

the nature of being the remover; otherwise, there would be all anarchy. And there would be the absurdity of the Vedānta passages not being the authority, by the non-production of cognition about that object. Further, you cannot say that it has the nature of being the remover of *ajñāna* and by that very nature, being the remover of that *ajñāna,* its being the object is stated metaphorically. Because there is the fault of mutual interdependence—there is the nature of being the remover of *ajñāna* owing to its being the object of that; and by that (being the remover of *ajñāna*) it is the object of that. Further, nowhere is it established that one is the remover of *ajñāna,* merely by being the object. Because that itself is now being considered. If it be argued that the nature of being an object which is imagined, cannot lead to its being the object—(our reply is) no; because nowhere have we admitted the real nature of the object, its being there for mere practical dealings is common (to both).

47. In this connection we say—Though it is impossible for Brahman to have the nature of the object of knowledge, the knowledge has Brahman for its object, and that (having Brahman for its object) is either the nature of perceiving the original object or quite something else indescribable. Nor should it be argued—How can the nature of an object be residing in knowledge on account of something apart from a substance, not being the resort of the Dharmas produced? And if they are not produced there would be just anarchy, and that cannot bear scrutiny—for, the knowledge also is a substance because it is a transformation of the inner sense-organ, and even though it has no nature of a substance, there can be no contradiction regarding the resort of the Dharmas produced, and the terminology 'substance' etc. serves no purpose. The nature of an object is some form, and that too is different for each object. Therefore, because of the removal of *ajñāna* not overextensive being quite possible by the direct right knowledge itself in the form of Brahman, the qualifying attribute—not having the mode of generality—is not wanted as the direct right knowledge having the form of the nature of being the remover of *ajñāna* persists everywhere. And further, it is not possible even to think of the cognition in the form 'this' as 'having the form of jar', because the difference in form is directly perceivable by the Witness quite distinctly. Otherwise it would be possible to state shamelessly that both these cognitions have just only one mode. In such cases, realisation alone is the (last) resort. And that is equally available in the present case.

49. . . . As the mode has for its counter-entity, the particular nature of what is being presented, the object of knowledge has got to be spoken of as particularised. And further, the knowledge not being the remover of its object, there would not be the removal of its mode—an undesirable contingency. And in the case of what is not perceivable by the pure sentiency, there could not be the possibility of its being the remover of the *ajñāna* perceivable by the pure sentiency; and because

only the presentation by the sentiency not tinged by anything else, has the capacity of removing the *ajñāna* in the aforesaid manner. In the case of being the object, however, the state of being perceivable by sentiency not tinged by anything else is proper, because though it is fit to be known by the Witness who presents that knowledge, it is not the object of that knowledge—that is the difference (between the *viṣaya* and *prakāra*). Therefore, it is proper that the modeless knowledge can have Brahman for its object. For this very reason, although at the first moment, the functioning and the object functioning are fit to be presented by the Witness, there is no contradiction of the functioning with the indeterminate nature. Because that (functioning) being produced from the words fortified by logical reasoning investigating the meaning of the word, has the form of mere Sentiency without a second, this same is spoken of as the state of the result of the means of proof. At the second moment, however, by the functioning gathering strength by the grasping of the form of mere '*cit*' is removed the *ajñāna*, associated with the pure '*cit*', as by the functioning of grasping the form of the rope, the *ajñāna* concerning it. Thereupon follows the removal of the super-imposition of the divisions, *ahaṁkāra*, *jīva*, Brahman etc., because the destruction itself of the constituent cause is the cause of the destruction of the unscreened constituents, and *ajñāna* itself is the constituent cause of that (super-imposition). Thereupon (follows) along with that, or subsequent to that, the removal of the manifesting functioning of the sentiency, which is the constituent of that. Thus comes about also the removal of the super-impositions of the body, sense-organs etc. Thus, over and above that, there being no limiting factor, only the unscreened *caitanya* remains, void of the divisions *jīva*, Brahman and the world, with the *ajñāna* and its products all swallowed up, and flashing up always in the form of self-illumination and the highest bliss,—this same is spoken of as the Salvation-state. As *ajñāna*, again, being beginningless is not something produced, and another beginningless *ajñāna* is not admitted; when the only one *ajñāna*-individual, which is the constituent cause of everything is totally removed, the paraphernalia, its effect, knower etc. also being totally removed, there is no return again of the *saṁsāra*.

50. By this argument is removed also the doubt whether that knowledge is removable by itself or by something else, because that is fit to be removed by the destruction of its cause. It is a matter beyond dispute for all, that the destruction of the constituent cause causes the destruction of the effect. There is no blemish either even though (it is held that) it is fit to be removed by itself along with the *avidyā* in its form as the perceivable. If there is the identity of the limitations of the nature of thing to be removed and that of the remover, there would be the violation of the rule about moments. In this case, there is the removing nature on account of the particularised right knowledge mentioned before and the nature of being fit to be removed on account of its being perceivable,—so there is no fault referred to.

(The objector says)—Well then, when the *ajñāna* which is the cause of the super-imposition in dream etc., is removed by the knowledge of the means of proof, the waking state etc., there would not be again the super-imposition in dream etc., because the reasoning adumbrated (by you) is the same. If it is admitted that there are many ajñānas there, the same is possible in the case of Ātman as well, and so there would be the unwelcome result—the absence of relief in Salvation. (Another objector says)—It is for this very absence of propriety, that the removal of *ajñāna* is not accepted there. Like the screening of illusion about a stream of water by the illusion about the serpent on one and the same unknown rope, here is effected merely the screening of the illusion about dream etc., even by the illusion about the waking state etc. The removal of *ajñāna*, however, is from the realisation itself of the identity of Brahman and Ātman, and so there is not the unwelcome result,—the absence of relief in Salvation. . . .

CHAPTER 17

Sadānanda

Sadānanda (ca. 1450 A.D.) is the author of *Vedāntasāra*, a widely read introductory text in Advaita. It is a highly syncretistic work which systematically presents the main doctrines of Advaita without dialectical controversy. The following selections are from *Vedāntasāra or the Essence of Vedānta of Sadānanda Yogīndra*, 3d ed., translated by Swami Nikhilananda (Advaita Ashrama: Mayavati, Almora, Himalayas, 1949).

VEDĀNTASĀRA

I, 6. The competent student is an aspirant who, by studying in accordance with the prescribed method the Vedas and the Vedāṅgas (the books auxiliary to the Vedas), has obtained a general comprehension of the entire Vedas, who, being absolved from all sins in this or in a previous life by the avoidance of the actions known as *kāmya* (rites performed with a view to attaining a desired object) and *niṣiddha* (those forbidden in the scriptures) and by the performance of actions called *nitya* (daily obligatory rites) and *naimittika* (obligatory on special occasions) as well as by penance and devotion, has become entirely pure in mind, and who has adopted the four sādhanas or means to the attainment of spiritual knowledge.

I, 15. The means to the attainment of Knowledge are:—discrimination between things permanent and transient; renunciation of the enjoyment of the fruits of actions in this world and hereafter; six treasures, such as control of the mind etc.; and the desire for spiritual freedom.

II, 32. *Adhyāropa* is the superimposition of the unreal on the real, like the false perception of a snake in a rope which is not a snake.

II, 33. Reality is Brahman which is without a second and is Existence, Consciousness and Bliss [*saccidānanda*]. Unreality is Nescience and all other material objects.

II, 34. However, ignorance is described as something positive though intangible, which cannot be described either as being or non-being, which is made of three qualities and is antagonistic to Knowledge. Its existence is established from such experiences as, "I am ignorant," and from such *śruti* passages as, "The power belonging to God Himself, hidden in its own qualities" (Śve. Up. 1. 3).

II, 35. This ignorance is said to be one or many according to the mode of observing it either collectively or individually.

II, 36. As, for instance, trees considered as an aggregate are denoted as one, *viz.*, the forest, or water is collectively named as the reservoir, so also ignorance, existing in jīvas, being diversely manifested, is collectively represented as one,—as in such scriptural passages as, "There is one unborn etc." (Śve. Up. 4. 5).

II, 37. This aggregate (of ignorance) on account of its appearing associated with Perfection (Pure Intelligence of Brahman) has a preponderance of pure *sattva*.

II, 38. Consciousness associated with this is endowed with such qualities as omniscience, universal lordship, all-controlling power, etc., and is designated as the undifferentiated, the inner guide, the cause of the world and Īśvara on account of Its being the illuminator of the aggregate of ignorance. As in the *śruti* passage, "Who knows all (generally) who perceives all (particularly)" (Mu. Up. 1. 1. 9).

II, 39. This aggregate of ignorance associated with Īśvara is known as the causal body on account of its being the cause of all, and as the *ānandamayakośa* (the blissful sheath) on account of its being full of bliss and covering like a sheath; it is further known as the Cosmic sleep as into it everything is dissolved, and, for this reason, it is designated as the state of dissolution of the gross and subtle phenomena.

II, 40. As a forest, from the standpoint of the units that compose it, may be designated as a number of trees, and as a reservoir from the same point of view may be spoken of as quantities of water, so also ignorance when denoting separate units is spoken of as many; as in such *śruti* passages as, "Indra through *Māyā* appears as of many forms" (*Ṛgveda* 6. 47. 18).

II, 41. Ignorance has been designated as individual and collective on account of its pervading the units and the aggregate.

II, 42. The individual ignorance, on account of its association with the inferior being, is characterised by impure *sattva*.

II, 43. Consciousness associated with this has limited knowledge and is devoid of the power of lordship; it's called *prajñā* on account of its being the illuminator of individual ignorance.

II, 44. It is called *prajñā* as it is deficient in illumination on account of its association with a dull limiting adjunct.

II, 45. The individual ignorance, associated with it, is also known as the causal body on account of its being the cause of egoism etc., and as the blissful sheath as it is full of bliss and covers like a sheath; it is further known as dreamless sleep as into it everything is dissolved and for this reason it is also designated as the state of dissolution of the gross and subtle phenomena.

II, 46. In the state of dreamless sleep both Īśvara and *prajñā*, through a very subtle function of ignorance illumined by Consciousness enjoy happiness, as in the *śruti* passage: "*Prajñā*, the enjoyer of bliss, with Consciousness for its aid (is the third aspect)" (Māṇḍ. Up. 5); as also from such experience of a man awaking from dreamless sleep as, "I slept happily, I did not know anything."

II, 47. This aggregate and individual ignorance are identical like a forest and the trees, or a reservoir and the water.

II, 48. As the *Ākāśa* enclosed by the forest is identical with the *Ākāśa* enclosed by the trees, or as the *Ākāśa* reflected in the water is the same as the *Ākāśa* reflected in the reservoir, similarly Īśvara and *prajñā* associated with these (aggregate and individual ignorance) are identical. There are such *śruti* passages as, "He is the Lord of all, (He is omniscient, He is the inner controller, He is the source of all, He is the cause of the origin and destruction of creatures)" (Māṇḍ. Up. 6).

II, 49. Like the unlimited *Ākāśa* which is the substratum of the *Ākāśa* enclosed by the forest and the trees, or of the *Ākāśa* which is reflected in the water and the reservoir, there is an unlimited Consciousness which is the substratum of the aggregate and the individual ignorance as well as of the Consciousness (Īśvara and *prajñā*) associated with them. This is called the "Fourth". As in such *śruti* passages as, "That which is (tranquil), auspicious and without a second, That the wise conceive of as the Fourth aspect. (He is the Self; He is to be known)" (Māṇḍ. Up. 7).

II, 50. This Pure Consciousness which is known as the "Fourth," when not discriminated, like a red-hot iron-ball, from ignorance and the Consciousness with which it is associated, becomes the direct meaning of the great Vedic dictum, and when discriminated, it gives us its implied meaning.

II, 51. This ignorance has two powers, *viz.*, the power of concealment and the power of projection.

II, 52. Just as a small patch of cloud, by obstructing the vision of the observer, conceals, as it were, the solar disc extending over many miles, similarly ignorance, though limited by nature, yet obstructing the intellect of the observer, conceals, as it were, the Self which is unlimited and not subject to transmigration. Such a power is this power of concealment. It is thus said:—"As the sun appears covered by a cloud and bedimmed to a very ignorant person whose vision is obscured by the cloud, so also That which to the unenlightened appears to be in bondage is my real nature—the Self—Eternal Knowledge" (*Hastāmalaka* 10).

II, 53. The Self covered by this (concealing power of ignorance) may become subject to *saṁsāra* (relative existence) characterised by one's feeling as agent, the experiencing subject, happy, miserable etc., just as a rope may become a snake due to the concealing power of one's own ignorance.

II, 54. Just as ignorance regarding a rope, by its inherent power, gives rise to the illusion of a snake etc. in the rope covered by it, so also ignorance, by its own power creates in the Self covered by it, such phenomena as *Ākāśa* etc. Such a power is called the power of projection. It is thus said:—"The power of projection creates all from the subtle bodies to the cosmos" (*Vākyasudhā* 13).

II, 55. Consciousness associated with ignorance, possessed of these two powers, when considered from its own standpoint is the efficient cause, and when considered from the standpoint of its *upādhi* or limitation is the material cause (of the universe).

II, 56. Just as the spider, when considered from the standpoint of its own self, is the efficient cause of the web, and when looked upon from the standpoint of its body, is also the material cause of the web.

II, 122. Now will be considered, in particular, how people variously superimpose on the innermost Self such ideas as "I am this," "I am this," etc.

II, 123. (Thus for example) an extremely deluded man speaks of his son as his own Self, on account of such *śruti* passages as, "Verily the Self is born as the son," owing also to the fact that one loves one's son as one's own Self, and further because of the experience that one feels oneself prosperous or ruined according as one's son fares well or ill.

IV, 137. As a snake falsely perceived in a rope is ultimately found out to be nothing but the rope; similarly the world of unreal things, beginning with ignorance, superimposed upon the Reality, is realized, at the end, to be nothing but Brahman. This is known as de-superimposition (*apavāda*).

IV, 138. Thus it has been said: *vikāra* is the actual modification of a thing altering into another substance; while *vivarta* is only an apparent modification.

IV, 139. To illustrate: The four kinds of physical bodies which are the seats of enjoyment; the different kinds of food and drink etc., which are the objects of enjoyment; the fourteen planes such as *bhur* etc., which contain them; and the universe (*brahmānda*) which contains these planes—all these are reduced to their cause, the five gross elements.

IV, 140. These five gross elements, together with the five objects such as sound etc., and the subtle bodies—all these are reduced to their cause—the uncompounded elements.

IV, 141. The five uncompounded elements, together with the tendencies of *sattva*, *rajas*, and *tamas*, in the reverse order to that of creation, are reduced to their cause, namely Consciousness associated with ignorance.

IV, 142. This ignorance and the Consciousness associated with it, such as Īśvara etc., are resolved into the transcendent Brahman unassociated with ignorance, which is the substratum of them all.

IV, 143. By this process of superimposition and de-superimposition the precise significance of "That" and "Thou" is clearly determined.

IV, 144. To explain: Collective ignorance and the rest, Consciousness associated with it and endowed with omniscience etc., as also the Pure

Consciousness unassociated with any attribute—these three, when appearing as one and inseparable like a red-hot iron ball, become the primary meaning of the word "That."

IV, 145. The unassociated Consciousness which is the substratum of the limiting adjuncts and of Īśvara which they limit, is the implied meaning of "That."

IV, 146. Individual ignorance and the rest, Consciousness associated with it and endowed with partial knowledge etc., as also the Pure Consciousness unassociated with any attribute—these three when appearing as one and inseparable like a red-hot iron ball, become the primary meaning of the word "Thou."

IV, 147. The unassociated transcendent Consciousness—the inward Bliss—which is the substratum of the limiting adjuncts and of the *jīva* which they limit, is the implied meaning of the word "Thou."

IV, 148. Now is being described the meaning of the great Vedic dictum (*mahāvākyam*):—This dictum is a proposition conveying identity, by virtue of the three relations of its terms, *viz.*, "Thou art That."

IV, 149. The three relations are:—*sāmānādhikaraṇya* or the relation between two words having the same substratum, *viśeṣana-viśeṣyabhāva* or the relation between two words qualifying each other (so as to signify a common object); and *lakṣya-lakṣaṇabhāva* or the relation between two words and an identical thing implied by them, here, the Inner Self.

IV, 150. Compare—(The relations are:) The relation between two words having the same substratum; that between two words qualifying each other (so as to signify a common object), and the relation between two words and an identical thing implied by them (here the Inner Self).

IV, 151. *Sāmānādhikaraṇya* is the relationship between two words having the same locus:—For instance, in the sentence, "This is that Devadatta," the word "That" signifying Devadatta associated with the past, and the word "This" signifying Devadatta associated with the present, both refer to one and the same person called Devadatta. Similarly in the sentence, "Thou art That," the word "That" signifying Consciousness characterized by remoteness etc., and the word "Thou" signifying Consciousness characterized by immediacy etc., both refer to one and the same Consciousness, *viz.*, Brahman.

IV, 152. The second relation, that of *viśeṣana-viśeṣyabhāva* is this:—In the same sentence ("This is that Devadatta"), the meaning of the word "That" is Devadatta existing in the past and the meaning of the word "This" is Devadatta existing in the present. They are contrary ideas, but still they qualify each other so as to signify a common object. Similarly in the sentence, "Thou art That," the meaning of the word "That" is Consciousness characterized by remoteness etc., and the meaning of the word "Thou" is Consciousness characterized by immediacy etc. They are contrary ideas, but still they qualify each other so as to signify a common object.

IV, 153. The third relation, that of *lakṣyalakṣaṇabhāva* is this:—In that very sentence ("This is that Devadatta"), the words "This" and "That" or their meanings, by the elimination of contrary associations of past and present time, stand in the relation of implier and implied with Devadatta who is common to both. Similarly in this sentence ("Thou art That") also, the words "That" and "Thou," or their meanings, by the elimination of contrary associations of remoteness and immediacy etc., stand in the relation of implier and implied with Consciousness which is common to both.

IV, 154. This is also called *bhāgalakṣaṇā.*

IV, 155. The literal meaning, in the manner of the sentence, "The blue lotus," does not fit in with the sentence, "Thou art That."

IV, 156. In the phrase ("The blue lotus"), the meaning of the word "blue" is the blue colour, and the meaning of the word "lotus" is the flower called lotus. They respectively exclude other colours such as white etc., and other objects such as cloth etc. Thus these two words mutually stand in the relation of qualifier and qualified. And this relation means their mutual qualification or their unity. This interpretation of the sentence, since it does not contradict any other means of knowledge, is admissible.

IV, 157. But in this sentence ("Thou art That"), the meaning of the word "That" is Consciousness associated with remoteness etc., and the meaning of the word "Thou" is Consciousness associated with immediacy etc. If it is maintained that these two ideas, since they eliminate their mutual distinction, stand to each other in the relation of qualifier and qualified, meaning their mutual qualification or their unity, it involves a contradiction with direct perception and other means of knowledge, and therefore is inconsistent.

IV, 159. Again in the sentence ("Thou art That"), *jahallakṣaṇā* is not also admissible as in the sentence, "The cowherd village is on (literally *in*) the Ganges."

IV, 160. In that sentence, as it is altogether absurd to construe the words, "Ganges" and "cowherd-village," literally, in the sense of container and contained respectively, that meaning of the sentence must be entirely abandoned, and it should refer by implication to the *bank* of the Ganges. Hence in this case the application of *jahallakṣaṇā* is admissible.

IV, 161. But this sentence ("Thou art That") meaning the identity of Consciousness characterised by immediacy or remoteness involves contradiction in one part only. Therefore it is not proper to abandon the other part as well and indicate something else by implication (*lakṣaṇā*). Hence in this case *jahallakṣaṇā* is not admissible.

IV, 162. Nor can it be urged: Just as the word "Ganges" (in the sentence in question), gives up its direct meaning and implies the "bank," so may the words "That" and "Thou" (in the sentence, "Thou art That") give up their direct meaning and mean by implication the contents of "Thou" and "That" respectively. So why should it not be a case of *jahallakṣaṇā*?

IV, 163. In that sentence the word "bank" is not mentioned, and therefore the meaning, which is not explicit, can only be derived through implication (*lakṣaṇā*). But in the other sentence ("Thou art That"), the words "That" and "Thou" are mentioned and their meanings are explicit; therefore it is not proper to use *lakṣaṇā* here in order to indicate through either of them the sense of the other (Thou or That).

IV, 164. Nor is *ajahallakṣaṇā* applicable in this sentence as in the sentence, "The red colour is running."

IV, 165. The literal meaning of that sentence, namely, the running of red colour, is absurd. This absurdity can be removed without abandoning the meaning of the word "Red," by interpreting it to imply a horse of that colour. Therefore in this case *ajahallakṣaṇā* is admissible.

IV, 166. But here (in the sentence, "Thou art That") the literal meaning, conveying an identical Consciousness associated with remoteness, immediacy, etc., is self-contradictory. If, without abandoning this meaning, any other idea connected with it be implied, still the contradiction will not be reconciled. Therefore in this case *ajahallakṣaṇā* is inadmissible.

IV, 167. Nor can it be urged: Either of the words "That" or "Thou" may exclude that portion of its meaning which conflicts with the other word and imply a combination of the other portion with the meaning of the other word (Thou or That). Therefore no necessity arises of admitting *bhāgalakṣaṇā*.

IV, 168. Because it is impossible to conceive the same word as indicating a part of its own meaning as well as the meaning of another word. Moreover when the meaning is directly expressed by the other word, it does not require the application of *lakṣaṇā* to the first word to indicate it.

IV, 169. Therefore, as the sentence, "This is that Devadatta," or its meaning, on account of the contradictions involved in one part of their import, *viz.*, Devadatta as existing in the past and in the present implies, by abandoning the conflicting portion which has reference to time, only the non-conflicting portion, *viz.*, the man Devadatta,—similarly, the sentence, "Thou art That," or its meaning, on account of the contradictions involved in one part of their import, *viz.*, Consciousness characterised by remoteness and immediacy, implies, by abandoning the conflicting portion which has relation to remoteness, immediacy etc., only Absolute Pure Consciousness which is common to both "Thou" and "That."

IV, 170. Now is being described the meaning of the sentence, "I am Brahman" (Bṛh. Up. 1. 4. 10), expressive of intuitive experience.

IV, 171. When the teacher in this way clears the meaning of the words "That" and "Thou" by the removal of superimpositions, and makes the qualified student grasp the import of the sentence, "Thou art That," which is Absolute Unity, there arises in his mind a state of absolute Oneness in which he feels that he is Brahman, by nature eternal, pure, self-illumined, free, real, supremely blissful, infinite and one without a second.

IV, 172. That mental state, illumined by the reflection of Pure Consciousness, makes the Supreme Brahman, unknown but identical with the individual self, its object and destroys the ignorance pertaining to Brahman. Then, just as a cloth is burnt when the threads composing it are burnt, so all the effects of ignorance are destroyed when their cause, *viz.*, ignorance, is destroyed. Hence the mental state of absolute Oneness, which forms part of those effects, is also destroyed.

IV, 173. As the light of a lamp cannot illumine the lustre of the sun but is overpowered by it, so Consciousness reflected in that state of the mind is unable to illumine the Supreme Brahman, self-effulgent and identical with the individual self, and is overpowered by it. And on the destruction of this state of absolute Oneness with which that Consciousness underlying it come into contact with the jar. The intellect identical with the individual self, just as the image of a face in a looking-glass is resolved into the face itself when the looking-glass is removed.

IV, 174. Such being the case, there is no contradiction between the following *śruti* passages: "By the mind alone It is to be perceived" (Bṛh. Up. 4. 4. 19), and "That which cannot be thought of by the mind" (Ken. Up. 1. 5). We are to suppose that the unknown Brahman is brought into contact with only the mental state, but not with the underlying Consciousness.

IV, 175. Thus it has been said:—"The authors of the scriptures have refuted the idea that the individual Consciousness can manifest the Brahman. But they admit that the Brahman associated with ignorance is brought into contact with the mental states only for the purpose of dispelling ignorance regarding It" (*Pañcadaśī* 6. 90).

IV, 176. "Brahman, being self-luminous, does not depend on the individual Consciousness for Its illumination" (*Pañcadaśī* 6. 92).

IV, 177. But there is a difference when the mental state assumes the form of material objects.

IV, 178. Because, in the case of the experience, "This is a jar," the mental state assumes the form of the jar, makes the unknown jar its object, and dispels the ignorance regarding it. Then the Consciousness underlying the mental state manifests the material jar.

IV, 179. Thus it has been said:—"Both the intellect and the Consciousness underlying it come into contact with the jar. The intellect destroys the ignorance (regarding the jar) and the underlying Consciousness manifests the jar" (*Pañcadaśī* 7. 91).

IV, 180. Just as the light of a lamp coming into contact with a jar or cloth existing in darkness, dispels the darkness which envelops them and through its own lustre manifests them as well.

CHAPTER 18

Dharmarāja

For Śaṁkara and his immediate followers the various areas of philosophy (metaphysics, ethics, etc.) were not separated into distinct disciplines, rather the various problems associated with any one area were treated in close relationship with the problems in another area. Epistemological issues, in particular, were intimately bound up with metaphysical ones and any radical separation of these domains simply did not take place in their work. In the later development of Advaita, however, epistemological questions were often at the forefront of discussion and assumed a pronounced position in the literature. This may be illustrated by the work of Dharmarāja, a seventeenth-century advaitin. His *Vedāntaparibhāṣā* is widely read by Indian students of Advaita as it offers, together with an analysis of ontological problems, a clear and precise summary of advaitic epistemology. It discusses the pramāṇas, or means of valid knowledge, in close detail and it analyzes the nature, source, and validity of knowledge. The following selection deals with *svataḥprāmāṇyavāda*, the theory of the intrinsic validity of knowledge, which is fundamental to the Mīmāṁsā justification of *śruti* and to the advaita relationship between Brahman-knowledge and other forms of knowing. The following selection is from *Vedāntaparibhāṣā*, translated by S. S. Suryanarayana Sastri (Adyar: Adyar Library, 1942).

VEDĀNTAPARIBHĀṢĀ

Of the pramāṇas thus stated, the validity is intrinsically generated and cognised. It is thus: validity is that which is common to recollection and experience, is favourable to successful appetition and consists in being cognition of a predicate in respect of what has that (predicate). And this is determined by the entire causal complex of cognition as such, but does not require an extra excellence, since there is no excellence common to all valid cognition.

Nor is there in perceptual valid cognition contact between the sense-organ and a multitude of parts, since this does not exist in the perception of colour and in the perception of the self; further, even where there is that (contact with a multitude of parts), there is delusiveness of the perception, 'The conch shell is yellow'.

For the same reason, even consideration of a sound *probans* is not the excellence, in valid inferential cognition etc.; for even where the consideration is of a *probans* that is not sound, there is validity for the inferred cognition etc., because of non-sublation.

Nor may it be said that thus even invalid cognition would be valid cognition, there being no distinction in respect of (the presence of) the causal-complex of cognition as such; for, absence of defect too is admitted to be a cause. Nor is there thus extrinsic nature (for validity), since there is extrinsic nature only when there is dependence on *positive* extraneous causes.

And validity is cognised too intrinsically. To be intrinsically apprehended is to be apprehended, when there is no defect, wherever there is the causal-complex for apprehending the locus of that (validity) itself. The locus of that itself is the cognitive psychosis; the apprehender of that is the witness-cognition; when by this the cognitive psychosis is apprehended, the validity present therein is also apprehended.

Nor thus is there unintelligibility of doubt as to validity; for, in conformity with the doubt as to that (validity), defect too exists; hence, since there is not the apprehender of its own locus as linked up with the absence of defect, validity is not apprehended at all in respect of that (cognition).

Or else, intrinsic nature (in respect of cognition) consists in competency to be apprehended wherever there is the apprehender of its own locus. In a case of doubt, though there is for validity the said competency, since it is yet not apprehended because of defect, there is no unintelligibility of doubt.

Invalidity, however, is not determined by the causal complex of cognition as such, because of the contingence of invalidity even in valid cognition; rather is it defect-determined.

Nor is invalidity apprehendable wherever there is the apprehender of its own locus; for, the non-existence of that (predicate) etc., which accounts for invalidity, not being brought in by the cognitive psychosis, is not capable of being apprehended by the witness.

But it (invalidity) is the content of inferred cognition etc., whose *probans* is unsuccessful appetition etc.; hence invalidity is both generated and cognised only extrinsically. (Chapter 7)

CHAPTER 19

Appaya Dīkṣita

During the last general phase of the development of Advaita Vedānta in its classical form, a number of compendia were written in which the authors, together with showing their own preferences for various ideas, summarized a vast amount of the doctrinal differences which had developed between the sub-schools of Advaita and between various individual thinkers. The *Siddhāntaleśasaṁgraha* by Appaya Dīkṣita (who lived in the sixteenth century) is among the better known of these works.

Appaya Dīkṣita was most favorably disposed towards the Bhāmatī reading of Advaita, but in his *Siddhāntaleśasaṁgraha* he treats the rival doctrines in a straightforward, objective manner. The following brief selections are from the translation of S. S. Suryanarayana Sastri (Madras: University of Madras, 1935) and deal primarily with the controversy over the multiplicity or singularity of the *jīva* and whether a doctrine of "subjective idealism" (*dṛṣṭi-sṛṣṭi-vāda*) is compatible with Advaita.

SIDDHĀNTALEŚASAṀGRAHA

Now, is this *jīva* one or many?

Some . . . adopt the unity of the *jīva* and say thus: the *jīva* is one; and therefore, it is only one body that has a *jīva*; others, like the bodies seen in dreams, have no jīvas; the world is posited by the ignorance of that (*jīva*); for that (*jīva*) there is empirical usage as long as there is nescience, as in the case of dream perception; there is not even the distinction between the bound and the released, because of the unity of the *jīva*; even the release etc. of Śuka is assumptive, like the release etc. of persons other (than the dreamer) in dreams; and the washing off of the mire of all objections that may occur to this (view) is to be effected solely in the continuous torrent of the dream-analogy.

Others, however, not gaining mental faith in this view of a sole (animated) body and a sole *jīva*, and thinking that there is conflict with such aphorisms as "But (the Lord is) more, because of the designation of difference," "But as in the world, (the creative activity is) mere sport," which teach that the Lord, who is more than the *jīva*, is alone the creator of the universe, not the *jīva*, and that though, there is no fruit for Him, there is creation of the world merely in sport, adopt the (following) view of a single *jīva* with many distinctive bodies: Hiraṇyagarbha, the sole reflection of Brahman, is the principle *jīva*; others, however, which are of the nature of reflections of that (Hiraṇyagarbha), are apparent jīvas, similar to the apparent clothes put on the bodies of human beings sketched on an artistically worked cloth, and are subject to transmigration etc.

Yet others, however, thinking that, because of the difference of Hiraṇyagarbhas in each aeon, there is nothing to determine which Hiraṇyagarbhas is the principal *jīva*, prefer the (following) view of a single *jīva* (animating) many bodies without distinction: a single *jīva* alone controls all bodies without distinction; nor thus is there the contingence of the remembrance of one another's happiness, in spite of the difference in bodies, just as (there is remembrance) in the case of the different parts of the body; for, since there is not seen the remembrance of the happiness etc., of another birth, it is settled that difference of body is the cause of the non-remembrance of that; in the case of yogins, however, the remembrance of the happiness etc., of a host of bodies is, like the apprehension of objects at a distance, conditioned by the might of yoga, and hence that is not an instance (to the contrary).

Still others, however, who are dissatisfied . . . resort to the view of many jīvas, through the admission of the internal organ, etc. as adjuncts of the *jīva*, and obtain the distinction of the bound from the released.

Of these, some say thus: though ignorance, which has the pure Brahman for locus and content, is but one, and only the destruction of that is release, yet, because of the admission of the persistence of a trace of ignorance in the state of release while embodied, ignorance has parts; hence that itself, when, in some adjuncts, there is the rise of the understanding of Brahman, ceases in part, while in other adjuncts it persists as before through (its) other parts.

Others, however, say thus: just as, in the view of some Logicians, the determinant of the presence of the absolute non-existence of pot on the ground is non-existence of conjunction with the pot and hence the absolute non-existence of pot which exists in association with many places possessing that is not in association with some places, when by the rise of conjunction with pot that non-existence is removed, similarly, since for the presence of ignorance is intelligence the determinant is the mind, the ignorance that exists in association with parts of intelligence, through that adjunct, is not in association with some when, by the rise of the realization of Brahman, the mind is removed, in the manner declared by the Scriptural text "The knot of the heart is cut"; elsewhere it remains as before; it is only the association and non-association with ignorance that constitute bondage and release.

Yet others, however, say thus: ignorance does not have pure intelligence as locus, but has the *jīva* for locus and Brahman for content; and that (ignorance) being, like generality in the particulars, separately realized in all the jīvas which are reflections in the internal organ, abandons some one for whom knowledge has arisen, as generality (abandons) a destroyed particular; this alone is release; in others it resides as before; this is the distinction.

Still others, however, establish the distinction between bondage and release only by admitting a different nescience for each *jīva*, and the persistence and removal of that (individual nescience).

On this view, by whose nescience is the world effected? If this be asked, (the reply is), since there is no determining consideration, it is effected by the nesciences of all, and is on a par with a cloth caused by several threads. When, on the release of one (person), his nescience is destroyed, then, as for the cloth when a single thread is destroyed, there is destruction of the world common to him; even at that time, like (the origination of) another cloth by the other existing threads, there is the creation of another world, common to all the rest, by the other nescience: thus say some.

Like the merely apparent silver produced by the respective (individual) ignorances, and like the duality which, in the view of the Logicians, is produced by the respective (individual) enumerative cognitions, the universe of ether etc., produced by the respective (individual) nesciences, is different for each individual; there is only the delusion of identity, as (in saying) in respect of nacre-silver "The silver seen by you that itself (is seen) by me too"; thus say others.

Māyā alone, which is different from the host of nesciences located in the jīvas and is (itself) located in the Lord, is the cause of the universe; as for the nesciences of the jīvas, they are of service in bare obscuration and in the projection of the merely apparent nacre-silver etc.: thus say yet others. (2:32) (pp. 176–181)

Those, however, who maintain that perception is creation (*dṛṣṭi-sṛṣṭi-vādins*) accept, for the whole world of waking, creation contemporaneous with perception, since the uncognised reality of what is assumptive is unintelligible; and they say that even the waking experience of elephant etc., is not an object of the sense of sight, since the cognition of the concomitance of the perception of pot etc. with the contact with the sense of sight, which (concomitance) is irreconcilable with the non-existence of pot etc., prior to the perception, is justified by them, only as in the case of dreams.

Now, if basing oneself on (the view of) perception as creation, one admits of the whole world of waking that it is assumptive, who is he that posits it? Is it the unconditioned self or the self conditioned by nescience? Not the first; for, since, even in release there exists the person who posits without the need of any other instruments, the world would persist, and there would be non-distinction from the state of migration.

Not the second; for, since nescience has itself to be posited, the establishment of the person who posits has to be declared even prior to the assumption of that (nescience).

To this some say thus: he who is conditioned by the earlier posited nesciences is he who posits the subsequent nesciences. And since, in the case of the stream of positer and posited, it cannot be said "This is the first", there is not the defect of infinite regress. . . . (3:711) (pp. 298–99)

CHAPTER 20

Summary

Advaita Vedānta has had a rich and varied history—and its doctrines are constantly being reconstructed and adapted to new situations and cultural problems. A number of basic principles, however, are affirmed throughout its history and they will continue to be affirmed so long as Advaita retains its distinctive nature and quality. For the sake of greater clarity in our understanding of Advaita we may sum up this common core of Advaita thinking, together with some of the specific teachings that were developed after Śaṁkara, as follows:

METAPHYSICS

Brahman

1. Brahman is Real and, in essence, is without quality or distinction.

2. "Brahman" stands for undifferentiated being, for pure unqualified consciousness. "Brahman" means *nirguṇa* Brahman, qualityless reality.

3. Brahman may, for purposes of orienting the mind towards it and for pointing out the basic features of one's experience of it, be represented or designated as *saccidānanda*—as the fullness of being (*sat*), awareness (*cit*), and joy of being (*ānanda*). In its status of pure being, though, no attribution can be made with respect to Brahman. It is *neti neti*, not this, not that; it is the negation of everything that is thinkable.

The World

1. Brahman is the sole Reality, and consequently the world of duality, of multiplicity, of change, and process is less than "real." It is a product of, and is constituted by, a creative illusion, *māyā*.

2. *Māyā* is beginningless (*anādi*) and indescribable (*anirvacanīya*) in terms of being and non-being. From the standpoint of the subject, *māyā* is *avidyā*—ignorance. It has the power of concealing reality (*āvaraṇa-śakti*) and of misrepresenting or distorting it

(*vikṣepa-śakti*). Man not only fails to perceive Brahman but he also substitutes the world in its place.

3. The world is taken by men to be real, and properly so, until such time as Brahman is realized. But like the snake erroneously seen in the rope, the world lacks real substantiality; it is mere name and form (*nāma-rūpa*).

4. It is not, however, completely unreal, like the "son of a barren woman," for it is experienced by men. The world is thus distinguished from true reality (*sat, paramārtha*) and from complete non-reality (*asat*), and is said to have a practical reality (*vyavahāra*).

5. It arises, in the final analysis, because of ignorance (*avidyā*), of superimposition (*adhyāsa*) of the attributes of one thing on another thing, of falsely identifying the true self with its association with the limiting adjuncts (upādhis) of the body and mind.

Īśvara or *Saguṇa* Brahman

1. When seen from the standpoint of *māyā* or *avidyā*, the world must be seen as having an intelligent principle as its creative source. This is Īśvara, Lord, or *saguṇa* Brahman, Brahman with attributes. The world is not self-explanatory; it refers back to an intelligent cause as its creative ground.

2. Īśvara is the creator of the world when Brahman is the locus of all superimposition: when we confound the infinite and the finite, and it is natural that we do this, Brahman, as Īśvara, is the material and the efficient cause of the world.

3. The "effect" always pre-exists in its (material) cause (*satkāryavāda*)—for there is no other way by which the causal relation can be made intelligible. Creation is thus not a bringing into existence of something that is radically new or different from its source, rather it is the bringing into being of that which is pre-existent in Īśvara. The world is a manifestation of Īśvara; it is brought forth and it is re-absorbed in recurring cycles. The world is without an absolute beginning in time.

4. Īśvara does not give rise to the world from any motive or purpose. Creation is *līlā*, play or sport. It is a spontaneous release of energy for its own sake, and hence no consequences attach to Īśvara's action in creating the world. Īśvara's action is precisely different in kind from all human action which follows the law of *karman*.

5. Still Īśvara is compelled, when creating, to distribute to souls the merits of their past actions. He must fulfill the dictates of *karman* for men.

6. From the standpoint of Reality, though, there is no creation and there is no creator god. The effect is really only an *apparent* manifestation of the cause (*vivarta*); in reality, there is only Brahman.

7. An illusion has reference to a substratum (*adhiṣṭhāna*) which is, in relation to the illusion, real. The rope is the substratum of the snake falsely perceived in it; Brahman is the substratum of the world falsely imagined (but necessarily so from the standpoint of sense-experience) to be created from it.

META-PSYCHOLOGICAL

Ātman

1. The Self is self-luminous (*svaprakāśa*) and cannot be established on any basis other than immediate experience. It cannot though be denied, for who would the denier be?

2. The Self, Ātman, is timeless and spaceless; it is unqualified consciousness.

3. The Self is one with Brahman.

Jīva

1. Most men do not realize what they essentially are and take themselves to be individual persons, jīvas. In reality the *jīva* is Ātman, but in the state of ignorance it regards itself as something finite, conditioned, and relative.

2. The *jīva* is seen to be separate from Brahman, from Ātman, because of the limitations (upādhis) which it falsely imposes upon itself or because, being a mere reflection of Brahman, it fails to realize the true identity between itself as a reflection (*pratibimba*) and Brahman as its prototype (*bimba*).

3. As a *jīva*, a man is constituted by various levels of consciousness, each of which is a reflection of the self as pure witness (*sākṣin*), and by various "sheaths" (kośas) or layers of his being which arise from a series of false self-identifications. These are: (*a*) waking consciousness (*jāgarita*)—the consciousness of the empirical world with its multiplicity; the self as identified with its physical body (*annamayakośa*—"the sheath made up of matter"). (*b*) dream consciousness (*svapna*)—the state of fancy and wish fulfillment, the level of "subconscious" motive and intention; the self as identified with its vitality (*prāṇamayakośa*), its sense-mind (*manomayakośa*), and its understanding (*vijñānamayakośa*), the three together constituting the "subtle body" (*sūkṣma-śarīra*) of the self. (*c*) deep sleep (*suṣupti*)—the state of harmonious awareness wherein all distinctions are held in abeyance; the self as iden-

tified with joy (*ānandamayakośa*); the self as constituted by the "causal body" (*kāraṇa-śarīra*).

EPISTEMOLOGICAL

Brahman-Knowledge

1. Braham is "unknowable" by means of reason and perception, but it is nevertheless the highest form of knowledge (*parā vidyā*).

2. Brahman is realized immediately and thus Brahman-knowledge is *sui generis* and self-certifying; it has a unique quality of ultimacy and no criterion drawn from other lesser forms of knowledge can be applied to it.

Empirical-Rational Knowledge

1. All lower knowledge (*aparā vidyā*) involves a threefold distinction between the knower (*pramātṛ*), the object known (*viṣaya*), and the means of knowledge (*pramāṇa*).

2. All empirical knowledge (*vṛttijñāna*) must meet these conditions: (*a*) the consciousness must undergo a modification or assume a mode (*vṛtti*) which enables it to appropriate the form of the object to be known; (*b*) it must synthesize the formal sense-contents into a meaningful concept through the activity of the intellect (*buddhi*); and (*c*) the consciousness of the subject must, through the instrumentality of the "internal organ" (*antaḥkaraṇa*) illumine the object.

3. The pure consciousness of the self as "witness" (*sākṣin*) cannot be an object of knowledge to itself. It is present, though, in every act of the knowing mind, as every act of knowledge presupposes it.

4. The means of valid knowledge (pramāṇas) are sixfold: perception (*pratyakṣa*), inference (*anumāna*), comparison (*upamāna*), non-cognition (*anupalabdhi*), postulation (*arthāpatti*), and testimony (*śabda*). No *pramāṇa* contradicts *śruti* when the latter is dealing with the nature of Brahman or the Self.

Criteria of Knowledge

1. All knowledge is intrinsically valid. One can falsify a judgement by experience which is contradictory to it, but one can never completely verify a judgement by external means.

2. All knowledge acquired through the various pramāṇas is valid in its own proper sphere, but insofar as it is subject to contradiction by another qualitatively different kind of experience it is necessarily "relative" knowledge. Brahman-knowledge is alone incapable of contradiction.

AXIOLOGICAL

1. The supreme value towards which all human effort should finally be directed is *mokṣa*—release from *saṁsāra*, from the cycle of ceaseless birth and death and rebirth. On its positive side *mokṣa* means perfect insight and self-determination.

2. Knowledge is the way to *mokṣa*. *Karman* or ritual action is neither a necessary nor a sufficient condition for its attainment. The practising of certain moral virtues (truthfulness, charity, etc.) are helpful auxiliaries to the path of wisdom (*jñāna-yoga*) but are likewise not conditions for its fulfillment.

3. *Mokṣa* is not something that is *attained*, rather it is an already existing state of one's being that needs to be realized as such. Knowledge only removes the obstruction to realization.

4. *Mokṣa* may be realized during one's life and when so realized one is a *jīvanmukta*. All the accumulated action which has not yet borne fruit (*saṁcita-karman*) and all action which would otherwise take place in the future (*āgāmi-karman*) is obliterated; action done in the past which has already begun to bear fruit (*prārabdha-karman*) must, however, be carried out. The *jīvanmukta* carries this out though without its affecting him, for he is unattached to it.

5. For the *jīvanmukta*, the enlightened man, complete liberation is obtained upon the death of the body (*videhamukti*): he is not reborn.

Bibliography

MAJOR PRIMARY SOURCES

Amalānanda (13th century) †	*Vedāntakalpataru* *Śāstradarpaṇa*
Ānandabodha (12th)	*Nyāyamakaranda*
Ānandagiri (9th)	*Nyāyanirṇaya*
Akhaṇḍānanda (14th)	*Tattvadīpana*
Appaya Dīkṣita (16th)	**Siddhāntaleśasaṁgraha*
Citsukha (13th)	*Tattvapradīpikā*
Dharmarāja (17th)	**Vedāntaparibhāṣā*
Gauḍapāda (7th)	**Kārikās on the Māṇḍūkya Upaniṣad*
Madhusūdana Sarasvatī (16th)	**Advaitasiddhi* **Siddhāntabindu* **Vedāntakalpalatikā*
Maṇḍana Miśra (9th)	*Brahmasiddhi*
Padmapāda (9th)	**Pañcapādikā*
Prakāśānanda (16th)	**Vedāntasiddhāntamuktāvalī*
Prakāśātman (13th)	*Pañcapādikāvivaraṇa*
Sadānanda (16th)	**Vedāntasāra*
Sarvajñatman (10th)	*Saṁkṣepaśārīraka*
Sureśvara (9th)	**Naiṣkarmyasiddhi* **Sambandhavārttika*
Śaṁkara (8th–9th)	**Aitareyopaniṣadbhāṣya* **Ātmabodha* **Bhagavadgītābhāṣya* **Brahmasūtrabhāṣya* **Bṛhadāraṇyakopaniṣadbhāṣya* **Chāndogyopaniṣadbhāṣya* **Īśopaniṣadbhāṣya* **Kaṭhopaniṣadbhāṣya* **Kenopaniṣadbhāṣya*

* Work has been published in English translation; see Major Primary Sources in English Translation.
† All dates indicated are approximate.

	**Māṇḍūkyopaniṣadbhāṣya*
	**Muṇḍakopaniṣadbhāṣya*
	**Praśnopaniṣadbhāṣya*
	Śvetāśvataropaniṣadbhāṣya
	**Taittirīyopaniṣadbhāṣya*
	**Upadeśasāhasrī*
	**Vivekacūḍāmaṇi*
Śrīharṣa (12th)	**Khaṇḍanakhaṇḍakhādya*
Vācaspati Miśra (9th–10th)	**Bhāmatī*
Vidyāraṇya (14th)	**Pañcadaśī*
	**Vivaraṇaprameyasaṁgraha*
	**Jīvanmuktiviveka*
Vimuktātman (13th)	*Iṣṭasiddhi*

MAJOR PRIMARY SOURCES IN ENGLISH TRANSLATION

Sureśvara

ALSTON, A. J., trans. *The Naiṣkarmya Siddhi of Śrī Sureśvara.* London: Shanti Sadan, 1959.

Śaṁkara

APTE, V. M., trans. *Brahma-Sūtra-Shānkara-Bhāshya.* Bombay: Popular Book Depot, 1960.

Gauḍapāda

BHATTACHARYYA, VIDHUSHEKHARA, ed. and trans. *The Āgamaśāstra of Gauḍapāda.* Calcutta: University of Calcutta, 1943.

Śaṁkara

CHATTERJEE, MOHINI M., trans. *Viveka-cūḍāmaṇi, or Crest-Jewel of Wisdom of Śrī Śaṁkarācārya.* Adyar, Madras: The Theosophical Publishing House, 1947.

Śaṁkara

DATE, VINAYAK HARI, trans. *Vedānta Explained, Śaṁkara's Commentary on the Brahma-sutras.* 2 vols. Bombay: Bookseller's Publishing Co., 1954.

Madhusūdanasarasvatī

DEVANJI, PRAHLAD CHANDRASHEKHA, trans. *Siddhāntabindu by Madhusūdanasarasvatī: A Commentary on the Daśaślokī of Śaṁkarācārya.* Gaekwad's Oriental Series, vol. 64. Baroda: Oriental Institute, 1933.

Śaṁkara

GAMBHĪRĀNANDA, SWĀMĪ, trans. *Eight Upaniṣads: with the Commentary of Śaṅkarācārya* [*Īśā, Kena, Kaṭha, Taittirīya* in vol. 1;

Aitareya, Muṇḍaka, Māṇḍūkya and Kārikā, Praśna in vol. 2]. Calcutta: Advaita Ashrama, 1957, 1958.

Sadānanda

HIRIYANNA, MYSORE, ed. and trans. *Vedānta-sāra (by Sadānanda): A Work on Vedānta Philosophy*. Poona: Oriental Book Agency, 1929.

Madhūsudanasarasvatī

JHA, GANGANATHA, trans. *Advaitasiddhi of Madhusūdana Sarasvatī* in *Indian Thought*, vol. 6, 1914–vol. 10, 1917.

Śaṁkara

———, trans. *The Chāndogyaopaniṣad (A Treatise on Vedānta Philosophy Translated into English with the Commentary of Śankara)*. Poona: Oriental Book Agency, 1942.

Śaṁkara

JAGADĀNANDA, SWĀMĪ, trans. *Upadeshasāhasrī of Srī Sankarāchārya (A Thousand Teachings)*. Mylapore, Madras: Sri Ramakrishna Math, 1961.

Gauḍapāda

KARMARKAR, RAGHUNATH DAMODAR, ed. and trans. *Gauḍapāda-Kārikā*, Poona: Bhandarkar Oriental Research Institute, 1953.

Madhusūdanasarasvatī

———, ed. and trans. *Vedāntakalpalatikā*. Poona: Bhandarkar Oriental Research Institute, 1962.

Śaṁkara

MADHAVANANDA, SWĀMĪ, trans. *The Bṛhadāraṇyaka Upaniṣad: with the Commentary of Śankarācārya*. Mayavati, Almora, Himalayas: Advaita Ashrama, 1950.

Sureśvara

MAHADEVAN, T. M. P., ed. and trans. *The Saṁbandha-Vārtika of Sureśvarācārya*. Madras: University of Madras, 1958.

Śaṁkara

NIKHILANANDA, SWĀMĪ, trans. *Self-Knowledge: An English Translation of Śaṅkarāchārya's Ātmabodha*. Mylapore, Madras: Sri Ramakrishna Math, 1947.

Śaṁkara

———, trans. *The Māṇḍūkhyopaniṣad with Gauḍapāda's Kārikā and Śaṅkara's Commentary*. Mysore: Sri Ramakrishnan Asrama, 1955.

Vidyāraṇya

ŚĀSTRĪ, S. SUBRAHMAṆYA, and AYYAṄGĀR, T. R. ŚRĪNIVĀSA, eds. and trans. *The Jīvan-Mukti-Viveka (The Path to Liberation-In-This-Life) of Śrī Vidyāraṇya*. Adyar, Madras: The Theosophical Publishing House, 1935.

Śaṁkara

SASTRY, A. MAHADEVA, trans. *The Bhagavad-Gita: with the Commen-*

tary of Sri Sankaracharya. Madras: V. Ramaswamy Sastrulu & Sons, 1961.

Vidyāraṇya

SHASTRI, HARI PRASAD, trans. *Panchadasi: A Treatise on Advaita Metaphysics by Swami Vidyaranya*. London: Shanti Sadan, 1956.

Appaya Dīkṣita

SASTRI, S. S. SURYANARAYANA, trans. *Siddhanta-leśa-saṅgraha by Appaya Dīkṣita*. Madras: University of Madras, 1935.

Dharmarāja

———, ed. and trans. *Vedāntaparibhāṣā by Dharmarāja Adhvarin*. Adyar: The Adyar Library, 1942.

Vidyāraṇya

SASTRI, S. S. SURYANARAYANA, and SEN, SAILESWAR, trans. *Vivaraṇa-prameya-saṅgraha of Vidyāraṇya*. Madras: The Sri Vidya Press, 1941.

Vācaspati

SASTRI, S. S. SURYANARAYANA, and RAJA, C. KUNHAN, eds. and trans. *The Bhāmatī of Vācaspati: on Śaṅkara's Brahmasutrabhāṣya (Catussūtri)*. Adyar, Madras: The Theosophical Publishing House, 1933.

Śaṁkara

THIBAUT, GEORGE, trans. *The Vedānta-sūtras with the Commentary of Śaṅkarācārya*. The Sacred Books of the East, vols. 34, 38. Edited by Max Müller. Oxford: The Clarendon Press, 1890 and 1896.

Padmapāda

VENKARARAMIAH, D., trans. *The Pañcapādikā of Padmapāda*. Gaekwad's Oriental Series, vol. 107. Baroda: Oriental Institute, 1948.

Prakāśānanda

VENIS, ARTHUR, trans. *The Vedānta Siddhāntamuktāvalī of Prakāśānanda* in *The Pandit*. Benares: E. L. Lazaras & Co., 1890.

SOME SECONDARY SOURCES ON ADVAITA VEDĀNTA

BELVALKAR, S. K. *Vedānta Philosophy*. Poona: Bilvakunja Publishing House, 1929.

BHATTACHARYA, ASUTOSH SASTRI. *Studies in Post-Śaṇkara Dialectics*. Calcutta: University of Calcutta, 1936.

BHATTACHARYYA, K. C. *Studies in Vedāntism*. Calcutta: University of Calcutta, 1909.

BHATTACHARYYA, KOKILESWAR. *An Introduction to Adwaita Philosophy*. Calcutta: University of Calcutta, 1924.

CHAUDHURI, AMIL KUMAR RAY. *Self and Falsity in Advaita Vedānta.*

Calcutta: Progressive Publishers, 1955.

DAS, RAS-VIHARI. *The Essentials of Advaitism.* Lahore: Motilal Banarsi Dass, 1933.

DAS, SAROJ KUMAR. *A Study of the Vedānta.* Calcutta: University of Calcutta, 1937.

DATTA, DHIRENDRA MOHAN. "Inward and Outward Advaita Vedānta." *The Philosophical Quarterly* 30 (1957): 165–172.

———. *The Six Ways of Knowing: A Critical Study of the Vedānta Theory of Knowledge.* 2d rev. ed. Calcutta: The University of Calcutta, 1960.

DEUTSCH, ELIOT. *Advaita Vedānta: A Philosophical Reconstruction.* Honolulu: East-West Center Press, 1969.

DEVARAJA, N. K. *An Introduction to Śaṅkara's Theory of Knowledge.* Delhi: Motilal Banarsi Dass, 1962.

GUÉNON, RENÉ. *Man and His Becoming according to the Vedānta.* Translated by Richard C. Nicholson. New York: The Noonday Press, 1958.

HACKER, PAUL. *Vivarta: Studien zur Geschichte der illusionistischen Kasmologie und Erkenntnistheorie der Inder.* Wiesbaden: Akademie der Wissenschaften und der Litteratur in Mainz, 1953.

HASURKAR, S. S. *Vācaspati Miśra on Advaita Vedānta.* Darbhanga: Mithila Institute, 1958.

INGALLS, DANIEL H. H. "Śaṃkara on the Question: Whose Is Avidya?" *Philosophy East and West*, 3 (1953): 69–72.

———. "Śaṃkara's Arguments against the Buddhists." *Philosophy East and West*, 3 (1954): 291–306.

IYER, K. A. KRISHNASWAMI. *Vedanta, or the Science of Reality.* Madras: Ganesh and Co., 1930.

IYER, M. K. VENKATARAMA. *Advaita Vedānta: According to Śaṁkara.* New York: Asia Publishing House, 1964.

LACOMBE, OLIVIER. *L'Absolu selon le Vedānta.* Paris: P. Geuthner, 1937.

LEVY, JOHN. *The Nature of Man According to the Vedanta.* London: Routledge and Kegan Paul, 1955.

MAHADEVAN, T. M. P. *The Philosophy of Advaita.* London: Luzac and Co., 1938.

———. *Gauḍapāda: A Study in Early Advaita.* Madras: University of Madras, 1954.

MALKANI, G. R. *Vedāntic Epistemology.* Amalner: The Indian Institute of Philosophy, 1953.

MURTY, K. SATCHIDANANDA. *Revelation and Reason in Advaita Vedānta.* New York: Columbia University Press, 1961.

RAO, K. S. RAMAKRISHNA. *Advaita as Philosophy and Religion.* Prasaranga: University of Mysore, 1969.

ROY, S. S. *The Heritage of Śaṁkara.* Allahabad: Udayana Publications, 1965.

SASTRI, KOKILESWAR. *An Introduction to Advaita Philosophy.* Calcutta: University of Calcutta, 1926.

SENGUPTA, B. K. *A Critique on the Vivaraṇa School.* Published by the author, 1959.

SINGH, RAM PRATAP. *The Vedānta of Śaṅkara—A Metaphysics of Value,* vol. I. Jaipur: Bharat Publishing House, 1949.

SIRCAR, MAHENDRANATH. *Comparative Studies in Vedāntism.* Bombay: Humphrey Milford, 1927.

STAAL, J. F. *Advaita and Neoplatonism: A Critical Study in Comparative Philosophy.* Madras: University of Madras, 1961.

SUNDARAM, P. K. *Advaita Epistemology: with Special Reference to Iṣṭasiddhi.* Madras: University of Madras, 1968.

UPADHYAYA, VEERMANI PRASAD. *Lights On Vedānta.* Varanasi: The Chowkhamba Sanskrit Series Office, 1959.

URGUHART, W. S. *The Vedānta and Modern Thought.* London: Oxford University Press, 1928.

Index

Abhāva ("negation," "non-existence"), 86n, 256
Action, in relation to inaction, 39, 40, 214–218
Ādhāra ("object of appearance"), 267, 268
Adharma ("unrighteousness"), 220
Adhiṣṭhāna ("substratum," "ground"), 267, 268, 290, 310
Adhyāropa ("superimposition"), 294. *See also Adhyāsa*
Adhyāsa ("superimposition"), 309; as defined and analyzed by: Padmapāda, 243–251; Sadānanda, 297; Śaṁkara, 138, 140, 151–154, 199–200; Sarvajñātman, 268; Vācaspati Miśra, 255–256, 264
Adṛṣṭa ("unseen principle"), 87, 87n, 88, 89, 95
Advaita, 10, 120; post-Śāṁkara, 223 passim; problems of, 73–76; and the purpose of *śāstra*, 221–222; school of, general definition of, 118; summary of school of, 308–312
Ahaṁkāra ("principle of individuation," "ego"), 79, 115; termed *Aniruddha*, 116
Ahiṁsā ("non-injury"), 104
Aitareya Āraṇyaka, 58, 160, 171, 183
Ajātivāda ("theory of no-origination"), 119
Ajīva ("inanimate nature"), in Jainism, 104
Ajñāna ("ignorance," "nescience"), 227; is beginningless, 292; is constituent cause of superimposition, 292; is removed by realization of identity of Brahman and Ātman, 293; the remover of, 290–291. *See also Avidyā*; Ignorance; Nescience
Ākāśa ("space"), 104, 296
Akṣapāda. See Gautama
Ālayavijñāna ("internal cognition"), in Buddhism, 103
Ālayavijñānapravāha ("the train of self-cognitions"), in Buddhism, 94
Ānandamaya, meaning of, 160–161
Ānandamayakośa ("sheath of bliss"), 282, 295, 311. *See also Kośas*
Anartha ("ills of life"), 243
Anekāntavāda ("theory of pluralism"), in Jainism, 104
Aniruddha, 115
Anirvacanīya ("inexplicable," "indescribable"), 249, 290, 308
Annamayakośa ("sheath of food"), 282, 310. *See also Kośas*
Antaḥkaraṇa ("internal organ"), 250, 282, 311; as called by different names, 193; existence of, 193–194
Antaryāmin ("inner ruler"), 54, 163, 285; definition of, 22–23. *See also* Self
Anumāna ("inference"), 6; example of, 108; ground of, 109; Nyāya definition of, 108–111; Nyāya model of, 108–111; two kinds of, 109; validity of, 110. *See also* Reason; *Tarka*
Anuśravaṇa ("Repeating"), 52

Aparā vidyā ("lower knowledge"), involves threefold distinction, 311
Āpastamba Dharmasūtra, 135
Apavāda ("de-superimposition"), 297
Appaya Dīkṣita, *Siddhāntaleśasaṁgraha,* 304
Apprehension, nature of, according to Śaṁkara, 144–148
Āraṇyakas, 7
Arjuna, dilemma of, in *Gītā,* 35
Asat ("non-being"), 309
Asatkāryavāda ("theory that effect is not pre-existent in its cause"), 87, 107, 183, 186. *See also* Causality; Cause and effect; Causes
Asiddha, logical fallacy of, 111
Āśraya ("locus"), 223, 227
Astikāyas ("categories"), in Jainism, 106
Ātman ("self"), 130, 131, 134–150 passim, 243, 269, 310; appears as many through nescience, 135; is Brahman, 30; composed of, 30; definition of, in *Upadeśasāhasrī,* 128; departure of, at death, 29; described as "not, not," 126; as free from social involvements, 129; identification with body in Śaṁkara, 127; light of, is pure consciousness, 145; by nature unrelated to rituals, 132; non-relational character of, 249; not an object, but appears as, 260–262; not composite, 139, 146; oneness of, with Brahman, 125; as perceiver in Gauḍapāda, 120; is self-effulgent and illumines entire aggregate of body, 205; is self-established, 144; transcendental changelessness of, 142; in *Upadeśasāhasrī,* 125–148. *See also Puruṣa*; Self; Soul; Spirit
Atoms, the, 89
Ātreya, 68
Auḍulomi, 61, 68
Avaccheda-vāda ("limitation theory"), 252
Āvaraṇa-śakti ("power of concealing reality"), 308. *See also Māyā*
Avidyā ("ignorance," "nescience"), 151, 214, 220 passim, 223, 235, 308, 309; cannot effect real knower, 222; conceals luminous nature of Brahman in *jīva,* 246; locus of, 242, 252, 267; is posited by implication, 246; and *Prakṛti,* 222; is *Prakṛti* predominated by *rajas* and *tamas,* 281; removal of, 289; as superimposition, 152. *See also Ajñāna*; Ignorance; Nescience
Ayutasiddha ("incapable of separate existence"), 91

Bādarāyaṇa, 61, 68. *See also Brahmasūtras*
Bādari, 61, 68
Bādhita, 111
Being, 8, 37; and non-being, 46
Bhagavadgītā, 4, 34, 67, 68, 72, 126, 130, 134, 135, 149, 150, 276; dissimilar to Upaniṣads, 34; exhibits strong theistic dimension, 213; rough chronology of, 35; Śaṁkara's commentary on, 213–222; status of, in Advaita Vedānta, 213; as a typology of Vedānta, 36; universalism of, 36
Bhāgavatas, 115; doctrine of the, 114
Bhakti ("devotion"), 35, 114, 213, 288. *See also* Devotion
Bhāmatī: criticisms of, by Vivaraṇa school, 224; question of locus of ignorance by, 223; school, 252; view of plurality of selves, 224

Bhāratītīrtha. *See* Vidyāraṇya
Bhartṛhari, 68
Bhāskara, 34, 36, 61, 71, 92; basic position of, 10
Bhautika ("elementary"), 93
Bhāva ("existence"), 256
Bhedābheda ("unity-and-difference"): no experience of, 276; Sureśvara's criticism of, 224–226
Bhūtas ("gross elements"), 79, 93, 128
Bible, the, 6
Bimba ("prototype"), in reflection theory, 242, 247, 310
Bliss (*ānanda*), 80; definition of, 267–268; as fruit of enquiry into Brahman, 154
Bodhāyana, 67, 68
Bondage, release from, 41
Brahmā: day of, 42; night of, 42; as primal creator, 46
Brahmajñāna ("knowledge of Brahman"), 243
Brahma-mīmāṁsā, 154
Brahman, 9, 10, 18, 29, 42, 50, 53–61 passim, 119, 121, 124, 126, 128, 130, 131, 134, 137, 170, 224, 259, 269, 297, 301, 310; absolute otherness of, 36; alleged break in nature of, due to ignorance, 190; always reflected in *prakṛti*, 281; as apprehended under two forms, 160; assigned an abode for purposes of meditation, 162; when associated with *māyā* becomes Īśvara, 284; as associated with nescience, different views of, 274–275; when associated with sheaths (*kośas*) becomes *jīva*, 284; is bliss, 19, 20, 41; as both differentiated and undifferentiated, 226; as breath, 20; called according to different relations, 286; called neither being nor non-being, 48; cannot be object of knowledge, 291; as cause, 156, 173–203 passim; continuity of, with world, 36; creative power of, 187; definition of, 19, 284; definition of, in relation to the world, 172–173; derivation of word, 155; as devoid of form, 197; is diametrically opposed to *prakṛti*, 281; discussion of definition of, 270–271; as efficient and substantial cause, 55; the enquiry into, 154; the enquiry into, antecedent conditions of, 155; essential nature of, 193; as eternal freedom, 188; as eternal pure cognition, 188; everything perceived by light of, 165; evolves names-and-forms, 57; as excluding other desire, 181; existence of, 155; experience of, 74; is fearlessness, 32; as food, 20; fruit of knowledge of, 202; Heaven of, 28; as highest state of wisdom, 49; the immortal, 31; inapplicability of inference to, 175; knowers of, 30, 150; knowledge of, 59, 75–76, 125, 155, 243, 311; is known as Īśvara when reflected in *māyā*, 281; as known through verbal testimony, 237–238; is locus of *avidyā* according to Sarvajñātman, 267; as locus of *avidyā* according to Vivaraṇa school, 224, 242; marks indicative of, 125; as material cause, 173; nature of, as intelligence, 171; is of the nature of knowledge, 241; negative qualities of, 58; as "neti, neti," 23; *Nirguṇa*, 73, 123, 270, 308; as not the object of knowledge according to Madhusūdana, 288; as not something to be accomplished, 235; nothing

existing different from, 199; is the object of ignorance, 252; is object of modeless knowledge, 292; as operative cause, 173; raised above apparent world, 190; is really unmodified, 266; as related to *tamas* and *sattva*, 283; *Saguṇa*, 73, 309; *Saguṇa*, is of a combined nature consisting of the real and non-real, 270; as something not to be attained, 157; as Soul of the universe, 30; is substratum of illusion according to Padmapāda, 247; as unable to be object of perception, 175; "unknowableness" of, 75; Vedāntic doctrine of, 85; viewed as cause of world, 171; what is meant by the term, 73

Brāhmaṇas, 7

Brahmasūtrabhāṣya, of Śaṁkara. *See Brahmasūtras*, Śaṁkara's commentary on

Brahmasūtras, 4, 10, 34, 51, 53, 66, 67, 68, 72, 114, 240; influence of, 9; Śaṁkara's commentary on, 8, 78; Śaṁkara's commentary on, *the* foundation work of classical Advaita Vedānta, 150; synopsis of topics of, 54–61. *See also* Bādarāyaṇa

Brahminism, 70

Brahmins, 17

Bṛhadāraṇyaka Upaniṣad, 21, 23, 24, 53, 54, 55, 58, 59, 60, 67; Śaṁkara's commentary on, 203–213; and transmigration, 16–17. *See also* Upaniṣads, the

Buddha, 93, 103

Buddhi ("intellect"), 79, 99, 162, 166, 182, 193, 282, 311

Buddhīndriyas ("organs of perception"), 79

Buddhism, 35, 69, 70, 71, 92; influence of, in Gauḍapāda, 119; objections of, to Vedānta teaching on Self, 207–213; Śaṁkara's criticism of, 92–93; 207–213

Buddhist, the: Idealists, 56; Realists, 56

Buddhists, the, 51

Caitta ("mental"), 94

Cārvāka, the, 248. *See also Lokāyatika*; Materialists

Causal body, 295. *See also Kāraṇa-śarīra*

Causality, 189; belongs only to consciousness, 269. *See also Asatkaryavāda*; Effect; *Pariṇāmavāda*; *Satkāryavāda*; *Vivartavāda*

Cause and effect, 116; basis of distinction of, 174; ideas of, not separate from ideas of substance and quality, 184; identity of, 178; simultaneousness of, 97

Causes: chain of, 95; which hinder grasping of knowledge, 125

Chāndogya Upaniṣad, 9, 21, 53, 54, 55, 58, 59, 67, 68, 183; and transmigration, 16–17. *See also* Upaniṣads, the

Christian church, 33

Cit ("pure consciousness"), 244, 285, 292

Citta ("mind," "thought"), 93, 193, 277

Cognition, 106; act of, 168–169; objective of, 267

Concealment, as power of ignorance, 296. *See also Āvaraṇa-śakti; Māyā*

Consciousness, 75, 99, 101, 200–201, 209–213 passim, 259, 295; act of, 100; distinction between waking and dream, 119; in a dream, 102; immediate, 102; levels of, 310; nature of, 93; as nature of self, 276; never pertains to body, 221; is permanent, 201; pure, 141, 143,

269, 301; pure, established without depending on any means of knowledge, 144; pure, known as the "Fourth," 296; reveals itself, 209; which persists in changing states is real, 277. *See also Cit*
Contemplation, 240; on knowledge of truth, 238
Contradictory attributes, impossibility of, 106
Conze, Edward, 93n
Creation, 309; circumstances of, are unequal due to merit and demerit of creatures, 192; knowledge of, 8; is not *ex nihilo*, 9; Ṛgvedic account of, 8; scriptural doctrine of, refers to apparent world only, 191. *See also* Causality
Creator, 172

Darśana (philosophical system), 114
DasGupta, Surendranath, 104n
Deep sleep: no nescience during, 277; state of, 143, 267; as state of seeing, 144. *See also* Consciousness
Definition, 270
Desire, 8, 30; destroyed only by discrimination, 233; as destroyer of spiritual and practical knowledge, 39; fivefold form of, 137; insatiable flame of, 39; role of, 8
Desireless, he who is, 30
Devotion, 36, 43, 50. *See also Bhakti*
Dharma ("righteousness," "duty," "law"), 5, 36, 49, 70, 214, 220; significance of, 35; in the smṛtis, 33
Dharmarāja, *Vedāntaparibhāṣā*, 302
Dharma-śāstras, 70
Discrimination, 125
Disembodiedness, state of, 158
Doubt, born of ignorance, 40
Drāmiḍa, 68
Dravya ("substance"), 104; definition of, 86
Dream, 100, 120; as distinct from empirical reality, 196; state of, 26, 143. *See also* Consciousness
Dreamless sleep, 284, 295; state of, 27
Dṛṣṭi-sṛṣṭi-vāda ("doctrine that perception precedes creation"), 224, 304, 306
Dualists, 225; problems of, 73–76
Duality: destruction of conception of, 157; the effect of nescience on, 135; originates from desire, 42

Education, Vedāntic, 51–52
Effect: form of, 186; has origin in speech only, 189; as a limiting adjunct, 178; as name only, 178; as non-different from cause, established by scripture, perception, reason, 182–187; as reabsorbed into cause, 175; as resulting from unreal cause, 181. *See also* Causality; Cause and effect; Causes
Efficient cause, 297. *See also* Causality; Cause and effect; Causes
Ego: notion of, is first *adhyāsa*, 245; viewed as agent, is a cause of *adhyāsa*, 246. *See also Ahaṁkāra*; Egotism
Egotism, 50; deluded by, 39
Ekajīvavāda ("theory of single self"), 224
Ekatva ("oneness"), 247
Empirical cognition, three factors of, 226
Enlightenment, 104, 228. *See also Mokṣa*; Liberation; Release
Epistemological, 302
Ether, 54

Evil, 76
Exegetes, the. *See* Mīmāṁsā, Exegetes
Existent, the, 11, 12, 125, 171; from Nonexistent, 21; as the root, 14; was in the beginning, 136
Experience, 111
External things: impossibility of, according to Buddhism, 99; non-existence of, cannot be maintained, 100
External world, existence of, 101

Faith, 40
Fearlessness, 126, 148; attainment of, 32
Field, the, briefly described in *Gītā*, 48. *See also Kṣetra*
Freedom. *See* Enlightenment; Liberation; *Mokṣa*; Release

Gauḍapāda, 68, 119
Gautama, 107. *See also* Nyāya
Gautamadharmasūtra, 230, 240
Gītā. See Bhagavadgītā
Gītā-śāstra, 219
God, according to Nyāya, 107; Lord of past and future, 31. *See also Brahman*; *Īśvara*; Lord
Godhead, both transcendent and immanent, 35. *See also Brahman* system
Govinda, 122
Grace, 46, 47, 50
Gross body, 55
Guṇas, 38, 39, 48, 81–86 passim, 213; as eternal though changing, 157; Vaiśeṣika definition of, 86. *See also Rajas*; *Sattva*; *Tamas*
Guru, 65
Guruparamparā, 65

Hetu ("cause"), member of inference, 109
Hetvābhāsa ("fallacy"), 110
Hinduism, 69, 70, 71
Hiraṇyagarbha (= god-Brahmā), is sole reflection of Brahman, 305

"I am Brahman": as expressive of intuitive experience, 300; meaning of, 300–301. *See also Mahāvākya*
Identity, 10
Ignorance, 76, 295; destroyed by knowledge, 41; has two powers, 296; as positive, 294. *See also Ajñāna*; *Avidyā*; Nescience
Illusion, power of, 42. *See also Khyāti*; *Māyā*
Immortality, 28, 31, 37, 163. *See also* Freedom; Liberation; *Mokṣa*; Release
Imperishable, the, 24
Impermanency, doctrine of, 95
Inaction, in action and *vice versa*, 40, 214–218
Individual soul, 10, 22, 54; as appearance of Self, 195; not created, 56; pain of, is not real, 194; as the product of nescience, 155. *See also Ātman*; *Jīva*; *Puruṣa*; Self; Soul; Spirit
Inference. *See Anumāna*
Ingalls, Daniel H. H., 77n, 108n
Inherence (*samavāya*), 112. *See also Samavāya*
Intellect, the, 143, 205, 272; is partial to truth, 262. *See also Buddhi*; *Citta*; *Manas*
Intelligence, motive power of, 83
Invalidity, 303
Islām, 33, 71
Iṣṭasiddhi, 290
Īśvara, 87n, 214, 216, 295, 309; as controller of *māyā*, 275; as distinct from *jīva*, 275; is the *Kṣetrajña*, 220; as a *saṁsārin*, 220; as superimposed on Brahman, 284; as supreme *puruṣa*, 275. *See also* God; Lord; *Brahman*

Īśvarakṛṣṇa, *Sāṁkhya-Kārikā*, 78
Itihāsa, 6

Jāgarita ("waking consciousness"), 310
Jaimini, 61, 68
Jainism, 35, 56, 103; categories of, 105–106; epistemology of, 104–105; philosophical doctrines of, 104; Śaṁkara's criticism of, 105
Janaka, 204
Jina ("conqueror"), 104
Jīva ("individual self"), 75, 80, 104, 118, 120, 182, 247, 262, 284, 292, 304–306 passim; is *Ātman*, 234, 310; becomes supreme *puruṣa* during deep sleep, 277; Bhedābhedavādin view of, as identical with Brahman in *saṁsāra*, 224; conditions of, being awake, 159; different grades of, 282; illusory manifestation of, 267; as locus of ignorance according to Maṇḍana Miśra, 223; as locus of *avidyā* according to Vācaspati, 252; is of the nature of *cit*, 248; nescience of, 274; as "reflection" of Brahman, 274; as result of differentiation of Brahman, 162; view of, as being different from Brahman, 225. *See also Ātman*; Individual soul; *Puruṣa*; Self; Soul; Spirit
Jīvanmukta ("one who is enlightened while living"), 312
Jñāna, can remove only *ajñāna*, 243. *See also* Knowledge; *Vidyā*
Jñānakāṇḍa, 7, 123
Jñāna-yoga ("the path of knowledge"), 35, 38, 218, 312; superiority of, according to Śaṁkara, 213
Judaeo-Christian, 74n

Kaṇāda, 90, 177; *Vaiśeṣika Sūtra*, 86. *See also* Vaiśeṣika
Kapila, 78, 177, 269. *See also* Sāṁkhya
Kāraṇa-śarīra ("causal body"), 282, 311
Kārikās on the Māṇḍūkya Upaniṣad, first available treatise on Advaita, 119, 176
Karmakāṇḍa, 7, 123, 179
Karman ("deed," "ritual action"), 28, 56, 57, 58, 88, 107, 108, 127, 224, 225, 226, 309, 312; cannot destroy ignorance, 224; as a category in Vaiśeṣika, 86; is an effect of ignorance, 225; final release from, 148; fruits of, 38; one exempt from, 60; performed as a sacrifice, 39; persistence of certain forms of, after knowledge of Brahman, 203; relation of, to *jñāna* for Maṇḍana Miśra, 229; three forms of, 312
Karma-saṁnyāsa, 219
Karma-yoga ("the way of the task"), 35, 38, 39, 41, 213, 214, 219; is impossible for one who has realised the Self, 219
Karmendriyas ("organs of action"), 79
Kāśakṛtsna, 68
Kaṭha Upaniṣad, 54, 55, 58. *See also* Upaniṣads, the
Kauṣītaki Upaniṣad, 54, 55. *See also* Upaniṣads, the
Khyāti ("error," "illusion"), analysis of problem of, according to Vimuktātman, 278–280
Knower, the, 145, 146
Knowledge, 20, 40, 100, 106, 148, 156; acquisition of, 65; act of, 99; annihilates good and evil works, 202–203; as concerned with non-duality, 235; criteria of, 311; destroys paths of renunciation and action, 228; discriminative, 149, 164;

empirical, 144, 146; empirical-rational, 311; enveloped by ignorance, 41; of field and knower of field, 48; has Brahman for its object, 291; illumines highest self, 41; kinds of, 164; is manifested quickly by exceptional means, 240; means to attain, 125, 294; not different from Brahman, 241; object and goal of, 48; obstacles of, 81; is the opposite of erroneous cognition, 236; originates from verbal testimony alone, 239; origination of, 203; perceptual, 75; perfect, 81, 195; recovery of, 65; relation to rites of, 231–241; right, 101, 153; the rise of, 236; as superior to action, 213; three fundamental means of, 6; true object of, 172; is verbal, 52; validity of ordinary sources of, 159; sought after for, 241

Kośas ("sheaths"), 19, 282, 310. *See also Ānandamayakośa; Annamayakośa; Manomayakośa; Prāṇamayakośa; Vijñānamayakośa*

Kṛṣṇa, 35, 114, 135; divided eightfold nature of, 42

Kṣatriya ("baron"), 16; class, special knowledge of, 17

Kṣetra ("field"), 221. *See also* Field

Kṣetrajña ("knower of the field"), the, as Kṛṣṇa, 219–220. *See also* Knower

Lakṣaṇā ("implication," "secondary meaning"), 300; *Ajahallakṣaṇā,* 300; *Bhāgalakṣaṇā,* 299, 300; *Jahallakṣaṇā,* 299; *Lakṣya,* 270; *Lakṣya-lakṣaṇabhāva* (type of relation between words), 298, 299; *Svarūpalakṣaṇa,* definition of, 270; *Upalakṣaṇa,* definition of, 270

Learning, 66

Learning tradition, vulnerability of, 66

Liberation: of self, 221; through knowledge, 225. *See also* Enlightenment; *Mokṣa;* Release

Līlā ("sport"), 309; as in creation of world without purpose, 191

Liṅga (*hetu;* "middle term"), 108

Liṅga-śarīra ("subtle body"), 282. *See also* Subtle body

Logicians, the, 306

Lokāyatika ("materialists"), 200. *See also Cārvāka;* Materialists

Lord: as dependent on names-and-forms, 182; no blame ascribed to the, 191–192; ruling, 94; is material as well as operative cause, 115; as not subject to pain of existence, 194; omniscience of the, 112, 113. *See also Brahman;* God; *Īśvara*

Madhusūdana: *Advaitasiddhi,* 288; *Vedāntakalpalatikā,* 288

Madhva, 68, 71

Mādhyamika, 92, 93, 208; refutation of, by Vedānta, 286

Magician, 188, 287; analogy of, with self, 176

Mahābhārata, 34, 68, 69

Mahāpralaya ("universal dissolution"), 169. *See also Pralaya*

Mahat ("principle of intellect"), 79, 83

Mahāvākya ("great statements"), 10, 242, 251. *See also* "I am Brahman"; *Tat tvam asi*

Mahāvīra, 104

Mahāyāna, relationship with Vedānta, 92

Māheśvaras (Śaivas), the, 111
Manas ("sense mind"), 79, 193, 205, 282
Maṇḍana Miśra: *Brahmasiddhi*, 223, 229; identification with Sureśvara, 223
Manomayakośa ("sheath of mind"), 282, 310. *See also Kośas*
Manu, 135
Manu, smṛti of, 33, 130, 135, 230, 233, 240
Material cause, 297. *See also* Causality
Material fallacies, five kinds of, 110
Materialists, the, 83. *See also Cārvāka; Lokāyatika*
Maṭhs, 92, 123
Māyā ("power," "illusion"), 40, 92, 118, 176, 247, 272, 274, 275, 295, 306; is *anādi* and *anirvacanīya*, 308; creates *jīva* and *Īśvara*, 287; as a creating and projecting power, 284; as a creative power according to Vidyāraṇya, 281; as divine power, 284; in Gauḍapāda, 119–121 passim; as indeterminable in terms of *sat* and *asat*, 283; makes ever-free *Ātman* appear to be attached, 287; nature of, as ignorance, 276; is *prakṛti* predominated by *sattva*, 281; is unaccountable from logical viewpoint, 286; is undefinable, 287. *See also Āvaraṇa-śakti;* Concealment; Projection; *Vikṣepa-śakti*
Meditation, 157
Mental impressions, variety of, 102
Mīmāṁsā: the, 5, 52–53, 67, 77; Exegetes, 6
Mind: assumes form of object it perceives, 285; as consisting of food, 129; as internal organ, 274. *See also Antaḥkaraṇa; Buddhi; Cit; Citta; Manas*
Mithyā ("false"), 118, 242; signification of word, 244
Mokṣa ("release"), 34, 38, 76, 123, 223, 229, 312; as eternal, 157; not a product of experience, 288; realization of, 130; is same as Brahman, 157. *See also* Freedom; Liberation; Release
Mokṣa Śāstras, the, 198
Momentariness, 103, 211; doctrine of, 96–98; and phenomenon of remembrance, 93. *See also* Impermanency, doctrine of
Moral behavior, 76
Moral judgements, 76
Muhammad, 33
Mūlāvidyā ("primal ignorance"), 224
Muṇḍaka Upaniṣad, 8, 54, 55, 58. *See also* Upaniṣads, the

Nāgārjuna, 92, 119
Naiyāyikas, the, 112
Nāma-rūpa ("name-and-form"), 12, 128, 129, 309; distinction of, from speech only, 190
Nayas ("standpoints"), 104
Nescience, 94, 96, 129, 136, 139, 148, 182, 273, 306; cycles of, 95; definition of, 138; is dependent upon Īśvara, 275; effects of, 135; explanation of, 137–138; in the form of duality, 164; locus and content of, 268; is the one enemy of man, 268; potency of, is in Brahman, 245. *See also Ajñāna; Avidyā;* Ignorance
Neti neti ("Not, Not"), 23, 308
Nigamana, member of inference, 109
Nihilists, the, 98, 139. *See also Śūnyavādin*

Nimbarka, 68
Nitya-karma ("obligatory duties"), 216
Non-being, 8, 37; and being, 46. *See also Asat*
Nondifference, 68
Non-dualism. *See Advaita*
Non-existence, Śaṁkara's definition of, 98
Nonexistent, the, 11, 171; in the beginning, 21
Not-self, 227; as object, 152
Nyāya, 73n, 77, 87n, 252; contributions of, to Indian philosophy, 108; two kinds of inference in, 109; *Kusumāñjali,* 107n; *Sūtra,* 67, 112; syllogism, 109; system, 107

Omniscience, 80; of Lord, 113
One, the, 8
Oral tradition, 65; primacy of, 66

Padārthadharmasaṁgraha, 86n, 87n
Padārthas ("categories"), 86
Padmapāda: a direct pupil of Śaṁkara, 242; *Pañcapādikā,* 242
Pakṣa ("minor term"), 108
Pañcadaśi, 301
Pāñcarātra, the, 56, 114
Pāṇini, *Aṣṭādhyāyī,* 67
Paramahaṃsa, 124, 127
Paramāṇus ("partless atoms"), 86
Paramārtha satya ("highest reality"), 119, 309
Paramātman ("supreme self"), 286. *See also Ātman; Brahman; Puruṣa;* Self; Soul; Spirit
Parārtha, as a kind of inference, 109
Parā vidyā ("higher knowledge"), 311
Pariṇāma ("transformation") 244
Pariṇamavāda ("the theory of the transformation of a cause into its effect"), 79, 87, 267. *See also* Causality; Cause and effect; Causes; *Vivarta*
Parisaṃkhyāna meditation, 148
Path of knowledge, the. *See Jñāna-yoga*
Path of works, the. *See Karma-yoga*
Perceiver, the, 132, 148
Perception, 100, 142; of *Ātman,* 143; object of, 101; and perceiver, non-distinction between, 142. *See also Pratyakṣa*
Perfection: how attained, 49; not attained by mere renunciation, 38. *See also* Enlightenment; Freedom; Liberation; *Mokṣa;* Release
Personal existence, basis of, 94
Phala ("result," "fruit"), as superimposed on *Ātman,* 246
Phenomenal world, non-different from its cause, 9
Philosophical problem, 72; axiological, 76; epistemological, 75; metaphysical, 73; meta-psychological, 74
Plurality: springs from wrong knowledge, 188; sublated by perfect knowledge, 188
Potter, Karl, 111n
Prābhākara theory of illusion, Vimuktātman's criticism of, 279
Practical distinctions, presuppositions of, 153
Pradhāna, 83, 85, 111–114 passim, 164; activity of, 84; existence of, 81; as non-intelligent, 82; spontaneous modification of, 84; transformation of, 83. *See also Prakṛti*
Pradyumna, 115
Prajñā, 282, 295
Prakāśānanda, 224

Prakṛti ("nature," "material force"), 10, 38, 39, 43, 48, 50, 54, 55, 79–81 passim, 281, 282; existence of, 79n; as material cause, 79. *See also* Guṇas
Pralaya ("state of dissolution"), 87, 88, 89. *See also* Brahmā, night of; *Mahāpalaya*
Pramāṇa ("means of valid knowledge"), 6, 108, 111, 254, 263, 272, 285, 302; are sixfold, 311; only the external world as content of, 271. *See also* Knowledge
Prāṇa ("breath"), 20, 29; fivefold function of, 282
Prāṇamayakośa ("sheath of vitality"), 282, 310. *See also* *Kośas*
Praśna Upaniṣad, 55. *See also* Upaniṣads, the
Pratibimba ("individual as reflection"), 242, 310; is *bimba,* 247. *See also* Bimba
Pratijñā, member of inference, 109
Pratyakṣa ("perception"), 6, 80, 111, 139, 220. *See also* Perception
Projection, as power of ignorance, 296–297. *See also Māyā*
Pudgala ("matter"), 104
Purāṇa, 6, 68, 69, 70
Purity, 70
Puruṣa ("self"), 10, 26, 29, 48, 79, 80, 130; is *Ātman,* 126; consists of desire, 30; existence of, 79n; is indifferent, 83. *See also Ātman; Brahman; Jīva;* Self; Soul; Spirit
Puruṣottama ("highest spirit"), 49. *See also Ātman; Brahman; Īśvara; Puruṣa;* Self; Soul; Spirit
Pūrvā Mīmāṁsā, 154. *See also* Mīmāṁsā
Quality (*guṇa*), Vaiśeṣika definition of, 86. *See also* Guṇas
Qur'ān, the, 33

Rajas, 79, 81, 213, 281, 282, 297. *See also* Guṇas
Rāmānuja, 21, 34, 36, 61, 67, 68, 71; basic position of, 10
Real, the, 273
Reason, 75; limits of, 175, 177. *See also Anumāna;* Inference; *Tarka*
Rebirth, 30, 42. *See also Saṁsāra;* Transmigration
Recollection, 69. *See also Smṛti*
"Reflexionism," theory of, 242; according to Sarvajñātman, 267
Release, 87, 95, 99, 116, 137, 203, 235; is contemporaneous with knowledge, 270; impossibility of, 85; means to, 124. *See also* Enlightenment; Liberation; *Mokṣa;* Perfection
Remembrance, 97; acts of, 102; needs unchangeable Self, 103
Renunciation: of actions, 41; as a duty, 218. *See also Saṁnyāsa*
Revelation. *See Śruti*
Ṛgveda, 8, 71, 135, 164, 295; philosophical hymns of, 8
Rite, as concerned with duality, 235. *See also Karman;* Mīmāṁsā
Ritual: action, 34; as effect of nescience, 137; use of, 131–132; Vedic injunctions as based on superimposition, 153. *See also Karman;* Mīmāṁsā
Rope-snake analogy, in *Upadeśasāhasrī,* 147
Rūpaskandha ("group of sensation"), 94

Saccidānanda, 294, 308
Sacerdotalism, Vedic tradition of, 34
Sadānanda, *Vedāntasāra,* 294

Sādhya ("major term"), 108
Śākhā (Vedic branch), 70
Sākṣin ("witness"), 226, 279, 285, 310, 311
Śakti ("power"), 169
Samādhi ("contemplation," "concentration"), 284
Sāmānādhikaraṇya, type of relation between words, 298
Sāmānya ("generality"), 86; definition of, 87
Samavāya ("inherence"), 86, 91, 184; definition of, 87
Saṁgrahanaya, Jain use of, as member of a class, 104
Saṁjñāskandha, according to Buddhism, 94
Śaṁkara, 8, 34, 36, 61, 68, 71, 77, 118; attack against the Śāṁkhya, 80–81; author of commentaries, 123–124; biographical sketch of, 122–123; *Brahmasūtrabhāṣya,* 150; combines exegesis and dialectic, 203; as different from Buddhists, 272; exegetical method of, 151; importance of *Bṛhadāraṇyaka Upaniṣad* to, 23; as revolutionary thinker, 123; *Upadeśasāhasrī,* 124
Sāṁkhya, 35, 54, 56, 73n, 77, 78, 87, 89, 90, 111, 157, 193, 252; arguments against Vedānta, 77n; general categories of evolution of, 80; *Kārikā,* 79n; as made use of by Vedānta, 281; system, 115; theory of evolution of world, 78–80; and Yoga are one, 41
Sāṁkhya-yoga, 113
Saṁnyāsa ("renunciation"), 122, 123, 219. *See also* Renunciation
Saṁsāra ("cycle of existence"), 95, 100, 170, 194, 196, 220, 221, 224, 225, 270, 286, 292, 296, 312; based on *avidyā,* 222; destroyed by knowledge, 228; release from, 114. *See also* Rebirth; Transmigration
Saṁskāra ("impression"), 158; as *upādhi,* 249
Saṁskāraskandha ("group of impressions"), 94
Saṁvṛtti-satya ("empirical truth"), 119
Saṁyoga ("conjunction"), 91, 112, 184
Saṅkarśaṇa, 115
Sanskrit, 69, 70; use of, 69
Saptabhaṅgīnaya, doctrine of standpoints in Jainism, 106
Śarīraka-mīmāṁsā-sūtras, 51; provide a system for Vedānta, 52
Sarvajñātman, *Saṁkṣepaśārīraka,* 267
Sarvāstitvādin ("Realists"), 93. *See also* Buddhism
Śāstra, 217
Sat ("Existence"), 9, 309
Śatapatha Brāhmaṇa, 8
Satkāryavāda ("theory that effect is pre-existent in its material cause") 79n, 309; doctrine of, 9. *See also* Causality; Cause and effect; Causes
Satpratipaksa, kind of fallacy, according to Nyāya, 110
Sattva, 79, 81, 213, 275, 281, 282, 295, 297. *See also* Guṇas
Savyabhicāra, kind of fallacy, according to Nyāya, 110
Scripture: cannot be opposed to experience, 253; content of, is final stage of direct knowledge, 239; range of, 177; validity of, 254; and validity of perception, 254. *See also Śruti*
Self, 19, 26, 50, 82, 120, 160, 221; as actionless, 215, 244; is always attained, 204; attainment of, as knowledge, 204; as becoming contents of consciousness, 207; as both *āśraya* and *viṣaya* of

avidyā, 227; is Brahman, 237; cannot be described as being "like this" or "like that," 283; cannot be object of experience, 283; as consisting of bliss (*ānanda*), 160; as consisting of breath, 20; as consisting of food, 20; as consisting of knowledge, 20; as consisting of mind, 20; as the controller of all, 31; corporeal, 28, 29; described as "not, not," 25, 31; difference between embodied self and highest self, 163; is different from individual soul in name only, 172; is differentiating owing to limiting adjuncts, 163; differentiation of, through ignorance, 228; is eternal witness, 226; ethical injunctions not pertaining to, 195; and the existent, 21; the five sheaths of, 282; as God, 31; identifications of, 205–207; as it identifies with sheaths, 282–283; as immortal inner controller, 22; as imparting selfhood to objects, 159; as knower, 283; knowledge of, eligibility for, 229–231; knowledge of, not for sake of something else, 234; knowledge of, is opposed to the performance of rite, 235; knowledge of, stills all sufferings, 233; nature of, 258; nature of, is pure consciousness, 227; not disturbed by good or evil, 32; obstructed by ignorance, 296; opinions about, 155; as separate from the body, 200; and sleep, 13; spoken of as embodied, 162; as subject, 152; is *svaprakāśa* (self-luminous), 310; true nature of, 254; unconnected with cause and effect, 222; as union of Indha (Indra) and Virāj, 25; Vedāntic view of, 155; as witness, 176. *See also Ātman; Brahman;* Consciousness; Īśvara; *Jīva; Kośas; Puruṣa; Sākṣin;* Soul; Spirit

Selfhood: empirical dimensions of, 74, 75; nature of, 74; spiritual dimensions of, 74. *See also* Self

Sense-experience. *See Pratyakṣa*

Senses, the, 37; objects of, 148

Similarity, perception of, 211

Sins, destroyed by knowledge, 41

Skandha ("groups," "aggregates"), 92, 94

Sleep, the doctrine of, 13

Smṛti ("Recollection"), 33, 55, 72, 115, 125, 126, 151; authority of, 33–34. *See also* Recollection

Soul, 56–58, 84; as agent, 53; cannot create, 57; description of, 37–38; devoid of action and qualities, 85; is of eternal intelligence, 193; merges with Brahman in dreamless sleep, 57; is a portion of supreme soul, 57. *See also Ātman; Brahman;* Consciousness; Īśvara; *Jīva; Kośas; Puruṣa; Sākṣin;* Self; Spirit

Speech, and creating, 10

Sphoṭa, nature of "word," 166–169 passim

Spirit, 26. *See also Ātman; Brahman;* Īśvara; *Jīva; Puruṣa;* Self; Soul

Śravaṇa ("listening"), 52

Śruti ("Revelation"), 5, 33, 69, 72, 74, 125, 126; area of authority of, 6; authority of, 7; as authorless, 5; classification of, 6; as containing meditative aids for those in ignorance, 151; conveys doctrine that Lord is universal cause, 174; passages in reference to Brahman of a

double character, 196; validity of, 232
Student, qualifications needed for competence, 294
Subject-object: distinction between, 151–152; mutual dependence of, 162
Sublation, 247–249 passim
Substance, Vaiśeṣika definition of, 86
Subtle body, 55, 57, 60. *See also* *Liṅga Śarīra*
Śūdras, 55, 170
Śūnyavādin ("Nihilists"), 92, 93. *See also* Nihilists
Supreme spirit, obtainable by devotion, 43
Sureśvara, 285; contrasted with Maṇḍana Miśra, 223; *Naiṣkarmya Siddhi*, 224
Suśumṇā, 61
Suṣupti ("deep sleep"), 310
Sūtra, 9, 65, 70; need explanation, 52; usages of, 51. *See also* *Brahmasūtras*
Svapna ("dream consciousness"), 310
Svārtha, kind of inference, 109
Svataḥprāmāṇyavāda ("theory of intrinsic validity of knowledge"), 302
Śvetāśvatara Upaniṣad, 54, 55. *See also* Upaniṣads, the
Syādvāda ("the doctrine of 'maybe' "), 105

Tādātmya ("identity"), 112
Taittirīya Āraṇyaka, 129, 134, 135
Taittirīya Upaniṣad, 19, 53, 54, 202. *See also* Upaniṣads, the
Tamas, 79, 80, 81, 213, 281, 282, 297. *See also* Guṇas
Ṭaṇaka, 68
Tanmātras ("subtle elements"), 79
Tarka ("reason"), explanation of, 250–251; function of, 251. *See also Anumāna;* Inference; Reason
Tat tvam asi ("Thou art that"), 14, 201–202, 238, 242, 247; explication of, in *Vedāntasāra*, 297–300. *See also* "I am Brahman"; *Mahāvākya*
Tattvas ("categories"), 105
Teacher, the, 125
Textual tradition, 66
Thomas, Edward J., 93n
Time and space, as effects of delusion, 228
Tīrthaṅkara ("prophet"), in Jainism, 104
Transfiguration: meaning of word, 274; theory, 273. *See also* *Vivartavāda*
Transformation theory: is preliminary to transfiguration theory, 273; nature of, 274. *See also Pariṇāmavāda*
Transmigration, 126, 131, 132; is axiomatic in *Bhagavadgītā*, 34; cause of, 137, 148, 252, 269; doctrine of, 17; ocean of, 127; release from, by knowledge, 137; results from, 130; root of, 136. *See also* Rebirth; *Saṁsāra*
Truth, 75; as dependent upon objects, 156; does not always remove illusory cognition, 238; relation of, to conduct, 238–239; Vedāntic attitude towards, 4

Udāharaṇa, member of reference, 109
Union, of field and knower of field, 49
Unity: doctrine of, 180; knowledge of, 157
Unmanifest, the, 42; hard for embodied to attain, 47
Unreal, the, 273; as not being within the sphere of experience, 258
Unreality, 294

Unseen Seer, 126
Upādāna ("material cause"), 9
Upadeśasāhasrī, 123, 133
Upādhi ("limitation"), 220, 248, 297, 309, 310; is the product of ignorance, 197
Upalabdhṛ ("the perceiving person"), 97
Upanaya, member of inference, 109
Upanayana ("initiation"), 51, 122; ceremony, 170
Upaniṣads, the, 4, 7, 36, 53, 67, 71, 72, 150, 234; are the concluding part of the Veda, 52; final authority of, 9; as quoted in texts presented: *Aitareya*, 125, 129, 134; *Bṛhadāraṇyaka*, 125, 126, 128, 130, 132, 133, 134, 135, 136, 150, 159, 160, 165, 171, 180, 190, 193, 197, 199, 230, 233, 238, 239, 240, 241, 249, 301; *Chāndogya*, 124, 125, 128, 131, 132, 134, 135, 136, 158, 162, 170, 171, 173, 178, 180, 183, 188, 196, 197, 202, 217, 234, 238; *Īśā*, 134, 136; *Jābāla*, 240; *Kaṭha*, 126, 129, 130, 134, 149, 150, 157, 197, 220, 233, 272; *Kauṣītaki*, 134, 240; *Kena*, 126, 301; *Māṇḍūkya*, 295, 296; *Muṇḍaka*, 124, 126, 134, 135, 136, 164, 197, 234, 235, 236, 238, 295; *Praśna*, 134, 170, 173; *Śvetāśvatara*, 134, 294, 295; *Taittirīya*, 126, 129, 134, 156, 161, 170, 171, 172, 178, 193; Tradition, 66
Upāsanā ("meditation"), 223
Upavarṣa, 68, 167
Uttara-mīmāṁsā ("the 'Second Enquiry' "), 52. *See also Vedānta*

Vācaspati Miśra, *Bhāmatī*, 252
Vaidikas, the, 70
Vaiśeṣika, 56, 73n, 107, 111; "atomic" theory of matter of, 86; categories of, 86, 90; nine substances distinguished by, 86; realistic and pluralistic system of, 86; *Sūtras*, 67, 86
Vaiṣṇaivism, 114
Validity, 302–303. *See also Svataḥprāmāṇyavāda*
Vallabha, 68
Vāsudeva, 135; four forms of, 115
Vāyu, 134
Veda, 4, 33, 47, 52, 294; Four, 7; language of, 69; statements about multiform Brahman in, as serving to direct attention, 198
Vedanāskandha ("group of feelings"), 94
Vedāṅgas, the, 294
Vedānta, the, 66, 234; also known as *uttara-mīmāṁsā*, the "Second Enquiry," 52; arguments of, 77; attitude of, toward the Veda and Upaniṣads, 8; basic problem of; 10; classical, 68, 69; the definite conclusion of, 120; exegetical methodology of, 77; as made synonymous with *Advaita*, 118; meaning of, 4; *Vedāntamīmāṁsā*, 4; most basic problem of, 72; was never a unitary system, 67; exegetical task of, 72; philosophical doctrines of, 77; as a philosophy, 67; primary pursuit of, 19; purpose of, according to Rāmānuja, 36; responses of, 71; Soul as agent according to, 53; and *śruti*, 53; system, the object of, 81; "theistic" criticism of Sāṁkhya, 81; three points of departure of, 4, 67; texts, culmination of, 243; traditional sources, 4
Vedāntasūtras, 51. *See also Brahmasūtras*

Vedāntins: basic positions of, 10; of classical period, 34
Videhamukti ("liberation at death"), 312
Vidyā ("knowledge"), 58–60, 220, 263, 289; as discrimination, 152. *See also Jñāna;* Knowledge; *Prajñā*
Vidyāraṇya: mainly concerned with cosmological or metaphysical themes, 281; *Pañcadaśī,* 281
Vijñāna ("intelligence," "understanding"), 29, 99, 193. *See also Jñāna;* Knowledge; *Prajñā; Vidyā*
Vijñānamaya, meaning of, 205
Vijñānamayakośa ("sheath of intellect"), 282, 310. *See also Kośas*
Vijñānaskandha ("knowledge-aggregate"), 94
Vijñānātman ("cognitional self"), 182
Vijñānavādin (Buddhist Idealist), 92, 93, 260; theory of illusion, Vimuktatman's criticism of, 280. *See also* Buddhism
Vikāra ("process of creation"), 11, 297
Vikṣepa-śakti ("power of distorting reality"), 309. *See also Māyā*
Vimuktātman, *Iṣṭa Siddhi,* 278
Virodha ("opposition"), characterized by, 244
Viruddha, 110
Viṣaya ("object"), 227, 244
Viśeṣa ("particularity"), 86; definition of, 87
Viśeṣaṇa, definition of, 270
Viśeṣaṇa-viśeṣyabhāva, type of relation between words, 298
Viṣṇu-Nārāyaṇa, 114
Vivaraṇa, 223, 252; founded by Padmapāda, 242
Vivarta ("illusory manifestation"), 266, 297, 310. *See also Pariṇāmavāda*
Vivartavāda, 267. *See also* Causality; Cause and effect; Causes
Vṛtti ("mental modification"), 284
Vṛttijñāna ("empirical knowledge"), 311
Vyāpti ("concomitance"), 109; kinds of: *asamavyāpti,* 109n; *samavyāpti,* 109n
Vyāsarājasvāmin, 288
Vyavahāra ("practical experience"), 244, 309
Vyavahāranaya, emphasis on individual features in Jainism, 104
Vyūhas ("levels," "forms"), 114, 115

Waking state, 143; as distinct from dream, 272
Way of the Gods, the, description of, 18
Way of the Insight, the. *See Jñāna-yoga*
Way of the Task, the. *See Karma-yoga*
Whole, in relation to parts, 184–185
Wisdom, as purifier, 40
Witness: requires no external proof of its existence, 227; theory of, leads to infinite regress, 226. *See also Sākṣin*
Word: as connected with species, 165; essence of, is power of denotation, 165
World: activity by which produced, 82–86; arrangement of, 82; beginninglessness of, 92; in *śruti,* conflicting statements concerning, 172; created without reference to purpose, 191; as existing in ignorance,

164; as illusion, 189; is a manifestation of Īśvara, 309; is non-different from Brahman, 10; is non-existent, 179–180; as true prior to knowledge of Brahman, 180; as not having an independent existence, 179; as originating from word, 166–169. *See also* Causality; *Līlā; Saṁsāra*

Yajña ("sacrifice"), 214

Yājñavalkya, 206

Yoga, 40; Kṛṣṇa's divine, in *Gītā*, 44; of meditation, 50; of renunciation, 44; and *Sāṁkhya* are one, 41; as skill in action, 38; school, 35; system, 111. *See also Bhakti-yoga; Jñāna-yoga; Karma-yoga*

Yogasūtrabhaṣya, 233